PEARLS OF WISDOM

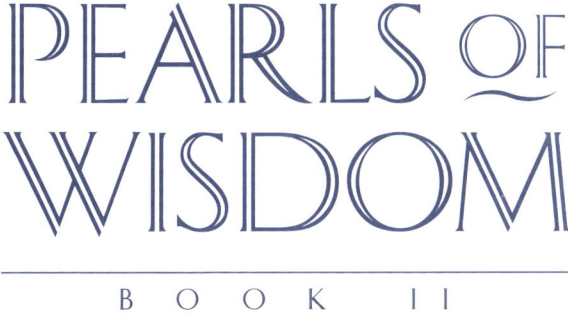

BOOK II

featuring
KABBALAH: KEY TO
YOUR HIDDEN POWER

Part Two:
MYSTERIES OF THE SOUL

Elizabeth Clare Prophet

TEACHINGS OF THE ASCENDED MASTERS
Mark L. Prophet • Elizabeth Clare Prophet
VOLUME THIRTY-FIVE • 1992

PEARLS OF WISDOM®
featuring
KABBALAH: KEY TO YOUR HIDDEN POWER
Part Two: Mysteries of the Soul
Elizabeth Clare Prophet
1992 Volume Thirty-Five Book II
Published by
The Summit Lighthouse® for Church Universal and Triumphant®

Copyright © 1992, 1995 by Church Universal and Triumphant.
All rights reserved.

No part of this book may be used, reproduced or transmitted in any manner whatsoever, except by a reviewer who may quote brief passages in a review. For information, write or call Summit University Press, Box 5000, Livingston, MT 59047-5000. Telephone: (406) 222-8300.

Pearls of Wisdom, The Summit Lighthouse, Church Universal and Triumphant, Summit University Press, and ♆ are registered trademarks of Church Universal and Triumphant. All rights to their use are reserved.

LIBRARY OF CONGRESS CATALOG CARD NUMBER: 95-070202

INTERNATIONAL STANDARD BOOK NUMBER: 0-922729-16-6

To preserve the Teachings of the Ascended Masters for posterity, this book has been printed on acid-free paper which meets the requirements of ANSI/NISO Z39.48-1992 (Permanence of Paper), and is rated to last several hundred years without significant deterioration under archival storage conditions.

Printed in the United States of America

Summit University Press®
First Printing

Dust jacket illustration: Adapted from woodcut of astronomer printed by Johann Weissenburger, Nuremberg, 1504.

Frontispiece: The Tetragrammaton, the most sacred name of God in the Old Testament, from a Bible in Sefardi hand, 1385.

*To the Ascended Master
El Morya
Preserver of Kabbalah
and the Truth of the Ages*

At the time that the Holy One, blessed be He, was about to create the world, he decided to fashion all the souls which would in due course be dealt out to the children of men. . . . Each one in its due time the Holy One bade come to him, and then said: "Go now, descend into this and this place, into this and this body."

Yet often enough the soul would reply: "Lord of the world, I am content to remain in this realm, and have no wish to depart to some other, where I shall be in thralldom and become stained."

Whereupon the Holy One would reply: "Thy destiny is, and has been from the day of thy forming, to go into that world."

THE ZOHAR

Contents

I	**KABBALAH: KEY TO YOUR HIDDEN POWER**	
4	*A Portrait of the God Within*	100
	Adam Kadmon: Our Divine Blueprint	103
	The I AM Presence: the Personal Presence of God	107
	Your Unique Identity in God	109
	The Holy Christ Self: Your Inner Teacher	113
	The Flame of God in Your Heart	116
	Your Soul and Four Lower Bodies	117
	The Sefirot and the Chakras	118
5	*Mysteries of the Soul*	126
	The Three Parts of the Soul	128
	The Difference between Your Soul and Your Divine Spark	131

	Soul Travel to Celestial Academies "With My Soul Have I Desired Thee in the Night"	134
	Twin Flames and Soul Mates	141
	Devekut, Mystical Cleaving to God	145
	The Soul's Journey after Life	150
	The Soul's Final Ascent	152
6	*The Origin of Evil*	158
	Evil Emerged from Gevurah/Din	160
	The Counterfeit Din	162
	Balancing the Masculine and Feminine Qualities of Hesed and Gevurah	163
	Escaping the Clutches of the Other Side and the Evil Urge	167
	Why Does God Allow Evil to Exist?	171
	Aiding and Abetting the Other Side	174
	Adam's Sin	177
	The Kings That Died	179
	The Breaking of the Vessels	180
	Parallels with Hindu Cosmology	182
	Liberating the Sparks	184
	The Hasidic View: Your Unique Role in Rescuing the Sparks	186

The Exile Takes on New Meaning		189
Notes		193
Picture Credits		203

Chapters 1–3 of *Kabbalah: Key to Your Hidden Power* are published in Book I of the 1992 *Pearls of Wisdom* and the remaining chapters are published in Book III.

II PEARLS OF WISDOM

Pearl Number		Date Dictated	Page Number

GAUTAMA BUDDHA
Wesak Address 1992

20 Have Mercy!
The Thoughtform of the Anchor
(May 16, 1992, Royal Teton Ranch, Montana) 249

MAHA CHOHAN
Pentecost Address 1992

21 The Process of the Purging
Expand the Capacity of the Heart!
(June 7, 1992, Royal Teton Ranch, Montana) 273

ELIZABETH CLARE PROPHET

22 Karma, Reincarnation and Christianity 6   285

WILLIAM ALAN MALEK

23 "And a Man's Foes Shall Be They
of His Own Household" —Jesus   305

LAURIE ALEXANDER BLACK

24 A Battle of Mind and Heart   325

FREEDOM 1992 *"Joy in the Heart"*

June 26 – July 5, 1992 • Royal Teton Ranch, Montana

I EL MORYA AS THE PATRIARCH ABRAHAM
25 Friendship with God
    Take the Leap in Consciousness!   (June 26, 1992) 353

II SAINT JOSEPH
26 "I Am Not Done with Pisces!"
    Turn Back the Adversary in Defense of the Child!
                                                (June 27, 1992) 365

III LORD LANTO
27 Turn the World Around!
    A Replica of the Great Causal Body   (June 28, 1992) 377

IV MIGHTY VICTORY WITH JUSTINA
28 Break the Spell of Non-Victory!
    A Moment when All Could Be Won and All Could Be Lost
                                                (June 28, 1992) 387

V HOLY JUSTINIUS
29 See What You Can Do!
    *For the Acceleration of Earth
    without the Destruction of Earth*   (June 28, 1992) 395

VI ELIZABETH CLARE PROPHET
30 Become Shiva!   (June 30, 1992) 399

VII LORD SHIVA
31 *Only Make the Call, "Shiva!"*   (June 30, 1992) 409

VIII OMEGA

32 Do Not Doubt God!
Love God and Love One Another (July 1, 1992) 421

IX ALPHA

33 The Fourth Woe
"I Will Become the Example!" (July 1, 1992) 429

X ELIZABETH CLARE PROPHET

35 The Light of Persia—
Mystical Experiences with Zarathustra (July 1, 1992) 453

XI ZARATHUSTRA

36 Thou Purging Fire!
Do Not Quench the Flame (July 1, 1992) 471

XII A SPOKESMAN FOR THE DELEGATION OF THE PRIESTHOOD OF MELCHIZEDEK IN ATTENDANCE

37 The Great Mystery of the Violet Flame
Give a Cup of Cool Violet Flame in Christ's Name
(July 1, 1992) 485

XIII ELIZABETH CLARE PROPHET

38 The Worship of the Goddess—
The Path of the Divine Mother (July 2, 1992) 493

XIV GODDESS SARASVATI

39 We Do Work!
Illumination—the Only Cure for Earth (July 2, 1992) 501

XV GODDESS LAKSHMI

40 Let the Egos Fall!
The Torch Must Be Passed to the Children (July 2, 1992) 507

MOTHER MARY
Mother Mary's Ascension Day Address 1992
34 "Be Careful!"
   Hold Fast to Me   (August 22, 1992, Royal Teton Ranch, Montana) 439

I AM the Witness

The Memory and Fulfillment of Community	283
"Jesus Loved the Little Children Most!"	383
To Become the Bride of Christ	384
Divine Love Heals the Anger of Separation from Our Source	386
A Terrible Accident Proves God's Deliverance	407
Pray for Visualizations!	419
The Tangible Tube of Light	420
The Burning Flame of the Son of God in My Heart	426
The Blessed Mother Wanted Me to Go to Summit University	452
The Power of Shiva's Third Eye	479
A Poem to Archangel Michael	480
Is Your Electric Blanket Sapping Your Strength?	482
My Heart Is the Heart of Christ	484

For a Safe and Swift Delivery Call upon the Messengers	491
El Morya Takes Students on a Field Trip to See God	506
I Shall Not Be Moved by Earthquakes	511
My Dream of the Blue Room	511
"Your Heart Is Fine"	513
The Mercy of the Law	535
The Process of the Re-Creation of Self	541

Prayers, Affirmations and Decrees

The Prayer of Teresa of Avila	259
I AM Receiving Now the Holy Spirit of Helios and Vesta	280
A Challenge to the Hosts of Darkness	367
The Power of God Shall Not Fail Us	371
Be Still and Know That I AM God	372
Om Namah Shivaya	403
Archangel Michael, Help Me, Help Me, Help Me!	407
Only Make the Call, *"Shiva!"*	415
I Cannot Rest Here!	417
I AM the Violet Flame	419

Alpha's Judgment of the Persecutors
of the Divine Mother and Her Seed   438

My Lord Jesus Christ, Have Mercy upon My Soul!   440

Bind the Forces of Antichrist in the Earth!   475

O Mighty Threefold Flame of Life   478

The Bija Mantras to the Feminine Deities   499

Letters

ELIZABETH CLARE PROPHET
    FREEDOM 1992—"Joy in the Heart"
                                    (June 1, 1992)   *follows page* 304

MARY ELLEN MAUNZ AND NANCY J. MCNABB
    Montessori Education Workshops
                                    (June 2, 1992)   *follows page* 304

ELIZABETH CLARE PROPHET
    Columbus Day Retreat   376

ELIZABETH CLARE PROPHET
    The 500th Anniversary of Christopher Columbus'
    Discovery of America   (September 12, 1992)   *follows page* 484

Index   515

Illustrations

Black-and-White Illustrations

The Tetragrammaton	*Frontispiece*
Adam Kadmon *from Qabbalah by Isaac Myer*	100
Astronomer *printed by Johann Weissenburger*	126
The New Jerusalem *by Gustave Doré*	136
The Grand Teton	140
Twin Flames	142
The Prophetess Deborah *by Edwin Austin Abbey*	147
The Serpent *by Gustave Doré*	158
Portia	165
Eve Tempted *by Lucien Lévy-Dhurmer*	170

Abram Draws Near to Shechem in the Promised Land
by Julius Schnorr   172

Israel in Egypt
by Sir Edward J. Poynter   173

Jeremiah at the Fall of Jerusalem
by Eduard Bendemann   188

The Sorrowing Jews in Exile
by Eduard Bendemann   189

Figures

Figure 9. *Adam Kadmon*   104

Figure 10. *Tzimtzum* and the Emanation of the *Sefirot*   106

Figure 11. The *Sefirot* and the Causal Body   110

Figure 12. Kabbalah's Tree of Life Superimposed over the Chart of Your Divine Self   114

Figure 13. The *Sefirot* and the *Chakras*   120

Figure 14. Attributes of and Correspondences to the *Sefirot*   122

Figure 15. A *Yod* Cleaving to a *Yod*   154

Figure 16. The Fiery Ovoid Uniting God and the Soul   155

Color Plates
following page 122

The Chart of Your Divine Self

The Seven *Chakras* and the Secret Chamber of the Heart

I

Kabbalah: Key to Your Hidden Power

PART TWO

Mysteries of the Soul

MYSTICAL PATHS
OF THE WORLD'S RELIGIONS

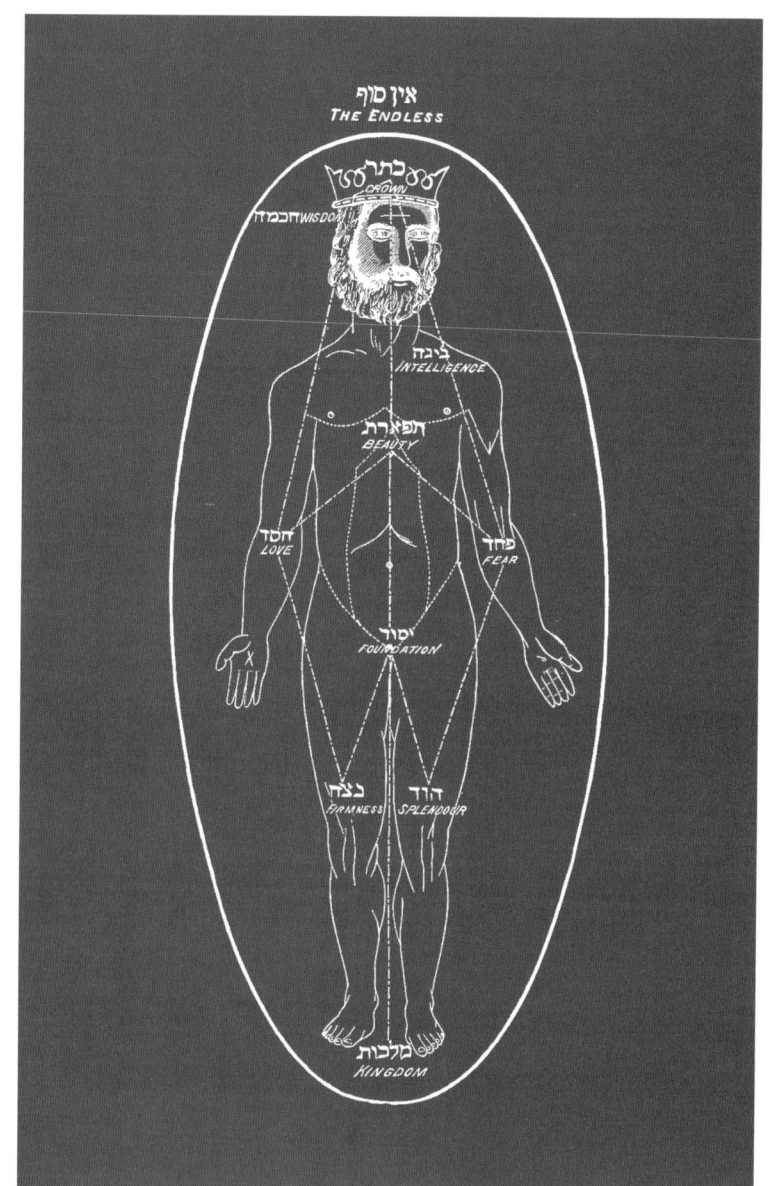

CHAPTER FOUR

A PORTRAIT OF THE GOD WITHIN

He stretched forth His right hand and created the world above.
He stretched forth His left hand and created this world....
He made this world to match the world above, and whatever
exists above has its counterpart below.

THE ZOHAR

Kabbalists tell us that the *sefirot* are the divine model for all of creation and that we ourselves contain the ten *sefirot*. Everything in the universe, including man, is created "according to the form that is above," says the Zohar. "[God] made the lower world on the pattern of the upper world, and they complement each other, forming one whole, in a single unity."[1]

The *sefirot* relate to you personally on many different levels. They are at once the archetypes of your inner, spiritual being and of your outer, physical body. "[The *sefirot*] are the causes and 'models' of all the intellectual lights which spring

Adam Kadmon *from* Qabbalah *by Isaac Myer, 1888.*

up in [man's] mind, of all the positive faculties and powers of his soul, of all the principal organs and members of his body," writes author Leo Schaya.[2]

Contemporary students of Kabbalah have described our relationship to the *sefirot* as follows:[3] *Keter* (Crown) is our divine essence. It also represents our free will and our awareness of God as the Divine Presence and First Cause. *Hokhmah* (Wisdom) in us is our knowledge of God. It is pure, undifferentiated thought. *Hokhmah* correlates with the right brain and is manifest as genius, inspiration, revelation and originality.

Binah (Understanding) represents the left brain, our ability to reason and discriminate. As a step-down from the internal thought processes of *Hokhmah* and *Binah*, *Da'at* (Knowledge) is our ability to express our thoughts. It is also spiritual knowledge and the omniscience and universal consciousness of God.

Hesed (Love/Mercy) manifests as love, tolerance, mercy and unconditional, unrestrained giving. *Hesed* is our "luminous nature which is always aspiring to the divine," says Schaya.[4] *Gevurah* (Justice/Judgment) is discipline, discrimination and true judgment. Rabbi Aryeh Kaplan says *Gevurah* can manifest as the ability and the strength to overcome one's self, or it can be rigid, noncaring, withdrawn and totally self-contained.[5]

Tiferet (Beauty/Compassion) is the heart or core of each of us, our essential nature. It manifests as our inner and outer beauty and as harmony, balance and serenity. "*Tiferet* is a balanced giving," says Kaplan, "the ability to create a harmonious relationship."[6]

Netzah (Victory) governs our instinctual and involuntary processes and sustains our health. Some describe it as achievement or spiritual power. When out of balance, *Netzah* can manifest as dominance. *Hod* (Splendor/Majesty), on the other hand, applies to our voluntary processes. It is that part of our nature that learns, communicates and controls. When out of balance, *Hod* can manifest as passivity and submissiveness.

Yesod (Foundation) is the foundation of spiritual birth, physical procreation and the ego. It is the seat of physical and spiritual pleasure. By mastering the attribute of *Yesod,* says Kaplan, the righteous are able to penetrate spiritual realms and attain an intimate union with God. *Malkhut/Shekhinah* (Kingdom/Divine Presence) represents our physical body and our receptivity, for as the last *sefirah* it receives the emanations of the preceding *sefirot.* It is the point where spiritual and physical forces meet.

Adam Kadmon: Our Divine Blueprint

In Kabbalah, the divine archetype of man and woman is known as *Adam Kadmon,* literally "Primordial Man." Some Kabbalists teach that when the *sefirot* emanated from *Ein Sof,* they first took the form of *Adam Kadmon.* Kabbalists describe him as "the concealed shape of the Godhead itself."[7] *Adam Kadmon* is androgynous; in him the male and female forces are in complete harmony and balance.

Kabbalists usually depict *Adam Kadmon* so that we are viewing his back. This is based on the passage from Exodus where Moses asks God to show him his glory but the LORD reveals only his back to Moses, saying: "Thou canst not see my face: for there shall no man see me and live.... And thou shalt see my back parts: but my face shall not be seen."[8]

Although Kabbalists do not always agree on how the *sefirot* correlate to *Adam Kadmon,* the most common scheme is shown in figure 9. *Keter, Hokhmah* and *Binah* (the three highest *sefirot*) represent *Adam Kadmon's* head. Some Kabbalists assign *Da'at,* the quasi-*sefirah* of Knowledge, to *Adam Kadmon's* face and throat.[9] *Hesed* (the fourth *sefirah*) is his right arm and *Gevurah* (the fifth *sefirah*) is his left arm. *Tiferet* (the sixth *sefirah*) is associated with the trunk of *Adam Kadmon's* body. *Netzah* (the seventh *sefirah*) is his right leg, and *Hod* (the eighth *sefirah*) is his left leg. *Yesod* (the ninth *sefirah*) relates to the male sexual organ. *Malkhut* is at times depicted at the feet or mouth of *Adam Kadmon*. Sometimes *Malkhut* is not included in diagrams of *Adam Kadmon* at all but is entirely separate.

Rabbi Isaac Luria teaches that the body of *Adam Kadmon* was created when *Ein Sof* emitted a line or ray of light that

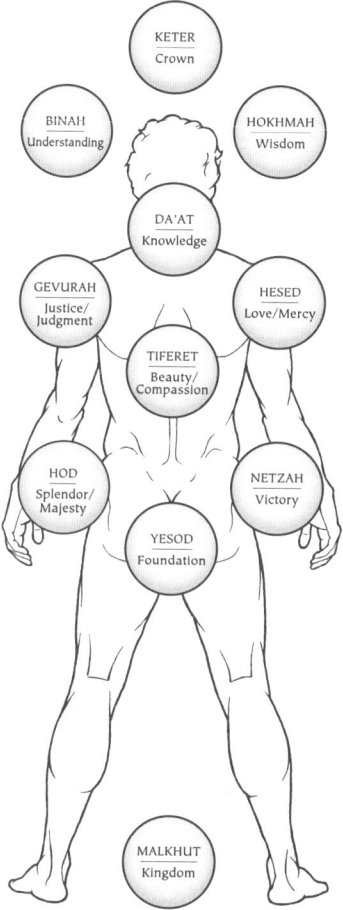

FIGURE 9. Adam Kadmon *(literally "Primordial Man") is the androgynous divine archetype of man, the primordial image and likeness of God in which we were made. Some Kabbalists teach that when the sefirot emanated from* Ein Sof, *they first took the form of* Adam Kadmon.

became a series of concentric spheres that are the *sefirot*. (fig. 10) Rabbi Hayim Vital, Luria's closest disciple, describes the process:

> [The] first concentric sphere which adheres closely to *Ein Sof* is called *Keter* of primordial man. Then, the straight line continues briefly, then retreats and forms another concentric sphere within the other. This sphere is called the *Hokhmah* of primordial man.

This process is repeated as all the *sefirot* are unfolded. Vital says:

> That which joins all the spheres together is the subtle thin line which spreads out from *Ein Sof,* traversing, descending and joining each sphere to another until it reaches the very last.
>
> Next, the line spreads out in a straight way from the top to the bottom, from the highest point of the highest sphere to the very lowest and last of the spheres. It consists of ten *sefirot* arranged mysteriously in the image of an upright human figure.[10]

The Adam of the Garden of Eden was the anthropological counterpart of *Adam Kadmon*. Before he sinned, Adam's body was spiritual and ethereal. After he fell from his divine state in Eden, Adam took on a material body. But *Adam Kadmon* never descended below the realm of heavenly perfection. He remained at what the ascended masters call the "etheric plane." His was the perfect body, the "etheric body."

I believe that *Adam Kadmon* was the primordial image and likeness of God in which we were made and that his body is the blueprint for the bodies of all sons and daughters of God. We have strayed from that blueprint, compromising our bodies by our negative thoughts, feelings, words and deeds. But the original matrix of perfection, the divine image and likeness, is there, sealed in our Higher Self.

Kabbalists say we can return to that divine image. "According to Genesis 1:27, the human being is created in the image of

God," writes Daniel Matt. "The *sefirot* are the divine original of that image. As Primordial Adam, they are the mythical paragon of the human being, our archetypal nature. The human race has lost this nature, but if one were to purify himself, he would reconnect with the *sefirot* and become a vessel for them. This is what the Patriarchs attained and, to a greater degree, Moses."[11]

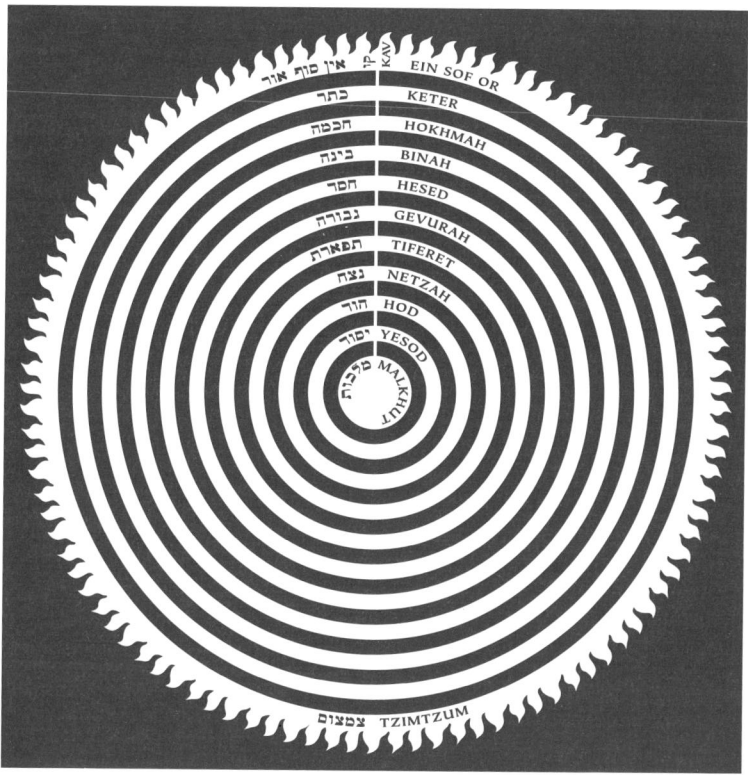

FIGURE 10. *The process of creation, according to sixteenth-century Kabbalist Isaac Luria, started when* Ein Sof, *the Infinite, contracted itself to its centermost point and then withdrew to the sides surrounding that point in order to leave a vacuum in which its creation could exist. This process is called* tzimtzum. *Next, from the Infinite Light* (Ein Sof Or) *that enveloped the vacuum,* Ein Sof *emitted a ray of light* (Kav) *that formed a series of concentric spheres. These spheres are the ten* sefirot, *which compose the body of Primordial Man,* Adam Kadmon.

In later chapters I will be reviewing techniques you can use to purify yourself spiritually, reconnect with the *sefirot* and make yourself a vessel for the divine light.

The I AM Presence: the Personal Presence of God

Like the Kabbalists of old, the ascended masters have drawn a diagram that illustrates our divine nature and our relationship to God and the *sefirot*. This diagram is called the Chart of Your Divine Self. (facing p. 122) The ascended masters also refer to it as the Tree of Life.

The upper figure in the chart represents your I AM Presence. The I AM Presence corresponds to the Father-Mother God *(Elohim)*, who is the Divine Us of Genesis 1:26.[12] The I AM Presence is the Presence of God individualized for each one of us. It is your personalized I AM THAT I AM. I AM THAT I AM is the name God revealed to Moses at Mount Sinai when he called to him out of the midst of the burning bush. In Kabbalah, I AM THAT I AM *(Ehyeh Asher Ehyeh)* is the name of God associated with *Keter*. So you can think of *Keter* (Crown) as corresponding to your I AM Presence.

What about *Ein Sof*, the "divine nothingness," the indescribable "Cause above all causes"? *Ein Sof* is hidden as the Sun behind the sun of the I AM Presence. That is why Kabbalists call *Ein Sof* the unmanifest and why the Zohar says "no trace may be found, nor can thought by any means or method reach it."[13]

A simple way to understand the relationship of *Ein Sof* to the I AM Presence is to think of *Ein Sof* as the sun and the I AM Presence as the moon during an eclipse of the sun. During a solar eclipse, the moon is positioned directly between the earth and the sun. The moon is smaller than the sun, but because it is closer to us it appears to be about the same size as the sun and therefore blocks the sun's light from our view. But even though we don't see the sun during an eclipse, we know that it is there, radiating its light and energy to sustain life on earth.

In the same way, the brightness of our I AM Presence eclipses the light of *Ein Sof*. And even though we don't perceive *Ein Sof* behind our I AM Presence, it is nevertheless the eternal, immutable source of life that continually sustains the created world through the agency of the *sefirot*.

Our I AM Presence is thus the closest and most personal Presence of God we can know while we are yet in our mortal body. Only when our soul has become one with *Keter* and I AM THAT I AM and has returned to the cosmos of pure Spirit will she be called to enter *Ein Sof*, the indescribable and unknowable God—the Supreme Source.

The light of I AM THAT I AM and *Keter* is a transforming light. Mark Prophet, my late husband and teacher, said that when the LORD told Moses, "Thou canst not see my face: for there shall no man see me and live," that meant: No man can see God and still live as man. If he survives the experience, he will be God in manifestation. Such is the power of the light of I AM THAT I AM and *Keter*. We may not yet be ready to stand in that Presence of God, but by reconnecting with the *sefirot*, by daily walking and talking with God, we are getting ready.

Before we can receive the light of *Keter* we must assimilate the essence of the nine lower *sefirot*. We can accomplish this under the tutelage of the ascended masters, who initiate us through the ten stages of the *sefirot* from the root of *Malkhut/ Shekhinah* to the crown of *Keter*. The soul's assimilation of the light of the *sefirot* may take numerous incarnations, perhaps with karmic digressions along the way. But, as Jesus said, "Blessed is the man that endureth temptation: for when he is tried, he shall receive the crown of life *[Keter]*, which the Lord hath promised to them that love him."[14]

Your Unique Identity in God

If the Presence of God is individualized for each of us, then what makes one soul different from another? How you color, or qualify, the interpenetrating spheres of light surrounding your I AM Presence determines what's unique about you. Together, these spheres make up the Causal Body, also known as the Body of First Cause, which exists in higher levels of Spirit.

The spheres of your Causal Body are the storehouse of everything that is real and permanent about your unique identity. They contain the records of the virtuous acts you have performed to the glory of God and the blessing of man through your many incarnations on earth. These good works are your treasure stored in heaven.[15] Whenever you judiciously exercise your free will in love, harmony and creative endeavor, these energies, multiplied by your service to life, ascend to one of the seven spheres of your Causal Body.

Each sphere of the Causal Body is a different color, representing one of the seven "rays." "Rays" are frequencies of light, and each one is associated with a different attribute or aspect of God's consciousness. In addition to the seven primary rays, there are five "secret" rays, which are "hidden" within the center sphere of the Causal Body. I have discovered that the five secret rays are embodied by the Five Dhyani Buddhas, each of whom presides over one of the five "Buddha families" delineated in Tibetan Buddhism.[16]

The progression of the spheres of the Causal Body, from the center sphere to the outermost sphere, corresponds to the progressive emanation of the *sefirot* that emanated from *Ein Sof* to form *Adam Kadmon*. (figs. 10, 11) The line, or ray of light, that connects the *sefirot* and runs right through the body of Primordial Man may be compared to the shaft of white light ("the crystal cord") that connects the three figures in the Chart of Your Divine Self. (facing p. 122)

When you embrace the attributes of each of the *sefirot,* you are creating a cosmic connection between your world and the heaven world. When you make the qualities of each of the *sefirot* your own, you increase the power and dominion of the corresponding sphere of your Causal Body as day by day the energy you have used for good ascends to the Causal Body. At the same time, your imitation of the divine attributes compels the corresponding frequency of God's light from the heaven world

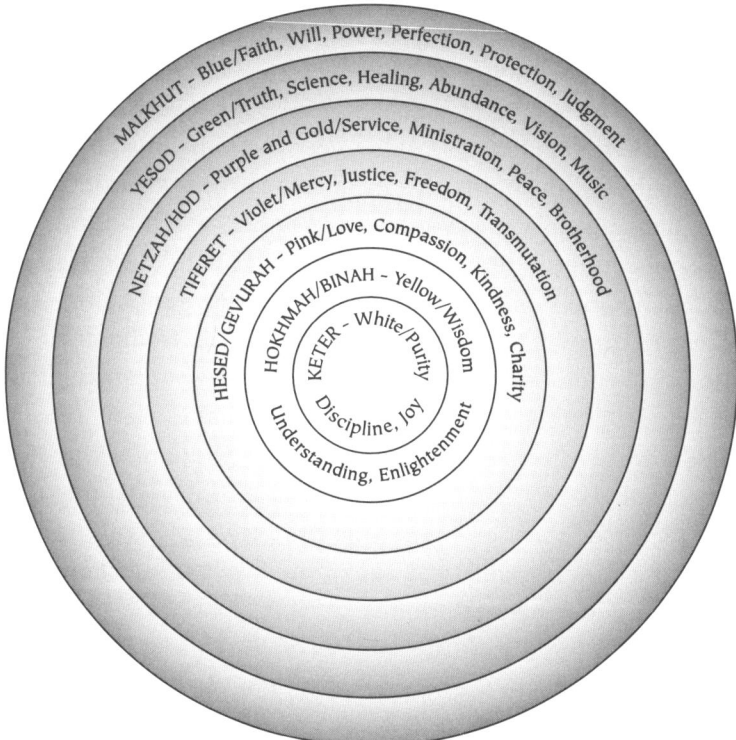

FIGURE 11: *The* sefirot *correspond to the colored spheres of your Causal Body that surround your I AM Presence (the Presence of God that is individualized for each one of us). As you imitate the divine attributes of the* sefirot, *you increase the power of the corresponding sphere of your Causal Body and you compel the corresponding frequency of God's light to descend into this world.*

to descend through this world over the circuit of the *sefirot*.

For example, *Keter* (Crown) corresponds to the white sphere in the center of the Causal Body. The white sphere is the sphere of divine purity, discipline and joy. Whenever you act with a pure heart and an unblemished motive, desiring only to glorify God, you are multiplying the power of your white sphere and you are stimulating the flow of *Keter's* light into the world.

Hokhmah (Wisdom) and *Binah* (Understanding) correspond to the yellow sphere of divine wisdom, understanding and enlightenment. Whenever you bring spiritual understanding and the illumination of the Mind of God to his children on earth, you are multiplying the power of the yellow sphere of your Causal Body and increasing the flow of God's wisdom and understanding (the light of *Hokhmah* and *Binah*) into the world. The same pattern of interaction is true for each of the following spheres and attributes.

Hesed (Love/Mercy) and *Gevurah* (Justice/Judgment) correspond to the pink sphere of divine love, compassion, kindness and charity. *Tiferet* (Beauty/Compassion) corresponds to the violet sphere of divine mercy, justice, freedom and transmutation. *Netzah* (Victory) and *Hod* (Splendor/Majesty) correspond to the purple-and-gold sphere of divine service, ministration, peace and brotherhood. *Yesod* (Foundation) corresponds to the green sphere of divine truth, science, healing, abundance, vision and music. *Malkhut* (Kingdom) corresponds to the blue sphere of divine faith, will, power, perfection, protection and judgment. The quasi-*sefirah*, *Da'at* (Knowledge), corresponds to the spheres of the five secret rays that are within the center sphere.

No two Causal Bodies are exactly alike because their shimmering spheres reflect the unique spiritual attainment of the soul. One person may have a greater momentum on expressing the love of *Hesed,* having perfected that quality over many lifetimes. Therefore the pink sphere of his Causal Body may be larger than the pink sphere of someone who has not developed that quality. One who embodies the attributes of *Hokhmah* and *Binah* may excel as a teacher of wisdom, and thus the yellow sphere of his Causal Body will shine as a star of great magnitude.

Furthermore, the particular attributes we have developed through hard work in our previous lives determine the gifts and talents we will be born with in our succeeding lives. These talents are sealed in our Causal Body and made available to us through our Holy Christ Self (the middle figure in the Chart of Your Divine Self) so we can multiply them again and again for the good of all.

In my meditations, God has shown me that the progression of the Causal Body spheres is a logical unfoldment of the identity of our soul as God provides us with what we need to fulfill our assignment on earth. In the beginning (representing the white sphere), each of us is created out of a single white-fire ovoid with our twin flame, our "other half" with whom we share a unique blueprint. Together twin flames embody the masculine/feminine polarity of the Divine Whole.[17]

Next, we are clothed with the Mind of God (yellow sphere) and the love of God (pink sphere). Then God bestows upon us the gift of free will, which includes the freedom and ability to create (the violet sphere). Endowed with free will, we will be able to use our talents to serve others (purple-and-gold sphere).

The next step is setting the foundation of our physical form, the blueprint of *Adam Kadmon* (green sphere). And lastly, God gives us power, will and faith, qualities we need to evolve physically and spiritually in the physical dimension.

If we return to the vision of Ezekiel—the vision of the throne-chariot of God that the *Merkabah* mystics yearned to behold—what he saw sounds like nothing less than his own

I AM Presence surrounded by the concentric spheres of his Causal Body. He saw the likeness of a man surrounded by "the appearance of fire" and a "brightness round about" the fire that resembled a rainbow.

Ezekiel describes his vision as "the appearance of the likeness of the glory of the LORD,"[18] and that is exactly what our Causal Body is. Each day, as we become closer and closer to God and reconnect with the ten *sefirot,* we are adding to that glory. And one day, when our soul has fully attained her goal of reunion with God, we will enter into the Causal Body and abide in the house of the LORD forever, nevermore to go out.

The Holy Christ Self: Your Inner Teacher

The middle figure in the Chart of Your Divine Self represents the "only begotten Son" of the Father-Mother God. That Son is the Universal Christ, corresponding to *Tiferet.* (fig. 12) There is only one Son of God, one *Tiferet,* but God gave you and me and every son and daughter of God an exact replica of the original. The ascended masters call this likeness the "Holy Christ Self" or "Higher Self."

Your Holy Christ Self is your soul's advocate before the Father-Mother God. He is your inner teacher, guardian and dearest friend. He is also the voice of conscience that speaks within the precincts of your heart and soul.

Another name for the Holy Christ Self is the LORD Our Righteousness. Jeremiah prophesied that the LORD Our Righteousness would reign as king, executing judgment, justice and righteousness in the earth.[19] Thus the prophet depicted the LORD Our Righteousness as a Mediator. Your Holy Christ Self acts as the Mediator between you and I AM THAT I AM. He divides the way between good and evil within you, teaching you right from wrong.

Before sin/karma descended upon us, our souls were bonded to the Universal Christ, *Tiferet,* and we were clothed

114 *A Portrait of the God Within*

in the original, etheric pattern of *Adam Kadmon* in which we were made. But through succeeding incarnations in an imperfect world, we descended to the level of the lower figure in the chart and lost the enlightenment we had. Today our Holy Christ Self sustains for us the blueprint of *Adam Kadmon,* which Kabbalists say we are destined to manifest again.

We can return to that archetypal pattern of perfection by bonding to our Holy Christ Self. This is the goal of every soul on the mystical path. What does it mean to be bonded to your Holy Christ Self? It means that through the steps and stages of the spiritualization of your consciousness, your soul has returned to the perfect pattern of your Holy Christ Self. This is "the alchemical marriage," whereby the soul attains union with her Bridegroom.

As you imitate the great spiritual teachers and rabbis of all time and as you develop the qualities of each of the *sefirot,* you can begin to know a greater fusion with your Holy Christ Self. Another way you can bond to your Holy Christ Self is to balance your karma. You do this by paying the debts you owe to those you have in some way wronged during this and past lifetimes. The most effective ways to balance karma are through (1) heartfelt prayer, including affirmations that invoke the violet flame of the Holy Spirit (see pp. 117–18), and (2) serving God, family and community.

FIGURE 12. *Kabbalah's diagram of the ten* sefirot *and the ascended masters' Chart of Your Divine Self are both referred to as the Tree of Life. Here the Kabbalists' Tree of Life is superimposed over the Chart of Your Divine Self. The uppermost* sefirah, Keter, *corresponds to the upper figure in the chart, the I AM Presence (the I AM THAT I AM individualized for each of us). The middle* sefirah, Tiferet, *corresponds to the Holy Christ Self (the Universal Christ individualized for each of us). The lower figure in the chart, representing your soul, corresponds to* Malkhut/Shekhinah—*the* sefirah *that represents the physical universe, the physical body, the soul, and the point where spiritual and physical forces meet.*

The Flame of God in Your Heart

The Chart of Your Divine Self shows a shaft of white light descending from the I AM Presence through the Holy Christ Self to the lower figure in the chart. This is the "crystal cord." In Ecclesiastes 12:6 it is referred to as the silver cord. Through this umbilical cord flows a cascading stream of God's light, life and consciousness. It is called the "lifestream." The lifestream empowers you to think, feel, reason, experience life, work, play, grow and wax strong in spirit.[20]

As you exercise your freedom to be what you choose to be, you are making your mark on your lifestream. You are coloring that crystal-clear stream with your thoughts, feelings, words, works and desires. Either you color the stream with pure colors, representing talents and virtues from God that you are developing day by day, or you taint the stream with the putrid, muddied perversions of an off-color state of consciousness.

The energy of your crystal cord also nourishes and sustains the flame of God that is ensconced in the secret chamber of your heart. This flame is called the "threefold flame" or "divine spark." It is literally a spark of sacred fire from God's own heart. It is your soul's point of contact with the Supreme Source of all life, *Ein Sof*.

In a discourse on the threefold flame and the secret chamber of the heart, the Ascended Master Saint Germain says:

> Your heart is indeed one of the choicest gifts of God. Within it there is a central chamber surrounded by such light and protection that we call it a "cosmic interval." It is a chamber separated from matter, and no probing could ever discover it. It occupies simultaneously not only the third and fourth dimensions but also other dimensions unknown to man. It is thus the connecting point of the mighty silver cord of light that descends from your God Presence to sustain the beating of your physical heart, giving you life, purpose and cosmic integration.[21]

The threefold flame has three "plumes" that embody the three primary attributes of God and that correspond to the Trinity. The blue plume (on your left) embodies God's Power and corresponds to the Father. The yellow plume (in the center) embodies God's Wisdom and corresponds to the Son. The pink plume (on your right) embodies God's Love and corresponds to the Holy Spirit. By accessing the Power, Wisdom and Love of the Godhead anchored in your threefold flame, you can fulfill your reason for being.

Your Soul and Four Lower Bodies

The lower figure in the Chart of Your Divine Self represents your soul. Your soul is sheathed in four different "bodies," called the "four lower bodies": (1) the etheric body, (2) the mental body, (3) the desire, or emotional, body and (4) the physical body. These are the vehicles your soul uses in her journey on earth. (They are called "lower bodies" in contrast to the three "higher bodies," which are the I AM Presence, Causal Body and Holy Christ Self.) The lower figure in the chart corresponds to the Holy Spirit, for your soul and four lower bodies are intended to be the temple of the Holy Spirit.[22]

Your etheric body, also called the memory body, houses the blueprint of your identity. It also contains the memory of all that has ever transpired in your soul and all impulses you have ever sent out through your soul since you were created. Your mental body is the vessel of your cognitive faculties. When it is purified it can become the vessel of the Mind of God. The desire body houses your higher and lower desires and records your emotions. Your physical body is the miracle of flesh and blood that enables your soul to progress in the material universe.

The Chart of Your Divine Self shows the lower figure standing in the violet flame. (facing p. 122) The violet flame is the spiritual fire of the Holy Spirit that can help your soul find her way back to God. It has the purifying power to consume negative thoughts, negative feelings and negative karma. As you invoke it, the violet flame will penetrate your mind and heart, your unconscious and subconscious to transmute your past "sins" (or misuses of the light of the ten *sefirot*) and bring all things into harmony and balance.

When you use the violet flame to transmute the imperfections of your etheric, mental, emotional and physical bodies, you are clearing the way for the blueprint of *Adam Kadmon* to be manifest in those bodies. And you will find that you are able to anchor in your body greater and greater increments of light to offset the darkness in the earth. (See the last chapter for affirmations you can use to invoke the violet flame.)

The Sefirot and the Chakras

We have seen how the *sefirot* correspond to the spheres of the Causal Body that surround the upper figure in the Chart of Your Divine Self. The *sefirot* also relate to the lower figure in the chart because they correspond to your *chakras,* a Sanskrit term for the centers of light in your etheric body. Your chakras receive the energy that flows from *Ein Sof* through your I AM Presence and the *sefirot,* and then they distribute it to your four lower bodies. Each *chakra* regulates the energy flow to a different area of the body, and each *chakra* externalizes that energy flow through one of the endocrine glands.

Although Kabbalists did not use the term *chakra,* Perle Epstein notes that they meditated on the body's energy centers to enhance their meditation. She says one way Kabbalists meditated on the body centers

> was to visualize the spinal column as the *lulav* (palm branch) and the heart as the *etrog* (citron)—ritual objects used during the Feast of Tabernacles at the harvest season. Regarding his body as the Tabernacle containing the Divine Spirit, the Kabbalist meditated on the fragrant-smelling citron, visualizing it

at his heart's core. The single pillar extending from heaven to earth which led the Israelites through the wilderness became synonymous in his mind with the *lulav* visualized as his spine.[23]

The seven major *chakras* are positioned along the spinal column from the base of the spine to the crown (see p. 120 and facing p. 123). Just as the *sefirot* are step-down transformers that transform God's energy for our use, so the *chakras* are internal step-down transformers that regulate God's energy according to the needs of our four lower bodies.

Chakra means "wheel" or "disc." The more energy that flows through a *chakra*, the faster it spins. Each *chakra* has a unique function and frequency and represents a different level of consciousness. These differences are denoted by the number of petals of each *chakra*. The more petals the *chakra* has, the higher its frequency.

Some modern Kabbalists have correlated the *sefirot* to specific *chakras*. The Ascended Master El Morya has told me that the system proposed by Rabbi Yonassan Gershom, as follows, is correct.[24] (fig. 13) (When I talked earlier about the Causal Body, I correlated the spheres and their corresponding rays to the *sefirot*. What follows is a different way of correlating the rays to the *sefirot*, but one that also has value for your meditation on the *sefirot*.)

Keter (Crown) corresponds to the crown *chakra*. The crown *chakra* has 972 petals and is located at the top of the head. The yellow flame of illumination is focused in the crown *chakra*. *Hokhmah* (Wisdom) and *Binah* (Understanding) correspond to the ninety-six-petaled third-eye *chakra*, located at the center of the brow. The green flame of truth, science, healing, abundance, vision and music is focused in this *chakra*.

Hesed (Love/Mercy) and *Gevurah* (Justice/Judgment) correspond to the sixteen-petaled throat *chakra*, where the blue flame of God's will, faith, power, protection, perfection and judgment is focused. *Tiferet* (Beauty/Compassion) corresponds

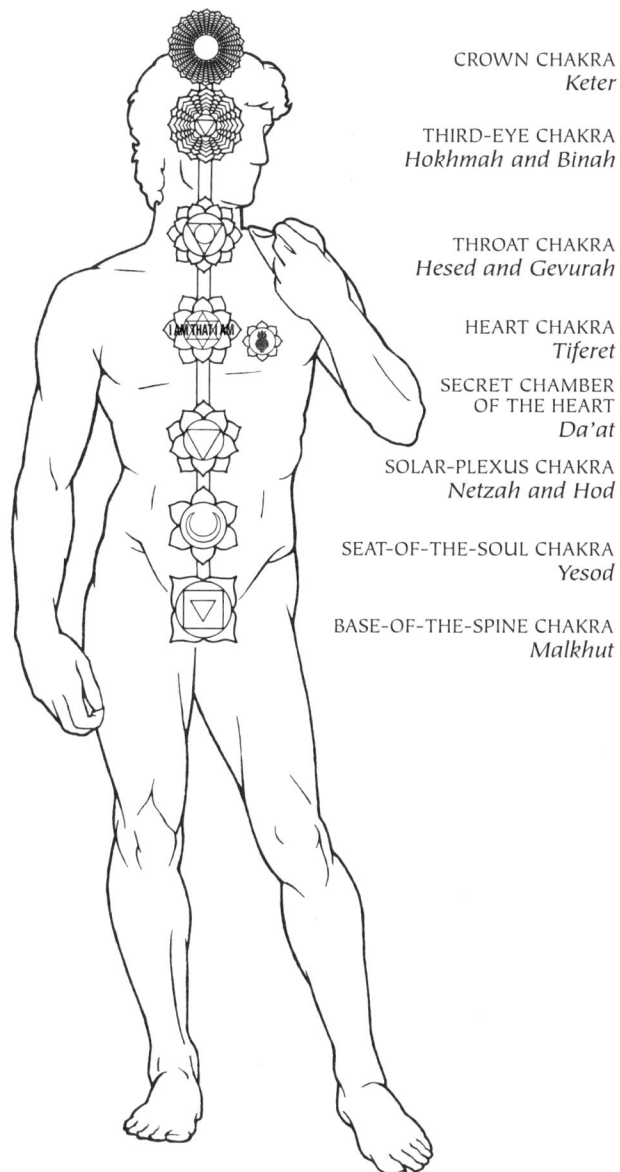

FIGURE 13. *The sefirot correspond to the chakras (the centers of light in your etheric body). Both the sefirot and the chakras step down God's energy for our use.*

to the twelve-petaled heart *chakra,* where the roseate flame of divine love is focused.

Netzah (Victory) and *Hod* (Splendor/Majesty) correspond to the ten-petaled solar-plexus *chakra* at the navel. The purple-and-gold flame of ministration and service is focused there. *Yesod* (Foundation) corresponds to the six-petaled seat-of-the-soul *chakra,* located halfway between the navel and base of the spine. Here the violet flame of transmutation is focused.

Malkhut (Kingdom) corresponds to the four-petaled base-of-the-spine *chakra,* the lowest *chakra* on the spinal column. The white flame focused in this *chakra* is known as the sacred fire and the flame of the ascension. When a soul pays off her karma, fulfills her divine plan and bonds to her Holy Christ Self, she returns to God in the ritual of the ascension, as Jesus and the ascended masters have done.

According to Gershom, *Malkhut* can correspond to the base of the spine or the feet. "Through the *sefirah Malkhut* you touch the physical world," he says. "It is the connection to the earth. Yogis sit on the ground, but in Kabbalah *Malkhut* corresponds to the point of the feet because we stand when we pray."[25]

In the beginning, the great mercy of God allowed the Divine Mother, *Malkhut/Shekhinah,* to descend to the level of the base-of-the-spine *chakra*. If God as *Malkhut* had not descended to that level, our souls could not have taken incarnation and we would not have had the opportunity to realize our own divine potential on earth.

As for the quasi-*sefirah, Da'at,* I believe it corresponds to the eight-petaled secret chamber of the heart, that special place where you commune with your Holy Christ Self and fan the fires of your threefold flame. Here you can also invoke the light of *Da'at* to gain self-knowledge, truly the knowledge of your inner child, your very soul.

You automatically intensify light in a *chakra* when you

SEFIRAH	ATTRIBUTE	ADAM KADMON'S BODY	CHAKRA	SPHERE OF CAUSAL BODY
KETER	Crown	Head	Crown	White/Purity, Discipline, Joy
HOKHMAH	Wisdom	Head	Third eye	Yellow/Wisdom, Understanding, Enlightenment
BINAH	Understanding	Head	Third eye	Yellow/Wisdom, Understanding, Enlightenment
DA'AT	Knowledge	Face and Throat	Secret Chamber of the Heart	Spheres of the Five Secret Rays
HESED	Love, Mercy	Right Arm	Throat	Pink/Love, Compassion, Kindness, Charity
GEVURAH	Justice, Judgment	Left Arm	Throat	Pink/Love, Compassion, Kindness, Charity
TIFERET	Beauty, Compassion	Trunk	Heart	Violet/Mercy, Justice, Freedom, Transmutation
NETZAH	Victory	Right Leg	Solar Plexus	Purple and Gold/ Service, Ministration, Peace, Brotherhood
HOD	Splendor, Majesty	Left Leg	Solar Plexus	Purple and Gold/ Service, Ministration, Peace, Brotherhood
YESOD	Foundation	Male Sexual Organ	Seat of the soul	Green/Truth, Science, Healing, Abundance, Vision, Music
MALKHUT/ SHEKHINAH	Kingdom/ Divine Presence	Feet or Mouth	Base of the spine	Blue/Faith, Will, Power, Perfection, Protection, Judgment

FIGURE 14. *Attributes of and Correspondences to the* Sefirot

PLATE 1. *The Chart of Your Divine Self*

PLATE 2. *The Seven Chakras and the Secret Chamber of the Heart*

perform the good works that accrue to the corresponding sphere of your Causal Body. For example, when you perform good works that accrue to the white sphere of your Causal Body, you also intensify the light in your white (base-of-the-spine) *chakra;* when you perform good works that accrue to your yellow sphere, you also intensify the light in your yellow (crown) *chakra.*

If you misuse the energies of your *chakras*—through selfishness, hatred, criticism, anger or any perversion of the virtues of the *sefirot*—your *chakras* will become clogged. This blocks the currents of *Ein Sof's* energy that vitalize your four lower bodies and can cause sluggishness or illness in your mental, emotional and physical bodies.

Although diagrams of the *chakras* and the *sefirot* of necessity depict them as static forces, when you meditate on them remember to see them as vibrant and dynamic. God's energy is constantly pulsing through your body and the network of your *chakras,* just as it is pulsing through the network of the *sefirot*. The *sefirot*, says Isaiah Tishby, are not like

> fixed, solid rungs on the ladder of the progressive revelation of the divine attributes. They are, on the contrary, dynamic forces, ascending and descending, and extending themselves within the area of the Godhead....They are in continuous motion, involved in innumerable processes of interweaving, interlinking, and union....The lower *sefirot* elevate themselves in their yearning to return and cleave to their source, and the upper *sefirot* move downward in order to give sustenance to the lower, and to transmit divine influence to the worlds below.[26]

The more we attune to the activity of the *sefirot*, which undergirds the entire universe, the more the Tree of Life of the *sefirot* will become a part of our daily walk with God. "Gradually, as the aspirant comes to appreciate the interaction of Laws—the flows, circulations, interchanges, transformations and levels—the Tree becomes less and less like an external abstraction and more like a living organism," writes Halevi. "When it has begun to be part of the aspirant's own being, he can say that he knows something of Kabbalah."[27]

The Kabbalists, along with mystics of all the world's religions, never lose sight of the principle that the divine pattern of the world above is reflected in their own bodies and souls and in the world all around them. The mystic lives and breathes the truth of the ancient Hermetic axiom, "As Above, so below." And as Ralph Waldo Emerson once said, "What lies behind us and what lies before us are tiny matters compared to what lies within us."

CHAPTER FIVE

MYSTERIES OF THE SOUL

*From the beginning of Time, through eternities, I was among
His hidden treasures. From Nothing He called me forth,
but at the End of Time I shall be recalled by the King.*

RABBI NAHMANIDES

Since we are patterned after the *sefirot*, Kabbalists believe that the more we know about our human form and our soul, the more we will know about the divine world of the *sefirot*. "The man who intends to penetrate the royal palace needs first to know his own soul...[which] is modeled on its Creator who created it," writes Rabbi Moses de León. "Therefore, when man knows the eminence and nature of the soul, his thoughts and understanding will spread from there to the secrets of royal matters,"[1] that is, the secrets of the *sefirot*.

What is the soul? According to Kabbalists, the soul is a mirror in which the *sefirot* are reflected, a spark of the divine

Kabbalists teach that if we desire to penetrate the secret world of the sefirot, we must first explore the mysteries of our own soul and spirit, for we are patterned after the sefirot. (Astronomer, printed by Johann Weissenburger, Nuremberg, 1504.)

essence. De León writes, "The body is not an image of the Creator....What, then, is His image and His counterpart? The soul, without a doubt." The soul, he says, is God's "own essential being."[2]

The Zohar tells us that our body is nothing more than a garment for our soul: "How does Scripture describe the creation of man? 'You have clothed me with skin and flesh' (Job 10:11). What then is man? If you say that he is nothing but skin and flesh, and bones and sinews, you are wrong; for, in actual truth, the real part of man is his soul. Clothes belong to man, but they are not man, and when man departs he is stripped of the clothes that he has put on."[3]

The Three Parts of the Soul

The Zohar says the soul has three parts: *nefesh, ruah* and *neshamah*. Each part comes from a different *sefirah*. *Nefesh* is the part of the soul that gives life to and sustains the body. Its source is the *sefirah Malkhut*. The Zohar says the *nefesh* stimulates the body to observe the commandments.

The second part of the soul, *ruah,* is the spirit, the seat of intellect and reason that allows us to transcend mere human existence. The *ruah* originates in *Tiferet*. It is "the ethical power to distinguish between good and evil," writes Scholem.[4]

The third part of the soul, *neshamah,* is known as the spiritual soul, holy soul or divine spark. It is described in the Zohar as a spark of *Binah*, for it comes from that *sefirah*.[5] Sidney Spencer writes:

> *Neshamah* is literally "breathing": it is the "breath of higher spirituality, the bridge which connects man with the heavenly world." It is an emanation of *Binah*, the divine Intelligence, and unites man with God.
>
> ...It is an individualized expression of the divine. As the Zohar says, it is in its essence "the Supernal Soul, the Soul of all souls, inscrutable and unknowable, veiled in a covering of

exceeding brightness" (2:245a). In entering into the depths of his own being, man thus becomes aware of the presence of God.[6]

We all have the potential to realize the three grades of the soul, say Kabbalists, but these grades are not automatically active in all people. The *nefesh* is active in everyone, but the other two parts are activated only when merited. Scholem says that the *ruah* and *neshamah*

> are found only in the man who has awakened spiritually and made a special effort to develop his intellectual powers and religious sensibilities. The *ruah*... is aroused at an unspecified time when a man succeeds in rising above his purely vitalistic side. But it is the highest of the three parts of the soul, the *neshamah* or *spiritus*, which is the most important of all. It is aroused in a man when he occupies himself with the Torah and its commandments, and it opens his higher powers of apprehension, especially his ability to mystically apprehend the Godhead and the secrets of the universe.[7] By acquiring *[neshamah]*, the Kabbalist thus realizes something of the divine in his own nature.[8]

The Zohar says that the *neshamah* is activated within us when we strive for righteousness and purity and that by observing the grades of the soul we can learn about the *sefirot*:

> The *nefesh* and the *ruah* are intertwined together, whereas the *neshamah* resides in a man's character—an abode which cannot be discovered or located. Should a man strive towards purity of life, he is aided thereto by a holy *neshamah*, whereby he is purified and sanctified and attains the title of "saint." But should he not strive for righteousness and purity of life, he is animated only by the two grades, *nefesh* and *ruah*, and is devoid of a holy *neshamah*. What is more, he who commences to defile himself is led further into defilement, and heavenly help is withdrawn from him. Thus each is led along the path which he chooses.[9]...
>
> Happy are the righteous in this world and in the next,

> because they are altogether holy. Their body is holy, their soul *(nefesh)* is holy, their spirit *(ruah)* is holy, their super-soul *(neshamah)* is holy of holies. These are three grades indissolubly united.
>
> If a man does well with his soul *(nefesh)*, there descends upon him a certain crown called spirit *(ruah)*, which stirs him to a deeper contemplation of the laws of the Holy King. If he does well with this spirit, he is invested with a noble holy crown called super-soul *(neshamah)*, which can contemplate all.[10]...
>
> From observing these grades of the soul, you will obtain an insight into the higher Wisdom, and everything is Wisdom, so that you might perceive in this way matters that are sealed[11] [i.e., perceive the *sefirot*[12]].

The Zohar goes on to say that Abraham attained the highest level of the soul. It interprets certain events in Abraham's life as symbolic of the soul testings he had to face as he sought to cleave to God. These teachings are profound and they are immediately relevant to your soul's ascent up the Tree of Life today. For every soul who seeks to cleave to God must pass through the same initiations that Abraham did.

> At the time when Abram [Abraham] entered the land, God appeared to him and he received there a *nefesh*, and built an altar to the corresponding grade (of divinity) [to the corresponding *sefirah*]. Then "he journeyed to the South," receiving a *ruah*. Finally he rose to the height of cleaving to God through the medium of the *neshamah*, whereupon he "built an altar to the Lord," indicating the most recondite grade corresponding to the *neshamah*.
>
> He then found that it was requisite for him to test himself and endow himself with grades, so he went down to Egypt [a country of magicians, symbolizing the domain of evil forces and magic; worldliness; the material world]. There he preserved himself from being seduced by those bright essences, and after testing himself he returned to his place: he "went up" from Egypt literally, strengthened and confirmed in faith,

and reached the highest grade of faith. Thenceforth Abram was acquainted with the higher Wisdom and clung to God and became the right hand of the world.[13]

What happens to the parts of the soul after death? Since the *neshamah* is a spark of the divine, the Zohar says that it cannot sin and therefore cannot be punished after death. The *nefesh* and sometimes the *ruah* can be punished after death. Scholem says Kabbalists teach that after death "the *nefesh* remains for a while in the grave, brooding over the body; the *ruah* ascends to the terrestrial paradise in accordance with its merits; and the *neshamah* goes directly back to its native home."[14]

Kabbalists after the Zohar, including Rabbi Isaac Luria, name two additional levels of the soul that are higher than the *nefesh*, *ruah* and *neshamah*: the *hayyah* and *yehidah*. These two tiers of the soul, writes Scholem, "were considered to represent the sublimest levels of intuitive cognition and to be within the grasp only of a few chosen individuals."[15]

The Difference between Your Soul and Your Divine Spark

Like the Kabbalists, mystics the world around believe that a part of God resides within each of us. The apostle Paul told the Corinthians: "Know ye not that ye are the temple of God, and that the Spirit of God dwelleth in you?"[16] Peter said that through the goodness and glory of Christ we could be "partakers of the divine nature."[17]

In a teaching that resembles that of Kabbalah, fourteenth-century Christian theologian and mystic Meister Eckhart taught: "There is something in the soul that is so akin to God that it is one with Him.[18] God's seed is within us.[19] There is a part of the soul that is untouched by time or mortality: it proceeds out of the Spirit and remains eternally in the Spirit and is divine.... Here God glows and flames without ceasing, in all His abundance and sweetness and rapture."[20]

Similarly, Buddhists teach that all men have within them the potential for Buddhahood, which they call the Buddha-nature or the "Germ of Buddhahood." One Buddhist text says, "The road to Buddhahood is open to all. At all times have all living beings the Germ of Buddhahood in them."[21]

Hinduism calls the indwelling God "the Atman." The Atman is the imperishable, undecaying core of man. It is identical with Brahman, the Absolute, hence the famous Hindu affirmation: *Tat Tvam Asi,* "That thou art," meaning: Thou art the Absolute. Thou art Brahman. Thou art God. *That* is what thou art.

Although mystics like Meister Eckhart sometimes refer to the soul and the divine spark as identical, there is a difference between them. The Jewish mystics approach this understanding when they make a distinction between the holy spark, *neshamah,* and the other two grades of the soul, *nefesh* and *ruah.*

The ascended masters teach that the divine spark is pure Spirit. It can never die. But the soul can be lost; she can self-destruct by her own actions. If the soul does not exercise her free will to realize her potential, she may ultimately lose that potential and cease to exist.

The Book of Ezekiel and the Book of Revelation explain what happens to the soul in this case: "The soul that sinneth, it shall die."[22] "He that overcometh shall inherit all things; and I will be his God and he shall be my son. But the fearful and unbelieving and the abominable and murderers and whoremongers and sorcerers and idolaters and all liars shall have their part in the lake which burneth with fire and brimstone: which is the second death."[23]

Mark L. Prophet and I explain the difference between the soul and the Spirit in *Climb the Highest Mountain:*

> God is a Spirit and the soul is the living potential of God. The soul's demand for free will and her separation from God resulted in the descent of this potential into the lowly estate of

the flesh. Sown in dishonor, the soul is destined to be raised in honor to the fullness of that God-estate which is the one Spirit of all Life. The soul can be lost; Spirit can never die....

The soul, then, remains a fallen potential that must be imbued with the Reality of Spirit, purified through prayer and supplication, and returned to the glory from which it descended and to the unity of the Whole. This rejoining of soul to Spirit is the alchemical marriage which determines the destiny of the self and makes it one with immortal Truth. When this ritual is fulfilled, the highest Self is enthroned as the Lord of Life; and the potential of God, realized in man, is found to be the All-in-all.[24]

Mark Prophet liked to cite the metaphor of a drop in the ocean to describe the relationship of the soul to God. In a lecture he once gave he said:

> I like to think that God is a Spirit—like a great big ocean. And I like to think of all of us as being like drops of water in a vast sea of Light.
>
> Reciting the great mysteries of the universe, the Hindu sage used to say: "God is the ocean..."—it was his favorite similitude, and he would hold up his finger with one little drop of water glistening on the end of it as he continued—"and this drop is the soul. This is a part of the ocean of God. It lacks only the quantity of God, but none of the quality."
>
> ...Do you know that all of the elements of the whole ocean are to be found in that drop of water?
>
> So you see, you have all of the shining qualities of God, of the Creator of a living soul which has the real potential—the *real*izable potential—of the Spirit....
>
> That means that you have within yourself a glisteringly beautiful spark of the Son of God, of the Christ consciousness —of Reality. It's right there in front of you. That's you! You're a drop in an infinite ocean of God. Isn't that something to think about![25]

The concept in Kabbalah that we have within us a part of God and that we are composed of the ten *sefirot* has far-reaching implications. Our divine nature confers upon us unparalleled opportunities: we not only have tremendous power to change our own lives and the world around us, but, astonishingly, we have the power to change the world of the Godhead as well. Scholem writes:

> Man is the perfecting agent in the structure of the cosmos; like all the other created beings, only even more so, he is composed of all ten *sefirot* and "of all spiritual things," that is, of the supernal principles that constitute the attributes of the Godhead. If the forces of the *sefirot* are reflected in him, he is also the "transformer" who through his own life and deeds amplifies these forces to their highest level of manifestation and redirects them to their original source. To use the neoplatonic formula, the process of creation involves the departure of [the] all from the One and its return to the One.[26]

In short, Kabbalists have come up with the very unique idea that we can use our spiritual power to strengthen or to weaken, to unite or to disrupt the divine world. This is a subject I will discuss further in later chapters.

Soul Travel to Celestial Academies
"With My Soul Have I Desired Thee in the Night"

The Zohar and other Kabbalistic writings describe the mystic ascent of the soul to heavenly realms. They say that while the body is asleep the soul can take flight to "celestial academies," where she is tutored in the sublime mysteries of God. Rabbi Hayim Vital says that Luria was one whose soul was worthy to ascend to the celestial academies nightly. Vital writes:

> Troops of angels would greet him to safeguard his way, bringing him to the celestial academies. These angels would ask him which academy he chose to visit. Sometimes he said that he

wished to visit the academy of Rabbi Simeon bar Yohai, or the academy of Rabbi Akiva or that of Rabbi Eliezer the Great or those of other *tannaim* and *amoraim*,[27] or of the prophets. And to whichever of those academies he wished to go, the angels would take him. The next day he would disclose to the sages what he received in that academy.[28]

Moshe Idel, a contemporary expert on Kabbalah, says, "This perception of Luria is no doubt closely connected to the huge amount of Kabbalistic material he communicated that produced the extensive Lurianic literature."[29]

Idel says that the Kabbalist Rabbi Shem Tov ibn Gaon also speaks of sharing knowledge gained during mystic ascents. "Rabbi Shem Tov mentions the need to fathom intellectually the secrets of the *Merkabah* [the throne-chariot of God] and the structures of the Creation," writes Idel. "The result is not only beatific or divine visions but also an impressive explosion of literary creativity, consisting in 'copying' the contents revealed in his mind as if from a book. The affinity of this description to Luria's own creativity is startling."[30] The ideal for the mystic, according to Rabbi Shem Tov, is "to ascend from the lower academy to the supernal academy and to subsist from the splendor of the *Shekhinah*."[31]

Idel also cites an entry made by Vital in his diary that alludes to the soul's ascent to spiritual realms to commune with heavenly beings. Here Vital is recording the dream of Rabbi Isaac Alatif.

> Once I fainted deeply for an hour, and a huge number of old men and many women came to watch me, and the house was completely full of them, and they all were worried for me. Afterwards the swoon passed and I opened my eyes and said, "Know that just now my soul ascended to the seat of glory, and they sent my soul back to this world in order to preach before you and lead you in the way of repentance and in matters of charity."[32]

The celestial academies that the Jewish mystics write about are what the ascended masters call "retreats" or "universities of the Spirit." They are located in the heaven world, known as the etheric plane. As your soul takes leave of your body while you sleep at night, you can travel to these academies to study with angels and masters of wisdom who have gained mastery in their fields of specialization.

If you keep your mind and heart attuned to the sendings of your soul, you may recall the lessons you have learned at

Kabbalists say that while the body is asleep, the soul can take flight, escorted by angels, to "celestial academies." At these academies the soul is tutored in the sublime mysteries of God. (The New Jerusalem by Gustave Doré.)

night in the etheric retreats or you may awaken in the morning with a clear direction to do this or that. You may even feel that the burdens you have prayed to God about the night before are resolved, or you will arise knowing precisely what steps to take to resolve them.

Keep a journal with pen or pencil handy on your nightstand. Record instructions and revelations you receive right away, either when you are awakened in the night or when you arise in the morning. Some dreams are encoded material presented symbolically by your Holy Christ Self. Ask your Holy Christ Self to decode your dreams and to show you how to apply their lessons to your daily life. Sift through the material and act on what feels right to you and is consistent with ethical standards. Discard what is neither plausible nor rational.

The Zohar wisely warns that the ascent of the soul during sleep is not without its dangers. In one passage it describes how "certain bright but unclean essences" attempt to prevent the soul from soaring to the heights:

> Rabbi Simeon was on a journey with Rabbi Eleazar, his son, Rabbi Abba, and Rabbi Judah. As they went along Rabbi Simeon said: It surprises me how people fail to pay attention to the study of the words of Torah, and of the very foundation of their lives.
>
> He proceeded to discourse on the text: "With my soul have I desired thee in the night, yea, with my spirit within me will I seek thee early" (Isa. 26:9). He said: The inner meaning of this verse is as follows.
>
> When a man lies down in bed, his vital spirit *(nefesh)* leaves him and begins to mount on high. But do all [souls] really ascend [that is, reach the highest levels[33]]? No. Not every one sees the countenance of the king [that is, contemplates the divine *sefirot*[34]]. But the soul does ascend, leaving with the body only the impression of a receptacle which contains the heartbeat. The rest of it tries to soar from grade to grade, and in

doing so it encounters certain bright but unclean essences.

If [the *nefesh*] is pure and has not defiled itself by day, it rises above [the unclean essences] to the higher realms, but if not, it becomes defiled among them and cleaves to them and does not rise any further. There they show her certain things which are going to happen in the near future: and sometimes they delude her and show her false things. Thus she goes about the whole night until the man wakes up, when she returns to her place. Happy are the righteous to whom God reveals His secrets in dreams, so that they may be on their guard against sin! Woe to the sinners who defile their bodies and their souls![35]

As you travel out of your body at night on your way to the etheric realm, call to God's angels to protect you so you don't get caught in the astral plane. Here bright essences of disembodied spirits will try to lure you to their level with baubles and trinkets. These spirits are also called "discarnate entities." Some have lost their souls and would draw you to themselves to steal your light. Do not allow them to pull on you. Resist their animal magnetism.

The above passage from the Zohar tells us that whatever we bring back from the astral plane and from the "bright but unclean essences" is not reliable and is not a revelation from God. Rather than seeking communications from disembodied spirits on the astral plane, seek the direct communication of your God Presence through your Holy Christ Self. Pray to the Holy Spirit for the gift of discernment of spirits and heed the warnings of your Holy Christ Self. Accept his guidance to stay away from the negative influences of the astral plane.

Beware not only of the soulless ones on the astral plane but of people who may have already lost their souls while yet in the flesh. They are hangers-on, ready and waiting to steal your light. Discarnate entities attach themselves to them like barnacles on the hull of a boat. These entities leech the life-essence of those to whom they cling as well as the life-essence of their close companions. For example, people who are possessed by discarnate entities can catch you off guard by introducing argumentation and accusation into a conversation. When you get defensive and allow yourself to be sucked into an argument, the entities in turn suck your light.

Aware of the wiles of these malevolent spirits, Paul said:

> Be strong in the Lord, and in the power of his might. Put on the whole armour of God, that ye may be able to stand against the wiles of the devil....
>
> Stand therefore, having your loins girt about with truth, and having on the breastplate of righteousness; and your feet shod with the preparation of the gospel of peace; above all, taking the shield of faith, wherewith ye shall be able to quench all the fiery darts of the wicked.
>
> And take the helmet of salvation, and the sword of the Spirit, which is the word of God: praying always with all prayer and supplication in the Spirit.[36]

A person who is possessed of discarnate entities can do what Paul told us to do. He can invoke the might of Archangel Michael to deliver him of controlling spirits. In the name of God you can also command Archangel Michael to protect your soul from getting entangled with the bright essences of disembodied spirits as you journey out of your body at night.* As you go to sleep, fix your mind straight as an arrow and let it fly unerringly to its mark. Focus your inner sight on your destination, preferably an etheric retreat of the Great White Brotherhood, such as the Royal Teton Retreat.

The Royal Teton Retreat, congruent with the Grand Teton near Jackson Hole, Wyoming, is the retreat the ascended masters recommend their students aim for. Put up a poster, painting or photo of the Grand Teton opposite your bed so it

---

*See the last chapter for commands you can give to invoke the intercession of God's angels.

The Royal Teton Retreat, a university of the Spirit in the heaven world, is congruent with the Grand Teton in the Teton Range near Jackson Hole, Wyoming. Souls travel to this retreat during sleep or between incarnations to be tutored by the ascended masters.

is the last thing you see just before you turn out your light. Then visualize your soul clothed in your etheric body of light being escorted to the Royal Teton Retreat by a cordon of angels assigned to you by Archangel Michael.

After warning of the bright but unclean essences that ensnare and delude souls who have defiled themselves during the day, the Zohar goes on to describe the ascent of pure souls.

> As for those who have not defiled themselves during the day, when they fall asleep at night their soul begins to ascend, and first enters those grades which we have mentioned, but it does not cleave to them and continues to mount further. And it moves on subsequently, rising in its own way [depending on the virtues that it has[37]]. The soul which is privileged thus to rise finally appears before the gate of the celestial palace and

yearns with all its might to behold the beauty of the King and to visit His sanctuary.

This is the man who ever hath a portion in the world to come, and this is the soul whose yearning when she ascends is for the Holy One, blessed be He, and who does not cleave to those other bright essences but seeks out the holy essence in the place from which she (originally) issued. Therefore it is written, "With my soul have I desired thee in the night," to pursue after thee and not to be enticed away after false powers.[38]

Twin Flames and Soul Mates

Another mystery of the soul unveiled in Kabbalah is the mystery of you and your soul partner. The Zohar teaches that your soul has a twin who was created with you in the beginning. God will bring the two of you together, it says, if you live a life of purity and good works.

> All the souls in the world, which are the fruit of the handiwork of the Almighty, are mystically one, but when they descend to this world they are separated into male and female, though these are still conjoined.
>
> When they first issue forth, they issue as male and female together. Subsequently, when they descend [to this world] they separate, one to one side and the other to the other, and God afterwards unites them—God and no other, He alone knowing the mate proper to each. Happy the man who is upright in his works [or pure] and walks in the way of truth, so that his soul may find its original mate, for then he becomes indeed perfect,* and through his perfection the whole world is blessed.[39]

Centuries before the Zohar was written, Plato taught that each of us is half of a divine whole and that is why we are always searching for our original partner. In his *Symposium* he writes:

---

*also translated "for if he performs good deeds, he is the proper, whole man." (Tishby, *Wisdom of the Zohar* 3:1382)

Ancient is the desire of one another which is implanted in us, reuniting our original nature, making one of two, and healing the state of man.

Each of us when separated, having one side only, like a flat fish, is but the indenture [indentation] of a man, and he is always looking for his other half....

When one of them meets with his other half, the actual half of himself,...the pair are lost in an amazement of love and friendship and intimacy....These are the people who pass their whole lives together; yet they could not explain what

God originally created each soul with a mate, says the Zohar, but they became separated when they descended into this world. God will bring soul partners together again if they live a life of purity and good works.

they desire of one another. For the intense yearning which each of them has towards the other does not appear to be the desire of lover's intercourse, but of something else which the soul of either evidently desires and cannot tell.[40]

Plato's image of the lone soul as a flat fish, having only one side, reminds me of statues of the Hindu god Shiva that depict him as half man and half woman. According to legend, Shiva was determined that there be no separation between himself and his consort Parvati. He therefore decreed that his right side represent Shiva and that his left side represent Parvati in an eternal union. That eternal union with one's divine counterpart and with God is what every soul, consciously or unconsciously, yearns for.

Like the Zohar, Plato says our search for our divine partner will end only if we are pious and avoid evil:

> Human nature was originally one and we were a whole, and the desire and pursuit of the whole is called love. There was a time, I say, when we were one, but now because of the wickedness of mankind God has dispersed us....
>
> Wherefore let us exhort all men to piety, that we may avoid evil, and obtain the good, of which Love is to us the lord and minister; and let no one oppose him—he who opposes him is the enemy of the gods. For if we are friends of the god [Love] and at peace with him, we shall find our own true loves, which rarely happens in this world at present....
>
> I believe that if our loves were perfectly accomplished, and each one returning to his primeval nature had his original true love, then our race would be happy....We must praise the god Love, who is our greatest benefactor, both leading us in this life back to our own nature, and giving us high hopes for the future, for he promises that if we are pious, he will restore us to our original state, and heal us and make us happy and blessed.[41]

The term the ascended masters use to describe you and your "other half" is "twin flames." God created your twin flames out of a single "white fire body." He separated this ovoid into two spheres of being—one with a masculine polarity and the other with a feminine polarity. For the purpose of the soul's evolution, each half of the divine whole has its own Causal Body, I AM Presence, Holy Christ Self and soul. Twin flames are twin flames because they have the same spiritual origin and unique pattern of identity.

We would have continued to share the beauty of the relationship of cosmic lovers with our twin flame throughout our many incarnations on earth if we had remained in harmony with each other and with God. But we fell from the state of perfection by misusing God's light. In the process, we created negative karma—coils of energy and layers of density in our aura that have separated us from our twin flame. We found ourselves farther and farther apart until we passed as ships in the night, not knowing how near and yet how far we were from one another.

Thus before God can bring you and your twin flame together, you may have karmic obligations to others that you must fulfill. The sooner you balance your karma through service to life, the sooner you and your twin flame will be liberated for the next step in the saga of your destiny. This is one of the reasons why we find ourselves inexplicably drawn into certain circumstances, relationships or marriages. We may have something very important to give to another or to receive from another before we can move on with the divine plan of our twin flames.

In chapter 4, I said that the most effective way to fulfill karmic obligations is through prayer, especially by invoking the violet flame, and through service to God, family and the world community. This is what Plato and the Zohar mean when they say we must be pious and upright in our works in order to be reunited with our other half.

I have always taught that the first step toward your soul's union with her twin flame is to seek union with your Holy

Christ Self and I AM Presence, to cleave to God as the Jewish mystics would say. For you want to be able to bring to your twin flame the highest gift of your love, your true self and your spiritual attainment. And it is the light of God you garner as you ascend the ladder of the *sefirot* that will magnetize your twin flame to you or liberate you both to move closer to that goal.

Not all beautiful and soul-fulfilling loves are those of twin flames. There is also the love of kindred souls, whom the ascended masters call "soul mates." Whereas twin flames share a common spiritual origin, soul mates share a complementary calling in life. They are mates in the sense of being partners for the journey, co-workers. Soul mates are very compatible and very much alike. They are in a sense playmates in the schoolroom of life. You may have a number of such associations in the history of your soul's incarnations. But you only have one twin flame. And your twin flame is your greatest love.

Although you may be separated from your twin flame on earth, you are always one in Spirit. If karma must keep you apart for a season, at spiritual levels you may still work with your twin flame, amplifying the combined momentum of your love to minister to life.[42]

The Baal Shem Tov, founder of Hasidism, a Jewish religious movement that began in Poland in the eighteenth century, expressed the beauty and power of the relationship of twin flames when he wrote: "From every human being there rises a light that reaches straight to heaven. And when two souls that are destined to be together find each other, their streams of light flow together and a single brighter light goes forth from their united being."

Devekut, Mystical Cleaving to God

Kabbalists believe that because the soul has her origin in the divine realm, she naturally desires to return to her source.

Kabbalists seek this return through *devekut,* mystical cleaving to God. *Devekut* is the ultimate goal of the Jewish mystic. Scholem says *devekut* is "continuous attachment or adhesion to God," "a perpetual being-with-God, an intimate union and conformity of the human and the divine will."[43]

Isaac of Acco delineates degrees of *devekut,* including equanimity (the indifference of the soul to praise or blame), concentration or solitude (being alone with God), the Holy Spirit (a general term for enlightenment and inspiration), and prophecy.[44]

The thirteenth-century mystic philosopher Rabbi Nahmanides says that *devekut* means that

> you should remember God and the love of Him always, that you should not cease thinking of Him, when you are on a journey, when you lie down or when you arise; so that when you converse with people you should do so with your mouth and your tongue, but your heart should be with God. And it is possible that the souls of men who achieve this state are bound up in the bond of eternal life even during their lifetime, for they are in themselves the abode of the *Shekhinah.*[45]

Nahmanides says that if you cleave to your Creator in this way, you are eligible to receive the Holy Spirit.[46] The twelfth-century Jewish philosopher and scholar Maimonides says that the person who has merited receiving the Holy Spirit is transformed and can perceive things that are not normally accessible:

> His soul becomes bound up on the level of the angels...and he becomes a completely different person. He can now understand things with a knowledge completely different than anything that he ever experienced previously. The level that he has attained is far above that of other men, who can merely use their intellect. This is the meaning of what [the prophet Samuel told] King Saul, "[The spirit of God shall descend

The ultimate goal of the Jewish mystic is an intimate oneness with God, known as devekut, *or mystical cleaving to God. Some Kabbalists describe prophecy as the highest level of* devekut. *The prophetess Deborah (above) was one of the greatest judges of Israel. The judges were charismatic leaders and military heroes, deliverers endowed with the Spirit of God. Deborah with Barak led the Israelites into battle and foretold their victory.* (The Prophetess Deborah *by Edwin Austin Abbey.*)

upon you,] you shall prophesy with them, and you shall be transformed into a different man" (I Sam. 10:6).[47]

Rabbi Moses Luzzatto also describes the Holy Spirit as a form of enlightenment that is above human reason and intellect. He calls it "bestowed enlightenment." "Bestowed enlightenment consists of an influence granted by God through various means," says Luzzatto. "When such influence enters a person's mind, certain information becomes fixed in his intellect. He perceives this information clearly, without any doubt or error, understanding it completely, with all its causes and effects, as well as its place in the general scheme."[48]

Like Isaac of Acco, Luzzatto describes an even higher form

of *devekut* than enlightenment—"the level of true prophecy." He says:

> This is a degree of inspiration in which the individual reaches a level where he literally binds himself to God in such a way that he actually feels this attachment. He then clearly realizes that the One to whom he is bound is God. This is sensed with complete clarity, with an awareness that leaves no room for any doubt whatsoever. The individual is as certain of it as he would be if it were a physical object observed with his physical senses.
>
> The main concept of true prophecy, then, is that a living human being achieves such an attachment and bond with God. This in itself is an extremely high state of perfection. Besides this, however, it is also often accompanied by certain information and enlightenment. Through prophecy, one can gain knowledge of many lofty truths among God's hidden mysteries. These things are perceived very clearly, just as all knowledge gained through bestowed enlightenment. Prophecy, however, comes with much greater intensity than *Ruah HaKodesh* [Holy Spirit].[49]

Kabbalists say that the opportunity to receive the Holy Spirit is not limited to Kabbalists or Jews. Elijah is said to have taught his disciples, "I call heaven and earth to bear witness that any person, Jew or Gentile, man or woman, freeman or slave, if his deeds are worthy, then *Ruah HaKodesh* will descend upon him."[50]

Kaplan also points to the promise in the Book of Joel as evidence that God intends all humanity to receive his Holy Spirit: "I will pour out my spirit upon all flesh; and your sons and your daughters shall prophesy, your old men shall dream dreams, your young men shall see visions. And also upon the servants and upon the handmaids in those days will I pour out my spirit."[51]

According to Scholem, Kabbalists unanimously agree that *devekut*, mystical cleaving to God, is the ultimate goal of the spiritual path. However, there is disagreement among scholars as to whether Kabbalists taught that *devekut* leads to total union with God.

Moshe Idel notes, "Gershom Scholem stressed, time and again, that a total union with the Divine is absent in Jewish texts."[52] Scholem wrote in his book *Major Trends in Jewish Mysticism:* "It is only in extremely rare cases that ecstasy signifies actual union with God, in which the human individuality abandons itself to the rapture of complete submersion in the divine stream. Even in this ecstatic frame of mind, the Jewish mystic almost invariably retains a sense of the distance between the Creator and His creature."[53]

However, as Idel points out, Scholem was such a fine scholar of Jewish mysticism that many other scholars have accepted his views uncritically.[54] Using Kabbalistic texts for evidence, Idel shows that some Kabbalists did in fact pursue complete union with God.

For instance, Rabbi Isaac of Acco uses a variation of the drop-in-the-ocean metaphor to describe the soul's union with God: "[The soul] will cleave to the divine intellect, and it will cleave to her... and she and the intellect become one entity, as if somebody pours out a jug of water into a flowing spring, so that all becomes one.... And this is the secret meaning of [the phrase] 'a fire devouring fire.'"[55]

In the same text Rabbi Isaac writes: "This [rational] soul will cleave to the *Ein Sof* and will become total and universal, after she had been individual, due to her [experience in the] palace, while she was yet imprisoned in it, and she will become universal because of the nature of her real source."[56]

The Hasidic master Rabbi Menahem Nahum of Chernobyl also speaks of the union of the soul with its source: "He becomes attached to the divine unity by means of the union of the part to the all, which is *Ein Sof*. Consequently, the light of the holiness of *Ein Sof* shines in him, as the part cleaves to its root."[57]

The Soul's Journey after Life

The Zohar says the soul's journey beyond her earthly life is determined by the type of *devekut* she pursues in her life on earth. The soul chooses her own fate by cleaving to holy forces or to unholy forces.

> Blessed are the righteous, whose desire is perpetual *devekut* to the Holy One, blessed be He, and as they cleave to Him continually, so He cleaves to them and never leaves them. Alas for the wicked, whose desire and *devekut* separate them from Him. And it is not enough that they separate themselves from Him, but they cleave to "the other side" [the domain of demonic powers]....
>
> When the righteous depart from the world, their souls all ascend, and the Holy One, blessed be He, prepares for them another form that they can put on, and that reflects their existence in this world.[58]

Tishby interprets this to mean that "the garment that the souls don after death in the Garden of Eden is woven from the commandments that were fulfilled and the good deeds that were done in the physical world."[59] The Zohar continues:

> It is the path taken by man in this world that determines the path of the soul on her departure. Thus, if a man is drawn towards the Holy One, and is filled with longing towards Him in this world, the soul in departing from him is carried upward towards the higher realms by the impetus given her each day in this world.[60]

Elaborating on the same theme, Rabbi Abba says in the Zohar that when he was in a town inhabited by descendants of the "children of the East," they imparted to him "some of the Wisdom of antiquity with which they were acquainted." One of the things they told him was that after the death of the body the soul who has cleaved to holiness while on earth will stand among "holy beings," but the soul who has cleaved to uncleanness while on earth will be attached to "unclean company." Rabbi Abba says:

> They showed me one [of their books of wisdom] in which it was written that, according to the goal which a man sets himself in this world, so does he draw to himself a spirit from on high. If he strives to attain some holy and lofty object, he draws that object from on high to himself below. But if his desire is to cleave to the other side, and he makes this his whole intent, then he draws to himself from above the other influence. They said, further, that all depends on the kind of speech, action, and intention to which a man habituates himself, for he draws to himself here below from on high that side to which he habitually cleaves.
>
> I found also in the same book the rites and ceremonies pertaining to the worship of the stars, with the requisite formulas and the directions for concentrating the thought upon them so as to draw them near the worshipper. The same principle applies to him who seeks to be attached to the sacred spirit on high. For it is by his acts, by his words, and by his fervency and devotion that he can draw to himself that spirit from on high.
>
> They further said that if a man follows a certain direction in this world, he will be led further in the same direction when he departs this world; as that to which he attaches himself in this world, so is that to which he will find himself attached in the other world: if holy, holy, and if defiled, defiled.
>
> If he cleaves to holiness he will on high be drawn to that side and be made a servant to minister before the Holy One among the angels, and will stand among those holy beings....Similarly if he clings here to uncleanness, he will be drawn there towards that side and be made one of the unclean company and be attached to them. These are called "pests of mankind."[61]

The ascended masters, like the Jewish mystics, teach that the goal of the soul is to reunite with God. When the soul passes on through the change called death but is not ready for this ultimate reunion, she will spend time on interim planes before her next incarnation. Advanced souls who have led a life dedicated to God are taken by angels to retreats in the heaven world. Here they progress spiritually and prepare to meet the challenges of their next life.

Not everyone, however, reaches these schoolrooms between their incarnations. Some souls get stuck in the astral plane, which the Zohar describes as the side of uncleanness. In the astral plane they become entangled with disembodied spirits (what the Zohar calls the "pests of mankind"), whose energies vibrate at the lowest common denominator of humanity.

The formula that the Zohar spells out is simple: if you cleave to earthly things while you are on earth—material goods, power, position, ambition, base desire—when you die your soul will not be free to rise to the realms of light. If you get into the habit of cleaving to heavenly things—meditating on the *sefirot*, communing with ascended masters, befriending the angels—then when your soul departs this world you will be magnetized to the light and, as the Zohar says, you will stand among holy beings.

The Soul's Final Ascent

Mystical cleaving to God is a day-by-day process of attaching oneself to God through prayer, devotion, meditation and good works. But, as I said, Kabbalists also speak of the soul's ultimate cleaving to God when she ascends back to her source at the end of her tenure on earth. Like Plato, de León describes the soul as a prisoner in the body.[62] The Zohar frequently depicts the soul as a fugitive or exile who has only one longing: "for the place from which it was taken."[63] Spencer writes:

> As an emanation from the *sefirot*, the soul pre-exists in the heavenly world, "hidden in the divine Idea." Before its descent to earth, it vows to fulfill its task—to re-unite itself with God. During its earthly life, it weaves the garment of light, which it is to wear after death in the "realm of radiance," from its righteous acts. In its final blessedness, when it has completed its growth, the soul ascends to its source, and is re-united with God.

This union is described in terms of love. The soul is united with "the Queen," the *Shekhinah,* or with the "heavenly King, the Holy One," in "the Palace of Love." But it is only "if a man is drawn towards the Holy One, and is filled with longing for Him in this world" that the soul is "carried upwards towards the higher realms" (Zohar 1:99). Otherwise men have to undergo reincarnation on earth, or to be purified in "the fiery stream of Gehenna," or even destroyed. Reincarnation, first taught in the Bahir, is apparently an exceptional destiny in the Zohar, though regarded by later Kabbalists as universal.[64]

Scholem says that as Kabbalah developed, "transmigration [reincarnation] ceased to be considered merely a punishment and came also to be viewed as an opportunity for the soul to fulfill its mission and make up for its failures in previous transmigrations."[65] The soul may go through numerous incarnations before she is perfected and is thereby worthy to reunite with God. If she does not willingly undergo the tests of the Holy Spirit lifetime after lifetime, her opportunity to do so will come to an end and she may ultimately cease to retain any identification with God. This is what is meant by the second death.[66]

The ascended masters teach that the soul is made permanent when after lifetimes of service to life she ascends back to God and reunites with her I AM Presence. This Jesus and other ascended masters have done. The prerequisites for this graduation from earth's schoolroom are (1) the soul must be bonded to her Holy Christ Self, (2) she must have balanced at least 51 percent of her karma, and (3) she must have fulfilled her mission on earth according to her divine plan. The reunion with the I AM Presence through the ascension is the ultimate goal of life for every living soul.

Kabbalists interpret certain Bible passages as referring to the union of the soul and God. Idel cites a passage from a work by one Jewish mystic: "He told me: 'Thou art my son, this day I have begotten thee' [Ps. 2:7], and also: 'See now that I,

FIGURE 15. *A disciple of the thirteenth-century Kabbalist Abraham Abulafia said that a* yod *cleaving to a* yod *symbolized union with God. The* yod *(above left) is the tenth letter of the Hebrew alphabet. The union of the two* yods *forms a circle (middle), resembling the ancient Chinese* yin-yang, *or T'ai Chi, symbol (right). The* yin-yang *symbol represents the harmonious interaction and integration of the* yin *(female) and* yang *(male) forces in the universe.*

even I, am He' [Deut. 32:39]. And the secret [of these verses] is the cleaving of the power—that is, the supernal divine power called the circle of prophecy—with the human power." Idel says that "I, even I, am He" stands for "the union of the Divine with the human."[67]

Idel also cites the work of one of the disciples of the Spanish Kabbalist Abraham Abulafia, which gives an interesting image for the soul's ascent and ultimate union with God. Abulafia's disciple says that the Hebrew letter *yod* stands for a person seeking union with God: "He is the *yod* in this world who has received the power from the all, and he comprises the all, like the *yod* in [the realm of] the *sefirot*. Understand, therefore, that there is no discernible difference between this *yod* and that *yod* but a very fine one, from the aspect of spirituality.... And this is the secret [of] 'and cleave unto Him' [Deut. 13:4]—the cleaving of *yod* to *yod* in order to complete the circle."[68] (fig. 15)

FIGURE 16. *The Fiery Ovoid Uniting God and the Soul. Mystical cleaving to God is portrayed here by the flow of light over the figure eight between the I AM Presence and the soul through the nexus of the Holy Christ Self. As your soul (the lower figure) bonds to your Holy Christ Self (the middle figure, corresponding to* Tiferet), *you are becoming one with God.*

The Soul's Final Ascent   155

The metaphor of the circle, explains Idel, is a symbol of the union of the human and the divine. He writes: "Each of the two *yods* are explicitly defined as halves of the circle, which is completed by the ascension of the lower man and his turning into 'the higher man, the man who [sits] on the throne and shall be called: "The LORD our righteousness."' Man, then, is but half of a greater unit, the circle, and by his ascent he can reconstruct it."[69]

The "cleaving of *yod* to *yod*" is the God in you below cleaving to the God in you above. In other words, by accessing the power of God that is within you, you can transform your lower self into your Higher Self. You can become one with the LORD Our Righteousness, your Holy Christ Self, and ultimately one with your I AM Presence.

When you look at the Chart of Your Divine Self, in your mind's eye draw an ellipse around it and see inside the ellipse a figure eight. (fig. 16) The I AM Presence represents the upper half of the figure eight and the soul represents the lower half. At the nexus of the figure eight is the Son of God, *Tiferet*, the LORD Our Righteousness. Through *Tiferet*, your soul (the *yod* below) is magnetized to your I AM Presence (the *yod* above), until you are no longer two but one.

Cleave to your I AM Presence. Cleave to the rock of your Divine Reality. For that which you cleave to, you shall become.

CHAPTER SIX

THE ORIGIN OF EVIL

Know that when all of God's works are each in its place, they are good in this place of their creation, as assigned to them and predetermined for them; but when they rebel and leave their legitimate places, then they are evil.

RABBI JOSEPH GIKATILLA

Where does evil come from? And why does God allow it to exist? For these age-old conundrums Kabbalists have offered innovative answers—extraordinary in their implications.

Kabbalists speak about the "evil urge," the dark side of human nature that entices man to sin, and about demonic powers, whose domain they call the "Other Side." But if a cardinal principle of Kabbalah is that everything ultimately has its roots in the Infinite God, *Ein Sof,* how do Kabbalists account for evil in the universe?

The Zohar uses the image of the snake to symbolize the power of evil that ambushes human beings, entices them to sin and persecutes Shekhinah. (The Serpent by Gustave Doré.)

They give several different explanations. One of the most prevalent is that evil is rooted in judgment untempered by love and mercy. This view is presented in the Zohar and then reappears, with a new twist, in the influential doctrines of Rabbi Isaac Luria.

Evil Emerged from Gevurah/Din

The Zohar says that evil emerged out of the fifth *sefirah*, *Gevurah* (also called *Din*), the *sefirah* of Power, Judgment and Justice. Specifically, the Zohar portrays evil as a by-product of the emanation of the *sefirot*. As I outlined in chapter 2, *Ein Sof* emanated *Keter*, *Keter* emanated *Hokhmah*, and *Hokhmah* emanated *Binah*. The remaining *sefirot* emanated from *Binah* starting with *Hesed* (Love/Mercy) and *Gevurah* (Justice/Judgment). Rabbi Arthur Green explains the Zohar's conception of how evil was born as the by-product of the creative tension between *Hesed* and *Gevurah/Din:*

> [There is a] necessary tension that exists as the fourth and fifth *sefirot*, *Hesed* and *Din*, emerge from *Binah*. *Din*, the force of divine rigor or judgment, resents being tied to *Hesed*, the unmitigated flow of love. In the very moment of its emanation it broke forth from the *sefirotic* system, saying, in the words of the Zohar, "I shall rule!" The measuring rod of the *sefirot*... used the power of *Ein Sof* to quickly force *Din* back into line, but in that moment of escape some portion of its power was released that could not be retrieved. That portion of *Din*, now turned against God, began its own *sefirotic* emanation in mocking imitation of the divine world. It too has ten emanated rungs....
>
> ...The Zohar sees evil as originating in justice itself, when that justice is not tempered with compassionate loving-kindness. The force of *Din* within God has a legitimate role, punishing the wicked and setting out to limit the indiscriminate love-flow of *Hesed,* which itself can be destructive if not held in proper balance. But once *Din* has escaped the demands of

love, it is no longer to be trusted. It then becomes a perversion of God's justice, one that would use his punishing powers to wreak destruction without cause.[1]

The counterfeit emanation that resulted from the rebellion of *Din* is what Kabbalists refer to as *Sitra Ahra,* the Other Side. It is also called the Emanation of the Left Hand or the Emanation of the Left because it emanated from *Din,* which is on the left side of the Tree of Life. The Zohar teaches that everything in the divine world, including the *sefirot,* has its counterpart on the Other Side: "Just as there are ten crowns of faith above, so there are ten crowns of sorcery of uncleanness below."[2]

The Zohar portrays the creation of the Other Side from *Gevurah/Din* as a single point that rises from the smoke of anger:

> When the smoke started to come out of the furious anger, the smoke spread farther and farther, anger after anger, one upon another, and one rode upon and dominated the other, like the appearance of male and female, so that all was a furious anger. And when the smoke began to spread it emitted from the anger the emission of a single point, that it might spread. Subsequently, the smoke of the anger spread out in a curling fashion, like the cunning snake, in order to do evil.[3]

Just as Genesis depicts the snake as the seducer of Eve and Jewish legend portrays Satan as a primordial snake, the Zohar uses the image of the snake to symbolize the Other Side. The snake, sometimes male and sometimes female, lures human beings into licentiousness, persecutes *Shekhinah* (the feminine aspect of God), and is the source of witchcraft. In one passage, the primordial snake is surrounded by his emissaries—a troop of snakes, including "the small snake that brings up the rear." These snakes "go out to ambush mankind with sins that repel them backward."[4]

The Counterfeit Din

The original act of rebellion took place when *Din* said, "I want to be the supreme judge without being forced to qualify my judgment with mercy." Fallen angels who personify stern judgment have attempted to usurp the authority of the true *Gevurah/Din*.[5] By refusing to qualify judgment with mercy, they have stripped *Gevurah* of its garments of Divine Justice, deposed it from its throne and blackened the name *Hesed*. Their battle cry is that of the rebellious *Din*, "I shall rule!"

The evil angels who are aligned with the counterfeit *Din* perpetrate wrongful judgment in all areas of life—judgment that rears its ugly head as racism, bigotry and prejudice. Judgment that ends in bloodbaths between Jews and Arabs, Catholics and Protestants, Hindus and Muslims, Serbs and Croats, Hutus and Tutsis. Judgment that maligns the innocent and glorifies the guilty through the misuse of the power of the bench and the press. Judgment that tears down the soul's self-esteem, destroys lives, and defies hope and faith and charity.

Think about stern judgment in your own life: If you judge another but your judgment is not just, you are sowing seeds of evil between you and your brother. You have arrived at the gate of bitterness and some part of you has become the slave of the unjust *Din*.

The Ascended Master El Morya has warned us again and again that we must not criticize, condemn or judge others. Jesus said, "Judge not, that ye be not judged."[6] Because we are not yet fully bonded to *Tiferet*, we do not always have the wisdom or the discernment to rightly judge another. But the portion of *Din* that turned against God is more than willing to enter into collusion with us to unjustly judge our neighbor. And once we enmesh ourselves in the roots of the counterfeit *Din*, we will have to wage war against it to extricate ourselves from its tangles.

If we become enslaved by *Din*, or if we have become the

victims of those who are enslaved by it, we must turn to *Tiferet*. For it is only through the compassionate heart of *Tiferet* (Beauty/Compassion) that we can balance and harmonize the contending forces of *Hesed* (Love/Mercy) and *Gevurah* (Justice/Judgment). Jesus Christ and all Sons of God who have embodied the compassion of *Tiferet* were sent by God to counteract the forces of harsh judgment. As John said, "God sent not his Son *[Tiferet]* into the world to condemn the world, but that the world through him might be saved."[7]

As we imitate the path of Jesus Christ and other rabbis and teachers who have become one with *Tiferet,* we are increasing the light of *Tiferet* within us. It is this light that will turn back the force of wrongful judgment. And as we develop the inner beauty and compassion of *Tiferet,* we will be able to judge true and righteous judgments, because our Holy Christ Self will counsel us as we separate out the Light from the Darkness, the Good from the Evil.

Balancing the Masculine and Feminine Qualities of Hesed and Gevurah

Some Kabbalists refer to *Gevurah/Din* as a feminine *sefirah*. It is on the left, or feminine, pillar of the Tree of Life. This connotes that the true and exalted nature of Justice as well as the perversion of Justice is feminine. Interestingly, Justice is traditionally symbolized by the female figure who holds a sword in one hand and scales in the other. To ensure impartiality, she is blindfolded.

Shakespeare gave Justice a body and breathed life into her when he created the character Portia in *The Merchant of Venice*. Portia disguises herself as a young lawyer and argues a case for her husband's friend Antonio, who after forfeiting a bond payment to Shylock is legally bound to give him a pound of flesh. In her plea for Antonio's life, Portia extols mercy when it seasons justice:

> The quality of mercy is not strained;
> It droppeth as the gentle rain from heaven
> Upon the place beneath. It is twice blest;
> It blesseth him that gives and him that takes.
> 'Tis mightiest in the mightiest; it becomes
> The thronèd monarch better than his crown.
> His scepter shows the force of temporal power,
> The attribute to awe and majesty,
> Wherein doth sit the dread and fear of kings;
> But mercy is above this scept'red sway;
> It is enthronèd in the hearts of kings,
> It is an attribute to God Himself,
> And earthly power doth then show likest God's
> When mercy seasons justice.[8]

As Portia says, earthly power is most like God's when, like *Tiferet,* it balances the opposing qualities of the masculine *Hesed* (Love/Mercy) and the feminine *Gevurah* (Justice/Judgment).

There is an ascended master named Portia who personifies Divine Justice. She epitomizes feminine strength and the mastery of the masculine and feminine principles. Her consort is the Ascended Master Saint Germain, who was embodied as Francis Bacon, the great scholar, scientist and true author of the Shakespearean plays.[9] Portia has been ascended for thousands of years. Perhaps when Bacon wrote *The Merchant of Venice,* he saw Portia as his muse in his visions or dreams.

Like the Kabbalists, mystics of many of the world's religions recognize that everything in the spiritual and material worlds moves to the rhythmic dance of male and female forces. Chinese philosophy also speaks of two opposite but complementary energies—*yin* and *yang*—whose interaction produces all phenomena in the universe. In their ideal state, *yin* (feminine) and *yang* (masculine) are in balance. These same forces are at work within our own body and soul and the components of our identity.

Shakespeare's Portia champions the balance of the masculine and feminine virtues of Justice (Gevurah) and Mercy (Hesed) when she eloquently pleads for Antonio's life, saying, "Mercy... is an attribute to God Himself, and earthly power doth then show likest God's when mercy seasons justice" (The Merchant of Venice, act 4, sc. 1).

All of us, both men and women, have a part of our nature that is masculine and a part of our nature that is feminine. Carl Jung called the feminine side of a man his anima and the masculine side of a woman her animus. The masculine side of our nature, corresponding to the left brain, is mental, reasoning and analytical. The feminine side of our nature, corresponding to the right brain, is caring, nurturing, sensitive and intuitive, and therein lies its strength. Yet this intuitive *(yin)* quality is what also leaves the feminine part of us vulnerable, because she must remain open.

In the account of Adam and Eve in Genesis, Eve represents our feminine, intuitive side. In her openness, Eve was receptive to the serpent. But she lost her objectivity and got sucked in to the perversion of the left-brain, male logic of that cunning agent of the Other Side.

Whether we are male or female, our goal is to balance the masculine and feminine parts of ourselves and bond to the great harmonizer, *Tiferet*, the Universal Christ. Only then will we be whole. When we have bonded to *Tiferet*, we will be open to others, yet we will have the discrimination to reject false logic with the authority of a son or daughter of God.

Shakespeare's Portia balanced the feminine and masculine sides of her nature. She showed an impeccable knowledge of the law and a commitment to justice, yet pleaded for mercy, saying to Shylock, "Though justice be thy plea, consider this: that, in the course of justice, none of us should see salvation."[10]

The battle between stern judgment and mercy that the Zohar pictures in mythical terms is not just a symbolic one. The battle goes on within and without. It takes place in ourselves as we struggle to balance our masculine and feminine sides to become spiritually and psychologically whole. It takes place in the streets and in the courts of law and in the schools every day as sons and daughters of God champion the meek of the earth. Everyone who takes a stand for truth, wherever it is found, is reinforcing the divine power of *Gevurah/Din*.

The equation is simple: Whenever someone champions justice, the power of the divine *Gevurah/Din* is amplified and the power of the Other Side is diminished. And whenever someone aligns with the unjust judges of the fallen *Din,* the power of the Other Side intensifies and the power of Divine Justice declines. As the Zohar puts it, our sins restore legs to the serpent, who was punished for seducing Adam and Eve by having his legs cut off. The serpent, representing the Other Side, literally had "no leg to stand on" after the episode in the

Garden of Eden. But when we sin, says the Zohar, we "give him supports and legs to stand upon, and he derives strength from them."[11]

Defeating the forces of the counterfeit *Din* is the work God has set before us. When we have accomplished it, the Other Side will be rolled up as a scroll and put to the torch of Divine Justice. May she reign supreme and may we, her children, know the glory of vindicating her cause.

Escaping the Clutches of the Other Side and the Evil Urge

In the Zohar, the evil urge, or "evil inclination," is the agent of the Other Side. At times the Zohar depicts the evil urge as an internal power that perpetually wars against our "good inclination." (The good inclination springs from the *neshamah,* the spark of the divine that resides within us.) But the Zohar also depicts the evil urge as an external power—a demonic person, a snake or a harlot who lies in wait to ensnare and annihilate the soul.

The war between good and evil has been symbolized in the literature of the world since ancient times. In a popular, contemporary setting, we can see the powers of the Other Side symbolized in Walt Disney's *Snow White and the Seven Dwarfs.* The beautiful princess Snow White escapes from her stepmother, the wicked queen, because the kindhearted huntsman warns her that the queen is jealous of her and has ordered him to kill her. Snow White flees, running through the forest. The tree trunks sprout evil faces, their branches grow fingers and they try to grab her. Snow White keeps running, but finally falls to the ground weeping.

Fortunately Snow White has friends in the forest—the gentle animals who escort her to the cottage of the seven dwarfs. The dwarfs invite Snow White to stay in their cottage, where she will be safe. When they leave for work the next morning, they warn her to be careful not to let anyone inside.

But the queen transforms herself into an old peddler woman and tricks the naive princess into eating a poisoned apple. Snow White falls into a deep sleep, and the dwarfs think she has died. Only when the handsome prince finds Snow White and gives her "love's first kiss" is the spell broken.

The wicked queen represents the fallen *Din* and the evil urge, the evil spirits of the forest represent the deputies of *Din*, and Snow White represents the soul. Like the queen and the evil spirits, *Din* and its agents are jealous of the light of God within us. They try to snag our soul and steal our light. The kind animals, the dwarfs and the prince are like the Kabbalists, the ascended masters and the angels. They awaken us to the dangers and the illusions of the Other Side. They give us the knowledge, the guidance and the love we need to survive the wiles of the Tempter and the circumstances of our karma.

The first line of defense against the evil urge is to be aware that it exists. Like Snow White, the soul has to be warned that someone is after her. The Baal Shem Tov teaches that the wise are always alert to the trickery of the evil urge:

> The righteous man who serves God...is fully aware of the battle waged by the evil urge. [The evil urge is like] the robber lying on the path [that leads] to the worship of God. [The righteous man] is aware of the danger, and is constantly alert to avoid a trap. He also knows how to warn others of the danger of these robbers....The wicked man, however,...constantly enjoys the snares of the evil urge, and says, "I am at peace—there is no danger in this world."[12]

Those who are blind to the snares of the evil urge are like the unwary people of Judah, who were lulled to sleep by the false prophets who proclaimed, "Peace, peace," when there was no peace.[13] That is what the evil urge whispers in our ear as it tempts us to stray from the path of oneness with our Higher Self.

According to the Kabbalists, we can escape the clutches of the evil urge and attract angels of light to protect us by observing the commandments *(mitzvot)* outlined in the Torah. The Zohar says:

> When a person sees that evil imaginings are assailing him, he should occupy himself with Torah and they will pass away.[14]...
>
> Whenever man goes toward the right, the protection of the Holy One, blessed be He, is always with him, and the Other Side can have no power over him. This evil is humiliated before him and cannot dominate him. But when the protection of the Holy One, blessed be He, passes from him, because of his attachment to evil, then this evil, seeing that he is without protection, immediately takes control of him, and comes to destroy him. Then authority is given to [evil], and he takes away his soul.[15]

When we keep the commandments of God and have compassion toward our brother, we are one with the Son, *Tiferet,* the Universal Christ. Our oneness with *Tiferet* brings us to the feet of I AM THAT I AM and connects us to *Keter*. And when we are one with *Tiferet* and *Keter,* we are empowered to defeat the fallen *Din*.

The Zohar warns that we must be careful not to give any part of ourselves to the Other Side:

> It is forbidden to a man to abandon any vessel of his house into the possession of the Other Side, for many emissaries [of the Other Side] are ready to receive it, and from that time blessings do not rest upon him—all the more if he assigns to the Other Side the most precious part of himself. For from that time he belongs to [the Other Side], and when the time comes for the celestial form which has been given to him to depart from this world, the evil spirit to which he had become daily devoted comes and takes it, and it is never again restored to him.[16]

This sounds very much like the proverbial "selling your soul to the devil." In light of Kabbalah and the teachings of the ascended masters, the vessels of our house that we should not abandon to the Other Side can be interpreted in several ways. We can think of our vessels as our four lower bodies, mentioned in chapter 4 (the etheric, mental, desire and physical bodies). These are the vehicles our soul uses to increase in the strength of the Lord and to fulfill her reason for being.

We can think of our *chakras* as vessels because they receive and distribute the light of God to our four lower bodies. When we misuse the light of our *chakras,* we stop up the flow of God's light and increase the power of the Other Side.

We can also think of our organs as our vessels. When they are working properly, our organs are instruments for the dynamic interchange of *yin/yang* energy in our body. When we abuse our organs by eating unhealthy foods, we reduce the quotient of God's light our body can carry. The Zohar goes so far as to say that "man's soul can be known only through the organs of the body," for the organs "are the levels that perform the work of the soul."[17]

Remember, you—body, mind and soul—were created by *Elohim* to be a vessel for the sacred energies of *Ein Sof*. You have a divine spark. The seed of Abraham is alive within your very breast. You are nobly endowed, and you must not surrender any part of yourself to the evil urge or to the Other Side.

Why Does God Allow Evil to Exist?

We have seen how the Zohar answers the question, Where does evil come from? But once evil emerges, why does God allow it to exist?

Some Kabbalists believe that rather than destroy evil outright, God assigns the righteous to destroy evil in his name. I believe that we are in the lower world because sometimes, somewhere we gave a part of ourselves to the Other Side. God sends us back to the lower world so that we might balance the karma we made when we allowed the light of the *sefirot* to be stolen by the forces of the fallen *Din*. The process of balancing our karma must include the championing of justice and the challenging of stern, unmerciful judgment.

The Zohar also teaches that God uses evil to punish the wicked and to test the mettle of our determination to return to the Tree of Everlasting Life. The Zohar uses an allegory of a prince who is tested by his father to illustrate how God uses the evil inclination to initiate us. The king commands his only son not to consort with an evil woman. Out of his love for his father, the son agrees to obey his father's will. One day the king decides to test his son. He orders a beautiful seductress to entice the prince.

If the son is worthy and attentive to his father's commands,

Evil literally has no leg to stand on, says the Zohar, because the serpent's legs were cut off as punishment for seducing Adam and Eve. Our negative thoughts, feelings, words and deeds are what empower the Other Side and restore legs to the serpent. (Eve Tempted *by Lucien Lévy-Dhurmer.*)

says the Zohar, he will rebuke her and send her away. Then the king will rejoice, invite his son into the innermost room of the palace and give him gifts and great honor. Who will have brought all this glory upon the son? asks the Zohar. "The whore, without a doubt!...She should be praised on every side...because she enabled the son to earn all this goodness and the deep love of the king."[18]

When you are tempted to stray from the paths of righteousness and violate God's laws in small ways or great, think of the king, the prince and the whore. And remember that God has a right to test us, we have a right to be tested, and we have a right to pass—or fail—our tests.

The Zohar also cites the trials of Abraham and the Israelites in Egypt to show that God uses evil to test and purify his children.

> Abraham went down to the "lower degrees" in Egypt, and probed them to the bottom, but clave not to them and returned unto his Master. He was not seduced by them, as was Adam,

who reached that level and was then seduced by the serpent, and brought death into the world. Nor was he seduced like Noah, who became intoxicated.... But of Abraham it is written, "And Abram went up out of Egypt" (Gen. 13:1). He went up and not down, and returned to his place, to the upper level to which he had attached himself at the beginning [that is, the *sefirah Hesed* (Love), the first of the seven lower *sefirot*[19]]....

The mystery of the matter is: If Abram had not gone down into Egypt and had not been purified there first, he would not have had a portion in the Holy One, blessed be He. Similarly with his descendants: the Holy One, blessed be He, wished to make of them a single people, a perfect people, and to draw them near to Him. But if they had not gone down into Egypt first and been tested there, they would not have been God's chosen people.[20]

In Kabbalah, Abraham's and the Israelites' journeys to Egypt are symbolic of the tests and trials we, too, must face in our encounters with evil. Abraham successfully passed his tests and so emulated the divine attribute of Love that Kabbalists say he actually embodied and represented the sefirah Hesed. *(Left:* Abram Draws Near to Shechem in the Promised Land *by Julius Schnorr. Above: from* Israel in Egypt *by Sir Edward J. Poynter.)*

"Abraham's descent into Egypt and safe return is a rite of passage," writes Daniel Matt. "Having confronted and experienced the Abyss, he is transmuted into a divine hero, apotheosized as *Hesed*, the Love of God."[21] Kabbalah teaches that Abraham embodied the *sefirah Hesed* and that he represents the attribute of Love, just as Isaac represents *Gevurah/Din* and Jacob represents *Tiferet*. This means that Abraham, by his spiritual attainment, was the vehicle through which the light and energy of *Hesed* was able to come to earth.

Tishby says the Zohar's teaching on Abraham's and the Israelites' descent into Egypt means that we are all tested and purified through our contact with the power of evil. "In order to achieve perfection in his desire to serve God, man must first enter the domain of evil and purify himself there as in a refiner's crucible," he writes. "Only after this can he ascend to the level of perfect goodness....Man has to prove his devotion to God by going out to fight God's adversary, and by returning victorious from the fray."[22]

Aiding and Abetting the Other Side

Although the Zohar says that God allows evil to exist in order to punish the wicked and to test us, it reminds us that it is not God that empowers evil but man. The Other Side was cut off from *Ein Sof's* life-giving energies, says the Zohar, and therefore evil has no power of its own. It literally lives off of the energies we feed it.

We energize the Other Side when we channel the precious energy God gives us daily into negative thoughts, feelings, words and deeds. And it is not just the "big" sins, like stealing or murder, that energize the Other Side. When we mentally put people down or make fun of them, when we curse them or are jealous of their accomplishments, we knowingly aid and abet the forces of the counterfeit *Din* and thereby join the enemy to the destruction of our soul. Conversely, when we generate good works, kind thoughts and daring deeds in defense of Truth and Justice, we vitalize the world of the *sefirot* and fasten our soul to the Tree of Life.

A powerful mantra that I often recite (in multiples of nine) to challenge the appearance of evil and its claim to power is "In the name of God, *Elohim:* Evil is not real and its appearance has no power!" Evil cannot exist unless we feed it the divine energies that come to us from *Ein Sof* through our I AM Presence and the ten *sefirot*. The fallen angels who align with the fallen *Din* are also cut off from the Tree of Life; we must not turn around and give them our precious lifeblood by perverting the light of any one of the ten *sefirot*.

Now we can see that the real reason we should avoid "sinning" is not for fear of roasting in "Hell" for eternity. It is because the energy that we misuse empowers the forces of wrongful judgment in the earth—the same evil forces that kill and maim children, that rape and harass women, that cause brother to kill brother. Yes, the same forces that engineered the Holocaust.

So before we attempt to climb the Tree of Life, we must make sure that we are not a sieve, that we are not allowing the emissaries of the Other Side to receive the windfall of *Ein Sof's* light that comes to us through the *sefirot*. We must protect the light we have garnered in our *chakras* by disciplining our mind and heart so that only God lives within us.

The Hasidic leader Menahem Mendel of Kotsk once asked some visitors, "Where is the dwelling place of God?" They laughed and replied, "What a thing to ask! Is not the whole world full of God's glory?" But he replied that this was not true, because God only dwells where people let God in. When we think the thoughts of God and do his deeds on earth, God dwells within us. When we think negative thoughts and do negative deeds, the forces of the Other Side control our soul.

The Zohar says that because evil requires a steady flow of God's energy to exist, it tempts us to keep sinning. Once evil convinces us to commit a sin of injustice, it tries to make us reinforce that injustice by doing it again and again. Its hold on us becomes stronger and stronger. Finally we are its prisoner and it is able to siphon off our life-essence as easily as sipping cider through a straw.

The Zohar compares the evil inclination to a man who breaks into a house and takes control of it when no one challenges him.

> When the evil inclination starts to attach itself to a man it is like someone coming to the door [of a house]. When he sees that no one tries to stop him, he enters the house and becomes a guest. He notices that no one tries to stop him or send him on his way. Once he has entered the house, and still no one tries to stop him, he gains the upper hand and becomes the master of the house, so that in time he exercises control over the whole household. . . .
>
> So it is with the evil inclination. He approaches a man like someone coming to the door. He interests him in a minor sin, and is then like a mere passer-by. . . . He then interests him in graver sins for a day or two, like a guest who is invited to stay in the house just for a day or two. [When he sees that no one tries to stop him] he becomes. . . the master of the house. The man has enslaved himself to him.[23]

If we do not challenge the evil inclination when it first knocks at our door, it will step by step gain the upper hand and eventually become the master of our soul.

In other passages, the Zohar depicts how the Other Side continually tries to subjugate *Shekhinah,* the divine mother who sustains our world, and how our actions on earth can spell defeat or victory for the Other Side. Tishby writes:

> The large amount of sin in the world helps [the Other Side] to reach its goal, while the power of the commandments and good deeds protects the *Shekhinah,* and helps to defeat the Other Side. In other words, human conduct holds the balance

in this conflict between good and evil. When the power of the Other Side is at its greatest, it subdues the *Shekhinah*. This means that the light of the upper *sefirot* is removed from the *Shekhinah,* the channels that transmit the flow of influence to the lower worlds are stopped up, and the powers of the *Shekhinah* are transferred to the Other Side and give it additional strength.[24]

As Tishby puts it, our world is a kind of "battle zone in the war between the two contestants"—the side of holiness and the Other Side.[25] The Zohar says, "When this side, the holy side, begins to prevail, *Sitra Ahra* [the Other Side], the unclean side, grows weak. One prevails; the other grows weak. . . .When one is full, the other is ruined."[26]

In short, Kabbalah teaches that we determine how much power evil exercises over the world. Since the advent of evil, we have been faced with two choices: we can submit to the evil urge and fortify the power of evil or we can obey the precepts of the Torah and strengthen the power of good.

Adam's Sin

As we have seen, the Zohar's first theory of the origin of evil is that evil was a by-product of the emanation of the *sefirot*. A second view of the origin of evil stated in the Zohar and by the Gerona Kabbalists is that evil can be traced back to Adam's sin in the Garden of Eden. But they describe Adam's sin very differently than do most interpreters of the Genesis story, for to Kabbalists the words of scripture are symbolic of much deeper mysteries.

According to this theory, Adam sinned by worshiping *Malkhut/Shekhinah* apart from the other *sefirot*. "Instead of penetrating the vast unity and totality of the *sefirot* in his contemplation," writes Scholem, "Adam, when faced with the choice, took the easier course of contemplating only the last *sefirah* (since it seemed to represent everything else) separately from the other *sefirot,* and of mistaking it for the whole of the Godhead."[27] As a result *Shekhinah,* the feminine aspect of God, was cut off from the upper *sefirot,* divorced from her husband, *Tiferet,* and forced to go with Adam into exile.

How did Adam's sin affect mankind? Before Adam sinned, he had enjoyed a steady, direct contact with God. But his sin severed that tie. "Had it not been for Adam's sin," writes Scholem, "the supreme divine will would have continued to work unbroken in Adam and Eve and all their descendants, and all of creation would have functioned in...harmony, transmitting the divine influx downward from above and upward from below, so that there would have been no separation between the Creator and His creation."[28]

The exile of *Shekhinah* symbolizes the separation of the masculine and feminine principles of God. The reunion of God and his *Shekhinah* will reunite the masculine and the feminine principles and restore harmony and the unimpeded flow of God's life between the divine and human realms.

The reunion of God and his *Shekhinah,* and God and man, is the goal of the Kabbalist. Scholem writes:

> It is the function of good in the world, whose tools are the Torah and its commandments, to bridge the abyss of separation that was formed by man's sin and to restore all existence to its original harmony and unity. The final goal, in other words, is the reunification of the divine and the human wills....Unlike [the] Christian dogma of original sin, the Kabbalah does not reject the idea that every man has the power to overcome this state of corruption, to the extent that he too is affected by it, by means of his own innate powers and with...divine aid.[29]

It is up to us to reestablish the tie between God and man. With the help of the ascended masters, who have attained union with God, and by accessing the power of the *sefirot* and our own inner, spiritual power, we can bring harmony and wholeness to both the divine and human worlds.

The Kings That Died

A third theory of the origin of evil found in the Zohar is that the Other Side originated from the leftovers of previous worlds that had been destroyed because they contained the forces of stern judgment untempered by mercy. These imperfect worlds emanated from *Keter* before the other *sefirot* were emanated. The Zohar says: "Before *[Keter]* prepared his attributes, he constructed kings, inscribed kings, and conjectured kings [that is, *Keter* attempted to set up the structure of emanation], but they could not survive, so that after a time he concealed them."[30]

The Zohar goes on to say that our world was not able to survive until the emanation of the *sefirot* had been completed in the form of Primordial Man, *Adam Kadmon*. Why? Because in Primordial Man there was a harmonious balance of male and female forces, and only through a balanced partnership of male and female, mercy and judgment, could the world sustain itself.

Tishby explains the Zohar's theory of how the Other Side sprang from the leftovers of defective worlds:

> These early judgments [that existed in the imperfect worlds] ...contained the root of evil in the form, as it were, of refuse. And the properly ordered system of emanation could not be established until the refuse had been removed from the divine realm. This removal was effected when the worlds were destroyed. The holy lights that were extinguished during this destruction were then rekindled and included among the *sefirot*, while the fragments of the destroyed worlds that were beyond repair were left mutilated and covered in darkness outside the divine system. It is from these fragments that the system of *Sitra Ahra* [the Other Side] was constructed.[31]

The Zohar refers to the previous worlds that had to be destroyed as "the kings that died."[32] It says these imperfect worlds are symbolized in Genesis 36 as the kings who were descendants of Esau and who reigned in Edom before there were kings in Israel. As Tishby notes, "one of the root meanings of *Edom* is 'red,' which is the color of strict judgment."[33] The Zohar's image of the death of the primordial kings was reinterpreted by Luria.

The Breaking of the Vessels

In the sixteenth century, Luria conceived yet another theory of the origin of evil, the most intricate and novel of any Kabbalist. Evil, he said, emerged from *Ein Sof* itself. Furthermore, he claimed that both the domain of evil and our world were born as a result of a cosmic catastrophe that accompanied the Creation.

Luria wrote down little of his own teachings, and the writings of his disciples give differing and even conflicting versions of his profound doctrines. Some of Luria's students view the disaster that spawned evil as an unplanned mishap. Others believe that God planned this catastrophe as a way to cleanse himself of the harsh elements of judgment *(Din)*. Here is what happened according to this theory.

The Creation was a two-step process of contraction and emanation. Luria starts with the premise that *Ein Sof,* who is infinite, could not create a finite world without first creating a space apart from its infinity where its creation could exist. In order to do that, *Ein Sof* first contracted itself to its centermost point and then withdrew to the sides surrounding that point, leaving an empty sphere. This process is called *tzimtzum.* Although *tzimtzum* is commonly referred to as "contraction," for Luria it does not mean that God is contracting, or concentrating, himself *in* a place, but that he is withdrawing *from* a place.

The space that was left behind after *Ein Sof's* withdrawal contained a residue of the divine light *(reshimu)*. Luria says this is like the residue of oil or wine left in a bottle after it is emptied of its contents. In the process of *tzimtzum, Ein Sof* separated out from itself "roots of judgment," or roots of *Din,* and left them behind in the empty space as well. Some Lurianic Kabbalists say that *Ein Sof* discharged the roots of judgment to purge itself of these elements of inharmony, elements of potential evil.

But the question still remains: How could *Ein Sof*—the infinite, perfect God—have had within itself any elements of inharmony in the first place? Some Kabbalists claim that the act of *tzimtzum* created the inharmony. Before *Ein Sof* contracted itself, all the forces within it were in perfect balance, including the opposing forces of *Din* (Judgment) and *Hesed* (Love/Mercy). These elements were in such harmony that they were not distinguishable from each other.

However, when *Ein Sof* contracted, *Din* became concentrated and crystallized. The reason for this is that the very act of *tzimtzum,* whereby *Ein Sof* was limiting and restricting its infinity, was an act of *Din,* the force of limitation and restriction. Thus as *Ein Sof* contracted itself, *Din* automatically became more powerful.

The activation of *Din* upset the delicate equilibrium of forces within *Ein Sof.* The only way to restore harmony to the Godhead was to separate out and expel the "roots of *Din.*" These roots of *Din,* or judgment, which were left in the empty space after *Ein Sof's* contraction, were what eventually took shape as the forces of evil.

Ein Sof's contraction and withdrawal was step one in the process of the Creation. Next *Ein Sof* began to emanate within the empty space that contained the mixture of light and the roots of judgment. When the divine light of *Ein Sof* first flowed forth, the *sefirot* took the form of *Adam Kadmon,* Primordial Man. Luria says that lights burst from the ears, nose and mouth of *Adam Kadmon* in an undifferentiated form. But the light that issued from his eyes was different. It separated into distinct *sefirot*, each requiring its own vessel to hold its light.

The light flowed into the vessels of the first three *sefirot*—*Keter, Hokhmah* and *Binah*—without any problem. But the vessels that were supposed to contain the light of the lower *sefirot*, from *Hesed* through *Yesod*, were not strong enough to hold the light and they shattered. The vessel containing *Malkhut* cracked but did not shatter. In this disaster, shards of the broken vessels scattered and fell. Some Kabbalists believe that the vessels were weak and broke because they were made up of the roots of judgment.

What happened to the light that was in the vessels? Some of it found its way back to its source. Some of the light, however, fell along with the shards of the broken vessels and became attached to them. From these shards, the dark forces of the Other Side were formed. These dark forces are called *kelippot*, "shells" or "husks" of evil. The husks of evil have no power of their own, says Luria. It is the sparks of light that are trapped among the husks that give life and power to the Other Side. Luria teaches that the breaking of the vessels not only animated evil but also inaugurated the creation of the material world, for the broken shards are the basis of all matter.

Luria associates the breaking of the vessels with the death of the primordial kings, the name the Zohar gives to the early, imperfect worlds that were destroyed because they contained an excess of stern judgment and lacked a harmonious balance of male and female forces. The same can be said of Luria's breaking of the vessels, where the out-of-balance force of judgment, activated through *Ein Sof's* contraction, had to be expelled from God.

Parallels with Hindu Cosmology

Luria's theory that the Creation was a two-step process of contraction and expansion resembles the theory in Hindu cosmology that the universe is continually evolving through alternating cycles of creation and dissolution.

According to Hindu cosmology, the universe evolves during the day of Brahma, the God of Creation. This is followed by the night of Brahma, during which all matter in the universe is absorbed into the Universal Spirit. The day of Brahma is thus a period of expansion, and the night of Brahma is a period of involution, or contraction. This rhythm of expansion and contraction is repeated as the universe continues to evolve during each day of Brahma and to dissolve during each night of Brahma.

Kabbalists, too, say that the two steps of contraction and expansion are cyclically repeated. Scholem says that in Lurianic Kabbalah, "just as the first movement in creation was in reality composed of two movements—the ascent of *Ein Sof* into the depths of itself [contraction, *tzimtzum*] and its partial descent [that is, expansion] into the space [left behind after] *tzimtzum*—so this double rhythm is a necessarily recurring feature of every stage in the universal process."[34] Kabbalists term this ebb and flow "regression" and "egression." Regression is *Ein Sof*'s desire to return to itself (its contraction), and egression is the expanding movement of *Ein Sof*.

Another way Hindus describe creation and dissolution is to portray it as the outbreath and inbreath of Brahma. Creation occurs during the outbreath, or exhalation, of Brahma and dissolution occurs during his inbreath, or inhalation. Scholem uses the same terminology to describe Kabbalah's drama of creation: "Just as the human organism exists through the double process of inhaling and exhaling and the one cannot be conceived without the other, so also the whole of Creation constitutes a gigantic process of divine inhalation and exhalation."[35] I see this cosmic process as the eternal movement of the Great Tao as all of creation dances to the rhythm of *yang* and *yin*—contraction and expansion, dissolution and creation.

Liberating the Sparks

Luria teaches that with the catastrophe of the breaking of the vessels, nothing has remained in its proper place. "Everything is somewhere else," says Scholem. "Since that primordial act, all being has been... in exile, in need of being led back and redeemed."[36] As David Biale writes, *tzimtzum* and the breaking of the vessels can be seen as "two stages in the same process where God is shattered and parts of him are exiled from the rest."[37]

Following the breaking of the vessels, the *sefirot* reorganized themselves in an attempt to restore their original harmony. But, Biale writes, "in place of the *Adam Kadmon* (primordial man) out of which emanated the original *sefirot,* a series of 'faces' *(partzufim)* constitute the divine realm. Luria suggests that the *sefirot* system described in the earlier Kabbalah does not exist in its ideal form after the [breaking of the vessels]. In general, the whole order of creation is demoted to a lower level as a result of the breaking of the vessels."[38]

Luria says the first man, Adam, had the opportunity to completely separate the sparks from their shells and set the world back in order because his body was a microcosm of *Adam Kadmon*. But he failed. In Luria's scheme, Adam's sin was not the origin of evil but a second fall that repeated and reinforced the original catastrophe that had given birth to evil. Scholem writes:

> Adam was by nature a purely spiritual figure, a 'great soul,' whose very body was a spiritual substance, an ethereal body, or body of light.[39] The soul of Adam was composed of all the worlds and was destined to uplift and reintegrate all the sparks of holiness that were left in the *kelippot* [shells or husks]. [His soul's] garment was of spiritual ether and it contained within it all of the souls of the human race in perfect condition. ...Had Adam fulfilled his mission through the spiritual works of which he was capable, which called for contemplative action and deep meditation,...the power of evil, the *kelippah,* would

have undergone...complete separation from holiness....

Instead of uplifting everything, however, he caused it to fall even further....As a result...Adam assumed a material body....His soul shattered and its unity was smashed to pieces. ...The bulk of the souls that were in Adam...fell from him and were subjugated by the *kelippot*....In a manner of speaking, Adam's fall when he sinned was a repetition of the catastrophe of the breaking of the vessels.[40] Each sin [of man] repeats the primordial event in part, just as each good deed contributes to the homecoming of the banished souls.[41]

According to Luria's theory, Adam's soul contained all the souls that were ever to be a part of humanity. Each of these souls, including our own souls, is a spark of Adam's great soul. Luria also taught that the souls within Adam are divided into a number of groups, or "soul families," and that each family shares a common "root." "Only sparks from the same root... are able to assist and strengthen one another," writes Scholem. "They suffer with one another, and anything done by one of them, good or bad, affects all the others. Their destiny is determined by a deep, invisible connection of 'soul affinity.'"[42] It is the task of man to seek out...the sparks of his root."[43]

The goal of the Kabbalist is to repair the cleavage that took place in the Godhead as a result of the breaking of the vessels and Adam's fall. The process of restoring the universe to its original design is called *tikkun,* which means literally "fixing," "repair" or "restoration."

Tikkun is essentially the work of man not God. To perform *tikkun,* we must find the sparks embedded here, there and everywhere and liberate them to return to their divine source. *Tikkun* will not only "repair" the Godhead, but it will spell defeat for the Other Side. For it is the sparks of light which are attached to the shells of evil that give power to the Other Side. Once the sparks are liberated, the Other Side cannot continue to exist.

Luria teaches, then, that there are two kinds of sparks to rescue: the sparks that fell when the vessels broke and the sparks that were once a part of Adam's soul. Luria says that anyone can strive to raise up the sparks of light that fell when the vessels broke. As for the sparks of Adam's soul, we can raise up only those sparks that belong to our own soul family, or soul root.

Therefore, in Luria's scheme our task is to raise up the sparks of the *sefirot* that are scattered throughout the creation, to raise up the sparks that belong to our soul family, and to perfect and thereby liberate our own soul. All who are part of the mystical body of God have a collective mission to rescue the sparks, but each son and daughter of God has a unique role to play in that great drama.

How do we perform *tikkun?* Through prayer and obedience to the commandments of God. This brings us full circle to the Zohar's equation: When we obey the commandments and do good, we energize the divine world and diminish the power of the Other Side; when we disobey the commandments and do evil, we energize the Other Side and weaken the harmony of the divine world.

"Every evil deed not only keeps the holy sparks imprisoned among the *kelippot* but also sends baneful impulses on high to disturb further the harmony among the *sefirot*," writes Rabbi Louis Jacobs. "Conversely, every good deed sends beneficent impulses on high to promote harmony among the *sefirot* and to reclaim the holy sparks."[44]

The Hasidic View:
Your Unique Role in Rescuing the Sparks

The Hasidic movement that blossomed in the eighteenth century transformed Luria's teaching on uplifting the sparks of light. According to Hasidism, the sparks that you and you alone can liberate are to be found in your environment—in food, drink and other material objects as well as in the people you come in contact with. As twentieth-century Kabbalist Hillel Zeitlin puts it, "Every man is the Redeemer of a world that is all his own."[45]

The idea that each person is responsible to redeem the sparks within his own personal sphere is well-developed in the teachings of the Baal Shem Tov. He says that God makes certain that we will meet the sparks that belong to the root of our soul. The grandson of the Baal Shem Tov writes:

> I have heard from my grandfather that all that belongs to a man, be it his servants and animals, be it even his household effects—they are all of his sparks which belong to the root of his soul and he has to lift them up to their upper root. For the beginnings of a thing are tied to its ultimate end, and even the lowest sparks still have some communion with their beginning within the infinite being. If, then, the man to whose root they belong experiences spiritual uplift, they all rise with him, and this is brought about through *devekut* [mystical cleaving to God], for it is *devekut* that enables him to lift them up.[46]

For the Baal Shem Tov, cleaving to God, *devekut*, is the key to our fulfilling our mission of redeeming the sparks. The Baal Shem says of the man who is not in a state of *devekut*, "If a man walks irregularly with God, . . . then [God] walks irregularly with him and does not prepare for him clothing and food that contain sparks of his own soul root so that he may perform their *tikkun* [restoration]."[47]

Rabbi Jacob Joseph of Polonnoye, a disciple of the Baal Shem, writes: "As is well known from the writings, all that a person eats and his house and his business and his contemporaries and his wife—all these come to the person according to his nature, that is, from his sparks. If a person deserves it by his good deeds, then he meets the sparks which by his very nature belong to him in order that he may restore them to their rightful place."[48]

188   *The Origin of Evil*

Hasidism's personal approach to rescuing the sparks led to a unique understanding of how to pursue the spiritual quest midst the challenges of living in the world. The Hasidic devotee believes that the rescue operation does not take place exclusively while we pray, study, and observe the commandments; it also takes place while we engage in necessary worldly pursuits, as long as our mind is stayed on God. "When attending to his material needs for the sake of God, the Hasid is

The exile and dispersion of the Jews took on new meaning with Isaac Luria's theory that sparks of God had scattered with the breaking of the vessels of the sefirot. Kabbalists no longer saw the exile of the Jews as a punishment or a test but as a way to fulfill their mission of rescuing the sparks that had been scattered throughout the creation. (Above: Jeremiah at the Fall of Jerusalem *by Eduard Bendemann. Right:* The Sorrowing Jews in Exile *by Eduard Bendemann.)*

carrying out acts of divine worship," writes Jacobs. "The Hasidic ideal, to which all else is subordinated, is that of *devekut,* wherein the total concentration of the mind is on God."[49]

As eighteenth-century Hasidic rabbi Levi Isaac of Berdichev says, "When you desire to eat or drink, or to fulfill other worldly desires, and you focus your awareness on the love of God, then you elevate that physical desire to spiritual desire. Thereby you draw out the holy spark that dwells within. You bring forth holy sparks from the material world. There is no path greater than this. For wherever you go and whatever you do—even mundane activities—you serve God."[50]

The Exile Takes on New Meaning

Luria's theory of the exile of the divine sparks from the rest of God struck a responsive chord among the Jews of his age. Ever since the Assyrians had deported the Israelites in 734 B.C. and 722 B.C. and the Babylonians had burned the Temple in Jerusalem and deported the people of Judah in 586 B.C., the Jews had been exiled from their homeland and scattered among the nations. But with Luria's theory of the shattering of the

vessels, the exile of the Jews became a symbol for something larger. It signified the crisis of cosmic proportions that God himself was still experiencing—the exile of his sparks of light.

Furthermore, for Luria the Jewish exile is no longer a punishment or a test. It is a mission. In fact, the exile and dispersion are crucial to the redemption of souls. "One needed the exile of Israel among all the seventy nations, where the sparks fell," says Rabbi Jacob Joseph of Polonnoye. "Each individual in Israel must be exiled... in that place which contains sparks from the root of his soul, [in order] to separate and uplift them."[51]

"In the course of its exile Israel must go everywhere, to every corner of the world, for everywhere a spark... is waiting to be found, gathered, and restored by a religious act," says Scholem. "Fundamentally every man and especially every Jew participates in the process of the *tikkun*."[52]

Scholem also notes that the exile of the Jews "has its parallel in the exile of the soul in its migrations from embodiment to embodiment, from one form of being to another. The doctrine of metempsychosis [reincarnation], as the exile of the soul, acquired unprecedented popularity among the Jewish masses of the generations following the Lurianic period."[53]

From this perspective, in each of our incarnations we must play the role of the shepherd who goes after the lost sheep, those souls for whom we are responsible and to whom we are tied, by good karma or bad or because they belong to our soul family. Thus, the circumstances into which we are born—including those who are destined to be our parents or children, our work mates, playmates or soul mates—are no accident.

I think of the process of *tikkun* as taking a cosmic tweezer and pulling out little specks of gold embedded in dense matter. Kabbalists regard *tikkun* primarily as the work of the Jews, but I believe that *tikkun* is the mighty work of the mystics of all ages and all religions.

Thus, our daily striving to cleave to God is not merely to exalt our soul or even to escape from the concerns of this world. It has a far greater purpose. Our mystical cleaving to God will confer upon us the spiritual empowerment we must have to rescue the souls, as well as the sparks, who cry out to us for help in the name of God.

Note: The remaining chapters of *Kabbalah: Key to Your Hidden Power* are published in Book III of the 1992 *Pearls of Wisdom*.

NOTES

CHAPTER 4 *A Portrait of the God Within*

Opening quotation: Zohar 2:20a, *Midrash ha-Ne'elam.*

1. Zohar 1:38a, quoted in Tishby, *Wisdom of the Zohar* 1:273.
2. Schaya, *Universal Meaning of the Kabbalah,* p. 34.
3. See Schaya, *Universal Meaning of the Kabbalah,* pp. 34–35, 116–19; Halevi, *Introduction to the Cabala,* pp. 35–50; Halevi, *Kabbalah,* pp. 6–7, 50; Aryeh Kaplan, *Innerspace: Introduction to Kabbalah, Meditation and Prophecy,* ed. Abraham Sutton (Jerusalem: Moznaim Publishing, 1990), pp. 52–54, 61–68.
4. Schaya, *Universal Meaning of the Kabbalah,* p. 35.
5. Kaplan, *Innerspace,* p. 62.
6. Ibid., p. 64.
7. Scholem, *Mystical Shape of the Godhead,* p. 39.
8. Exod. 33:20, 23.
9. See Halevi, *Kabbalah,* p. 12.
10. Hayim Vital, *Sefer Etz Hayyim* 12a, quoted in Ariel, *The Mystic Quest,* pp. 169–70.
11. Matt, *Zohar,* p. 34.
12. In the Old Testament, *Elohim* is the generic term for the Deity. *Elohim* is a plural word, but when used as a name for God it is singular in meaning. Grammarians call this singular usage of a plural noun "the plural of majesty." Gen. 1:26, 27

shows this usage: "And God *[Elohim]* said: 'Let us make man in our image, after our likeness.'...So God *[Elohim]* created man in his own image, in the image of God *[Elohim]* created he him; male and female created he them."

13. Zohar 1:21a, quoted in Poncé, *Kabbalah,* p. 239.
14. James 1:12.
15. Matt. 6:19, 20; Luke 12:33.
16. The Five Dhyani Buddhas are celestial Buddhas who symbolize universal divine principles or forces. Tibetan Buddhists believe that each Dhyani Buddha presides over one of the five Buddha families. Each Dhyani Buddha also embodies one of the five wisdoms, which antidote the five deadly poisons that are of ultimate danger to our spiritual progress.

    Vairochana presides over the *Tathagata* (Buddha) family. His All-Pervading Wisdom of the Dharmakaya, or the Wisdom of the Dharmadhatu, reveals the realm of highest reality and overcomes the poison of ignorance.

    Akshobhya presides over the *vajra* (diamond) family. His Mirrorlike Wisdom reflects all things calmly and uncritically and reveals their true nature. His wisdom antidotes the poison of hatred and anger.

    Ratnasambhava presides over the *ratna* (jewel) family. His Wisdom of Equality enables one to see all things with divine impartiality and recognize the divine equality of all beings. His wisdom transmutes the poison of spiritual, intellectual and human pride.

    Amitabha presides over the *padma* (lotus) family. His Discriminating Wisdom enables one to discern all beings separately yet know every being as an individual expression of the One. His wisdom conquers the poison of the passions—all cravings, covetousness, greed and lust.

    Amoghasiddhi presides over the karma family. His All-Accomplishing Wisdom, or Wisdom of Perfected Action, confers perseverance, infallible judgment and unerring action. His wisdom antidotes the poison of envy and jealousy.

    For further information, see *Mandala of the Five Dhyani*

Buddhas, 16-page booklet, published by Summit University Press.

17. See chapter 5, pp. 141–45.
18. Ezek. 1:26–28.
19. Jer. 23:5, 6; 33:15, 16.
20. Luke 1:80; 2:40.
21. Saint Germain, "A Trilogy On the Threefold Flame of Life," in *Saint Germain On Alchemy* (Livingston, Mont.: Summit University Press, 1985), p. 350.
22. I Cor. 3:16, 17; 6:19, 20; II Cor. 6:16.
23. Epstein, *Kabbalah,* p. 61.
24. Telephone interview with Rabbi Yonassan Gershom, 12 May 1992.
25. Ibid.
26. Tishby, *Wisdom of the Zohar* 1:272.
27. Z'ev ben Shimon Halevi, *The Way of Kabbalah* (New York: Samuel Weiser, 1976), p. 142.

CHAPTER 5 *Mysteries of the Soul*

Opening quotation: From a hymn by Rabbi Nahmanides.

1. Moses de León, *Sefer ha-Nefesh ha-Hakhamah,* quoted in Tishby, *Wisdom of the Zohar* 2:683.
2. Ibid., pp. 681, 680.
3. Zohar 2:75b–76a, quoted in Tishby, *Wisdom of the Zohar* 2:680.
4. Scholem, *Kabbalah,* p. 156.
5. The predominant view of the Zohar is that the *nefesh, ruah* and *neshamah* correlate to *Malkhut, Tiferet* and *Binah* respectively. However, a few passages in the Zohar say that these three parts of the soul are images of *Tiferet, Gevurah* and *Hesed* respectively. Other Kabbalists associate the *nefesh* with *Binah,* the *ruah* with *Keter,* and the *neshamah* with *Hokhmah.* (See Tishby, *Wisdom of the Zohar* 2:687–88, 692.)

6. Spencer, *Mysticism in World Religion,* p. 194.
7. Scholem, *Kabbalah,* p. 155.
8. Scholem, *Major Trends in Jewish Mysticism,* p. 241.
9. Zohar 1:62a, in Sperling, Simon, and Levertoff, *The Zohar* 1:203.
10. Zohar 3:70b, in Sperling, Simon, and Levertoff, *The Zohar* 5:67.
11. Zohar 1:83b. Translation from Sperling, Simon, and Levertoff, *The Zohar* 1:278; and Tishby, *Wisdom of the Zohar* 2:732.
12. Tishby, *Wisdom of the Zohar* 2:683.
13. Zohar 1:83b, in Sperling, Simon, and Levertoff, *The Zohar* 1:278–79.
14. Scholem, *Kabbalah,* p. 161.
15. Ibid., p. 157.
16. I Cor. 3:16.
17. II Pet. 1:3, 4.
18. Meister Eckhart, quoted in Spencer, *Mysticism in World Religion,* p. 245.
19. *Meister Eckhart: Sermons and Treatises,* trans. and ed. M. O'C. Walshe (Longmead, Shaftesbury, Dorset: Element Books, 1987), 3:107.
20. Meister Eckhart, quoted in Joseph James, comp., *The Way of Mysticism* (New York: Harper and Brothers Publishers, n.d.), p. 64.
21. *Ratnagotravibhāga* 1.28, in Edward Conze et al., eds., *Buddhist Texts through the Ages* (1954; reprint, New York: Harper and Row, Harper Torchbooks, 1964), p. 181.
22. Ezek. 18:4, 20.
23. Rev. 21:7, 8.
24. Mark L. Prophet and Elizabeth Clare Prophet, *Climb the Highest Mountain,* 2d ed. (Livingston, Mont.: Summit University Press, 1972), pp. 8–9.
25. Mark L. Prophet and Elizabeth Clare Prophet, *The Lost Teachings of Jesus 1* (Livingston, Mont.: Summit University Press, 1986), pocketbook edition, pp. 56–57.

26. Scholem, *Kabbalah,* p. 152.

27. *tannaim* (sing. *tanna*): literally "teachers"; the name for over two hundred rabbis who contributed to the Mishnah, a collection of Jewish laws and the rabbis' commentaries on them, compiled around A.D. 200.

    amoraim (sing. *amora*): literally "speakers," "interpreters"; the title given to Palestinian and Babylonian rabbis who interpreted the Mishnah from A.D. 200 to 500. The Mishnah and the commentary of the *amoraim* compose the Talmud, the authoritative body of written Jewish tradition.

    Rabbi Simeon bar Yohai, second century: eminent *tanna* who is traditionally believed to have written the Zohar.

    Rabbi Akiva (or Akiba), c. 50–c. 135: the most prominent *tanna* and Jewish leader of his time. He championed the Jewish patriot Bar Kokhba and his revolt against the Romans. The Romans subsequently martyred Akiva for breaking an ordinance forbidding the teaching of the Jewish law. A *Merkabah* mystic, Rabbi Akiva wrote some of the most important *Merkabah* literature.

    Rabbi Eliezer the Great (or Eliezer ben Hyrcanus), first–second centuries: teacher of Rabbi Akiva and one of the most important *tannaim.*

28. Hayim Vital, quoted in Perle Besserman, comp. and ed., *The Way of the Jewish Mystics* (Boston: Shambhala, 1994), pp. 160–61; and Meir Benayahu, *Sefer Toldot ha-'Ari,* quoted in Moshe Idel, *Kabbalah: New Perspectives* (New Haven, Conn.: Yale University Press, 1988), p. 92.

29. Idel, *Kabbalah,* p. 93.

30. Ibid.

31. Shem Tov ibn Gaon, quoted in Idel, *Kabbalah,* p. 93.

32. Hayim Vital, *Sefer ha-Hezyonot,* quoted in Idel, *Kabbalah,* p. 93.

33. Tishby, *Wisdom of the Zohar* 2:818 n. 22.

34. Ibid. 2:818 n. 23.

35. Zohar 1:83a. Translation from Tishby, *Wisdom of the Zohar*

2:818; and Sperling, Simon, and Levertoff, *The Zohar* 1:277.

36. Eph. 6:10, 11, 14–18.
37. Tishby, *Wisdom of the Zohar* 2:819 n. 32.
38. Zohar 1:83a. Translation from Sperling, Simon, and Levertoff, *The Zohar* 1:277; and Tishby, *Wisdom of the Zohar* 2:819.
39. Zohar 1:85b. Translation from Sperling, Simon, and Levertoff, *The Zohar* 1:285–86; Tishby, *Wisdom of the Zohar* 3:1381–82; and Ariel, *The Mystic Quest*, p. 131.
40. Plato, *Apology, Crito, Phaedo, Symposium, Republic*, trans. B. Jowett (Roslyn, N.Y.: Walter J. Black, 1942), pp. 180, 181.
41. Ibid., pp. 182, 183.
42. For more information about twin flames and soul mates, see the following Summit University Press publications: Elizabeth Clare Prophet, *Twin Flames in Love II*, 3-audiocassette album, #A82155; condensed in 1-audiocassette album *Twin Flames and Soul Mates: A New Look at Love, Karma and Relationships*, #S86005. Elizabeth Clare Prophet, *The Union of Twin Flames*, 1 videocassette, #HL88031. *The Coming Revolution: The Magazine for Higher Consciousness*, Summer 1986, #2001.
43. Scholem, *Major Trends in Jewish Mysticism*, pp. 233, 123.
44. Scholem, *Kabbalah*, pp. 174–75; Idel, *Kabbalah*, pp. 49–50.
45. Nahmanides, *Commentary to the Torah*, Deut. 11:22, quoted in Tishby, *Wisdom of the Zohar* 3:986.
46. Scholem, *Kabbalah*, p. 175.
47. Maimonides, *Yad, Yesodey HaTorah* 7:1, quoted in Aryeh Kaplan, *Meditation and the Bible* (1978; reprint, York Beach, Maine: Samuel Weiser, 1988), p. 22.
48. Moses Luzzatto, *Derekh HaShem*, quoted in Kaplan, *Meditation and the Bible*, p. 23.
49. Ibid., pp. 23–24.
50. *Tana DeBei Eliahu* 9, quoted in Kaplan, *Meditation and the Bible*, p. 21.
51. Joel 2:28, 29. Kaplan, *Meditation and the Bible*, p. 21.

52. Idel, *Kabbalah,* p. 59.
53. Scholem, *Major Trends in Jewish Mysticism,* pp. 122–23.
54. Idel, *Kabbalah,* pp. 59–60.
55. Isaac of Acco, *'Ozar Hayyim.* Translation from Idel, *Kabbalah,* p. 67; and Daniel C. Matt, "*Ayin:* The Concept of Nothingness in Jewish Mysticism," in Robert K. C. Forman, *The Problem of Pure Consciousness* (New York: Oxford University Press, 1990), p. 136.
56. Isaac of Acco, *'Ozar Hayyim,* quoted in Idel, *Kabbalah,* p. 48.
57. Menahem Nahum of Chernobyl, *Me'or 'Eynaim,* quoted in Idel, *Kabbalah,* p. 66.
58. Zohar 2:11b; 1:91a, in Tishby, *Wisdom of the Zohar* 3:995, 2:742–43.
59. Tishby, *Wisdom of the Zohar* 2:743 n. 178.
60. Zohar 1:99b, in Sperling, Simon, and Levertoff, *The Zohar* 1:324.
61. Zohar 1:99b–100a, in Sperling, Simon, and Levertoff, *The Zohar* 1:324–25.
62. Tishby, *Wisdom of the Zohar* 2:683.
63. *Zohar Hadash, Bereshit* 18b *(Midrash ha-Ne'elam),* quoted in Tishby, *Wisdom of the Zohar* 2:683.
64. Spencer, *Mysticism in World Religion,* p. 194.
65. Scholem, *Kabbalah,* p. 161.
66. Rev. 2:11; 20:6, 11–15; 21:7, 8. See p. 120.
67. Idel, *Kabbalah,* p. 64.
68. *Sha'arey Zedek,* quoted in Idel, *Kabbalah,* p. 63.
69. Idel, *Kabbalah,* p. 63.

CHAPTER 6 *The Origin of Evil*

Opening quotation: Rabbi Joseph Gikatilla, *Sod ha-Nahash u-Mishpato (The Mystery of the Serpent and Its Sentence).*

1. Green, "The Zohar," p. 125.

2. Zohar 3:41b, quoted in Tishby, *Wisdom of the Zohar* 2:450.
3. Zohar 2:242b, in Tishby, *Wisdom of the Zohar* 2:475.
4. Zohar 1:243b, in Tishby, *Wisdom of the Zohar* 2:499. For a discussion of the Zohar's use of the imagery of the snake to represent evil, see Tishby, 2:467–70.
5. See Elizabeth Clare Prophet, *Forbidden Mysteries of Enoch: Fallen Angels and the Origins of Evil* (Livingston, Mont.: Summit University Press, 1983). Contains the entire Book of Enoch and all the other Enoch texts plus an introduction on why church fathers suppressed the real story of the fallen angels.
6. Matt. 7:1; Luke 6:37.
7. John 3:17.
8. William Shakespeare, *The Merchant of Venice*, act 4, sc. 1, lines 183–96.
9. Two ciphers, contained in the works of various Elizabethan writers and in the original editions of the Shakespearean plays, reveal that Francis Bacon wrote the plays attributed to William Shakespeare. See Orville W. Owen, *Sir Francis Bacon's Cipher Story*, 5 vol. (Detroit, Mich.: Howard Publishing Co., 1893–1895). Elizabeth Wells Gallup, *The Bi-literal Cypher of Sir Francis Bacon*, 3d ed. (Detroit, Mich.: Howard Publishing Co., 1901). Margaret Barsi-Greene, comp., *I, Prince Tudor, Wrote Shakespeare: An Autobiography from His Two Ciphers in Poetry and Prose* (Boston: Branden Press, 1973). Penn Leary, *The Second Cryptographic Shakespeare*, enl. 2d ed. (Omaha, Nebr.: Westchester House Publishers, 1990); and *Are There Ciphers in Shakespeare? A Supplement to the Book "The Second Cryptographic Shakespeare"* (n.p., 1993).
10. Shakespeare, *The Merchant of Venice*, act 4, sc. 1, lines 197–99.
11. Zohar 1:171a, in Tishby, *Wisdom of the Zohar* 3:1146.
12. Baal Shem Tov, quoted in Besserman, *Way of the Jewish Mystics*, pp. 144–45.
13. Jer. 6:14; 8:11; Ezek. 13:10.
14. Zohar 1:190a, in Matt, *Zohar*, p. 85.

15. Zohar 1:208b–209a, quoted in Tishby, *Wisdom of the Zohar* 2:456.
16. Zohar 3:43a. Translation from Sperling, Simon, and Levertoff, *The Zohar* 5:5; and Tishby, *Wisdom of the Zohar* 2:789.
17. Zohar 1:103b, in Tishby, *Wisdom of the Zohar* 1:400.
18. Zohar 2:163a, in Tishby, *Wisdom of the Zohar* 2:806.
19. Matt, *Zohar*, p. 220.
20. Zohar 1:83a. Translation from Tishby, *Wisdom of the Zohar* 2:457; and Sperling, Simon, and Levertoff, *The Zohar* 1:276.
21. Matt, *Zohar*, p. 220.
22. Tishby, *Wisdom of the Zohar* 2:457, 458.
23. Zohar 2:267b–268a, in Tishby, *Wisdom of the Zohar* 2:803–4.
24. Tishby, *Wisdom of the Zohar* 2:452.
25. Ibid.
26. Zohar 2:238b, quoted in Tishby, *Wisdom of the Zohar* 2:452.
27. Scholem, *Kabbalah and Its Symbolism*, p. 108.
28. Scholem, *Kabbalah*, p. 153.
29. Ibid., p. 154.
30. Zohar 3:135a–b, in Tishby, *Wisdom of the Zohar* 1:332.
31. Tishby, *Wisdom of the Zohar* 2:458.
32. Ibid. See also Zohar 3:135a–b, in Tishby, *Wisdom of the Zohar* 1:332–33.
33. Tishby, *Wisdom of the Zohar* 1:332 n. 252.
34. Scholem, *Kabbalah*, p. 131.
35. Scholem, *Major Trends in Jewish Mysticism*, p. 263.
36. Scholem, *Kabbalah and Its Symbolism*, p. 112.
37. Biale, "Jewish Mysticism in the Sixteenth Century," p. 324.
38. Ibid., p. 325.
39. Scholem, *Kabbalah and Its Symbolism*, p. 115.
40. Scholem, *Kabbalah*, pp. 162, 163.
41. Scholem, *Kabbalah and Its Symbolism*, p. 115.

42. Scholem, *Mystical Shape of the Godhead,* p. 234.
43. Gershom Scholem, *The Messianic Idea in Judaism and Other Essays on Jewish Spirituality* (New York: Schocken Books, 1971), p. 187.
44. Louis Jacobs, "The Uplifting of Sparks in Later Jewish Mysticism," in Green, *Jewish Spirituality,* p. 106.
45. Hillel Zeitlin, *Ha-Hasidut,* quoted in Scholem, *The Messianic Idea in Judaism,* p. 190.
46. Ephraim of Sedylkov, *Degel Mahane Efrayim,* quoted in Scholem, *The Messianic Idea in Judaism,* p. 189.
47. Baal Shem Tov, quoted in Scholem, *Mystical Shape of the Godhead,* p. 250.
48. *Toldot Ya'akov Yosef.* Translation from Scholem, *Mystical Shape of the Godhead,* p. 246; and *The Messianic Idea in Judaism,* p. 189.
49. Jacobs, "Uplifting of Sparks in Later Jewish Mysticism," pp. 116, 124.
50. Levi Isaac of Berdichev, *Qedushat Levi,* quoted in Daniel C. Matt, *The Essential Kabbalah: The Heart of Jewish Mysticism* (New York: HarperCollins Publishers, HarperSanFrancisco, 1995), p. 151.
51. Jacob Joseph of Polonnoye, *Ketoneth Passim,* quoted in Scholem, *Mystical Shape of the Godhead,* p. 248.
52. Scholem, *Kabbalah and Its Symbolism,* pp. 116, 117.
53. Ibid., p. 116.

To order books and tapes from Summit University Press, write Summit University Press, Dept. 470, Box 5000, Livingston, MT 59047-5000, or call (800) 245-5445; outside the U.S.A., call (406) 222-8300.

Picture Credits

frontispiece *The Name of God from Bible in Sefardi Hand,* 1385, by permission of the British Library, London.

173 *Israel in Egypt* (portion) by Sir Edward J. Poynter, Guildhall Art Gallery, London.

188 *Jeremiah at the Fall of Jerusalem* by Eduard Bendemann, Foto Marburg/Art Resource, N.Y.

189 *The Sorrowing Jews in Exile* by Eduard Bendemann, Rheinische Bildarchiv, Cologne.

II

Pearls of Wisdom

BOOK II

Teachings of the Ascended Masters
Mark L. Prophet · Elizabeth Clare Prophet
VOLUME THIRTY-FIVE · 1992

BELOVED GAUTAMA BUDDHA
Wesak Address 1992

20

Have Mercy!
The Thoughtform of the Anchor

My beloved, receive me as I AM—as I AM and not as you think I am. Allow me to be who I AM, the Buddha of your heart. Allow my Messenger to also be, and to be who she is. Allow your soul to go free. Let the soul be free to respond in the spontaneity of the flame of the Buddha.

I am come to you to bring you to the sameness of the inner Light and to the uniqueness of your individualization of that Light. I raise my hand and release the power for the trembling and then the crumbling of worlds within that are not you, that are not even of you.

Let go, beloved, for the Divine Id-Entity descends. Know this Identity as the I AM of God, as the "I" of God. Know your being, beloved, and then daily and hourly claim your freedom in the ritual of creation to be that being.

Each time you turn the page of a Buddhist text you understand a new freedom. It is the hour, then, to cast the anchor of your being into the Great Causal Body above. You have anchored your hopes and dreams in the astral sea. So accustomed have you become to anchoring yourself in lower levels that you do not realize how many anchors of desire you have dropped beneath that deep blue sea, which grows black as you descend the fathoms.

Cross this sea! Do not be anchored in it or to it. Yes, cast your hopes and your dreams, your longings but above all your will into the great sea of Light, the sea of Light that is the Causal Body of your I AM Presence. All elements of Light are in this Causal Body, this great, great firmament of Light.

How do you cast an anchor up, high up—up in the sense of in the very accelerated vibrations of consciousness of your I AM Presence?

The Presence resists anything that is less than the light of your perfection of soul. Thus, imagine pulling against the gravity of karma and against the lesser self, knowing that with all of your might you must heave this anchor of pure hope into the very highest octaves. The thirty-three planes await the arrival of your anchor with a mighty thud, as you have hurled it with the assistance of Hercules and Amazonia.

I come to speak to you of this concept this night, beloved, because the astral sea does rise.[1] It is a treacherous sea. As boisterous as the wind might be and as threatening as the waves, the astral sea does not reveal what is beneath the surface. Thus, your moorings must be elsewhere and you must pull from the depths, from the very deep itself, substance of your being that you have allowed to be tied to the lower levels of the astral plane.

This is the exercise of the hour and of the year: to withdraw yourself from the lowest levels to which you have descended, thoughtlessly or thoughtfully, premeditatedly or without even a care. It is dangerous, I say, for you to have any portion of yourself tied to these lower realms. [This subject] is worthy of [your] consideration.

Think as I speak to you now, beloved: What portion of yourself have you left behind? What desire that is not of God have you clung to, have you kept, that is pulling you down to those lower levels? I repeat, beloved, it is dangerous.

Now I would like to read to you from an ancient text so that you might see yourselves this night sitting at the feet of the Teacher and knowing that these texts are inspired by myself. They are for you and all disciples, all monks and sisters on the Path.

The first part is entitled "The Ship."

> "Revered Nāgasena, when you say three qualities of a ship must be adopted, which are these three qualities that must be adopted?"
>
> "As, sire, a ship, because of the combination of the many kinds of timber of which it is constructed takes many people across, even so, sire, the yogin, the earnest student of yoga, because of the combination of good habits, morality, special qualities, various practices and many kinds of mental states of which he is constructed, should cross over the world with the devas. This, sire, is the first quality of the ship that must be adopted.

"And again, sire, a ship endures the force of many kinds of thundering waves and the force of far-flung whirlpools; even so, sire, the yogin, the earnest student of yoga should endure the force of the waves of the many kinds of defilements, the gains, honours, renown, fame, veneration, salutation, the reproach and the praise of other families; and the force of the waves of the many kinds of defects in happiness and anguish, and the respect and the contempt (that he experiences). This, sire, is the second quality of the ship that must be adopted.

"And again, sire, a ship moves over the great and mighty ocean which is immeasurable, unending, without a farther shore, unperturbed and deep, of a great and mighty noise and confused with crowds of great ocean fishes and sea-monsters; even so, sire, the yogin, the earnest student of yoga should make his mind move about in the penetration and understanding of the four Truths with their three sections and twelve modes. This, sire, is the third quality of the ship that must be adopted. And this, sire, was said by the Lord, the deva above devas...: 'When you, monks, are thinking you should think: This is anguish. You should think: This is the arising of anguish. You should think: This is the stopping of anguish. You should think: This is the course leading to the stopping of anguish.'"

The next section is "The Anchor."

"Revered Nāgasena, when you say two qualities of the anchor must be adopted, which are these two qualities that must be adopted?"

"As, sire, the anchor holds the ship and keeps it where it is in an expanse of waters that is agitated and confused by the turmoil of many waves and does not let it be carried in one direction or another; even so, sire, should the yogin, the earnest student of yoga hold his mind in the great and mighty battle with thoughts in the turmoil of the waves of attachment, aversion and confusion, and not let it be carried in one direction or another. This, sire, is the first quality of the anchor that must be adopted.

"And again, sire, a ship's anchor does not float; it sinks down in the water even for a hundred cubits, holds the ship and keeps it in place; even so, sire, the yogin, the earnest student of yoga should not float among gains, renown, honours, reverence, salutation, veneration and the homage (paid to him) even if he be at the height of gain, the height of renown, but he should keep his mind fixed merely on keeping his body going. This, sire, is the second quality of the anchor that must be adopted. And this, sire, was said by the Elder Sāriputta, the General under Dhamma:

> 'As the anchor floats not on the sea, but sinks down,
> So float you not on gains and honours, but sink down.'"

The next section is "The Mast."

"Revered Nāgasena, when you say one quality of the mast must be adopted, which is this one quality that must be adopted?"

"As, sire, the mast carries ropes and braces and sails, even so, sire, the yogin, the earnest student of yoga must be possessed of mindfulness and clear consciousness; whether he is setting out or returning (from his alms-gathering), looking in front or looking around, stretching out or bending back (his arm), carrying his outer cloak, his bowl and robe, eating, drinking, chewing, tasting, obeying the calls of nature, walking, standing, sitting, asleep, awake, talking or silent, he must be one acting in a clearly conscious way. This, sire, is the one quality of the mast that must be adopted[—acting in a clearly conscious way]. And this, sire, was said by the Lord, the deva above devas: 'Monks, a monk should abide mindful and clearly conscious—this is our instruction to you.'"

The next section is "The Navigator."

"Revered Nāgasena, when you say three qualities of the navigator must be adopted, which are these three qualities that must be adopted?"

"As, sire, a navigator, night and day, constantly and continually, diligently and with strenuous care, makes the ship go, even so, sire, the yogin, the earnest student of yoga, when he is controlling and restraining his mind, (then) night and day, constantly and continually, diligently and with considered attention, should he control his mind. This, sire, is the first quality of the navigator that must be adopted. And this, sire, was said by the Lord, the deva above devas, in the Dhammapada:

> 'Be those who delight in diligence, guard your own
>   minds,

Each pull yourself out of the wrong way as an elephant sunk in mud.'

"And again, sire, whatever is in the great ocean, whether it be lovely or evil, is all known to the navigator; even so, sire, the yogin, the earnest student of yoga should discriminate between skill and unskill, between what is blameworthy and blameless, between what is low and excellent, between what is dark and bright and evenly mixed. This, sire, is the second quality of the navigator that must be adopted.

"And again, sire, the navigator puts a seal on the mechanism, saying: 'Let no one touch the mechanism'; even so, sire, the yogin, the earnest student of yoga should put a seal on control over his mind, thinking: 'Think not any evil unskilled thought.' And this, sire, was said by the Lord, the deva above devas . . .: 'Do not, monks, think evil unskilled thoughts, that is to say thoughts of sense-pleasures, thoughts of malevolence, thoughts of harming.'"

The next section is "The Handyman," the ship's carpenter.

"Revered Nāgasena, when you say one quality of the handyman must be adopted, which is this one quality that must be adopted?"

"As, sire, the handyman reflects thus: 'I am a hireling, I am working in this ship, it is on account of this ship that I get my keep; nothing slack is to be done by me; this ship is to be made to go through my diligence'; even so, sire, the yogin, the earnest student of yoga must reflect thus: 'I, reflecting on this body that is derived from the four great elementals, constantly and continually diligent, with mindfulness aroused, mindful and clearly conscious, my mind composed and made one-pointed, think: I will be freed from birth, ageing, disease, dying, grief, sorrow, suffering, lamentation and despair—diligence is to be done by me.' This, sire, is the one quality of the handyman that must be adopted. And this, sire, was said by the Elder Sāriputta, the General under Dhamma:

> 'Do you reflect on this body, know it accurately, again and again;
> Seeing in body its own essence, you shall make an end of anguish.'"

The next section is "The Sea."

"Revered Nāgasena, when you say five qualities of the sea must be adopted, which are these five qualities that must be adopted?"

"As, sire, the great ocean does not associate with a dead body, a corpse, even so, sire, the yogin, the earnest student of yoga should not associate with the stains of attachment, aversion, confusion, pride, false views, hypocrisy, spite, jealousy, stinginess, deceit, treachery, crookedness, uneven and wrong faring or with the defilements. This, sire, is the first quality of the sea that must be adopted.

"And again, sire, the sea, though possessing a wealth of pearls, gems, lapis lazuli, mother-of-pearls, quartz, corals, crystal-gems and many kinds of jewels, yet covers them over and does not scatter them outside (itself); even so, sire, the yogin, the earnest student of yoga, having arrived at the Ways, the fruits, the meditations, the liberations, concentration and attainment, insight, super-knowledge, and the jewels of the many kinds of special qualities, must cover them over and must not drive them outside (himself). This, sire, is the second quality of the sea that must be adopted.

"And again, sire, the sea associates with great and mighty beings; even so, sire, the yogin, the earnest student of yoga should dwell near a fellow Brahma-farer, a lovely friend who is of few wants, contented, a preacher of asceticism, one living in submissiveness, possessed of good habits, modest, well behaved, revered, to be respected, a speaker,...one who reproves (for an offence), censuring evil, an exhorter, instructor, adviser, one who gladdens, arouses, incites and delights (his fellow Brahma-farers). This, sire, is the third quality of the sea that must be adopted.

"And again, sire, the sea, though full of fresh water from a hundred thousand rivers...and though filled with downpours of water from the sky, yet does not overflow its own margins; even so, sire, the yogin, the earnest student of yoga should not, even for the sake of his life, knowingly transgress against the rules of training on account of the gains, honours, fame, salutation, reverence and veneration (paid to him). This, sire, is the fourth quality of the sea that must be adopted. And this, sire, was said by the Lord, the deva above devas: 'And as, sire, the great ocean is stable and does not overflow its margins, even so, sire, my disciples do not transgress against the rules of training laid down by me, even for their life's sake.'

"And again, sire, the sea is not overfull with all the rivers... (that flow into it), with the downpours of water from the sky; even so, sire, the yogin, the earnest student of yoga should never have enough of the recitation (of the Pātimokkha), the interrogation, of listening to, remembering, and investigation of the Abhidhamma and Discipline, of the deep Suttantas, of the resolution (of compounds), of the placing of words, of the liaison of words, of the division of words, of hearing the excellent nine-limbed instruction of the Conqueror. This, sire, is the fifth quality of the sea that must be adopted. And this, sire, was said by the Lord, the deva above devas...:

> 'As a fire burning grass and sticks
> Never has enough, nor the ocean of rivers,
> So do these wise men, O best of kings,
> Never have enough of hearing what is well spoken.' " [2]

I instruct that these teachings be prepared for you each one, that you read them three times, invoking my Dharmakaya, Sambhogakaya, Nirmanakaya,[3] that I might manifest my mind in you, my love for the discipline of Truth, my understanding of the analogies of life. For to meditate upon the world with all of its richness of the creation of God is to see beyond the form unto the formless and to recognize that everything that is created of God contains its own stamp of virtue to be internalized by the contemplation of the formed.

Thus, in this contemplation of the beauty of God, do not rest your weary eyes with the mere fixing of them upon the form of the mountain or of the rain or of the river or of the sun or of the flower or of the tree or of the beautiful face of a child, of a loved one, of a soul purified and made white. Penetrate beyond the form lest you become worshipers of form. Discover the key, the inner pattern. And when you have the pattern, you will have the key to creation itself, for the pattern that you contain is the pattern that you can multiply.

I have chosen the thoughtform of the anchor for my discourse this night. And I desire that you contemplate this object so ancient—as ancient as the ancient mariner—so necessary to those who ply the seas. Consider the balance, consider what energy of self is embodied in the anchor. It is indeed the quality of hope. So it is hope of which the author of Hebrews speaks, even in connection with the Christian symbol of the anchor.[4]

Where have you anchored the self?

The anchor is that which precedes the self in realms of glory. What does precede you? Of course, it is your hope!

And if you hope for no thing instead of some thing, then your anchor will be idle. Cast your hopes unto the highest and let your energy flow with the anchor and the rope. For the rope is that filigree thread, that tie, that blessed tie that ties the soul to the Great White Brotherhood.

And you have been promised that when you give all of the decrees that have been given at this Easter conference past as they were given here, you may have that thread of contact.[5] The thread of contact must become by your devotion, by your one-pointedness, a rope, a rope that may hold the anchor that is the hope, even the faith, even the promise of your heart that as the rope is thrown into the great "cloud of knowing" (which some have called "the cloud of unknowing"), so the anchor will be hurled.

Think of how much rope you must have to cast the foreself, the self that precedes you, the self that is a portion of the etheric self, a portion of the astral self and of the mind, even a portion of the will that resides in the marrow of your bones—to be able to cast that portion into that Infinite.

And then, beloved, with that anchor firmly secured and never wavering, no matter what the sea of life does bring, you can pull on the rope, know the anchor is secure, and you can climb that rope by thought, by desire, by hope and again hope until all of you is rising and none of you is left in the treacherous sea of the astral plane that is rising.

Yes, beloved, would you be, one and all, anchorites? ["Yes!"]

The anchorite is a Christian hermit. Sometimes you think you are hermits, and then you go forth into the world. And the world becomes to you drier and drier, yet you return to your home of Light and you say, "I am not fulfilled, but it is not my home that is at fault any more than that chambered nautilus is at fault."

But what does the inhabitant make of the home?

Surely the home is the point of Light, the sacred fire breath, the inbreathing and the outbreathing. Surely the home is the place where you go up the spiral of the love of the Guru—[the Guru's love] for your soul and your soul's hope in the love of the Guru.

Have you sometimes felt, beloved, if the Guru did not have hope in you and love for you, standing by you day by day, that you yourself should lose all hope in life's way?

This sense, beloved, comes to every chela in those moments of despair when the real worth of the Guru is sensed. I AM that

Guru. Fortunate am I and fortunate are you that I may span the octaves and speak to you many thousands of years before you might accurately converse with me between the octaves.

Thus, in the Guru-chela relationship that includes a "two-way" Messenger, beloved, there is such a shortening of the days for the elect[6] that you may hope in God *and hope in God* and know that your hopes are being tangibly crystallized in the central sun of your being and that you shall arrive at that crystal gate and the twelve gates with their many crystals that signify the rays of the sun and the Central Sun and the hierarchies thereof.

I AM Gautama. And you know that you must cross the sea of *samsara*.[7] And you know the ship of Maitreya.[8] And you know that ships carry not one but many anchors. And [in ancient times] the greatest anchor of all was called the "sacred anchor"; and when it was cast at the last, that anchor, then, was the last hope of sailors that the ship would hold against the tides and the storms of the sea.

Yes, beloved, you hope in Christ, him the hope of glory. And your hope does not waver, for your hope in Christ is answered when you answer, when you dare to move closer to that Son of God, that Sun of being, fearing not but hearing the voice, "Come up higher!" Hope is being faithful in all things, not just a few but *all* things. That faithfulness, beloved, is rewarded. And again, you feel the tautness of the rope as though Christ himself were the very anchor that you have cast: "Christ in you, the hope of glory."[9]

Be the anchor in this world, beloved. Be the hope of many. Be steadfast. Be persevering. Hold on to the salt of the sea and the minerals and the jewels and all that the sea of life contains. Let your aura be rich in the gifts of the Spirit and in all those gifts that temper the quality of the earth, providing nourishment to the body that the soul may inhabit it with joy.

I come in an hour when many things in the earth are brewing beneath the levels of the astral sea. Thus, beloved, I come to give you [extended] "vision" of the All-Seeing Eye of God that you might with special lenses probe the astral depths and take your ["sonar"] readings as readings of sound returning to you the report of what is at many levels.

Yes, beloved, you can determine what is there and you must know that there is great agitation in the astral plane. This you have seen in your cities, even the eruption of anger on the part of some lifestreams, even the neglect on the part of others who could have long ago brought aid to the poor, to the needy, to those crying out to be educated, to be free to earn their daily bread and to come up higher.

Ought not a nation to consider the ancient law, the law of feeding the beggars? You cannot turn away those who come with begging bowls. And those who are too ignorant to know that a gun or a stone or the destruction of life and neighborhoods and buildings is not a begging bowl—those who know it not, those who know it not, teach them. Teach them, beloved! And if they will not be God-taught, let them receive justice for their crimes, but also let them be loved free [from their criminal tendencies]!

Hope is everywhere where there is life. And where there is life you must fan the fires of hope. It is just and right that those who carry karma, any karma, recognize the avenue of balancing karma by feeding the poor and the hungry, caring for the children, educating them and bringing life to a level of inner dignity. Where there is no dignity, destruction will increase, and mass destruction from many levels.

Pray, I say, for divine resolution in the hearts of the Lightbearers! Alpha has called you to pray for the Lightbearers.[10] These are the calls that may be answered. Many Lightbearers in the world are not pursuing their calling. They have not hope in Christ or Buddha yet retain hope in the vanity of the ego. How swiftly the egos file, as skulls and skeletons, to their graves!

Know that hope is in the inner Light and Life of Buddha, of Christ. Hope, yes, hope in trying instead of not trying, hope in not giving up on anyone—hope, beloved! For all souls who have become sinners by the influence of outside forces and even by their inner commitment to Darkness must be served. And there are many levels of society that need to serve [because their karma dictates it] but they turn their backs and consider that it is unjust that they [should be required to] give to those who are in the self-destruct mode, destroying themselves and their cities.

Blessed ones, *feed* the poor. *Clothe* their souls. Adorn the mind with the wisdom and the practical know-how of their daily livelihood. Set an example. Teach the children. Let them not be lost! When serving the public good and the order, there must be no discrimination between the ranks of those who have much or less karma or this or that. When you are a public servant—and you are all public servants—then your Lord is the Christ of every man. ["Judge not lest ye be judged."[11]]

And I remind you that the Great Teacher said, "The servant is not greater than his lord."[12] Thus, remember in humility that you are not greater than the Christ, even the Christ Self that might be far above the evildoer. Serve that Christ! Cast your anchor into the heart of that Christ and pull that Christ down and raise that soul up and let the marriage [of that soul and her Lord take place because you have interceded in Mercy's name]!

Much can be accomplished by visualization as you visualize this happening to millions of the disenfranchised, millions of those who do not know what it means to have a piece of the pie of the American dream. If you give them no hope, it means you give them no anchor, no anchor to cast into the bedrock of their own God-Reality.

Pray, then, for there is not one of you here tonight who in some embodiment past has not been at the very bottom of the heap, [at the lowest rung] of society's ladder. And there you should have remained had it not been for someone who had compassion and more, who when looking upon you had to have hope, beloved—hope of a greater vision of what you could become than even you yourself had for yourself. If someone had not had compassion and hope for you, hope that is conviction, a conviction that inspires one to act and to do something for the poor wretch lying in the gutter somewhere—namely you—had such a one not come to your aid, you should not have risen in that life and if not in that life, then perhaps not in a series of lives.

I will tell you the secret prayer of the Messenger, who continually praises God in Morya, who did pick her up as an orphan waif sometime, somewhere in the depths of the astral plane. Thus, beloved, understand how you may share in the prayer of Teresa of Avila, [which is also the prayer of the Messenger]: "I, a poor sinner, I, a poor sinner, am not worthy of thee, my Lord, and yet I serve and I pray."

See yourself, then, truly as that orphan. For are you not an orphan until the day and the hour when someone, perhaps some great one of the adepts, does take you and turn you around and set you on a course straight for the highest star? Does anyone here still think that he has done this of himself? ["No."]

It is well to remember that, beloved. For all have been wretched, all have been the downtrodden, all have been under [the boot of] civilizations, empires [that have been run as] absolute dictatorships.

Who did come and rescue you?

So it was Sanat Kumara, Saint Germain, the Holy One of God. Yes, beloved. Yes, beloved, remember these things when you see the peoples of this nation, the masses of humanity and so many who are under tyrants and helpless before oncoming armies, famines, droughts and the hopelessness of no change for the future. Think of those incarcerated across the nations of the earth.

I say this to all of you, for I give you the consciousness of the Buddha, and I want you to know that that portion that I give to you is the sensitivity to the pain of those who are not as well-off as you are. And when I speak of being well-off, I speak of the riches of the Spirit and the direct contact you have with the Ascended Masters and Almighty God if you exercise it.

Do you not know that some have indeed silenced the voice of conscience, snuffed out the threefold flame and have no momentum of contact with God? Yet somewhere deep inside there is a point of kindness, a point of goodness and the desire to be somebody who can accomplish something, who might ultimately do something for someone else. Have mercy. Have the quality of mercy within you. Be merciful toward life. For as God has forgiven you your sins, so know that the gift is given to you to extend that forgiveness to life.

And the disciples were given that gift: "Whosoever sins ye remit, they are remitted; whosoever sins ye retain, they are retained."[13] This is given to the true disciple, who has that Christ Flame burning brightly and has developed the sword of discrimination, cleaving asunder the Real from the Unreal and understanding when it is necessary for a man, a woman, a child to bear their karma and when, in their heart of hearts, it is not necessary for them to carry it longer.

Understand the mystery of the Law, the mastery of the Law and yourself in the whole scheme of things. I say, having all due humility, *you* shall pass your tests! But without [that understanding and that humility], beloved, you will be so dense as to not know that a test has come and gone or that you have failed it because you have not even engaged it.

Such a state of affairs, beloved, should leave you with a sense that there are more layers to peel away. Every day I knock, your Holy Christ Self knocks with a challenge or with the same old test that has been going on a long time to give you the opportunity for soul refinement, for the shedding of the snakeskin, for the cutting of the tie to the fallen angels.

Pass those tests, beloved! For the Great Teams of Conquerors are just on the other side of the wall, just on the other side of the wall waiting to initiate you in their ranks. Expect them! Pass them! Move on and be recognized for what you are (and should be manifesting): Teachers of righteousness! Teachers of righteousness!

May you be empowered by the Spirit [of the I AM THAT I AM], the Holy Spirit, when you come to the hour of Pentecost.*
May you know the obvious qualifications [of that Spirit, which you

---
*June 7, 1992

should embody in your soul and in your spirit, whereby you may be empowered by that Spirit]. Acquire them swiftly, for they are already seeds planted within you. Let them be present. Put together the elements of your Tree of Life, as Above, so below, and see how quickly that Spirit moves through you! Yes, indeed, take advantage of your access to the Messenger, for you can move mountains of the not-self and be ensconced in the flower of hope.

I AM Gautama Buddha. I shall continue speaking in this place for many hours to come, recording, embroidering on the ethers for you my nuggets of gold.

This night, O my beloved, I cast my anchor of hope into the heart of the true chela. And I say, if you were not a true chela five minutes ago, you may become one just that quickly! Simply surrender all to your Mighty I AM Presence and see how you, the true chela, will know the beauty of your true Guru.

I am in the flame of the Western Shamballa. I do a great deal of walking up and down the earth, up and down the mountains. I walk, beloved, and you should be surprised to see my resemblance.

I seal you in the flame of Wesak, of my birth, my enlightenment, my ascension. Cherish it, beloved. These are not mere words. I seal you in the flame of Wesak, of my birth, my enlightenment and my ascension.

Messenger's Comments:

Let us continue to express our gratitude to Lord Gautama as we have our love offering of gratitude to him, and immediately thereafter Buddha's pudding[14] will be served. While we eat that pudding, I will give you additional teachings of Gautama from the Masters.

Messenger's Blessing of the Love Offering:

Beloved Mighty I AM Presence, beloved Lord Gautama Buddha, receive the offering of our hearts, the offering of our hope, our faith, our charity, the offering of our souls to thee fearlessly, gently, lovingly and without reserve. For our hope is our trust in God, and thou art God-manifestation, O Lord!

Receive our Community! Purge our souls and beings this night! Let us hear with the inner ear your teachings that continue. Make us one body that is vibrant and strong, that we might serve as the spiritual elect. Let the rays of our hearts become the mighty beacons of our Summit Lighthouse, going out to all the world to draw in the Lightbearers, whereby this nucleus of Light shall surely represent your Nirmanakaya in the earth.

Receive us, O Lord! We have received your message. We send love by the great *antahkarana* of Life to all those who are keeping the flame of the Lord of the World, Gautama Buddha. O God, make us one! We are one on the inner. Make us one on the outer if it be thy will.

O Lord Gautama, make war this night[15] and bind all fallen ones who would prevent the great victory of the City of God on earth as it is in heaven.

In the name of the Father, the Son, the Holy Spirit and the Divine Mother, let this offering be multiplied and returned to the Great Giver and to each one who is his instrument. Let the gifts be used wisely for the sending of the message of the Buddha and the Christ.

O God, we wait upon thee for the solution to so many problems in the earth, known and unknown. Great All-Seeing Eye of God, let thy Light shine to the depths of the astral sea that we might know what we must deal with and that we might deal with it swiftly.

In the name of our Lord and Saviour Jesus Christ, Padma Sambhava, Lord Maitreya, Gautama Buddha, Sanat Kumara, the Five Dhyani Buddhas and the Buddha of the Ruby Ray, Amen.

The Messenger reads the Teachings of the Buddha given by the Ascended Masters:

The Maha Chohan said on July 1, 1960:

Children of God, keep your flame steady. Keep your consciousness anchored.

In the United States of America, at Annapolis, Maryland, there is an anchor outside the chapel of the United States Naval Academy. This anchor is a great symbol. All anchors can be symbols of "holding fast to that which thou hast that no one take thy crown."[16] Thy crown of eternal comfort is an eternal one. I long to bestow it on each of you.

Archangel Michael said on April 13, 1986:

Sweet hearts of Chamuel's bands, . . . receive now that portion of God-Love on every line of the Clock that will be there as a flame to multiply the twelve God-qualities within you. This, then, is the considered and concerted reward to all who have dared to stand in this sanctuary and in the courts of the world to defend our name and cause. For it is by love and only love that thou couldst have endured, showing, then, that thy treasure is truly in the heart of God and thy heart is in his.

Beloved, you who know you have fought the good fight and won, receive, then, this point of the Ruby Ray. And this fire is shaped like the anchor of a mighty ship. And that anchor, beloved, is as a lodestone. Call, then, for the flaming anchor of Love to multiply your God-Power, God-Love, God-Mastery, God-Control, God-Obedience, God-Wisdom—and especially God-Harmony, God-Gratitude and God-Justice. For these three must take you through the journey of the night through the astral plane of that karma that you will—I say, *you will*—balance perforce by the gain already achieved.

It is the dark night of the soul of personal and planetary karma of which I speak that all must face following the balancing of 51 percent of their karma if they would move on to the ascension after the 100 percent and then some. Realize, beloved, as you have been told, that the dispensation of the 51 percent was given because so many souls lost the ascension when the next initiation [they had to face] was the descent into Death and Hell [on the six o'clock line].

Therefore, this fiery anchor of Love will multiply the

Ruby Ray initiations as well as [the soul's] protection in that astral quadrant of the six, seven and eight o'clock lines. Now then, it does multiply your God-Reality, God-Vision and God-Victory. Beloved ones, in the next initiation you will place the missing anchor in the center of the circle of thy Christhood.[17]

Gautama Buddha, December 31, 1984:

There is passed to me now from the Keeper of the Scrolls the scroll of the thoughtform for the year 1985. It is the image of planet earth restored—karma balanced, axis straightened. It is sealed in the etheric sheath and thus appears as a shimmering sphere of light. The configurations of landmasses and seas are not exactly as they are today, signifying the true etheric matrix of that which is to be in the golden age.

Present in the canvas that is drawn, at the lower left, is an anchor, an anchor such as used by Maitreya in his clipper ship. It signifies the anchoring of planet earth in the bedrock of Maitreya's consciousness. In the upper right corner are the scales, signifying the balance of all forces and karmic cycles.

So the lower left is the anchor and the upper right is the scales. And the scales have equal sides, and the base of the anchor has equal sides.

In the lower right-hand corner is the Sacred Heart of [Jesus] Christ, full blossoming with a fleur-de-lis and the white rose of the Mother. Diamond and bejeweled with the gems of the City Foursquare, this heart is the sign of the disciples of the Path of the Ruby Ray who enter into the union of the cross of Sanat Kumara, Gautama, Jesus and Maitreya.

And in the upper left-hand corner there is the image of the City Foursquare, the New Jerusalem that descends out of heaven as the etheric matrix lowered for the Community of the Holy Spirit forged and won by the called-out ones. Beneath that symbol is the outline of the mountains of the Inner Retreat.

Thus, in these signs you may understand the mighty work of the ages of your souls to seal the earth in the bedrock of the path of Maitreya by the anchor itself for the conquest of sea and water. The balance that is held is in

Have Mercy!

the Mind of God through the scales. The sacred fire of the heart [of Jesus Christ] is the victory of the Spirit as the Word made flesh. Fire in Matter signifies the union of heaven and earth in the chakra supreme in the body temple, [which is the heart chakra. This fire in Matter is the Sacred Heart of Jesus one with our hearts]. And the descending city is the pattern and blueprint whereby the etheric octave becomes physical, proven once and then proven again and again as a formula of Life varying in each continent and place that shall spring up as the whole world receives the education of the heart.

May you pray for the precipitation of these four symbols in the hearts of all Lightbearers, that the cardinal points of earth and the gates of the city might be kept.[18]

So for your own sketch of this thoughtform, you simply draw a rectangle. In the lower left-hand corner is the anchor. In the upper right-hand corner are the scales. In the lower right-hand corner is the Sacred Heart of Jesus. And in the upper left-hand corner is the City Foursquare, the Holy City, which we know is the Retreat of the Divine Mother over the Inner Retreat.[19] These are four amazing and powerful thoughtforms.

Lord Maitreya said on December 4, 1980:

There is a little bird, snowy white, in a little golden cage in my heart chamber. He sings a song of love and The Song of the Homing.

This little white bird is not imprisoned but entered the cage voluntarily and shut the door, desiring to be an adornment at the altar where the chela may come to meditate—the chela whom I have chosen, not who has chosen me. This snowy white bird sings the love song of twin flames. And, do you know, he sings *the keynote of each one's I AM Presence* as that chela approaches the altar of initiation in my heart....

Contemplate the little bird and then determine whether it is "God and my right" as your own private interpretation of the Word or "God and my right" as your own Mighty I AM Presence and Christ Self that will become the leading authority in your life—the leading authority as the mighty Lifestream that not only connects you to the Great God Star but pulls you in year by year as you, the soul, are the anchor and God himself is the great mother ship.

O hearts of Light, indeed you are anchor points—

under the sea of the astral plane and in the heart of the earth—of the great, great light of the mother ship of our Brotherhood. So it is that the clipper ship is my symbol and the symbol of your soul's journey in time and in space.[20]

Gautama Buddha explained to me that the thoughtform of the anchor, and especially the one that is beaded upon my garment, is for you to look upon in the same manner in which the children of Israel looked upon the caduceus—the brazen serpent that Moses put upon a pole and held up in the wilderness. When the children of Israel looked upon it, they were healed of the bites from the fiery serpents, which the LORD had sent for their judgment.[21]

As you see this thoughtform of the anchor and visualize it, you can pour into it, as a matrix, all of your hopes, your plans, your destiny and the distillation from your being of all that is the transmuted essence of your karma and your psychology. And if you fix your hope upon the anchor, even as the anchor represents hope, you will find that you will retain what is real about yourself and discard the unreal as all things permanent coalesce in the thoughtform of the anchor.

Now, as we receive the thoughtform of the anchor and see it in that lower left-hand corner of the thoughtform for the year 1985, we can also make use of the other thoughtforms. We will enshrine the thoughtform of the Sacred Heart of Jesus (in the lower right-hand corner) at our First Friday devotions. We will embrace beloved Portia's mighty scales of Justice (in the upper right-hand corner) as the focus of the mighty action of the Law in our life and always respect that Justice is the champion of the Law in our behalf no matter what price we must pay.

We will meditate on the divine blueprint, the great lodestone of the Inner Retreat of the Divine Mother in the etheric octave over this place (upper left-hand corner) as the tangible, living, vibrant city of the saints of God that it is. And if we cannot reach our Mighty I AM Presence by casting our anchor of hope into it, we can cast our anchor of hope into the Holy City until we are able to sustain the tie to our Mighty I AM Presence.

This year's Wesak dictation from Gautama is for the coalescing of our forces, the distilling of our energy, the withdrawal of our energy from old, outworn, rotten matrices of psychology of this and past embodiments, so that we might release those matrices into the flame, extract the energy, transmute it into light and create out of it this mighty jeweled anchor. So I have worn this garment that is precious to me—not only as an outer symbol of this teaching but because it is actually similar to a garment that Gautama Buddha has also worn.

I would like you to think of Gautama Buddha as having a presence and a form not much larger than my own. Sometimes we visualize the Buddhas as filling the sky, as massive beings, and therefore we make them unapproachable. But if you think of Gautama as walking through these hills, simply attired, I think you will not fear to approach him, to walk with him and talk with him. So that is why I give you a vision of the simplicity of the great Lord of the World.

Whenever I am in the presence of Gautama Buddha, I remember the day in the early 1960s when I arrived at National Airport in Washington, D.C. I was alone. Mark had met me and I was seated for some time while he attended to errands.

Gautama Buddha's keynote began to play over the speaker, the song we sing to him, "Precious Gautama," to the melody of "Moonlight and Roses." And with my inner sight I saw Gautama Buddha walk through National Airport and come to me. He revealed to me many levels of world conditions and many things that were coming upon the earth at that time and which are still coming upon the earth and which have not yet come to pass.

It was my first impression of Gautama Buddha as a Master of action moving through the terminals of the world, the capitals, the crossroads. He was distinctly the Buddha—not a Buddha like other Buddhas, but the Buddha who is the one ultimately in charge of planet earth. He cares, he is involved, he is as much a statesman as he is a Buddha, a comforter, a friend, a person of many talents, a tremendous mind, a compassionate mind, a mind that embraces all things and circumstances. His Causal Body and aura literally contain the planet and every part of life on the planet. And yet I could see him, I could walk with him, I could talk with him person to person, heart to heart.

He made me to know that I had the seed of the Buddha inside of me. And that is something that you need to know if you desire to maintain a co-relationship with him. You need to know that you are (or you can be, if you are not) a chela worthy of being a Chela with a capital *C* and that you can be his counterpart because the reality of God is in you and the reality of you is God. And in the sense of God being your reality, you are so profoundly humble before that presence that you actually go into an "egoless existence" because God, the Divine Ego, has displaced yourself, hence is yourself.

And so, the process of distilling yourself, the essence of

yourself, into the thoughtform of the anchor, as I have explained its spiritual significance, is intended to give you the key that it is time to dispense with the substance of the not-self, the decay of it, the old forms of it. You are all alchemists. Every one of you here is an alchemist. You perform alchemy daily if you give but a single "Heart, Head and Hand" decree with the full fervor of your Buddhic nature.

So now extract the essence of yourself from the old mold, and begin by seeing this beautiful anchor as the focus of the new mold. And if you do as I have told you, you will think miracles are happening in your life, but they will not be miracles, because you will be applying a scientific formula. More of this formula and its action I cannot tell you. But the teaching that God gave to me for my personal path and the use of the anchor is surely a mighty teaching and a point of liberation, which you can discover for yourself.

I ask you to meditate on the anchor that you might receive a very personal teaching for your life from beloved El Morya. I would like to read, in closing, a few verses from the Book of Hebrews regarding the anchor and the quality of hope, which begins with Abraham. The symbolic meaning of the anchor comes from a passage in chapter 6, which reads:

> When God made a promise to Abraham, since he had no one greater by whom to swear, he swore by himself, saying, "Surely I will bless you and multiply you."
> And thus Abraham, having patiently endured, obtained the promise.
> Men indeed swear by a greater than themselves, and in all their disputes an oath is final for confirmation.
> So when God desired to show more convincingly to the heirs of the promise the unchangeable character of his purposes, he interposed with an oath, so that through two unchangeable things, in which it is impossible that God should prove false, we who have fled for refuge might have strong encouragement to seize the hope set before us.
> We have this [hope] as a sure and steadfast anchor of the soul, a hope that enters into the inner shrine behind the curtain, where Jesus has gone as a forerunner on our behalf, having become a high priest forever after the order of Melchizedek.[22]

This is the curtain that shielded the Holy of holies from the outer court.[23] "As a sure and steadfast anchor of the soul, a hope that enters into the inner shrine behind the curtain." We cast our anchor into the Holy of Holies of our being, behind that curtain that no man may enter except he have that Christ consciousness, "where Jesus has gone as a forerunner on our behalf, having become a high priest forever after the order of Melchizedek."

In Christian teaching, hope is an important virtue. Jesus is the unfailing hope of all who believe in him.

The word *anchorite* comes from the Greek word meaning "to withdraw." A female anchorite is called an anchoress. The word *anchorite* refers to an extreme type of Christian ascetic. (Viewed by the world, we are definitely extreme types!) The anchorites withdrew from the world to pursue spiritual perfection. They often subjected themselves to severe hardships.

I am smiling for the very next statement. *The Catholic Encyclopedia* notes: "In its extremest isolation, the life of the Christian anchorite is no Nirvana." I think they meant "picnic"— that's the Catholic view of nirvana. "[But] the soul occupied with divine thoughts freed from all distracting cares leads an existence... productive of the highest type of happiness obtainable on this earth."[24]

Encyclopaedia Britannica says:

> [The word] hermit... is used interchangeably with anchorite [I think Gautama is sending us a message], although the two were originally distinguished on the basis of location: an anchorite selected a cell attached to a church or near a populous centre, while a hermit retired to the wilderness.
>
> The first Christian hermits appeared by the end of the 3rd century in Egypt, where one reaction to the persecution of Christians by the Roman emperor Decius was flight into the desert to preserve the faith and to lead a life of prayer and penance....
>
> The excessive austerity and other extremes of the early hermits' lives were tempered by the establishment of cenobite (common life) communities. The foundation was thus laid in the 4th century for the institution of monasticism (*i.e.*, monks living a common life according to an established rule). The [hermitic] life eventually died out in Western Christianity, but it has continued in Eastern Christianity[—and at the Royal Teton Ranch adjacent to America's wilderness!][25]

And that's all the teaching I am going to give you tonight, because you're going to listen to Gautama Buddha as you go home and as you ask to be taken to the Retreat of the Divine Mother over the ranch and as you realize that all things that are mysteries will not be given to you by an outer voice but by the inner voice. And if I tell you everything, you see, then you will not develop your own inner ear or your own Christ discrimination that embraces the Light and eschews the Darkness.

Pondering the thoughtform of the anchor, may you find the true mystery of your soul's anchoring in God. And may you ponder all these words so you can begin to put all these things together and finally come to that teaching which El Morya has given me, which I shall not give you but which he is ready to give to you directly by your establishing your attunement with him.

I would be very happy to receive from you letters giving me your insights as to what you have discovered as you pondered this thoughtform.

Let us have our benediction.

Messenger's Benediction:

Beloved Mighty I AM Presence from the heart of God in the Great Central Sun, we are grateful for our beloved Lord Gautama Buddha in the heart of the earth, embracing the earth, containing the earth in his Great Causal Body. We are the children of his Sun. We are the anchor points of his being here below, even as we cast our anchor into the heart of God.

Our hope is in thee, O Lord! For there is no other hope but thee and in thee, Lord God Almighty, Lord Gautama, Lord Jesus, Lord Maitreya, Lord Padma Sambhava and our most beloved Lord Sanat Kumara.

In the name of the Father, the Son, the Holy Spirit and the Divine Mother, I anchor these hearts in the heart of Gautama, and Gautama in these hearts.

In the name of Sanat Kumara, we retire to the strains of *Finlandia*. Good night, everyone.

Let us give to our beloved Gautama the applause that is due him. [22-second standing ovation]

Have Mercy! 271

"The Summit Lighthouse Sheds Its Radiance O'er All the World to Manifest as Pearls of Wisdom." This dictation by **beloved Gautama Buddha** was **delivered** by the Messenger of the Great White Brotherhood Elizabeth Clare Prophet at the conclusion of the Saturday evening, **May 16, 1992 Wesak service** at the **Royal Teton Ranch, Park County, Montana.** The dictation and Messenger's teachings are available on 90-min. audiocassette ($6.50 plus $1.05 postage, A92033). [**N.B.** Throughout this *Pearl,* bracketed material denotes words unspoken yet implicit in the dictation, added by the Messenger under Gautama's direction for clarity in the written word.] Throughout these notes *PoW* is the abbreviation for *Pearls of Wisdom.* (**1**) **Rising astral sea.** See 1988 *PoW,* Book II, pp. 622–24, 625–26. (**2**) I. B. Horner, trans., *Milinda's Questions,* vol. 23 of *Sacred Books of the Buddhists* (London: Luzac and Company, 1964), pp. 246–53. (**3**) In Buddhism the Dharmakaya, Sambhogakaya and Nirmanakaya are the three "bodies" of the Buddha. The **Dharmakaya** is the Body ("kaya") of Law ("Dharma"), the Body of First Cause or the Body of Essence, which is one with Absolute Reality. It corresponds to the upper figure in the Chart of Your Divine Self, the Causal Body, including the I AM Presence. The **Sambhogakaya** is the Body of Bliss, Body of Inspiration or Spiritual Enjoyment, or Glorious Body. It is the form that a Buddha characteristically uses to reveal himself in his glory to bodhisattvas, enlightening and inspiring them. The Sambhogakaya corresponds to the middle figure in the Chart—the Holy Christ Self. The **Nirmanakaya** is the Body of Transformation or Created Body, i.e., the crystallization of the Dharmakaya in human form for the purpose of expounding the Teaching and saving other beings. It corresponds to the lower figure in the Chart and is employed at the plane of the soul incarnating the I AM. (**4**) Heb. 6:13–20. (**5**) See p. 247. (**6**) Matt. 24:22; Mark 13:20. (**7**) *samsara* [Sanskrit, literally 'wandering through', 'journeying']: passing through a succession of states; the indefinitely repeated cycles of birth, misery and death caused by karma; corporeal existence; worldly illusion; the universe of manifestation and phenomena as distinguished from the real existence which lies behind it; the veil of sorrow, pain and illusion. (**8**) **Ship of Maitreya.** The clipper ship is the symbol of Lord Maitreya. It is the ship of initiation—the ship the soul takes to travel over the sea of samsara. Lord Maitreya has said: "I am the captain of a mighty ship, a sailing vessel where I take you on journeys of the soul.... I AM that Law that does deliver thee. And the means of deliverance which you have seen as the clipper ship is truly my Causal Body" (July 2, 1978, March 24, 1985). (**9**) Col. 1:27. (**10**) **Alpha's call to pray for the Lightbearers.** See Alpha, July 5, 1987, "Alpha's Agenda," in 1987 *PoW,* pp. 387–88. (**11**) Matt. 7:1–5; Luke 6:37, 38. (**12**) John 13:16; 15:20. (**13**) John 20:23. (**14**) **Buddha's pudding.** Traditionally after Gautama's Wesak address, his devotees partake of rice pudding in commemoration of the rich rice milk that Sujata, a villager's daughter, served Gautama before his meditation under the Bo tree. The Gospel of Buddha records that when Gautama had partaken of the rice milk, "all his limbs were refreshed, his mind became clear again, and he was strong to receive the highest enlightenment." (**15**) **"Make war this night."** In a dictation given July 5, 1969, Zarathustra commanded angels of the sacred fire: "Take your mighty swords of Light and make war tonight with the hosts of Darkness. Vanquish them from the earth.... God and man desire it." On January 1, 1966, Gautama Buddha said: "And now we go to win the world—a mighty banner I unfurl.... We say to all the hordes of Dark: *Depart, depart* this very park! For

God is here and here to stay!" **(16)** Rev. 3:11. **(17)** 1986 *PoW*, Book II, pp. 427–28. **(18)** 1985 *PoW*, Book I, pp. 63–64. **(19) Holy City, Retreat of the Divine Mother.** See 1990 *PoW*, pp. 308, 514; 1991 *PoW*, pp. 96, 104 n. 15. **(20)** 1980 *PoW*, pp. 369–70. **(21)** Num. 21:5–9. **(22)** Heb. 6:13–20 (Revised Standard Version). **(23) Curtain shielding the Holy of holies.** Exod. 26:31–35; 30:6; 36:35, 36; Lev. 16:2; 21:23; Heb. 9, 10. **(24)** *The Catholic Encyclopedia,* ed. Charles G. Herbermann et al. (New York: Robert Appleton Company, 1907–14), s.v. "Anchorites." **(25)** *Encyclopaedia Britannica,* 15th ed., s.v. "hermit."

The Beloved Maha Chohan
Pentecost Address 1992

21

The Process of the Purging
Expand the Capacity of the Heart!

From my fingertips streams of fire flow, quickening the mind, exalting the heart. Thus does the Holy Spirit penetrate the substrata of being.

Gently, gently are the cups of consciousness emptied, then filled, emptied and filled as you would wash a pot that must be washed again and again. So the first stage of the receiving of the Holy Spirit is for the purging. Thus, the Holy Spirit comes and it does dislodge that substance that must not be allowed to commingle with the Light.

It is our goal, beloved, and thus we have called you personally to Maitreya's Mystery School, to prepare you day by day that you might one day receive and retain the Holy Spirit. The process of this hour, then, in which we [shall engage you, inasmuch as we] do have your cooperation (and for this we are grateful), is the process of the purging.

Therefore do not be discomfited, do not be upset, for much is coming to the surface. And it is in the etheric body and the mental body and in the desire body and in the physical.

Old encrustations of consciousness and records must come to the surface and flow out. This process, beloved, can be dangerous if you do not understand it, because the mind will arrest the process and begin to go over and relive and reexperience the old memories, desires, the old ways of thinking and reasoning, the old patterns of the physical body.

Blessed ones, it is safe to assume day after day that the Light is coming into your temple, that the Light does purge as much as you are able to release into the Flame. I come, the Maha Chohan, to seek your intense cooperation with this process. For when you understand it, beloved, you will so bind your heart to the flame of the altar, even the flame of the ark of the covenant, for you will know that the process is ongoing. And as you participate in the spiritualization of consciousness, you will be anchoring more and more of the Holy Spirit; and less and less of it will be for the purging, and more and more of it, which we give to you drop by drop, will be for your strengthening.

    Blessed ones, it is so wise to *hold* what thou hast received![1] Hold the position! When there is a cleansing, when there is a strengthening, when there is a grasping of a cosmic principle, hold fast to it. Write it down. Keep your journals of the discovery of the Mind of God and the unfolding process of that Mind within you.

    Your human mind is not capable of remembering or even containing the wondrous glimpses of the Mind of God that you receive. Therefore you must write them down with joy and read them in the hours when you are once again in the throes of the purging, as deeper levels of the astral body must come to the surface.

    This is an hour for great tenacity, for holding on as though you were on a ship at sea in a heavy storm and you should hold on to the mast, hold on to the bars that you would be not tossed overboard when the wind and the wave and the storm descended. So this is a likeness of what some experience [in the process of the purging]. And when there is this experience—for which you are surely cut out and which is the reason why this Mystery School is here—you sometimes think, "Life is so difficult, the only way to get through it is to depart." Beloved ones, this could be heartbreaking to us, if our hearts could break.

    You must understand that we must apply the pressure in order to answer the mandates of your decrees and fiats, the pressure of the *heat!* Blessed ones, there is no creation without the *heat* of fire and the sacred fire itself, and that *heat* is for the alchemy [of the soul's transformation].

    I AM the alchemist of the Holy Spirit and the Flame thereof. And when I have a body of initiates such as you are or can be—those of you who call yourselves Keepers of the Flame throughout the world, you who have the direct knowledge and the direct contact with the Hierarchy of Light—I say, we do everything that we can possibly do for you to bring you into that superb and sublime state of consciousness wherein you know your God and have that accuracy, that piercing Christ-discrimination whereby

The Process of the Purging 275

you are no longer tossed and tumbled by the human sympathies with this and that state or stage of consciousness, your own or another's. [For sometimes you are so colored by those sympathies,] beloved, that you do not perceive the Rock of Christ in the midst and you make such unwise and uncalled-for decisions.

These decisions are not [necessarily] a product of your karma. They are a matter of an absence of fastidiousness in the mastery of your own mind, the steadying of your own mind so that in the midst of these initiations, beloved, you remain whole, you remain unmoved. You know that as you are unmoved God will continue to apply the greater and greater pressure whereby the worlds were framed and you were created in the Beginning.

You are being tested daily to determine how much of the pressure of Light and the pressure of the Holy Spirit you can withstand. Beloved ones, you are our children and our sons and daughters. Shall we apply more pressure than you can receive and withstand and still hold the balance of sanity and the stilling of the emotions?

Well, of course not! We will give you that heat, and if it is too hot, we will withdraw it and wait again for another moment when you have the strength to receive it.

Now understand, beloved, with your eyes wide open, that whatever you can receive and deliver and deal with and still hold your harmony we shall give to you! And we shall give it to you as quickly as possible, for we have the Keeper of the Scrolls, we have the angels of the Keeper of the Scrolls at our disposal, and we know the timetable of your life and the cycles turning. Therefore, we seek to expand the capacity of the heart!

Would you not have a greater heart capacity, beloved? ["Yes!"]

I come to you this evening to tell you, oh, it is so possible! Stretch the heart muscle! Expand the petals of the heart chakra! Breathe upon the fire of the threefold flame and breathe upon it again and know that your breathing exercises are for more than meets the eye.

Blessed ones, here is how you expand the heart. Everyone has established a certain limit of patience, of tolerance, of indulgence of others. Most people, including yourselves, find that level of limitation. And when someone does try you or test you or torment you beyond a certain level, you, then, are no longer in that state of patience [or tolerance or indulgence]. And at that moment, because of the artificial barriers of the heart that you have erected, [you declare your limit, which] you do not go beyond. [You are unwilling to] walk another mile and another mile, caring for life—caring for life, beloved, loving and still loving, and yet that love is such a power of the discipline of the soul and of the fire of your own spirit. [This is surely *not* the way to expand the heart!]

Love is surely the greatest quality of God and the most misunderstood. Love is a purging fire! Love is self-discipline and the discipline of the child and the four lower bodies that have grown out of line. [Accept Love without limits and you *will* expand your heart.]

Yes, beloved, let us test the heart! Let us expand the capacity of heart for the power of God to bring all into submission to the Great Heart of Light! Thus, [there is the need for] the two-edged sword, the mighty sword of discrimination, beloved, whereby there is mercy, whereby there is justice and whereby Love does impel those who have gone out of the way to come back to that center!

We have sent our Messenger on this mission to perform this very task for you, and yet sometimes you are so resistant and you will not take that correction. It is like the correcting of the ship at sea that is no longer on course. It is the correcting, beloved, of the mind that has gone out of the way, that is not where it ought to be. It is the correcting of that plane that has strayed into foreign territory.

Do you understand, beloved, that you do not necessarily contain the discrimination to know when you are off course [according to] the chart that has been charted for you by your Holy Christ Self?

And sometimes [when] you think you are in the very center of that Christ Self, [that Christ Self must speak sternly to you: "Be ye far from me!"] But, beloved, it is because of the brittleness of the mind and the intellect and the fat hardened in the heart itself, even in the very physical heart.

Blessed ones, I come indeed with the Holy Spirit. I come with that portion that you can receive and still maintain harmony and then a little more! For if I did not give to you a little more than your capacity, beloved, you would not grow. And therein lies the very key to the path of initiation. You must be initiated just beyond your present level of ability so that you will stretch! For if you want this mortal to put on immortality,[2] you must stretch beyond its confines, beyond its thought matrices that are merely the thoughts of limitation and death.

Therefore, beloved, understand the peculiar quality of the human mind. It sets its position. It establishes its parameters. It establishes its comfortability. And you will find this [in those of every age]—from the newborn child to those on the way to the octaves of Light. There is the resistance to be pushed beyond the level that the individual is willing to go.

Why, therefore, do you have whips for horses? Why do you have all means to *move* those in the animal kingdom to exceed their capacity? [It is because some] will not *move* unless they are whipped!

So, you see, along comes the Guru and says, "You cannot remain at this level!" And it causes literally a cataclysm in your entire being as the untransmuted forces of the not-self rear up and say, "We will not be moved! We are in control here. We are in control of this soul in this child, in this person."

So, you see, beloved, the mantle of the Guru must have the capacity and the power to bind the force within you that resists the forward march of progress into the kingdom of God. Initiation always compels you to break barriers, to hear the shattering of the old pot, the old glass.

Yes, beloved, be willing to be taken a quarter of an inch each day! Be willing to let the cracks in the ceiling appear and the rafters begin to rot. Be willing to see the old house crumble. And be willing to get out of the way, for one day the intensity of that Holy Spirit will be so great that the structure *must* crumble.

In that day, beloved, will you be able to maintain your life and your soul in these four lower bodies? Or will the rigidity have so set in in the mind, in the astral body and especially in the physical and the etheric bodies that you will pass from the screen of life because you have not established this resiliency in all of your members and all of your sheaths of consciousness so that you are pliable and you will not break?

How far can we take you in this embodiment, beloved? That is the question. How far are you willing to go before you will to break rather than to submit to your own Holy Christ Self, who is represented in the Messenger?

You must understand that we could give you a much more intense path. But then, beloved, we would run the risk of losing sometimes a very fine chela who says, "I cannot understand this intensity. I will depart."

So, you see, beloved, we must make our decisions as wise teachers. And our decision this night is to speak to you of these things so that you will not be offended in me when I speak to you through the Messenger, through the voice of your own Holy Christ Self or your I AM Presence, so that you will rather be *expecting* the fire or the rebuke or the soft word or the turning upside down of your world until you struggle and mourn and become upset perhaps for months or years because you do not understand the seeming injustice of a situation that has come upon you through the disciplines of our retreat.

Beloved ones, please remember, *please remember* you have had thousands of lifetimes! And some of the karma of some of these lifetimes is holding you back—holding you back in such a dangerous way and at such dangerous levels that we must allow that karma to descend in the form of initiation instead of allowing you to go out into the world as your karma dictates. It is better to receive the initiation if you can. And there is no "if" about it, for truly you can *if you will*.

It is time to test the will and, each day when you see things that must be done that you don't want to do or you cannot do, to test the will and see how much fire of your Mighty I AM Presence you can draw down by will—the will to heal your body, beloved, the will to strengthen your mind. Oh, how Morya and the Maha Chohan need the strong mind!

So, beloved, the hour has come and the cycles have turned again and we approach the summer solstice. Remember, as I remind you, that this is the hour of initiation. This is the time to pass your annual test, the time to graduate to a new schoolroom in our retreats, the time to move forward.

Beloved ones, welcome, then, *welcome, then,* the fire of Hierarchy through our Messenger and through the part of you that is God. And when in doubt as to whose voice is speaking or which way is the right way, pause, then, and do your novenas to the will of God, to the Great Divine Director or consult the Messenger if it is appropriate.

Beloved ones, [if you] do not [want to] be fooled [by the human consciousness], do not allow the untransmuted self to mock God as the world does with all of its theories and reasonings as to how this and that should be and should not be, when they are so far from the center of the Sacred Heart of Christ's own love.

Receive us. Receive us through our Messenger, beloved, and allow, as we have said before, the Messenger to be your personal Messenger. There are many here whose service and work and devotion and purity of heart warrants acceleration.

Won't you put together that which I give you tonight? Won't you put it together in your own mind? Won't you remember that this land is consecrated, this land is holy?

It is consecrated, beloved. And therefore, when you pray and when you do your yoga postures as the greatest form of spiritual/ physical exercise, do them together with rejoicing. Do them on your breaks or in extra moments on your lunch hours.

Be still and know that I AM God within you[3] and that that I AM THAT I AM is the Holy Spirit and that you can walk and talk with God as the ancient prophets did, as the saints have done, as the humble of heart, the nameless ones, have done.

Do not lose the joy of the Mystery School. Do not lose it. This is an hour to expand your hearts, for as you do and as you expand that joy of Jesus in your heart and your joy in Jesus' heart, you will create that sun of joy, that mighty twelve-petaled chakra of the heart, which is the mandala of this class—FREEDOM 1992: "Joy in the Heart"—and the thoughtform for it. And many more will be able to come here because you are keeping that Flame.

Keep the Flame, beloved! Even allow your autoreverse tape recorders to continue to play the calls that you have given in the court when you had the hours to do so. Let that vibration sing through our retreat! Let the sound go forth! Let the clearing of the way *be!* And then when you are called from time to time, come together with great intensity to clear away that which has come to the surface in the larger body of the Community, that which has come out of the entire Community and worldwide body of the Lightbearers—the discarnates, the portions of the dweller that can be taken.

Let this happen, beloved, and then go for the binding [of the discard] by the power of Astrea. I cannot emphasize to you [enough] how important the call to Astrea is for those who must find their way back to God.

We consider this conference to be the greatest opportunity that has been provided in this century for souls of Light to reconnect to their Source. This demands that *you* reconnect to *your* Source.

They will come because they will follow *your star,* your individual star of your Mighty I AM Presence and Causal Body. They will follow that star right to the Heart of the Inner Retreat! And they will follow the single star that is the one star of the Body of Lightbearers of the earth. They will follow it!

And you must be so steadfast in upholding your consciousness that you might be a magnet. For when you let it drop and you lose the Holy Spirit that we give you, especially on this occasion, then you become part of the misqualification of energy that stands between the people and their coming to this gate.

O beloved ones, for a moment contemplate the seraphim of God who have gathered this night to love you, to love you and to love you! All that we do and say is to love you. You must understand Love that is a piercing fire that will suddenly separate you from the most cherished elements of yourself or your life. You must understand this and get on top of it and go beyond it, beloved.

You must understand that Love does come in 144,000 different flames, if you will. There is no limitation to how Love can be conveyed, and that Love does meet every human need. It does meet it, beloved. This is not an unworldly love or an otherworldly love. This is love that is God's love, which reaches every level of life. [Embrace it and you *will* expand your heart!]

O the mighty sunbeams of the Great Central Sun! Bask in them now. Bask in them now, beloved. For the light of the Sun caresses you, and these light rays so gently take from you now that which you are ready to give to your Father-Mother God.

Therefore let go. Give to God all that limits you. Receive the limitless light of the Sun, the sun rays, and on these golden beams, beloved, receive now the Holy Spirit.

Each day, think of your Father-Mother Helios and Vesta as you greet the sun. And even for a moment, as you bask in the light, simply say:

> I AM receiving now the Holy Spirit of Helios and Vesta
>   into my mind, into my heart, into my being,
>   into the organs of my body, into my entire self.
> And I AM made Whole
>   by the Whole-I-Spirit of Helios and Vesta.

In this Love abide. In this Love remain steadfast, unmoved, beloved, by all that would take it from you. See how your immovability is the key to your increase of the Spirit of God.

Oh, reach up and simply touch and take now the hand of your Mighty I AM Presence! Hold that hand and clasp it.

Yes, beloved, you are so very, very near to your victory. Treasure, oh, treasure the moments which you endow with the flames of your victory. Treasure the cups of consciousness. Treasure them, beloved, for the moments in the time frame shall be the elements of your eternity.

I AM the Maha Chohan. I woo you to the sacred heart of every ascended one. Make it your goal, beloved, to be that sacred heart and see how the world will truly receive the teaching you so love and you have so internalized. This is a love feast, beloved, a love feast in the Holy Spirit.

Go, then, to your place of rest. Go, then, beloved, and know that thou art blessed.

Keep the Flame! Keep the Flame! Keep the Flame, for I have given it to you. Do not lose it this time.

The Process of the Purging

Messenger's Invocation:
O Lord, we have received thy Spirit. We give thee thanks, O Lord God Almighty, that thou hast taken unto thee thy great power and hast reigned in our hearts.

Come, O Lord Holy Christ Self, Lord Padma Sambhava, Lord Jesus Christ, Lord Maitreya, Lord Gautama Buddha, Lord Sanat Kumara. Buddha of the Ruby Ray, Dhyani Buddhas, come now! Reign in our hearts. Take dominion in our hearts.

O God, we are grateful. O God, we seal, then, thy Spirit in these hearts. Let us, then, go forth to thy retreat this night, O Lord the Maha Chohan, that we might be instructed as children and continue to learn what it is to walk the earth in the full empowerment of the Holy Spirit.

We are thy servants, O God. Prune and purge us and make us ready, for the world has waited too long for us to make our decision to be all of thee, O God. We will make them wait no longer!

We come in thy name, Sanat Kumara. O receive us, Lord. Forgive us, Lord. Forgive us that we have hurt any part of life at any time in all of our incarnations. We call upon the law of forgiveness that we have offended thee at any hour or day of our lives, or one of thy little ones. May the heart of mercy go forth from us and the heart of mercy be upon us that we might always uphold life and in no way deny it.

O God, make us better servants day by day. In this feast day of the descent of the Holy Ghost we are of one accord and in one place and our accord as agreement is this, O God, that we live henceforth to be thy vessel. Come, Holy Spirit, enlighten us!

In the name of the Father, the Son, the Holy Spirit and the Divine Mother, Amen.

Messenger's Comments:
I seal you to go to your place of rest. Whether you are driving or walking, I ask you to call to Archangel Michael to protect you and take you to the retreat of the Maha Chohan at the island of Ceylon, Sri Lanka. I ask for you to be taken, upon your return, to the Retreat of the Divine Mother over this ranch and to the Western Shamballa. May there not be a night that goes by that you are not in the retreats.

As we leave, we will hear the strains of the music from our album *Sanctissima,* that we might be received by Mother Mary and the Maha Chohan for our souls' tutoring at inner levels.

God bless you for your presence in the earth and your presentation of yourselves in this life as temples for the Holy Spirit. May the peace of God be upon you. May God be with you and go with you always, guiding your thoughts and the words of your mouths and your compassion and your tenderness and, above all, your willingness to release into the fire this night all resistance to the path of your Christhood.

In the name of the entire Spirit of the Great White Brotherhood and our beloved Lanello, I seal you this hour in the Mighty Presence of the Lord. Go in peace.

"The Summit Lighthouse Sheds Its Radiance O'er All the World to Manifest as Pearls of Wisdom." This dictation by the **Maha Chohan** was **delivered** by the Messenger of the Great White Brotherhood Elizabeth Clare Prophet on **Pentecost Sunday, June 7, 1992,** at the **Royal Teton Ranch, Park County, Montana.** In the service prior to the dictation, the Messenger read Mark 16:14–20 and Acts 2:1–41; 4:24. [**N.B.** Throughout this *Pearl,* bracketed material denotes words unspoken yet implicit in the dictation, added by the Messenger under the Maha Chohan's direction for clarity in the written word.]   (**1**) Rev. 3:11. (**2**) I Cor. 15:53, 54. (**3**) Ps. 46:10.

I AM the Witness

The Memory and Fulfillment of Community

Beloved Mother,

As I have a few days and hours to rest and meditate during my vacation, I want to reflect on the joy and gratitude in my heart to you, the Ascended Masters, our community and friends of Light throughout the world for all the blessings I've received.

Many years ago when I was in the ninth grade, after having been introduced to reembodiment and karma through the Edgar Cayce readings, I felt that there existed somewhere a community of believers that I would be a part of one day. It would uphold the highest standards of spirituality and discipline but not lack in the joy and love of daily service. It would consist of those with the highest ideals, who could outpicture them in a practical way—living in the world but not of it.

I dreamt that we would have the purest organic food, a wonderful educational system (a "universe-city" as I penned it in a poem) and craftsmen of every sort who would strive for perfection in their lives through the loving work of their hands. It would truly be a Christian community in the truest sense of the word—just as in the early days after Jesus' ministry.

My search for this community had begun and I read every book on spiritual subjects I could find, from *The Prophet* by Kahlil Gibran to *The Impersonal Life* to *The Essene Gospel of Peace* to *Life and Teachings of the Masters of the Far East*. I retreated from the outer life I could have enjoyed through my talents in sports, music, math and science, searching instead for the Truth I knew I would one day find.

Then one day, shortly after Easter in 1974 during my senior year in high school, a friend returned from a year's work in the Los Angeles area to tell me of a conference he had attended there. He said that he'd found a teaching and an organization that outpictured everything we had been searching for. He sold me one of the first hardbound issues of *Climb the Highest Mountain,* which I began reading while riding to and from school on a bus. The joys of rediscovering truths I had known within but had never read greeted me whenever I dipped into that book—even amidst the raucous behavior of my fellow busmates.

Within a fortnight of graduation, my thoughts returned to my friend and the teachings he had introduced to me. That night I spoke to him in my mind and tried to telepathically elicit a response, as I didn't know his address or phone number. To my amazement, the next morning he called me and asked if I wanted to attend a conference in Spokane that he was going to drive to. I jumped at the offer and rode a train 300 miles the next day to meet him. We drove straight to Spokane with a brief respite in the Wyoming wilds. I attended my first conference and knew that my search for Truth had ended and had also begun anew.

As I pore over the memories of seventeen years in the Teachings, Summit University, and fifteen years on staff, I am awed at the wonderment of it all. Although I sacrificed my college education to serve, the higher education I've received has far surpassed my dreams. The Utopia I had been searching for is being daily won through the hearts of love I serve with.

Though I have experienced many trials, failed tests and had temporary setbacks, one thing stands above all: the love and faith I have in my Guru—our beloved Messenger—and in the Teachings of the Ascended Masters, the highest truth I know that exists on earth today. Many have joined the bandwagon for a ride only to discover that the Path was strewn with hardships they dared not endure. Yet the unceasing blessings we receive pale the specters of human concerns into nothingnesses.

Sure, the life on staff is not easy; it requires diligence, fortitude and one-pointedness. But the rewards of service—the daily fellowship with kindred souls of Light, the inner growth that is won through striving, and the awe of hearing, reading and living the true teachings of Christ—are worth any seeming sacrifice one makes.

The Masters have sent forth the clarion call for more students of Light to serve with us. Those who have answered the call are here. Our dreams far outweigh our ability to realize them, though if you'd ask, all of us would serve longer and harder if we could.

We need recruits to fill our ranks. We need the courageous, the spirit-filled ones who can help in the Lord's work. The fields are surely white to the harvest and the laborers are few. I would ask those of you who read this and know you should be here to please leave the nets that bind you to the world and come and serve with us.

Lovingly,
A humble fellow student of Light

N.B. Testimonies of disciples of Jesus Christ and the Ascended Masters stating their witness to the power of Truth in their lives will regularly appear in this column in the *Pearls of Wisdom*. If you would like to witness to the power of Truth in your life brought about through the Ascended Masters and their Messengers, we welcome your testimony for publication. Your letter will be kept on file in our archives but your name will be withheld from this page to protect your privacy and your progress on the Path.

22

Karma, Reincarnation and Christianity 6

The keystone of Jesus' teaching on reincarnation in the New Testament is our Lord's statement that John the Baptist was Elijah come again.

To set the stage: It was a popular belief among the Jews of Jesus' day that Elijah would come again as the forerunner of the Messiah, as the LORD had prophesied through the prophet Malachi:

> Behold, I will send my messenger, and he shall prepare the way before me....
>
> Behold, I will send you Elijah the prophet before the coming of the great and dreadful day of the LORD.
>
> And he shall turn the heart of the fathers to the children, and the heart of the children to their fathers, lest I come and smite the earth with a curse.* Mal. 3

Even Isaiah had foreseen his day:

> The voice of him that crieth in the wilderness, "Prepare ye the way of the LORD, make straight in the desert a highway for our God.
>
> "Every valley shall be exalted, and every mountain and hill shall be made low; and the crooked shall be made straight, and the rough places plain.

---
*The word *curse* here means "judgment," "the descent of their karma."

"And the glory of the LORD shall be revealed, and all flesh shall see it together. For the mouth of the LORD hath spoken it."   Isaiah 40

Was John the Baptist the prophet Elijah come again? That was a matter of great interest to the Jews, as the Gospel of John makes clear.

John the Beloved records the interchange that took place when the Jews sent priests and Levites from Jerusalem to investigate the baptizer at Bethabara. When they asked him "Who art thou?" he confessed that he was neither the Christ nor the prophet Elijah. When they pressed him to tell them something, anything about himself, that they might give answer to their superiors, John said: "I am the voice of one crying in the wilderness, 'Make straight the way of the Lord,' as said the prophet Isaiah."[1]

Despite his denial that he was Elijah, I believe that John was giving them and us a clue. He didn't say, "I am one crying in the wilderness." He said, "I am *the voice* of one crying in the wilderness, 'Make straight the way of the LORD,'"[2] quoting Isaiah.

Truly, Isaiah had prophesied the coming of John the Baptist and identified him as "the voice of him that crieth in the wilderness." But it was left to Malachi to name "the voice" as Elijah the prophet. So if John wasn't the voice of Elijah, whose voice was he?

My hypothesis is that by innuendo—by saying that his voice was the voice of another—John was letting them know that his voice was indeed the voice of Elijah "come again" and that he and Elijah were one and the same soul and one and the same prophet. What was new was that Elijah had a new coat of skins[3] (i.e., a new body) and a new name.

There is another angle to this that is worth mentioning. People who believe in reincarnation and know who they were in a past life do not identify themselves today as who they were yesterday. For instance, if you were to ask me, "Are you Martha, the sister of Mary of Bethany?" I would say, "No, I'm Elizabeth Clare Prophet but I *was* Martha in a past life." Even so, John the Baptist was John the Baptist. He *had been*

Elijah in a past life and in this life he was "the voice" of Elijah. But he could accurately say that he was not Elijah in the flesh—his was the spirit of Elijah who had *re-incarnated*,* that is to say, who had come again in the flesh. This time around he *was* John the Baptist.

The Pharisees saw through John's denial and his veiled confirmation that he was the voice of Elijah. "If you are not that Christ nor Elijah," they insisted, "then why are you baptizing?" John sidestepped the inquiry by pointing to the greatness of Jesus Christ, who would baptize them with the Holy Ghost and with fire, whereas he himself was baptizing them with water only.[4]

Had John professed himself to be either "that Christ" or the prophet Elijah, they might have stoned, imprisoned or killed him as they had done to the prophets before him and as they eventually did do to him. He did not answer them directly but indirectly. The truth is that it was not lawful for him, an initiate of the Great White Brotherhood, a so-called "Son of the Solitude,"[5] to reveal who he had been in a past life or what was his attainment today.

Furthermore, it was not lawful for his identity to be made known by anyone until he had "first come," before Jesus, to prepare the way of the Lord and to "restore all things," namely the law and the prophets. Once that assignment had been accomplished, Elijah's coming in the person of John the Baptist could be revealed.

Not once, but twice, did Jesus reveal that John was indeed Elijah come again. The more important of the two revelations came after John's death, on the occasion of Jesus' transfiguration. The other took place while John was yet in prison (after he had fulfilled his mission) when Jesus actually delivered a public tribute to John before the multitudes.

I will take up the more important first. The scene is our Lord's transfiguration on a high mountain, where he had taken Peter, James and John to witness his initiation. This is the heart of the passage as recorded by Mark:

> Jesus taketh with him Peter and James and John and leadeth them up into an high mountain apart by

---
*incarnate [from Latin *incarnatus*, past participle of *incarnare*, to be made flesh]: to give bodily form or substance to; embody. *reincarnate:* to incarnate again.

themselves. And he was transfigured before them.

And his raiment became shining, exceeding white as snow, so as no fuller on earth can white them.

And there appeared unto them Elijah with Moses and they were talking with Jesus. . . .

And there was a cloud that overshadowed them and a voice came out of the cloud, saying, "This is my beloved Son: hear him."

And suddenly, when they had looked round about, they saw no man anymore, save Jesus only with themselves. . . .

And they asked him, saying, "Why say the scribes that Elijah must first come?"

In other words, "If Elijah is appearing to you out of heaven in his celestial body, then why didn't he first go before you on earth as the prophet who should prepare the way for your coming? What's he doing in heaven when we haven't yet seen him on earth?"

And he answered and told them, "Elijah verily cometh first and restoreth all things; and . . . it is written of the Son of man that he must suffer many things and be set at nought.

"But I say unto you that Elijah is indeed come and they have done unto him whatsoever they listed, as it is written of him." Mark 9

Matthew records:

Then the disciples understood that he spake unto them of John the Baptist. Matthew 17

So when Jesus said, "Elijah is indeed come," he was saying that Elijah had already reincarnated in the mantle and the calling of the messenger of the LORD who should go before the face of the Son of God to prepare the way before him.[6] And Herod had done with him what he would. Tragically, he had imprisoned and beheaded John the Baptist for his outspokenness against Herod's unlawful marriage to his brother's wife.[7]

Thus we see that there are practical and spiritual imperatives against an initiate of the Great White Brotherhood revealing his true identity until the appointed time. Even Jesus, when he came down the Mount of Transfiguration, charged Peter, James and John that they should tell no man what things they had seen until the Son of man should be risen from the dead.[8] This was because it was not lawful for the initiation his disciples had just witnessed to be made known to anyone save those whom he had chosen to see it.[9]

The transfiguration served to ratify Jesus' ministry in the tradition of Moses and the prophets. Were it to have been noised abroad, the timetable of his crucifixion might have been advanced by his enemies; but his time, as in the case of John the Baptist, had not yet come.

All avatars, prophets, Christed ones and messengers of God choose the hour when they shall reveal who they are and what their mission is. They never allow that hour to be dictated by their interrogators or their accusers, even to the point of incurring public humiliation and disgrace. And until that hour they are obliged to fend such questions as they can, remain silent or even deny their true identity when directly confronted.

This is not a prevarication; it is the postponement of the telling of the truth to those who must be told, for they have neither eyes to see nor ears to hear[10] who stands before them speaking to them out of the mouth of God. The truth written in the aura of the avatars, which cannot be denied, goes before them heralding their true identity for all who have developed their inner sight and soul faculties to "see." Nevertheless, their verbal silence concerning who they are, where they have come from, and what their mission is, is their keeping of the sacred trust of their sponsorship under the hierarchy of Sanat Kumara.

It is perfectly clear what the powers-that-be did to John the Baptist when their moment came (see Matt. 14:1–12; Mark 6:14–29; Luke 3:19, 20) and it is perfectly clear what they did to Jesus when they finally caught up with him and one of his disciples could be bribed to identify him in the garden.[11]

The reason I digress on this point is that some have argued that because John denied he was Elijah at the beginning of his mission, Jesus would not have affirmed that John was Elijah at the end of his mission. They are mistaken only because they are mistaught. The time had come for the truth to be proclaimed far and wide that Elijah had come again in the person of John the Baptist. And no less than Jesus himself did the honors.

I have reviewed the revelation Jesus gave to the disciples as they came down the Mount of Transfiguration. Now I will take up Jesus' speech to the multitudes concerning John the Baptist that he delivered when John was yet in prison by order of Herod. We hear Jesus unveil the prophet as his promised messenger—and as the greatest of all on earth who had been born of woman. He also confirms the Old Testament prophecy concerning the coming of his messenger.

Jesus gives a stunning tribute to the prophet and messenger who had gone before him and who had once said of the Son of God, whom he baptized: "He must increase but I must decrease."[12] It is touchingly clear that Jesus thought more of John the Baptist than of any other personage of his time. Their relationship was old, very old, and their love for one another was beyond this world. Matthew records Jesus' words:

> What went ye out into the wilderness to see? A reed shaken with the wind?
>
> But what went ye out for to see? A man clothed in soft raiment? Behold, they that wear soft clothing are in kings' houses.
>
> But what went ye out for to see? A prophet? Yea, I say unto you, and more than a prophet.
>
> For this is he, of whom it is written, Behold, I send my messenger before thy face, which shall prepare thy way before thee.
>
> Verily I say unto you, among them that are born of women there hath not risen a greater than John the Baptist: notwithstanding he that is least in the kingdom of heaven is greater than he.

And from the days of John the Baptist until now the kingdom of heaven suffereth violence, and the violent take it by force. For all the prophets and the law prophesied until John.*

And if ye will receive it, this is Elijah, which was for to come. He that hath ears to hear, let him hear.

Matthew 11

The fact that Jesus affirmed publicly to the multitudes and then privately to three of his disciples that the true identity of John the Baptist was Elijah the prophet—and the fact that Matthew and Mark both record Jesus as saying, "This is Elijah come again"—should put to shame those who profess to be Christians yet deny Christ's own words concerning the reincarnation of Elijah as John the Baptist.

Note that when speaking to the multitudes Jesus qualified his announcement "This is Elijah, which was for to come," with the words "if ye will receive it" and "He that hath ears to hear, let him hear." Jesus knew that some of the multitudes would believe that Elijah had indeed come again and some would not.

He also knew that some of the Jewish authorities would receive this truth and some would vehemently deny it—not because they did not believe that Elijah would reincarnate, but because they did believe it and they feared the LORD's judgment which the greatest of all prophets would deliver upon them.

Witness Herod's superstition, reported by Mark, that Jesus himself was "John whom I beheaded...risen from the dead"![13] Note that it was his father, Herod the Great, who had had all the male babies killed "in Bethlehem and in all the coasts thereof" when it was known that the Christ was about to be born.[14] Truly, the fallen angels among us have feared the coming of the Christed ones since Archangel Michael and his legions cast them out of heaven into the earth[15] and into earthly bodies, which they wear to this day.

And their worst fears *did* come upon them when they heard the pungent pronouncements upon their heads such as

---
*Because it was towards John that all the prophecies of the prophets and of the law were leading. (Jerusalem Bible)

the following from John and a relentless string of others from Jesus:[16]

> O generation of vipers, who hath warned you to flee from the wrath to come?
> Bring forth therefore fruits meet for repentance.
> And think not to say within yourselves, "We have Abraham to our father," for I say unto you that God is able of these stones to raise up children unto Abraham.
> And now also the axe is laid unto the root of the trees: therefore every tree which bringeth not forth good fruit is hewn down and cast into the fire.
>
> Matthew 3

The suggestion that the transfiguration accounts in Matthew and Mark may infer a belief in reincarnation is not something new to this century. The fourth-century Church Father Jerome, for example, specifically argues in his commentary on Matthew that the transfiguration passage should *not* be interpreted as supporting reincarnation.[17] That Jerome makes such an argument tells us that some Christians of his day believed that Jesus and the disciples accepted, or were at least aware of, the concept of reincarnation.

Now I will give you the Christian refutation of "Elijah come again." In his book *Reincarnation and Christianity*, Dr. Robert Morey gives a standard orthodox Christian argument for denying that the "Elijah come again" passage speaks of reincarnation. He says, "Elijah, like Enoch, never died but was translated to heaven without ever tasting death." But then he says that "Elijah showed himself still alive and in his original body on the Mount of Transfiguration."[18] Apparently Morey and others do not understand the meaning of the word *translation.** Therefore they believe that Enoch, as well as Elijah, went into heaven in his physical body.

The actual translation of a soul to heaven in the ritual of the ascension involves the soul's union with the white-fire body of the I AM Presence. In the process of a physical

---

*translation, definition 1b in *Webster's Ninth New Collegiate Dictionary:* a change to a different substance, form, or appearance: conversion. *Translate* is defined as: (1a) to bear, remove, or change from one place, state, form, or appearance to another: transfer, transform; (1b) to convey to heaven or to a nontemporal condition without death.

ascension, the physical body is transformed by and superseded by the Ascended-Master Light Body (also called the Deathless Solar Body), in which the soul is permanently clothed during the ascension ritual.

Genesis records, "And Enoch walked with God and he was not, for God took him."[19] In truth, Enoch was translated—and by this I mean he went through the process of the physical ascension, which I have just described.

According to the dictionary definition and the Teachings of the Ascended Masters, the term *translation* describes the transformation of the physical body and the soul that takes place during the physical ascension and during cremation when the soul ascends but there is not a physical ascension.

II Kings records that Elijah "went up by a whirlwind into heaven." This whirlwind was the vortex of the ascension flame. Elijah had told his disciple Elisha, "If you see me when I am taken from you, you will receive a double portion of my Spirit"[20]—that is, you will receive the mantle of my Mighty I AM Presence and the empowerment of my calling and my mission.

What Elisha saw was the translation of Elijah. Before his very eyes the physical body of Elijah was transformed and Elijah was swept up in his Ascended-Master Light Body. Elisha saw the whirlwind and the chariot of Israel and the horsemen thereof. And then the scriptures say, "He saw him no more."

The ascension ritual was completed and Elijah was out of sight of mortal eyes. Nevertheless, his mantle and a double portion of his spirit fell upon Elisha. And Elisha rent his clothes, took up the mantle of his Guru and smote the waters of Jordan, saying: "Where is the LORD God of Elijah?" And the waters parted and Elisha went over.[21]

The reincarnation of Elijah as John the Baptist was the rare exception to the rule that Ascended Masters do not reincarnate. Today most people whose souls do qualify for the ritual of the ascension ascend from inner levels after the soul has departed the physical body. The soul attains union with the Mighty I AM Presence to become a permanent atom in the Body of God just as she does in a physical ascension.

When there is not a physical ascension, it is customary for the disciples of an initiate or the family and friends of a Keeper of the Flame* to consecrate and cremate the remains. Their motto is not "For dust thou art, and unto dust thou shalt return"[22] but "Out of the sacred fire thou hast descended and into the sacred fire thou shalt ascend." As Paul makes clear, earthly bodies are not suitable for the heaven-world. The soul does not retain a physical earth body once she has ascended to heaven.

Although the synoptic Gospels[23] only say that Moses and Elijah "appeared" to the disciples, Morey claims that "Elijah showed himself still alive and in his original body on the Mount of Transfiguration." (He doesn't mention what body Moses came in.) Has he overlooked Paul's chastisement to those who say: "How are the dead raised up? And with what body do they come?" Paul's answer to them is compelling. It is a lesson for us all:

> Thou fool, that which thou sowest is not quickened, except it die!...
>
> There are...celestial bodies and bodies terrestrial. But the glory of the celestial is one, and the glory of the terrestrial is another.
>
> There is one glory of the sun, and another glory of the moon, and another glory of the stars; for one star differeth from another star in glory.
>
> So also is the resurrection of the dead. It is sown in corruption; it is raised in incorruption.
>
> It is sown in dishonour; it is raised in glory. It is sown in weakness; it is raised in power.
>
> It is sown a natural body; it is raised a spiritual body. There is a natural body, and there is a spiritual body.
>
> And so it is written, The first man Adam was made a living soul; the last Adam was made a quickening spirit.
>
> Howbeit that was not first which is spiritual, but

Keeper of the Flame: a member of the Keepers of the Flame Fraternity, founded in 1961 by Saint Germain. The Keepers of the Flame Fraternity is an organization of Ascended Masters and their chelas, dedicated to keeping the flame of Life on earth and to the freedom and enlightenment of her people.

that which is natural; and afterward that which is spiritual.

The first man is of the earth, earthy: the second man is the Lord from heaven.

As is the earthy, such are they also that are earthy. And as is the heavenly, such are they also that are heavenly.

And as we have borne the image of the earthy, we shall also bear the image of the heavenly.

Now this I say, brethren, that *flesh and blood cannot inherit the kingdom of God; neither doth corruption inherit incorruption.*

Behold, I show you a mystery. We shall not all sleep, but we shall all be changed, in a moment, in the twinkling of an eye, at the last trump. For the trumpet shall sound, and the dead shall be raised incorruptible, and we shall be changed.

For this corruptible must put on incorruption, and this mortal must put on immortality.

So when this corruptible shall have put on incorruption, and this mortal shall have put on immortality, then shall be brought to pass the saying that is written, Death is swallowed up in victory.

O death, where is thy sting? O grave, where is thy victory?   I Corinthians 15

The akashic records[24] verify that Elijah was not in a corruptible, mortal body when he appeared to Jesus and the disciples on the Mount of Transfiguration some nine hundred years after he had challenged the 450 prophets of Baal at Mount Carmel.[25] They also verify that Moses did not present himself in a corruptible, mortal body for the occasion. There was no necessity for Elijah or Moses to appear to Jesus in a physical body because they could talk to Jesus perfectly well in their celestial bodies.

In addition to Paul's teaching on mutable and immutable bodies, another text that refutes Morey is Mark 9 (already quoted). Mark says that Peter, James and John all saw Elijah with Moses talking with Jesus. But "suddenly"—

after the voice of God out of the cloud announced, "This is my beloved Son: hear ye him"—the three "looked round about" and "saw no man anymore, save Jesus only." Had Elijah (or Moses) been in his corruptible body, he would not have suddenly disappeared. Have any of you here tonight ever seen a physical person "suddenly" disappear?

The conclusion of the matter is that the Ascended Master John the Baptist appeared to Jesus as Elijah the prophet in his Ascended-Master Light Body,* and the Ascended Master Moses also appeared to Jesus in his Ascended-Master Light Body.

Jesus was transfigured, his raiment was shining with a heavenly light, "exceeding white as snow, so as no fuller's earth can white them." Having been accelerated to that level of the white light (the definition of the transfiguration), he could talk to Moses and Elijah face-to-face and they could talk with him.

Jesus temporarily raised his three closest disciples to that exalted height so that they might bear witness of his transfiguration after his resurrection. He made certain that they saw not only his transfiguration but also the figures of Elijah and Moses "in glory," as Luke has it.[26] Matthew, Mark and Luke concur that neither of these two prophets were in the vibration or the plane of the earthly body.

According to Morey, when Jesus said that Elijah had "come already" as John the Baptist, "Jesus was simply saying that the *ministry* of John the Baptist was 'in the spirit and power' of Elijah's ministry."[27] ("In the spirit and power" of Elijah comes from Luke's account of the Archangel Gabriel appearing to Zacharias and prophesying that his son, John, would go before the Messiah "in the spirit and power" of Elijah.[28])

Some Christians say that Jesus was speaking figuratively and did not literally mean that Elijah was reincarnated as John the Baptist. Professor George Buttrick interprets Jesus' words as meaning that John had come "in striking likeness of the flesh and in [the] verity of the spirit [of Elijah]." He writes: "John, dressed like Elijah, lived in the desert as Elijah

---

*The student of the Ascended Masters should know, however, that an Ascended Master may appear to unascended disciples in the guise of any of his past incarnations, just as Saint Germain appears to Catholics as Saint Joseph.

had lived, and defied Herod and Herodias as Elijah had defied Ahab and Jezebel."[29]

So, as far as Buttrick is concerned, what looks like a duck, waddles like a duck and quacks like a duck is still not a duck!

For me Buttrick's argument, based on the parallels of John and Elijah, only buttresses the fact that not only the spirit and power of Elijah but also his very soul was fully embodied in John the Baptist. Yes, indeed, Elijah had already come; but the carnally minded were either too dense to recognize him or too superstitious to allow themselves to believe it was he.

It is as though they were convinced in their narrow-mindedness that even if he wanted to, God couldn't put Elijah's soul or your soul or my soul in a new body for a new mission. And because they were so convinced in their own conceit, they set up rules defining what God is allowed to do and what he isn't allowed to do.

Well, you know what? God can do anything he wants to anytime he wants to. He can put our souls in new bodies and he already has. He can create a meeting ground between Ascended Masters and unascended masters with their disciples, just as he did on the Mount of Transfiguration. And he can bring that mountain to us, just as he does every time we receive a dictation from one of the Ascended Masters at the altar of the Holy Grail!

God is practical. He's not a stuntman or a magician. What he does, he does within the framework of the expediency and the practicality of his law. And it was neither expedient nor practical to have Elijah in heaven in his physical body, nor was it expedient or practical for God to create a new soul to fulfill the mission of John the Baptist when the soul of Elijah was already fully trained and empowered for the mission.

First of all, it is much easier to create a new body than a new soul! Secondly, the soul increases in wisdom and love and adeptship with the cumulative experience of many soul journeys through many lifetimes. And the absolute necessity for that cumulative experience is the reason why God set up the system of reincarnation in the first place! It was ingenious, expedient and powerfully practical. A single lifetime, whether lived to age 9 or 90 or 900, is just not enough time for the soul to mature to the levels required for her to achieve the crowning victory of individual Christhood.

What was true for the soul of Elijah is true for you and me. We have "come again" to "restore all things"—that is, to make peace with every part of life, to embody God's law and the teachings of his ageless prophets, to balance our karma, fulfill our mission and ascend.

Such a God who loves us so much as to give us opportunity after opportunity to come to his knowledge and his glory is my kind of God. I can identify with a Father-Mother God who is infinitely merciful. I cannot identify with a one-chance God who would throw us into the fires of eternal damnation if we fail to make it in one lifetime.

My kind of God is smarter than that. And he is scientific. He has put the essence of himself in our hearts, his own divine spark (the threefold flame). It is the seed of a Christ or a Buddha to be. And he knows that this seed is the lodestone of himself that will ultimately woo the soul back to him.

Our Father-Mother God is confident that sooner or later we little lambs who have lost our way will come Home wagging our tails behind us. So there is no need for God to cast us into hell, because he is inside of us and he fully intends to pilot us Home—*when we are ready.*

Hell is a place reserved for the devil and his angels, who continue to make war against the Woman and her Manchild and the seed of Christ in the earth.[30] These self-styled gods who mock God while they mimic him have no eternal life because they deny that life, who is God, in their minds and in their bodies. By willfully extinguishing his flame in their hearts, they have chosen to commit spiritual suicide.

Rest assured that our Father-Mother have given to us who have chosen to magnify the LORD in all our members the gift of the abundant life, lifetime after lifetime, that we might return in mercy and in grace to our point of origin in God.

It was evident two thousand years ago and it is evident

today that some theologians go to great lengths to deny the doctrine of reincarnation that is plainly written in scripture:

> Elijah verily cometh first and restoreth all things; and...it is written of the Son of man that he must suffer many things and be set at nought.
> But I say unto you that Elijah is indeed come and they have done unto him whatsoever they listed, as it is written of him. Mark 9

These are Jesus' own words, yet some among the clergy will not receive them. In denying Jesus' words, they deny the Lord himself, who is the ultimate Word incarnate. Peter spoke of this when he referred to Paul's epistles, saying:

> Some things [are] hard to be understood, which they that are unlearned and unstable wrest,* as they do also the other scriptures, unto their own destruction.
> Ye therefore, beloved, seeing ye know these things before, beware lest ye also, being led away with the error of the wicked, fall from your own steadfastness.
> But grow in grace, and in the knowledge of our Lord and Saviour Jesus Christ. To him be glory both now and forever. Amen. II Peter 3

The unfortunate fact is that some theologians are simply not willing to come to grips with the doctrines of karma and reincarnation. Why do you think this is so? Are they fleeing from the wrath of their own karma that is not yet come? And is it not yet come because, as Jesus said, "If ye were [physically] blind, ye should have no sin [i.e., karma, because your blindness would be the means provided by the Great Law for the expiation of your karma], but now ye say, 'We see'; therefore your sin remaineth [i.e., your karma has not yet descended]"?[31]

The Pharisees then and now have physical sight but no spiritual understanding, and their unredeemed karma is the cause of their spiritual blindness.

I believe that today's Pharisees do not accept the twin

---
*wrest: to pull, force, or move by violent wringing or twisting movements; to gain with difficulty by or as if by force, violence or determined labor *(Webster's Ninth New Collegiate Dictionary).*

doctrines of karma and reincarnation because if they did they would have to accept accountability for their own actions in this life and all past lives. A large percentage of the people on earth today do not want to take responsibility for their karma. They've lived by the doctrine that says Jesus carries it all: "Jesus died for my sins. He is going to bear my sins and give me absolution and all I have to do is accept him as my Lord and Saviour and he will do the rest. And I am guaranteed entrée into the kingdom by my profession of faith."

This is a simplistic notion. Yet it's what the doctrine of the vicarious atonement, accepted by clergymen and churchgoers alike, is all about. And I tell you from my heart and from the Sacred Heart of Jesus, who has given to me this teaching by the Holy Spirit, that the doctrine that Jesus pays the whole price for our karma and we pay nothing is not the true doctrine of Jesus Christ. It is false doctrine and it is in violation of the laws of God set forth in the Bible from Genesis to Revelation.

Now, if it is not the doctrine of Jesus Christ, then, pray tell me, whose doctrine is it? Well, if you don't know, I'll tell you. It is the doctrine of the Adversary—Jesus' Adversary and yours and mine. And this doctrine that Jesus paid it all will deny you your own victory over death and hell if you continue to believe it.

Believing that you can commit any crime, break the laws of God and man, and not pay the price because Jesus already paid it for you is simply not what Jesus taught. Moreover, it is absolutely inconsistent with the law of karma set forth in the Old and New Testaments. And I will leave you to ponder why in the final analysis the doctrine of the vicarious atonement is neither expedient nor practical.

Think about that. And ask yourself:

Who is responsible for my soul? Is it the false pastors and false teachers who tell me I am saved because I respond to the altar call and confess that Jesus is my Lord? Or is it I?

Who will give accounting for my soul when I stand before my Lord at the end of this life? I myself, who with

God am the sole proprietor of my soul, or those pastors and teachers who will be long gone when I stand before the judgment seat?

Jesus is doing everything he can to help you. He will even help you carry your karma until you can not only carry it yourself but also transmute it by service to life and your daily decrees to the violet flame. (Just fifteen minutes a day with my tapes will bring you closer to God than you've ever been before.) But he sent his apostle Paul to tell you that it is your responsibility to "work out your own salvation with fear and trembling,"[32] for in the end "every man shall bear his own [karmic] burden."[33]

Now, if you will, ask yourself this question before you put down this *Pearl of Wisdom:* "Who will give accounting for my soul when I stand before my Lord?" And when you answer it, act on it.

to be continued

"The Summit Lighthouse Sheds Its Radiance O'er All the World to Manifest as Pearls of Wisdom." "Karma, Reincarnation and Christianity" is based on a lecture given by Elizabeth Clare Prophet on Friday, October 11, 1991, during the four-day *Class of the Golden Cycle* held at the New Orleans Airport Hilton. (**1**) John 1:19–23. (**2**) Elijah is regarded as a **"wilderness prophet,"** as he spent time in solitude in the wilderness and mountains. (**3**) Gen. 3:21. (**4**) **"I baptize you with water . . ."** John 1:24–27; Matt. 3:11; Mark 1:7, 8; Luke 3:16. (**5**) **The Sons of the Solitude** are an ancient Brotherhood of advanced adepts. In the book *A Dweller on Two Planets* by Phylos the Tibetan, we learn that they were the highest initiates on Atlantis. They were celibate, lived without families and often apart from civilization. The Sons of the Solitude attained their mastery through years of training in many lifetimes. Examples in scripture of the Sons of the Solitude include Abraham, Melchizedek, Jesus Christ and John the Baptist. (**6**) **"He shall prepare the way before me . . ."** Mal. 3:1; Matt. 11:10; Mark 1:2, 3; Luke 1:76–79; 7:27; John 3:28. (**7**) **John beheaded by Herod.** Matt. 14:1–12; Mark 6:14–29; Luke 3:19, 20. (**8**) Matt. 17:9; Mark 9:9. (**9**) **Jesus protects his identity.** There are also scenes in the New Testament where Jesus either refuses to say who he is or tells others not to reveal who he is. **Jesus to his disciples:** Once Jesus asked his disciples "Whom say the people that I am?" and they answered: "John the Baptist; but some say, Elijah; and others say that one of the old prophets is risen again." Then he asked them: "But whom say ye that I am?" And Peter answered, "The Christ of God." As Luke records, Jesus "straitly charged them and commanded them to tell no man that thing, saying, 'The Son of man must suffer many things and be rejected of the elders and chief priests and scribes and be slain and be raised the third day' " (Luke 9:18–22; see also Matt. 16:13–16, 20; Mark 8:27–30). **Jesus to the devils:** On one occasion, Jesus even commanded the devils not to say who he was. We read in Luke 4: "Now when the sun was setting, all they that had any sick with divers diseases brought them unto him; and he laid his hands on every one of them and healed them. And devils also came out of many, crying out and saying, 'Thou art Christ the Son of God!' And he rebuking them suffered them not to speak, for they knew that he was Christ" (Luke 4:40, 41). **Jesus to the chief priests, scribes and elders:** At another time, when Jesus was walking in the temple in Jerusalem, he refused to directly answer the chief priests, scribes and elders who asked him: "By what authority doest thou these things? And who gave thee this authority to do these things?" Jesus said: "I will also ask of you one question, and answer me, and I will tell you by what authority I do these things. The baptism of John, was it from heaven, or of men? Answer me." Mark records: "And they reasoned with themselves, saying, If we shall say, 'From heaven,' he will say, 'Why then did ye not believe him?' But if we shall say, 'Of men,' they feared the people. For all men counted John, that he was a prophet indeed. And they answered and said unto Jesus, 'We cannot tell.' And Jesus answering saith unto them, 'Neither do I tell you by what authority I do these things' " (Mark 11:27–33; see also Matt. 21:23–27; Luke 20:1–8). **Jesus before the Sanhedrin:** When Jesus was arrested and taken before the Sanhedrin for questioning, he would not directly affirm that he was the Christ. Luke gives the following account: "And as soon as it was day, the elders of the people and the chief priests and the scribes came together and led him into their council, saying, 'Art thou the Christ? Tell us.' And he said unto them, 'If I tell you, ye will not believe. And if I also ask you, ye will not answer me, nor let me go. Hereafter shall the Son of man sit on the right hand of the power of God.' Then said they all, 'Art thou then the Son of God?' And he said unto them, 'Ye say that I am.' And they said, 'What need we any further witness? For we ourselves have heard of his own mouth'" (Luke 22:66–71; see also Matt. 26:62–68). (10) **No eyes to see, no ears to hear.** Deut. 29:4; Isa. 6:9, 10; Ezek. 12:2; Matt. 11:15; 13:9–17, 43; Mark 4:9–12, 23; 7:16; 8:17, 18; Luke 8:8–10; 14:35; John 12:37–40; Acts 28:25–27; Rom. 11:8. (11) **Betrayal and crucifixion of Jesus.** Matt. 26:14–16, 36–68; 27:1, 2, 11–50; Mark 14:10, 11, 32–65; 15:1–37; Luke 22:1–6, 39–54, 63–71; 23:1–46; John 18:1–15, 19–40; 19:1–37. (12) John 3:30. (13) Mark 6:14–16. (14) Matt. 2:1–18. (15) Rev. 12:7–12. (16) See **"Confrontations: The Watchers vs. John the Baptist and Jesus Christ,"** in Elizabeth Clare Prophet, *Forbidden Mysteries of Enoch,* pp. 491–93; and Archangel Gabriel, *Mysteries of the Holy Grail,* pp. 197–210. **Jesus' pronouncements upon the seed of the wicked.** See Matt. 12:22–42; 23:13–36; Luke 11:16, 29–54; 16:14–17; John 5:39–47; 8:12–59; 10:22–39. (17) Jerome, cited by Quincy Howe, Jr., *Reincarnation for the Christian* (1974; reprint, Wheaton, Ill.: Theosophical Publishing House, 1987), p. 95. (18) Robert A. Morey, *Reincarnation and Christianity* (Minneapolis: Bethany House Publishers, 1980), p. 34. (19) Gen. 5:24. (20) II Kings 2:1–11. (21) II Kings 2:12–14. (22) Gen. 3:19. (23) **Synoptic Gospels.** The first three Gospels of the New Testament: Matthew, Mark and Luke. These are distinguished from the fourth, the Gospel of John, by their similarity in content, order and language. (24) **Akashic records.** All that transpires in an individual's world and all events in the physical universe are recorded in an etheric substance and dimension known as *akasha* (Sanskrit, from the root *kas* 'to be visible, appear', 'to shine brightly', 'to see clearly'). *Akasha* is defined as primary substance, the subtlest, ethereal essence, which fills the whole of space; etheric energy vibrating at a certain frequency so as to absorb, or record, all of the impressions of life. The akashic records can be read by adepts or those whose soul (psychic) faculties are developed. The Messenger has explained that an Ascended Master or an unascended adept can look at a record just the way an archaeologist would look through layers of the earth. He can look through layers of records and pinpoint any age or time since the earth was created and read the record of what happened at that particular point in time and space. The Messenger Mark L. Prophet said: "Man makes a record every time he thinks or speaks or feels. Just like a clock ticking twenty-four hours a day, the computers of heaven are ticking off and recording the events of our lives and bringing back to our own personal doorstep exactly what we send out." (25) I Kings 18:17–40. (26) Luke 9:30, 31. (27) Morey, *Reincarnation and Christianity,* p. 34. (28) Luke 1:17. (29) George A. Buttrick, exposition on Matthew, in *The Interpreter's Bible* (Nashville: Abingdon Press, 1951–57), 7:462. (30) Rev. 12. (31) John 9:41. (32) Phil. 2:12. (33) Gal. 6:5.

KARMA & REINCARNATION
Audio- and Videotapes by Elizabeth Clare Prophet

KARMA, REINCARNATION AND CHRISTIANITY
Did Jesus teach karma and reincarnation? Were they a part of early Christianity? In this unifying and healing message, Elizabeth Clare Prophet shows that both the Old and New Testaments contain teaching on karma and reincarnation. She examines the writings of the Christian gnostics on reincarnation and explains why reincarnation was excluded from Church doctrine for political reasons. She also reviews the amazing findings of doctors and therapists whose patients have remembered past lives.   **2 videotapes, 4 hr. 10 min. #GP92001 $29.95**
3-audiotape album, 4 hr. 10 min. #A92006 $21.95

THE REINCARNATION OF THE SOUL: Regressing and Remembering
Elizabeth Clare Prophet examines *Life Before Life* by Helen Wambach, Ph.D.—an extraordinary account of how, under hypnosis, 750 people remembered the time before birth and the birth experience itself. Learn the Ascended Masters' perspective on reincarnation and the results of this study. Includes questions and answers.   **2-audiotape album, 3 hr. #A8218 $14.95**

ON DEALING WITH DEATH, DISCARNATES AND MALEVOLENT SPIRITS
PART I, with commentary on the movie *Ghost*
What are the soul's options when it leaves the body? Topics include soul travel to the etheric and astral planes, how discarnate and mass entities influence people to become addicted, and the reasons for cremation. Dictation by Lady Master Leto.
2 videotapes, 2 hr. 40 min. #GP90117 $22.50   2-audiotape album, 3 hr. #A90040 $14.95
Lecture only: I videotape, I hr. 45 min. #HP90117 $14.95

PART II, with commentary on the movie *Flatliners*
This lecture will keep you on the edge of your seat as Elizabeth Clare Prophet discusses near-death experiences, what happens to the soul after death, and why it is important to balance karma in this lifetime. Dictations by Lady Master Nada and Astrea.   **2 videotapes, 2 hr. 45 min. #GP91053 $18.95**
2-audiotape album, 2 hr. 40 min. #A91049 $14.95

THE PHOENIX MYSTERY: KARMA AND REINCARNATION
The phoenix mystery is you, every day, meeting the challenge of your returning karma. It is you going through the process of growth, of refinement, of self-transcendence. Elizabeth Clare Prophet explains how your soul can successfully pass through the "trial by fire" and, like the phoenix, rise from the ashes of your karma. Includes a guided meditation and dictation by the Maha Chohan.
2 videotapes, 3 hr. 30 min. #GP91032 $29.90   Lecture only: 2 audiotapes, 2 hr. 35 min.
#A91042 $14.95   Dictation only: I audiotape, 70 min. #A91044 $7.50

THE PSYCHOLOGY OF ZAILM: A Study of Reincarnation and Karma
A fascinating study on how we must all come to grips with the forces of our psychology and karma. Using the life of Zailm of Atlantis from the book *A Dweller on Two Planets*, Mrs. Prophet gives invaluable keys for transcending your own subconscious patterns inherited from your family. Explores the dynamics of the mother-child relationship, the Oedipus complex, the anima and animus, and types of dysfunctional families.   **4 videotapes, 5 hr. #GP91022 $37.50**
4 audiotapes, 5 hr. 20 min. #A91014 $29.95

Prices, availability and postage are subject to change. To order call Summit University Press, Dept. 470, (800) 245-5445 in the U.S.A. or (406) 222-8300 outside the U.S.A.

Royal Teton Ranch

Box 5000, Corwin Springs, Montana 59030-5000 406/848-7441

June 1, 1992

Dearest Companion of the Great Inner Light,

When the psalmist said, "Be still and know that I am God," he was drawing us close as companions of the Great Inner Light. He was telling us to still the outer senses and listen, in the stillness of the secret chamber of the heart, to the soundless sound of the eternal flame, to God's own heartbeat, to the sacred breath and to the still small voice of our God within.

Dearest companion of that Inner Light, that Inner Christos, that Inner God, won't you be still for a moment, and for moments in eternity, and know that the I AM THAT I AM is within you, above you, all around you and that the God-flame burns brightly and joyously in the secret chamber of your heart?

Be still and <u>know</u>!—with all the fervor of your Higher Mind's knowing—that the Great I AM within you <u>is</u> <u>God</u>!

Today I am specifically empowered to establish a strong heart-tie from my heart to your heart, from the hearts of Jesus Christ and Gautama Buddha, Shiva and Shakti to your heart; from the hearts of Abraham, Moses, the great prophets and the apostles of the Lord to your heart; from the hearts of Zarathustra, the Yellow Emperor, Confucius and Lao Tzu to your heart; and from the hearts of Mohammed and the nameless ones who have achieved mystical union with God to your heart.

These Wayshowers and the mighty Archangels of the LORD are the constant companions of the Great Inner Light and they come to initiate us that we might also learn the art and the science of unceasing prayer and unbroken communion with the I AM THAT I AM.

To be a companion is to accompany another, to be a friend, a comrade, a cohort. Thus, we companions of the Great Inner Light will gather together in the Heart of the Inner Retreat for ten days of <u>Joy</u> and <u>Initiation</u> and <u>Right-Mindfulness</u> in the LORD our God, the I AM THAT I AM.

I am writing to you to invite you to discover <u>the place</u> where the world's religions meet—both in the Heart of the Inner Retreat and in your own heart.

The Heart of the Inner Retreat is the "Place Prepared" in ages past for the coming of the Divine Mother and her devotees, for the awakening of the Inner Child of each one, who so longs to be cradled in her arms and nestled in her heart—and to come Home! The Heart of the Inner Retreat is the place where, on April 18, 1981, Lord Gautama Buddha chose to establish his etheric retreat called the Western Shamballa. The Western Shamballa is congruent with our thirteen-thousand-acre Royal Teton Ranch and extends for miles in concentric rings around our secluded mountain valley.

On the enclosed flyer you see pristine forests rising from the Heart to Sportsman Peak, which I like to call Mount Kailasa, the Western abode of Shiva and Parvati. The Heart lies two and a half miles northeast of the peak. It is the mystical center of the Inner Retreat, the hub of Light that bonds our hearts across the miles and continents. Yes, from the Heart this filigree of our devotions expands to drape our dear earth in the prayers and mantras, the chants and affirmations of the name of God that pass from the lips and hearts of those who know what it means to be a companion to the LORD God in the earth.

Was not Abraham, great patriarch of the Hebrews, called the friend of God? And is it not the hour for you and me to acquaint now ourselves with the Mighty I AM Presence and be at peace in the Divine Friendship?

Yes, this Inner Retreat, also known as the "Place of Great Encounters," is the place where we encounter both the hosts of the LORD and Ascended-Master Gurus as well as dearest companions of Light whom we have known down the corridors of the centuries and across the lines of longitude around the globe.

Here time and space take on another dimension. They are defined by the beating of your heart, one with God's heartbeat, and by the twelve petals of the heart chakra. As an inhabitant of the Matter cosmos, you can only glimpse the cycles of eternity through the shavings of time and space. But through the threefold flame of Father, Son and Holy Spirit, sealed in the secret chamber of your heart, you can enter in to the cycles of eternity. This very flame of God is the source of the Great Inner Light. It is the only permanent reality of your being.

In my lecture on Christian mysticism we will take up Teresa of Avila's concept of the secret chamber of the heart as "the interior castle" to which the soul retreats in prayer and meditation. Thus, I welcome you to the Heart of the Inner Retreat to discover the open door to your own heart "which no man can shut" save one—yourself.

That threefold flame burning on the altar of your own "Inner Retreat" marks <u>the place</u> where the world's religions meet, for all the world's religions come out of and return to that single flame, that essence of our Father-Mother God.

This flame is the Shekhinah of Israel, the essence of the Mother, the fabric of the worldwide Community of the bearers of the Light. This flame is the Word that was with Brahman in the Beginning, incarnate in Jesus Christ. Out of this flame we and the heavens and the earth were formed.

Yes, all the rays of the world's religions lead to that single God-flame in your heart and in the heart of the Great Central Sun. Just as the Great Central Sun is the spiritual center of the Spirit-Matter cosmos, so your heart chakra and your threefold flame make up the spiritual sun center of your body temple.

Out of that flame, the Great Inner Light radiates Love and Joy and Wisdom and the Power of Be-ness right where you are! That central sun is sustained for you by your Real Self and Inner Teacher, known as the Holy Christ Self, and by the Beloved

Mighty I AM Presence, whose light rays penetrate all cosmos and connect us with the one flame of Life in all other servants of God.

The Heart of the Inner Retreat is the Lord's extension of our heart chamber in the physical octave. We gather here not because God is not in us and we seek him outside of ourselves; we gather here because <u>He is in us</u> and we desire to amplify our God-ness, flame to flame, to support and sustain all life.

To so convene for ten days of immersion in this Light and in direct contact with the ascended hosts and Cosmic Beings is to reinforce our oneness in the Mystical Body of God. It is to follow the rays of the world's religions back to the God-flame and the Great God Source, where all paths converge in the single Light and the single Doctrine—the "Light/Doctrine" of Divine Love manifest in the Word and Work of the Lord in his disciples.

When we finally arrive at the Central Sun we will no longer need the outer structure of man-made doctrines, for we will have fulfilled our reason for being as dearest friends and companions of the Great Inner Light. There, in the center of God's being, Love is the fulfilling of the whole law.

Welcome to FREEDOM 1992! Come to reestablish heart-ties, to reintegrate with the Great Inner Light and the God-flame within yourself and all other Keepers of the Flame! Come to reaffirm your inner vows, commitments made long, long ago! For now the hour of the fulfillment of all things is come. Come to be made the kindling wood of the Lord that you might be kindled and kindle, stick by stick, a conflagration of worlds within and worlds without.

Yes! Come and invoke the violet flame as never before and shake the bowers of heaven for an abundant harvest of violet flame immortelles to tuck in the hearts of unwanted and abused children and aborted babies!

Come and extol the virtues of our God! Come and love the law of the Mighty I AM Presence with all your heart and soul and mind! Come to be made one with the teachings of the avatars and, above all, to commune deeply with our Brothers and Sisters who are the saints in heaven, the Great Lights of all ages. For they are our heroes. They made their way to the altar of the heart, met their Lord and knew themselves as one in his Body and in his ever-flowing stream of Light.

Come! Let us follow in their footsteps. For it is their footsteps I shall trace as I unfold for you the mystical paths of the world's religions. This is for me truly the most exciting lecture series I have ever given. Surely the Holy Spirit will be upon us as we sit at the Lord's table and he anoints us with oil and our cup of the mysteries of God runneth over.

In addition to delivering the teachings of the holy hearts of the saints, I will minister at the high altar of God that we have erected in the wilderness under the tabernacle of the LORD. I come as the servant of the Great Inner Light of your soul and as a Messenger who goes before the face of your own Holy Christ Self to prepare your soul for her bonding to that Great Inner Light, to the Inner Christ and the Inner Buddha.

Jesus said, "The servant is not greater than his lord." Thus, I, the servant, am not greater than the Lord of your interior castle, who is Christ, who is Buddha, who is the I AM THAT I AM—who is Krishna. I come as the facilitator of your soul's union with God. I come to reconnect you to the Ascended Masters, who are our mentors of the Spirit, for they have preceded us into the octaves of Light and they are teaching us every day how we can get there from here.

The mantle of my calling has been upon me for many lifetimes. And in this lifetime I have received specific training under Jesus, the Ascended Masters El Morya and Saint Germain, the Blessed Mother, Saint Francis and the apostle Paul. I am guarded and guided by Saint Michael the Archangel. And by the grace of God, and only by that grace, I transmit to you the baptism of the Holy Ghost with sacred fire.

In the East this is called darshan. Communion with the ascended hosts of Light is darshan, a heart-to-heart contact with the immortal Gurus. I AM—the God in me is—the vessel for that Light. And how my cup overflows! So much that I could not possibly contain it but must give away this golden liquid light moment by moment, hour by hour. This is my joy in the heart of God, my joy in the Heart of the Inner Retreat and my joy in my interior castle as I commune with you, dearest companions of the Great Inner Light.

Won't you take a moment now to reread the program, to meditate upon the names of our Elder Brothers and Sisters, the Ascended Masters, who will deliver their teachings as freely as the golden liquid light is sent over the crystal cord from the Great Central Sun to sustain the threefold flame of Life that beats your heart? Establish your heart-tie to each one of them before you put this letter aside. And they will pull you right into the Great Inner Light of their hearts and your heart—and the Heart of the Inner Retreat.

O how tenderly, how closely, how strongly we are tied to God! Make the contact by making a fervent call to each one. Name their names and call for that miracle that will clear the way for you to be in your seat when Alpha and Omega address us on July 1. They will release you from financial limitation as you accept the abundant joy of the flame that burns on the altar of your heart. Have you not heard these lines from the Chandogya Upanishad:

> Where there is creation there is progress.
> Where there is no creation there is no progress:
>   Know the nature of creation.
> Where there is joy there is creation.
> Where there is no joy there is no creation:
>   Know the nature of joy.
> Where there is the Infinite there is joy.
> There is no joy in the finite.

Yes, we all need support on the personal path of joy that we follow sometimes so alone even in the midst of our closest companions. When tempted to join the crowd we must reaffirm our chosen path as the Katha Upanishad tells us: "There is the path of joy and there is the path of pleasure. Both attract the soul. The two paths lie in front of man. Pondering on them, the wise chooses the path of joy: the fool takes the path of pleasure."

Our goal of union with God must lead us to the place where all faiths merge in the Great Central Sun of Divine Love. We do not engage in doctrinal disputes, for we know that doctrine is but a means to an end. And at the end of the road we throw away our doctrinal road maps. Thus, Lao Tzu said, "He who loves does not dispute: He who disputes does not love."

FREEDOM 1992: "Joy in the Heart," our thirty-third international conference for spiritual freedom, has one goal: that each one in attendance, from the babe in the womb to those who are nearing the hour of transition into the Great Inner Light, might know and receive the oil of gladness.

What is this gladness that lightens my karmic load, that fortifies me to the initiation at hand?

It is the fount of love of my creator, the fount in my heart, which has become his heart because I abide in him and he abides in me. In the words of Sadi:

>In this world I feel joyful
>   because He is the source of joy:
>I am in love with all creation
>   because He is the Creator.
>I shall drink with joy the cup of sorrow
>   because my Beloved is the cup-bearer:
>I will bear pain with gladness,
>   because through Him I shall be healed.

As the old hymn goes, "Weeping may endure for a night, but joy cometh in the morning." Joy in the Lord is a dispeller of time and space, both of which create distance from our God. Where there is joy, there is no separation—not from one another and not from our True Self and the true and living God.

There is no future for us in the hereafter if we do not find him in the here and now. Remember the words of Kabir:

>O friend! hope for Him whilst you live,
>   know whilst you live,
>   understand whilst you live:
>   for in life deliverance abides.
>If your bonds be not broken whilst living,
>   what hope of deliverance in death?

> It is but an empty dream,
>   that the soul shall have union with Him
>   because it has passed from the body:
> If He is found now, He is found then.
> If not, we do but go to dwell in death.

The key to the path of mysticism that I will teach you, by God's grace, is direct contact with the living God and the living Ascended Masters in our midst, direct experience in the Holy Christ Self and in the furnace of Saint John of the Cross's living flame of Love. The saints have known this. Come, let us rekindle the fire and the sacred memory of our inner knowing of God.

"Joy in the Heart" is a true spiritual retreat and possibly the highest spiritual experience you will partake of in your lifetime. The great heavenly beings are dedicated to making it so. Our beloved staff and Keepers of the Flame are dedicated to making it so, as are our children and the elementals.

And I, as your servant, am wholly dedicated now and always to serving your soul's victory in God in this life.

> Welcome to My Heart!—
>   the place prepared where
>   I have encountered my Lord
>   in the unfed flame
>   of his Sacred Heart

Elizabeth Clare Prophet

P.S. GOOD NEWS! Airline fares in the United States have been reduced by up to 50% on major U.S. carriers for travel between June 5 and September 13 on tickets purchased by June 5. Some tickets already issued are eligible for re-ticketing at the new, lower rates. Call your travel agent right away or Roger's Travel at 1-800-657-5812 for substantial savings on flights to Montana!

For more information, write or call Summit University, Box 5000, Livingston, MT 59047-5000; 1-800-245-5445. Outside the U.S. call 406-222-8300.

Royal Teton Ranch
Box 5000, Corwin Springs, Montana 59030-5000 406/848-7811

ANNOUNCING MONTESSORI EDUCATION WORKSHOPS
9 a.m. to 11 a.m. during "Joy in the Heart"

Saturday, June 27:	**Religious Training for Children from Birth through Age 12**
Sunday, June 28:	**How to Teach Math and Algebra with Ease to Children from Birth through Age 12**
Monday, June 29:	**How to Teach Reading to Young Children**
Tuesday, June 30:	**How to Incorporate Montessori Principles into Your Home**
Wednesday, July 1:	**How to Give Your Child a Well-Rounded Cultural Literacy Program**
Thursday, July 2:	**Home-Schooling Your Children**

June 2, 1992

Dear Friend of the Child,

    It is our great privilege to invite you to our Montessori Education Workshops which we will conduct this summer during "Joy in the Heart." These six two-hour sessions are new additions to the program that were not listed in the brochure you received.

They will help you quickly develop new skills to teach your children or any child you know. If you can't come to the Montessori Parent and Teacher Education Course this summer, then these workshops are a must. They will be held on the mornings of Saturday, June 27, to Thursday, July 2, from 9:00 a.m. to 11:00 a.m. There is no charge for the workshops to registered conferees.

At "The Aquarian Age Child," the five-day seminar we held last June, we presented a quick overview of the techniques we use at Montessori International. The topics included the discoveries and work of Maria Montessori, Glenn Doman and Marva Collins and our own program of teaching reading, math, music and religion to young children.

If you attended "The Aquarian Age Child," you already have a wonderful background for the new information we will be giving you at the workshops this summer. If you missed "The Aquarian Age Child," then these workshops will give you another opportunity to hear about our educational methods. This may be your only chance for some time to come since the "Aquarian Age Child" seminar has not been published.

Following are some of the topics we will present at the workshops:

1) How to conduct First Holy Communion classes and Sunday School lessons to nurture the spiritual development of your child.

2) Simple materials you can use to teach math concepts from basic counting through algebra.

3) How to teach basic reading skills to young children using our Montessori International Reading Program.

    4) How you can organize your home to foster independence and optimum development in your child.

    5) Valuable ideas on how to impart a rich cultural heritage to your child.

    6) The benefits of home-schooling, how to go about it and keys to providing a successful home-schooling experience for your child.

If you are a parent, this information will be of immediate practical value. If you are a teacher or a home-schooler, you can incorporate many of the ideas into your classrooms this fall. In short, if you have children or know children (if you don't, you should), then this information is for you!

On July 3, 1991, Beloved Lord Lanto explained to us the assignment of all Keepers of the Flame:

> We place before you that <u>absolute necessity for Keepers of the Flame</u> in their Study Groups and Teaching Centers to make room in their hearts, in their homes, in their centers...<u>to bring in the children</u>, whatever children, <u>and to begin to teach them</u> and to show that children from all walks of life, all backgrounds, all economic classifications will prosper under this plan...
>
> I trust you will understand that there is no mission for any Ascended Master of this planet for the furtherance of a great golden age unless the foundations of true education be laid.

Come, let us share with you the fruits of our years of striving and discovery of the unlimited potential of the child. We at

Montessori International have pledged our lives to the fulfillment of all that the Masters have called forth for education.

<u>We don't have all the answers but we do know that the system we are evolving works!</u> We see it every day in our classrooms—joyous, eager children who work hard, love to learn and delight in their accomplishments. <u>It will work for you too!</u> Come and apply the fires of your heart to the task, that together we might manifest the victory for every Aquarian age child.

We look forward to seeing you in the Heart and at our educational workshops. We can't wait to talk to you about your children, share success stories and put our heads together to come up with the God-solution to the challenges that face us as parents and educators. Together we can form the Ascended Master Mind Alliance that our youth need to overcome all opposition to their education, their acceleration and life itself.

Join us for these workshops each morning from June 27 to July 2, 1992, and find out how you can make a difference in the life of one child and many children.

Dedicated to the freedom of the child, we are,

Mary Ellen Maunz
Mary Ellen Maunz

Nancy J. McNabb
Nancy J. McNabb

23

I AM the Witness

"And a Man's Foes Shall Be They of His Own Household"
—*Jesus*

It is a great joy to witness to the truth of the Teachings that instructed me in silence while I went through one of the worst tragedies in my life—an attempted deprogramming.

In 1978, at the age of twenty-two, my life was just beginning both professionally and spiritually. I was a senior at the University of California at Santa Barbara. One evening in April, I attended a lecture on campus about the effects of drugs, alcohol, nicotine and sugar, sponsored by the Summit Lighthouse Santa Barbara Teaching Center. I had learned of the lecture by reading a small two-line advertisement in the school newspaper at lunch that same day. Since I was practicing hatha yoga at the time, I was interested in finding out more about the physical side effects of these substances, which surrounded me at school.

As I walked into the 250-seat theater-style auditorium right on time at 7 p.m., I was startled to see that there was only one other person that had come to hear the lecture. I sat down hesitantly and waited to see if the lecture was going to be canceled due to lack of interest. Much to my astonishment, the speaker began his presentation and spoke as though the room were filled with people.

He was clean-cut, casually dressed and had a sincere and humble tone of voice. I was impressed by his well-documented facts, and I could identify with the personal experiences he shared about drugs, diet and healthy living. I felt obliged to stay through to the end because he really had his heart in his subject—and because, after an hour, I was the only one left in the audience.

Unlike other seminars I had attended, where I felt like someone was trying to sell me something, I knew this speaker was there because he had a genuine concern for people. His desire was to share information and offer another perspective. Besides presenting facts on the physical consequences of eating too much sugar, smoking marijuana and drinking alcohol, he opened my eyes to the potential impact these substances could have on my soul.

The interesting part about the whole evening was what happened to me when I returned to my dorm room. As I prepared to go to bed, I was overcome with a feeling akin to a religious conversion experience. I was profoundly moved by something deep within my soul and I sat on my bed and cried. However, I could not understand it because I did not consider myself to be a religious person.

The weeks following this experience, I rarely thought about that beautiful night until the morning of Easter Sunday. One of my daily rituals was to get up before dawn and run three to five miles on the beach since I lived so close and it was always peaceful. After running for a half-hour on a very clear blue-sky morning, totally oblivious to the fact that it was Easter morning, I started to get my second wind and was really feeling great as I rounded a cove heading East. The moment I turned the corner, I was headed directly into the brilliant sun just coming up over the mountains behind Santa Barbara.

Within moments I began experiencing a sudden weakening of my legs and had to slow down to a walk. I found myself caught in a rapture of an intense electric feeling in my soul and body. I ended up walking and watching the sun with tears of bliss streaming down my cheeks. My attention was firmly placed on everything that the sun represented as God. I was seriously beginning to wonder if God was trying to speak to me, given the two soul-moving events in one month.

Since I was into the yoga scene and was enamored with Eastern values and philosophy, I began reading every book I could find on the saints of India. Later that summer, I was sitting in a laundromat waiting for my clothes to dry when I glanced at a poster announcing a two-day weekend retreat on "Higher Consciousness" sponsored by the Summit Lighthouse Santa Barbara Teaching Center. If it had not been for the fact that I was completely engrossed in reading *Autobiography of a Yogi* at the time and wanting to know more, I might not have decided to attend. It was that September retreat in Santa Barbara that effectively introduced me to the Teachings of the Ascended Masters.

Afterward, I began reading Summit Lighthouse books—one right after another. As a neophyte to the Teachings with only the printed word to enlighten me, I was excited to find that these books struck a deep and profound chord in my soul. I began to give the rosary in *My Soul Doth Magnify the Lord!* every morning, and during the fall of 1978 I completed reading *The Chela and the Path, Climb the Highest Mountain, The Human Aura* and *The Great White Brotherhood.*

In October, I attended *The Touch of Shiva* conference at Camelot, the 240-acre headquarters of Church Universal and Triumphant, located in the Santa Monica Mountains near Malibu. Needless to say, I was awestruck as I experienced the meaning of "living sacred fire" through Mother's delivery on the teachings of Lord Shiva. I remember the simple truth that was given: "The becoming of Shiva is the very essence of life itself."

Having recognized so much hope and vision for humanity contained in the Teachings of the Ascended Masters, I developed a fiery zeal to tell everyone I knew about the greatest discovery anyone would ever want to make in a lifetime. I was not standing on the corner proselytizing, but I did introduce all of my yoga friends to the Chief Indian Guru of the Himalayas, El Morya.

As Christmas 1978 approached, I was preparing to graduate from the University of California with a bachelor of science degree in mechanical and environmental engineering. Four years earlier, I had graduated from high school as class valedictorian. Now, after four years of intense study, I had a thirst to understand more spiritual matters, so I made plans to attend Summit University—a twelve-week retreat to be held at Camelot—in January 1979. I thought it would be the perfect transition into my professional career.

The Jonestown People's Temple tragedy, which was to occur on November 18, 1978, would soon be influencing the minds of many—especially parents who had children involved in anything other than the mainline Christian orthodoxy. It was just prior to this event that Stanley Petrowski, a former member of Church Universal and Triumphant who had been dismissed from the Church in 1973, visited my parents.

I believe he was assisted by an anti-cult group called the Spiritual Counterfeits Project and/or the Cult Awareness Network (formerly known as the Citizens Freedom Foundation). I later discovered that the people in these groups helped spur my parents to plot a kidnapping and to subject me to a psychological terror I would never have dreamed possible in the land of the free.

The visit by Petrowski and his associates was tape-recorded and later played to me when I was home for Thanksgiving. On the tape, Petrowski alleged that Mark and Mother participated in demonic rages and false prophecy. He continued with a litany of the Christian fundamentalists' philosophy about "cults" and by the end of the meeting had everyone crying and praying for me—which was also recorded.

Since I take a scientific approach to life, I wanted to see for myself the truth or error of these allegations before I drew any conclusions on the matter. After all, my only association with the Church headquarters had been at a weekend conference in October, attended by thousands of other people. I had read some of the teachings in my apartment at college and attended the campus lecture back in April but, other than that, my only contact with the Church had been through the Santa Barbara Teaching Center. I had not even met Mother at the time. So I figured the best thing to do was to go to Summit University, where I could personally meet Mother and ask her about all these allegations and experience firsthand the day-to-day community life.

I am sure it was my decision not to postpone my going to Summit University right after graduation in January that led my gullible parents to pay three deprogrammers and two or three bodyguards to participate in my kidnapping eight days before Christmas. In fact, the deception that led me to get into a van to go out to dinner with my father and sister was done in the name of Christmas.

The phone rang Sunday morning, December 17. To my surprise, it was my father, inviting me to dinner. He said, "I'm in town with your sister and her boyfriend. We wanted to deliver some Christmas presents to you since you're not coming home for Christmas."

It seemed odd, but I thought such an innocuous event as going out to dinner certainly would be appropriate since they had traveled to see me and bring me gifts. I simply could not have fathomed what was going to take place as I got into my sister's boyfriend's van to go to dinner.

After we had driven three hundred yards from my driveway, my sister's boyfriend slammed on the brakes in the middle of the street and two men I had never met before jumped into the back of the van, where I was sitting with my father and sister. My sister then moved to the front seat and the two men blocked my exit. Startled, I demanded: "What is going on?"

One of the men looked like he had come right out of the Marines. He was stocky and well-built—not someone I would want to fool around with. His accomplice was only slightly less intimidating. He seemed gruff and immovable.

They said, "We're going to take you to see some people that just want to talk." I said, "I am not interested and I am going to return to my apartment." But I could see that that would be impossible—the van was speeding ahead and there was no way out.

One of the bodyguards shouted at me, "Sit down and shut up!" I blurted back, "Every one of you in this van will be responsible for taking me against my free will!"

They proceeded to drive for three hours straight to a Holiday Inn in San Bernardino, playing rock music the whole way. I asked them to turn it off but they refused. They knew that the Church taught that rock music was detrimental to the psyche, and I believe their intent was to disorient me during the drive.

I sat in silence for the entire trip—scared, confused and outraged that my own parents had betrayed our sacred trust as a family. I had been kidnapped at the age of twenty-two, after having lived on my own for four years. I was not even a Church member and had not attended Summit University.

When we arrived at the motel, one of the two bodyguards said, "You can cooperate and walk quietly into Room 235 or else we will carry you in." I said, "I'm a man of peace and I don't want you to touch me."

My parents had rented three motel rooms in a row. Room 235 was the middle room. A few moments after my arrival, three men professing to be spiritual counsellors were in the room with my father, armed with file folders and Bibles. The two bodyguards in the room positioned themselves between me and the only exit. One of them warned, "Don't give us any trouble." I demanded, "Why am I here and what do you want from me?"

Instead of answering, they gave me aliases and began questioning and challenging every aspect of my beliefs, my thoughts and my personal life. Here is just a sampling of their browbeating:

They asked: "Do you pray to Elizabeth Clare Prophet as God?"

I said: "No. Nothing I have seen or read leads me to believe that she professes to be God and that I must pray to her as such."

Another question: "Do you realize that your vegetarian diet and your meditation and chanting are destroying your reasoning ability and making you vulnerable to brainwashing?"

My answer: "I have been a vegetarian for at least a year and I have never felt better or more alert. My form of prayer is no more harmful than yours."

They also asked: "Do you realize your soul is in grave danger by not believing that Jesus Christ is the only Son of God?"

I responded: "Jesus knows my heart and I love him, but I will not deny the Christ in the saints who have become immortal."

I have no concrete proof that Stanley Petrowski was in the room, but one of the deprogrammers slipped and called the man who was leading the session "Stan." I participated somewhat cordially in the conversation, hoping that once we were done discussing all the issues thoroughly, we could conclude and I could return to my apartment.

I discovered that I could control the direction of the dialogue to some degree by asking provocative questions that kept them busy frantically thumbing through their Bibles for passages to quote to me. This also allowed me time to think of other questions to pose and to avoid being on the defensive.

I asked such questions as: Where in the Bible does it say we are not reincarnated? What did Jesus mean when he said that we would do greater things than he? Why in the first chapter of John does it talk about the power to become the Sons of God? In the Book of Revelation, who are the hundred and forty and four thousand? What will happen on the day of the rapture? Why can't we pray to God's angels? They quoted me verse after verse but none of their answers made much sense. I didn't buy any of it.

God and the angels truly helped me to see through this situation by instructing me in silence and showing me why various accusations and spiritual concepts had no basis in fact or common sense. My captors tried to destroy my newfound faith by telling me outrageous stories I had never heard before about Mark and Elizabeth Prophet bilking Church members' pocketbooks for their selfish interests, participating in Satanic rituals and breaking up families. They also read me a letter from a psychotic ex-member of the Church in a mental institution claiming he was brainwashed by Elizabeth Clare Prophet and still controlled by her. It became evident that the "deprogramming session" was actually a session in the character assassination of Mark and Elizabeth Prophet and that all they wanted to do was to destroy these two persons and their integrity in my eyes.

After about three hours, I realized that they had no intention of stopping. They kept repeating the same subjects and questions to me, alleging that I had been brainwashed and mentally incapacitated, that I had lost my free will, and that my soul was in grave danger because I believed the books written by Mark and Elizabeth Prophet.

It would have been silly to believe or even consider that they were being objective. I said to myself: "You are not going to come to any conclusions while you are held in this environment. You're going to wait to hear the other side of the story. You are in your right mind and there is no way that this woman (or anyone) you don't even know could be controlling you or brainwashing you over the 'air waves.' There is no way that someone miles away could be controlling you in your apartment or in your daily life in Santa Barbara." I simply could not believe that they thought I was that stupid or gullible!

The deprogrammers cited Bible passage after Bible passage, quoting the "right" answers to everything, yet they were the living hypocrisy of their own chosen faith. They told me directly that because of my association with the Church, they were justified in breaking the law in order to "bring me back to God." They not only wanted me to believe everything they said but they wanted me to embrace their religion as the solution to my predicament of being in that room.

After agreeing that we were in the "last days" as described in the Bible, I asked them if they agreed that the

Bible prophesied the appearance on earth of two witnesses in the last days. They said, "We agree." So I asked: "If Mark and Elizabeth Prophet are not the two witnesses, then who are?" They answered, "The two witnesses are growing up in the Middle East."

I thought to myself: "They are now either making up answers or they really believe what they are saying. If they are right, I don't see how mankind has even a remote chance of overcoming the accelerated decay of civilization without expedient divine intercession. In either case, I have a lot more questions than they have answers."

Having remained relatively calm throughout most of the evening, I began to get concerned when "Stan" told me, "We have enough information to go over to keep you here for as long as it takes." With three deprogrammers, a guard at the door and my father in the room, escape seemed very unlikely without a physical confrontation.

They relentlessly continued their attempts to break my faith, attacking the foundation of such basic principles as reincarnation, the law of karma and the hope of a New Age—all of which I had come to understand even before I discovered the Teachings of the Ascended Masters! Since they did not make progress on this ground, they began to subject me to their guilt-inducing accusations that I was destroying my family and causing them much grief because of my beliefs.

Enough was enough! I had endured over three hours of their emotionally draining barrage. A surge of righteous indignation sprang me to my feet and I delivered an oration of such intensity that they were momentarily stunned.

With a thundering voice, I severely rebuked them: "You hypocrites! How do you expect me to believe you when you do not even follow your own religion? Jesus never said that the ends justify the means, and you are all accomplices in my kidnapping. You are breaking the law and I am going to walk out that door! How dare you incite such fear and guile into the hearts of my parents with your half-baked, mealy-mouthed ideologies? And if you are the type of people who are going to be caught up in the rapture, then I would rather not be a part of it!"

I continued uninterrupted for at least five minutes, but I cannot quote all the things I said because I did call them a few nasty names! In the split second after I finished, I found myself instinctively dashing for the door. I opened it and ran about three feet before my father grabbed me from behind and pinned me on the second-floor railing outside of the room. He said, "You aren't going anywhere!" I started screaming as loud as I could: "Rape! Murder! Help me! Call the police! . . ."

I broke my father's grip and bolted down the walkway in an Olympic-style sprint. By the time I had reached the end of the walkway and was headed toward the stairs, I could hear the deprogrammers saying, "We have to get out of here fast." I thought to myself, "Such cowards!"

I ran down to the front desk to call the police. I then called the director of the Santa Barbara Teaching Center and she said she would call headquarters and have someone leave immediately to pick me up. It was after midnight. I talked to the police by phone and told them that I was OK and that I wanted to sleep before I decided what to do about the kidnapping. Around 3:30 a.m. I finally arrived at Camelot, where I spent the rest of the night.

The following day, I had my first opportunity to personally meet Mother and discuss the whole situation with her. I was surprised and moved by her kindness and genuine concern and I realized that she certainly was not the person the deprogrammers portrayed her to be. In fact, it was Mother's loving counsel that persuaded me not to sue my parents because, after all, they were my parents.

I spent the next three months at Summit University and discovered for myself that the allegations about Mark and Mother were distortions and blatant lies generated by the media and apostate ex-members. Over the years, I have observed that there are many reasons why people leave the Church. I have watched some come to the Church expecting Mother to empower them before the Community. And when their need for ego reinforcement was not met, I have seen them turn and become enraged. They eventually left because they never got what they wanted from Mother or the Community. They basically could not understand that the role of a Guru is to tear down the ego, not build it, so that the soul can be liberated to become the Real Self.

I have known Mother now for over thirteen years and have had the blessing to personally interact with her and observe her in many roles and situations both public and private. Never have I witnessed an act or word that would substantiate *any* of the deprogrammers' allegations. I am proud to be associated with her and can only say that she is one of the truest friends one could ever have or desire.

After Summit University, I moved to Los Angeles and began my career at a large natural gas utility, putting my degree to good use as an energy conservation engineer. Over the past thirteen years, I have lived on my own and had jobs working for highly respected companies. I served for four years on the Church staff in Montana as a consulting engineer. During that time I married my lovely wife. We presently reside in the Pacific Northwest, where I am working in an engineering firm full time.

Unfortunately, ever since the attempted deprogramming, my life and religious beliefs have been paraded through the media by my parents, Charles and Marilyn Malek. I have continually had to challenge their unmitigated public accusations regarding Mother, the Church and my own state of well being. They have used newspapers across America and radio and TV talk shows as their forum.

On *60 Minutes* my mother claimed she had lost me to a "cult," when in fact I was living in Minneapolis working full time in a large energy corporation. She was even quoted in Scotland's *Glasgow Herald* as saying, "Families break up because of freedom of religion that is permitted in the United States."

It is appalling to sift through the volume of material generated by my mother in her campaign to destroy the Church. Besides attempting to influence public opinion through a negatively biased media, she has worked closely with those who have brought civil suits against the Church and has bombarded congressmen and federal and state agencies with letters demanding legislation to curtail Church activities. In a letter to the mother of a Church staff member, she wrote: "To keep my sanity, I intend to keep on looking for a way to put pressure on Mrs. Prophet and C.U.T. and hope we find her Achilles' heel. I want to see this group totally closed if possible, regardless of what our son does."

Quite frankly, I have sometimes been burdened with shame and embarrassment in front of fellow Church members because of the efforts of my own mother, who has continually tried (and failed) to destroy everything that we hold dear and sacred to our hearts as a worldwide community of spiritual seekers who honor all the great religions and saints East and West.

This is particularly painful because I really do love my parents. I have tried many times to establish a relationship with them on the basis of family and love and mutual devotion, trying to leave religious matters entirely out of the picture. I have gone home several times to visit with my parents and have often talked with them on the phone in an effort to heal the rift between us. I invited them to visit me and we even had dinner together at The Ranch Kitchen. But they have erected barriers between us, setting up artificial terms for our relationship rather than just accepting me as their son and as an individual with a God-given freedom to pursue the religion of his choice.

My parents have stated on many occasions that if I did not leave and disaffiliate myself with the Church entirely, they would have no respect for me. They have denied my requests for the addresses and phone numbers of relatives and even refused to give me the small but significant silver coin collection I invested in as a young boy. They have told me: "Your involvement with the Church is a worse problem than if you were on drugs." From various actions they have taken over the years, it is clear that they have disinherited me.

It is easy to understand why there is no meaningful relationship between us. Although thirteen years have passed since the kidnapping, the violation of the sacred trust of the bond of family has never healed. This has been a great burden and source of grief to my soul. I would have preferred that things could have been different, but I have had to accept that the situation will probably never be fully resolved and that my parents will likely go to their graves harboring their unfounded animosity toward my Church.

I deeply regret that my parents still associate with the Cult Awareness Network (CAN). This anti-cult group is headed by Patricia Ryan (president) and Cynthia Kisser (executive director). According to CAN's literature, members include "mental health professionals, lawyers, physicians, legislators, clergy, law enforcement officers and educators."

CAN encourages and condones psychological raping of the heart and mind as well as the criminal activity of kidnapping. For this reason, I have studied the phenomenon of deprogramming in great detail and have given lectures on the subject over the years. I feel it is important that I share with you the names of those who are actively attempting to deprogram members of our Church—both those who are just discovering the Teachings and longstanding members.

Three of these deprogrammers came into the limelight recently when LaVerne Collins, a Church member of fifteen years, was kidnapped from her home in Boise, Idaho, and subjected to a week-long deprogramming attempt by Joseph Szimhart, Mary Alice Chrnalogar and Kenneth Paolini. These three individuals have been involved in numerous other attempts to deprogram Church members in the past.

Since the methods they use are similar to those that have been used in many documented cases of deprogrammings, I have included below summaries of a few of these, taken from a publication entitled *A Criminal Assault on Religious Freedom: the Anti-Religious Movement* and from the *Religious Freedom Alert* newsletter.* Although these particular examples do not involve members of our Church, most of the deprogrammers named have been involved at one time or

---

*A Criminal Assault on Religious Freedom is available through Church of Scientology International, 6331 Hollywood Blvd., Suite 1200, Hollywood, CA 90028-6329. *Religious Freedom Alert* is available through the Coalition for Religious Freedom, 5400 Eisenhower Blvd., Alexandria, VA 22304.

another in attempted deprogrammings of Church members.

In one extreme case, Ted Patrick, a deprogrammer and convicted felon who has a long track record of brutal violations of civil and constitutional rights, held Wendy Helander for eighty-six days! During this time he carried her to twelve different locations in an unsuccessful effort to persuade her to change her religious beliefs. Wendy later sued Patrick and was awarded monetary damages after the court determined that she had been "seized, restrained and subjected to frightful experiences" with "no legal justification."

In Patrick's own book, *Let Our Children Go*, he admits using violence and gives an account of kidnapping a born-again Christian who was resisting his abduction. As Patrick describes it, he forced his victim into the car by squeezing the man's genitals until he "let out a howl." His victim "doubled up," releasing his hold on the car roof, and then Patrick shoved him into the car, piling in on top of him.

As a side note here, I'd like to mention that Patrick, who calls himself "Black Lightning," was interviewed on the film *Deprogramming: Understanding the Issue,* produced by the Institute for the Study of Religious Movements. In a panel discussion, he referred to cult members as "mindless robots," giving as an example a Hare Krishna member who was also part of the panel. These are his words: "The young man over there right now—he just setting over there chantin' 'Hare Krishna,' which is self-hypnosis.... Now, this is his life's blood. He got to chant. And because if he doesn't chant, ... he'll start thinking."

I think that the anti-cult movement fears the science of the spoken Word and the use of mantras, affirmations and decrees because they know that these liberate people to become one with God—and when people are one with God and have a deep-seated faith, they cannot be "deprogrammed."

Patrick says cults "automatically destroy all your freedom, your human rights and your constitutional rights. And when a person deprogram, all of their rights are restored." This ludicrous statement epitomizes the twisted logic that the deprogrammer uses to rationalize his repugnant and criminal behavior. Patrick boasts that he has deprogrammed over two thousand people successfully. He says, "There's no law against talkin' to a person. That's all I do is talk to a person."

Steve Hassan, a well-known deprogrammer and supporter of the Cult Awareness Network, was accused by kidnap victim Arthur Roselle of tying him up for three days while trying to force him to renounce his faith. In an affidavit, Roselle claimed he was tied so tightly that his hands became badly swollen. He was not allowed to go to the bathroom unescorted or to bathe or shave.

Galen Kelly is another deprogrammer who has been involved with violent sessions. In a sworn statement, Joan Stedrak, a New Jersey woman, charged that she had been seized by Kelly and others and shoved into a van as she was leaving work late one night. As she screamed and struggled, her glasses fell off and her purse contents were scattered on the pavement. Joan claims she was held for four days and was not allowed to sleep or go to the bathroom alone. Kelly threatened her by saying, "I'll leave you to die in the wilderness if you try to escape." She eventually did manage to escape and Kelly was later convicted on the charge of assault and battery. He was given a sixty-day suspended prison sentence, one year probation and a $500 fine.

Rick Ross of Phoenix, Arizona, and two other self-styled deprogrammers seized a nineteen-year-old Pentecostal from Seattle in January 1991 by luring him to his mother's house and then handcuffing him. After throwing him into a van, they taped his mouth shut with duct tape. He was held for five days in a condominium with the windows blocked and doors locked at all times. During his captivity, he was forced to watch videos about cults and "cult behavior." He escaped by pretending to cooperate with his captors and then running away during a "celebratory" dinner.

Cliff Daniels, who has been known to charge up to $25,000 for a deprogramming, claims to have deprogrammed more than 250 people. He is one of the growing number of deprogrammers who specialize in Christian groups that he calls "Bible-based cults."

Before closing, I must add that my parents never told me exactly how much they paid the deprogrammers but in a newspaper article in the mid-eighties my mother was quoted as saying that if they were to try and deprogram me again, it would cost tens of thousands of dollars.

Over the thirteen trying years that have passed since the attempted deprogramming, I have learned a lot from all of the challenges to my chosen faith. Even though I seemed to be alone during that trial, I knew that God was there to defend and strengthen me in my hour of need. My victory was truly God's victory.

It is a sublime honor to witness to the Truth that has guided the saints who have gone before us and are among us. God has allowed me to experience just a little of what they have gone through and I can now appreciate how much more they have sacrificed for the right to follow their Path no matter what the opposition or persecution.

If my story can reach the heart and soul of just one family and forestall another deprogramming tragedy, then it is worth every word on this paper. All glory to God!

In the Defense of Religious Freedom, I Am,

William Alan Malek

Tips on What to Do If You Are Abducted against Your Will:

1. Demand your freedom and attempt to leave and regain your freedom.
2. Repeatedly state: "You are holding me against my will."
3. Inform your captors of the laws that they are violating, namely, kidnapping, false imprisonment, assault, battery, intentional infliction of emotional distress and federal civil rights violations.
4. Where possible, loudly and forcefully inform bystanders of your plight.
5. Demand to see and study a copy of any alleged court papers. Your captors are not shielded or legally excused for any criminal or civil wrong committed against you in spite of the existence of an alleged guardianship. You are not legally required to respect or remain under any illegal guardianship.
6. Do not sign any release absolving your captors of physical or psychological harm. It may cause you to forfeit certain legal claims later. Do not put your signature on any documents whatsoever.
7. Do not consent to any medical or psychological treatment and do not engage in argument or in defending your religion.
8. Each time you are questioned or intimidated, demand to speak with your own or any independent attorney.
9. Be alert and observant and memorize all details of your circumstances and the persons involved.
10. No matter what they say, your captors are intent upon destroying your freedom and your independent mind. Do not cooperate with them.
11. If your parents or other family members are part of the kidnapping and deprogramming, tell them you would be more than willing to discuss your church, its leadership

and its beliefs in the privacy of your own home, without the presence of outsiders. Invite them to speak with other Keepers of the Flame or Study Group leaders nearest you or to take a tour of the Royal Teton Ranch and North and South Glastonbury and meet the staff and families who are in the area. Tell them the voices of your friends are missing in the deprogrammers' discussion and presentation.

Organizations Fighting against the Anti-Cult Movement:

FRIENDS OF FREEDOM
Dr. George Robertson
72 Cranbrook Road, #194
Cockeysville, MD 21030-3404

VOICE OF FREEDOM
Rev. Jim Nicholls
P.O. Box 1005
York, PA 17405

RELIGIOUS FREEDOM
CRUSADE
Rev. Ken Hoden
5930 Franklin Avenue
Hollywood, CA 90028

NATIONAL TASK FORCE ON
RELIGIOUS FREEDOM
Rev. Isaac N. Brooks, Jr.
Executive Chairman
5900 Cable Avenue
Camp Springs, MD 20746

COALITION FOR RELIGIOUS
FREEDOM
Dr. Donald N. Sills, President
5400 Eisenhower Boulevard
Alexandria, VA 22304

AMERICANS UNITED FOR
THE SEPARATION OF
CHURCH AND STATE
Lee Boothby, Esq.
8120 Fenton
Silver Spring, MD 20910

NATIONAL COUNCIL OF
CHURCHES
Rev. Dean M. Kelley
475 Riverside Drive
New York, NY 10115

J. M. DAWSON INSTITUTE
OF CHURCH-STATE STUDIES
Dr. James E. Wood, Jr.
Director
Baylor University
Box 380
Waco, TX 76798

FACT (First Amendment
Crisis Task Force)
Henry Kriegel
Executive Director
P.O. Box 3051
Bozeman, MT 59772

Mr. and Mrs. William Alan Malek

THE SCIENCE OF THE SPOKEN WORD
Books and Tapes by Mark L. Prophet and Elizabeth Clare Prophet

The science of the spoken Word is a means to deep, heartfelt communion with God. This ancient science combines prayer, meditation and visualization with dynamic decrees—an acceleration of all prayer forms East and West.

THE SCIENCE OF THE SPOKEN WORD
By Mark L. Prophet and Elizabeth Clare Prophet. Step-by-step instruction on how to give effective prayers, mantras, affirmations and decrees. This handbook will teach you how to invoke God's intercession to solve specific personal and planetary problems and how to use the violet flame to unlock your unlimited creative potential. Includes seven full-color thoughtforms with special mantras, meditations and visualizations for healing. **Softbound. 218 pp. #104 $9.95**

PRAYERS, MEDITATIONS AND DYNAMIC DECREES FOR THE COMING REVOLUTION IN HIGHER CONSCIOUSNESS
Everything you need to apply the science of the spoken Word to personal and world needs, including decrees for protection and the will of God, wisdom, love, purity, abundance and healing, ministration and service, freedom, forgiveness and transmutation. Color-coded on loose-leaf pages.
**Section I: 104 decrees #105 $4.95   Section II: 75 decrees #1657 $4.95
7½" x 9" 3-ring binders: 2" rings, white, #1162 $5.75   1" rings, white, #1041 $3.85**

DEVOTIONS, DECREES AND SPIRITED SONGS TO ARCHANGEL MICHAEL
Summon Archangel Michael and his legions of light to guard and guide you, your loved ones, your community and nation. Given at a devotional pace with fervor. For beginners and children as well as advanced students.
1-audiotape album with 32-page booklet, devotional pace. 70 min. #A93090 $7.95

DECREES AND SONGS TO ARCHANGEL MICHAEL
1 audiotape, medium pace. 90 min. #B94083 $6.95

ARCHANGEL MICHAEL'S ROSARY FOR ARMAGEDDON
You *can* do something about world and community problems! With this rosary of prayers, decrees and hymns, you can call Archangel Michael and his legions into action to help solve the problems of our youth, education, crime, the economy. Given with intensity and ardor. Includes three dictations by Archangel Michael.
2-audiotape album with 32-page booklet, devotional pace. 2 hr. 45 min. #A93070 $14.95

HOW TO USE THE SWORD OF THE SPIRIT AND THE WORD OF GOD TO FULFILL GOD'S PLAN FOR YOU
By Elizabeth Clare Prophet. Those who would increase the light in their auras to bring love and healing to mankind need spiritual protection. Learn how to draw down your spiritual armour and use the "sword" of God—the sacred Word—to protect you, your livelihood, your family and nation.
2-audiotape album, 3 hr. #A93061 $14.95

Prices, availability and postage are subject to change. To order call Summit University Press, Dept. 470, (800) 245-5445 in the U.S.A. or (406) 222-8300 outside the U.S.A.

continued on page 352

24

A Battle of Mind and Heart

To My Brothers and Sisters on the Path:

This is the story of my mother's attempt at having me deprogrammed. It is also a witness to the power of Archangel Michael, who personally rescued me. I want to share with you what happened and all that I learned from the ordeal, but before I begin I think it is necessary to give you a little background on my life both before and after I found the Teachings of the Ascended Masters.

Background

My mother was the kind of person who cared for her children and wanted the best for them. But for whatever reason, she was not able to give me consistent discipline. This affected my sense of self-worth and made it hard for me to have self-discipline when I grew up.

My parents were divorced when I was about seven years old. We were living in Spain at the time and after the divorce my father left the country. When we finally moved back to the United States, I visited my father occasionally but never spent much time with him or really got to know him until I was in my teens. We became good friends and have maintained a close relationship to this day.

As a teenager, I began a serious quest for a path of Truth. I felt an emptiness within and a sense of hopelessness toward the world I saw around me. As I watched the Watergate trials on television, I thought about the fact that not only was our government corrupt but most of the adults I encountered operated on a very superficial level.

My soul longed for truth and reality. I did not want a mundane life with a nine-to-five job. I longed to live a life in which I could strive to become a better person. I wanted to do something to help others. I became depressed and felt totally lost. I longed for wholeness within and without. I longed for God.

In my search for Truth, I studied many spiritual teachings of the New Age movement. Since my mother also showed an interest in new ideas and spiritual teachings, I shared with her my discoveries. We maintained a rather liberal relationship as mother and daughter, and I looked at her more as a friend than a mother.

What I discovered about many of the New Age organizations I came across was that they built up the human ego. My mother was drawn to this type of philosophy but I could not respect it. And this is where we began going our separate ways.

Up until the time I found the Teachings of the Ascended Masters, I had never really held a job, as I didn't need to because I received a substantial income from my grandparents. During that period of my life I was free to go see my mother whenever she wanted and, for the most part, could be with her whenever she wanted to come and see me. I had no major commitments or responsibilities except those that I decided to create. I spent most of my time searching through New Age teachings.

Enter . . . Elizabeth Clare Prophet and the Ascended Masters

In December of 1981, a friend told me about the Teachings of the Ascended Masters and Church Universal and

Triumphant. I immediately decided to attend *The Class of Elohim*, which was held at Camelot, the Church headquarters in Malibu. I never left. Right after the conference I began Summit University. I completed Levels I, II and III and then joined staff in the audio-visual department in March of '83.

My soul was in bliss! Not only was I receiving the spiritual truths I had so longed for but I was also beginning to live a disciplined life-style as a staff member. I was joyous and felt good about myself. And in Mrs. Prophet I had found an example I could follow and respect. It was the example of Christ in her that I was so drawn to. Somehow I knew that through this woman I could find my own Christ-identity.

Mrs. Prophet's students, including myself, call her "Mother" because of her devotion to the flame of God as Mother. We use it as a title of respect similar to the Catholic "Reverend Mother."

Through Mother I was reintroduced to the Ascended Masters. I say "reintroduced" because I felt I had known them for many embodiments. Because of their recognizable dedication to truth, honor and goodness, I no longer felt depressed about the world I lived in. Somehow I knew these great beings oversaw mankind and directed them in many ways despite all the corruption and evil so apparent everywhere. Just their presence gave me peace, comfort and a sense of hope for all life.

At Camelot, I became a production assistant in the video department. I loved my work and I loved the idea that I was doing something to help the Brotherhood and ultimately all of mankind by getting the videos out to the world. For the first time in my life I felt I had a purpose.

Part of my job consisted of taking notes and changing tapes whenever we were recording Mother. So the busiest times for me were during conferences, which usually fell on holidays. I would rarely leave at those times to go and see my mother or any of my other relatives. My work meant more to me than anything because not only was it exciting—I got to hear all the teachings and dictations—but it was helping me gain a sense of worth and self-esteem. I was healing my soul. This, however, did not go over well with my mother.

When I began my commitment to Mother and the Church as a full-time staff member, I became less available to my mother. She began to get upset when I did not come home to see her for the holidays. The ironic thing is that she had never been big on holidays anyway. I think what really was bothering her was that I no longer chose to come whenever she wanted me. It was at this point that the tension in our relationship started to build.

Once when I did visit her she saw me reading a Keepers of the Flame lesson and asked to see it. When I told her she couldn't because she was not a member of the Keepers of the Flame Fraternity, she became so upset that she joined just so she could see what I was reading. When she came to see me at the Ashram of the World Mother in Los Angeles, where I was living at the time, she felt rejected because she was not allowed upstairs. (At the time there was a rule that no outside visitors were permitted upstairs.)

When one enters a spiritual community, one expects that there will be rules and regulations. To me it was perfectly natural. But to my mother, it was totally unacceptable.

The Deprogramming

I had been in the Teachings for nearly five years. We were in the process of moving our headquarters to Montana. Just before I was going to make the big move, I decided to spend Christmas with my mother in northern California.

The whole time I was there I noticed that she was acting a little strange. She was overly nice. She told me that she was arranging for someone to come and paint a portrait of her and all the children in the near future and she wanted to make sure I would come. Although I did not know it at the time, she was using this as a hook to get me to come back when she could arrange for the deprogrammers to be there.

I moved to Montana in January of 1987. I loved my new life at the ranch and I was happier than ever with my life on staff. Then, on February 15, I received the following letter from my mother:

Dearest Laurie,

I had a very enlightening trip to Texas, and am in the midst of some major decisions. I have gotten agreement from the others, and am sending tickets to all, so that it will be easier for you to get here. This is the best schedule I could get and I trust you can make it work.

I am hoping to coordinate the painting preparation at the same time, and that may be possible. There is a time factor that I need to coordinate with Daddy before tax time, and felt that it would be better that we all meet here rather than go to Texas.

All is well. What a busy year this is turning out to be! I did have fun seeing the whooping cranes in Texas! Hope you are well—I miss you, and am anxious to hear about your Montana adventures.

I love you,
Mother

Enclosed was a round trip ticket from Montana to California and a copy of a letter from my mother's tax attorney in which he told her she needed to bring all her five children together to discuss how certain new tax laws would affect her and any money her children might receive from her. He asked her to bring the children together so that he could discuss the issue with them. (The whole letter was a fraud.)

I think it's interesting that every letter I had ever received from my mother had always been signed "Mom." This was the first letter signed "Mother." During the deprogramming attempt I began to see how disturbed my mother was because she thought she was being displaced by Mother. This was a big issue with her.

The following day I called my mother to tell her that I was sensitive about discussing money issues with the family since in the past I had been looked down upon by various family members who thought I was giving all my money to the Church. I told my mother that whatever she decided to do with her money was fine with me and that I really didn't feel that I needed to be present for this meeting.

My mother became upset and asked me to reconsider because it meant a lot to her. I told her I would think about it and she said she would call me back the next day.

When she called the next day she was very emotional and said that she had had a bad dream during the night. She dreamed that she was hanging on to a train for her life and felt she could not hang on any longer. Then she told me that she thought she was preparing for her death.

She said that the real reason for getting us all together was that she wanted to be with all of her children together in one place just one more time. She said she felt that then she could let us all go. If I would just come for this visit, she would be satisfied. I told her I would think about it.

I think what got me was that Saint Germain had dictated the previous month and talked about how death had come knocking at Mother's door and how she had had to wrestle with it. Saint Germain said:

> One must know that though death be predestined by your karma and your stars and may surround and grip you, *predestination is not the law of Cosmos*. Nay, the free will of the individual to overcome a predestination of karma and to rise again—this is the law of the Great White Brotherhood whereby we have defeated Death time and again.
>
> Let the record be clear. As one has stood in your midst to defy the enemy, so when your hour does come, the full mantle of this experience may be upon you multiplying your Christhood.... I say to you, begin now and cast out Death and Hell from your consciousness.... Beloved hearts, you cannot have kept from you the testings of Death and Hell. You must be ready.

In the weeks that followed, Mother had given a series of teachings on not succumbing to the death entity. I thought my mother must be a victim of this death energy and I felt sorry for her. I decided to go see her not because I believed she was dying but because I thought she needed me to help her deal with the forces attacking her. I was coming to her as an assistant and a friend, as I had done so many times in the past. So on Tuesday evening, February 17, I called my mother to tell her that I would be coming.

On Thursday, February 19, at approximately 12:30 p.m. I arrived at the Eureka/Arcata airport, where I was greeted by my mother. The moment I saw her I got a funny feeling from her. I asked her where all my other brothers and sisters were and she said that my two sisters were in town shopping and that my brothers had not arrived yet. She seemed a little nervous.

When we had my bag, we got in her car and drove to her house in Mckindleyville, which is only about five minutes away from the airport. Aside from one house nearby, my mother's house is situated in a relatively isolated area. It is located at the end of a long driveway in a big field.

As we pulled up her driveway, I noticed that there were other vehicles in front of her house. However, I did not question this too much because the last time I had visited her she had had secretaries and yardmen working at the house. We sat in the car and talked for about ten minutes as I told her all about Montana and how much I loved it there. Finally we went in the house.

We went to a room in the back and she sat me in a chair and put my feet up, which I thought was strange. She asked me if I wanted a drink of water and I said no. She said she wanted one and left the room. When she came back she had a glass of wine and asked me if I would like a drink. She said that I might need one. Then she said, "Laurie, I have brought you home to stay. I will never let you go back. I will never let you go again."

As she spoke, I felt a great fear come over me. I was frightened because I knew that she had probably hired some deprogrammers. Suddenly I heard people moving around outside the room. I wanted to know what was going on out there so I told her I had to go to the bathroom. I got up and starting walking out of the room and my mother said that she would have to stay with me.

As I walked into the next room, I saw all kinds of people running around closing windows, guarding doors, et cetera. I walked into the bathroom and my mother accompanied me. I looked out the bathroom window and noticed a mean-looking lady sitting right outside the window.

I became more and more frightened and felt trapped. My mother proceeded to tell me that she had gone to great extent to do this. She said that she had hired three "counsellors" and some local people to be my bodyguards so that I could not get away. She told me that it was hard to get bodyguards for this kind of thing because nobody wanted to get involved in it. I asked her if the lady outside the window was a guard and she said yes.

She told me she was going to take me to a house in the mountains about an hour away. The reason for this was because she had been told that once the other members of my church found out that I was gone they would come looking for me. She said that she had been told that to attempt to deprogram me was a dangerous thing and that all the people involved knew that they were taking a risk. She also told me she had been planning this for six months.

Finally she said that it was time to go and she asked me if I would go voluntarily or if they would have to take other means. Because I did not want to be physically harmed, I told her that I would go voluntarily. I was feeling weak because I was tired from the trip and from not getting much sleep the night before. I also had a back injury that was causing me a lot of pain.

I did not feel that I was in any shape to physically fight off these people or to try to run at that moment. I also felt subdued by the feeling of imprisonment that these people had created all around me. It was terrifying. I decided to cooperate with them until I could think of what to do or until I knew I was strong enough to try and get away.

When I came out of the bathroom I was met by a muscular man who appeared to be in his twenties, two very masculine ladies and a woman by the name of Arlene Powers, whom I recognized as my mother's former secretary who had worked for her in Texas.

My mother and all these people escorted me to my mother's car. I was told to sit in the back seat of the car and my mother sat next to me. On my left there was no door, on my right was my mother, and in front of me was the muscular man, who drove the car. To his right sat Arlene Powers.

As we drove out of the garage, I noticed that there was a white car in front of us with the two masculine ladies who were to be my bodyguards. I found out later that their names were Cathy and Rachel. We followed the white car the whole way.

During the drive my mother kept reaching out her hand so that I would hold it. I was disgusted and revolted by her gesture and I just could not believe she was expecting me to be all lovey with her after what she was doing to me. Everyone in the car was silent the entire trip. I felt as if I were in some sort of nightmare. I could not believe this was happening to me.

About an hour later we arrived at an isolated house somewhere in the mountains. It was way out in the country, surrounded by many trees. There was hardly a house in sight. When we pulled in the driveway, I saw a big plastic bag over the mailbox. I was escorted into the house by all the people in my vehicle. As I was walking, I noticed a big river down the hill below the house.

At that point I was introduced to two of the deprogrammers—a fat man in his mid-forties named Bob, and a tall woman with dark curly hair who called herself Becky. When I asked them their last names they said that they would not tell me that right now.

I later learned that the man was Bob Brandyberry and that Becky's real name was Nan Henderson. She had been a member of my church at one time. "Becky" told me that this was the first time she had ever done this.

I asked them what they were planning to do with me and they said that they simply wanted to give me some information.

I asked them how long it would take and they said that depended on me. I asked them if they could hold me as long as a year and Bob said, laughing, "I hope it doesn't take that long!"

I then told them that I did not want to hear their information and that it was not my freewill choice to be there. I told them that I was being held against my will and I demanded to be let go. They said that they would not let me go until they had delivered their information. They told me that it was their job and they intended to do it. I was still too weak to try to have any physical confrontation or to try and run for the door.

Because I felt so tired and my back was really hurting, I told them I needed to rest. I was escorted to a small bedroom, where I was left alone. I could hear everybody bustling around the house and talking about me. I also heard people outside barring my window.

I was nervous and couldn't sleep. I lay in the bed wondering what to expect. I made fervent calls to Archangel Michael and then I remembered I had with me my little tape recorder and headphones and the Archangel Michael Rosary. So I hid it under my covers and gave it quietly in its entirety. I was able to give this rosary two times in the three days that I was held captive.

A couple of hours later I walked into the main room to get a glass of water. It was just getting dark outside. I saw the image of a man on the porch. As he turned toward me our eyes met and I knew this was truly my enemy.

This man was going to be my greatest challenge. He walked in and extended his hand to me and I wanted absolutely nothing to do with him. He was the most void-of-light person I had ever seen and his face conveyed so much hatred. This was my first encounter with Joseph Szimhart, the "expert" on Church Universal and Triumphant.

Joseph began to tell me about himself. I interrupted him and said, "You are all holding me against my free will and I demand to be let go. I want no part of this." Again they said they were just going to give me some information, and I said I didn't want it. They said they were going to give it to me anyway. Joe began asking me about my work in the Church. I did not answer his questions. They all began talking back and forth and then my mother demanded that I participate.

Bob told my mother not to worry because even if it wasn't the most pleasant way, they could still do their work of drilling the information into my head. He told her my subconscious would be taking it all in and at some point I would break.

So they began having dialogues with each other. Joe was sarcastic and hateful. They made fun of Mother and the Ascended Masters and anything about our church they could think of. This went on for about an hour, at which point I got up to go into the bathroom. I noticed one of the lady bodyguards standing outside the window while I was in there.

My first reaction to this entire situation was to try and outsmart all these people. I could tell by certain things that were said that they thought I was just a young, naive, happy-go-lucky person who was controlled by a cult. So the first thing I tried was to play that role so that they would never know what I was really thinking.

I felt it was important to never let them know where I was coming from. I noticed that if I just sort of laughed with them and acted a little bit interested, the energy in the room would lighten up considerably. The deprogrammers would not be so intense.

I thought that by acting this way I could eventually make them think that I would never go back to the Church and then when they released me I could go back home. I also thought that if I could make them think I was really interested in what they were saying, they would be unprepared when I tried to escape and therefore I would succeed. By 10:30 p.m. on Thursday night I had been listening to them talk back and forth for about three hours. I was exhausted and I kept nodding out in my chair, so finally they said I could go to bed.

On Friday morning they began by showing some videos. The first video was on Jim Jones. It showed how crazed he was and how he was responsible for taking the lives of everyone in his community. The anti-cult movement loves to compare Mother and the Church to Jim Jones, but anyone who has ever met Mother or visited our community knows how absurd such a comparison is.

The next video I remember was about the Rajneesh community. It showed all their strange sexual rituals. The whole thing was wild and chaotic. Then we watched *The Wave,* which is a true story about a teacher who demonstrated how he could control his students and make them do as he pleased. They also showed me several videos about Hitler and the Nazis and about totalitarian movements.

When the deprogrammers first began that morning, they did not discuss my church or me personally. Initially, their whole tactic was to get me to make my own comparison between the groups depicted in the videos and my church. That first day I managed to laugh with them and seem interested in what they were trying to show me, as I had planned. It was not too hard to maintain my act at that point since they were not really directly discussing me or the Church.

Bob Brandyberry was the one who had brought all the videos. He had been a member of the Unification Church at one time and often referred to the "Moonies" during our sessions. Nan Henderson's role was to play up Bob and Joseph. As they would speak, giving all their facts and logic, she would ask them questions that she thought might interest me. She would often say things like, "You guys are so loving for trying to help Laurie and give her all this information."

By Friday evening my attitude about how I was going to interact with this group had changed quite a bit. I had become exhausted, disgusted and angry at what they were trying to do to me. I had had enough of their nonsense and I didn't want to play games with them or give them any more of my energy at all.

I began to realize that trying to play a game with them wasn't going to work so I decided to take a stand and show a little more of my true colors. I was actually quite amazed at how I suddenly felt the great presence of El Morya and the Masters when I did finally take a firm stand.

This was a great lesson to me and it made me think about Sir Thomas More and other true saints who had taken their stand against the forces of Darkness. I am sure it wasn't easy for them and it brought much pain and suffering, but I know that they must have been greatly strengthened by the presence of God with them.

It would have been easier for these great souls to compromise and save their skins, but their love for God and the Truth was greater. They had to stand for what was right and there was no sense in trying to trick the enemy. In the end, God will always be the judge.

This experience taught me that the Masters cannot place on us their full mantle of power and protection until we take our stand for Truth with fearlessness in the face of Evil. I cannot compare myself to Sir Thomas More and the other saints who died at the hands of evil forces but my experience gave me a small taste of what they must have felt.

That evening when I came out of my room, the deprogrammers all noticed the change in me. I was very serious. From that point on, I didn't speak to them or engage with them in any way and I kept my head bowed down so that I wouldn't have to see the videos.

The deprogrammers became much more intense with me. They yelled at me and accused me of being a manipulator. They said to my mother, "See, this is how we were expecting her to act from the beginning! This is more like it. This is the normal way a brainwashed person reacts to us."

My mother tried to talk to me. When I did not respond she became really angry. The thing that seemed to disturb my mother the most was that she thought that I had left home to go search for a different mother figure. In one sense she was right but what she failed to understand was that I was searching for the example of Christ, not a new human mother. I wanted a teacher and a Guru who could show me the way back to God.

My mother had so much guilt about the fact that she was

not a good mother that she could not see that this deprogramming she had arranged was really an attempt to assassinate my soul. All she wanted was to force me to leave the Church and come back home to her.

Cathy, one of the lady bodyguards, asked the group if she could take me on a walk and they consented. We went down by the river and she became very sympathetic with me. She told me she knew that I was upset and that she never really wanted to do this.

Cathy confided that the only reason she had agreed to participate was because she was a good friend of my mother. She told me that my mother's parents and some of my brothers and sisters were behind this. Cathy had heard someone saying that if I did not come on this visit to my mother's house they would have to come to Montana to get me.

She told me that when I absolutely could not take it anymore I should let her know and she would try to speak to my mother. However, I knew that the deprogrammers had a lot more influence with my mother than she did. I did not know if I should trust Cathy but I decided to think about what she had said.

It began to get quite dark outside so Cathy said that she would take me back to the house. I considered trying to run as we were walking back. I began looking around for lights coming from houses so that I could see which way to run. The only lights that I could see, however, were coming from a house across the river. It was too dark to try and swim the river but I decided that this was the house that I would go for when I did get the opportunity.

When we returned from the walk, the deprogrammers were anxious to talk to me more. Joseph was quite irritated with me and accused me of being a spoiled brat for not participating in their discussions about my church. I went in my room to lie down because I was frightened and I wanted to be left alone.

My mother came in and said that she was sick and tired of me acting this way. She said that if I did not come back into the main room, they would carry me in. I told her that I would

A Battle of Mind and Heart

go if she would let me talk to Cathy alone for a minute.

Cathy came in the room and I told her that I could not take it any longer. She said I had to try. She did not keep her word and try to persuade my mother to let me go.

I went back into the main room and they kept me up till midnight. My mother threatened to hide me out for months so that my friends could not find me. She said that she would even hide me in Europe if necessary. She warned that she would go as far as selling her house in California to move somewhere else so that nobody would ever be able to find me.

This concerned me greatly. My mother and these deprogrammers were denying my rights as an adult in society. They were holding me prisoner against my will and now my mother was telling me that she would hide me for months and even take me to Europe. I knew she had the funds to do it if she wanted to. I became more and more desperate to escape.

After I went to bed I heard the deprogrammers rebuking Cathy. They told her that she could not be sympathetic with me anymore. That night as I lay in my bed I was able to do the Archangel Michael Rosary for the second and last time.

On Saturday, February 21, I was awakened at 7 a.m. and brought into the main room for a full day of hearing my church compared to Hitler's regime and other organizations. The deprogrammers showed me more videos. I noticed that since my attitude had changed they were much more alert about guarding me and they watched my every move. I didn't get the opportunity to try and run that day.

They began directly attacking Mother. Usually the main target of attack for a deprogrammer is the leader of the organization in question. Joseph told me that he had been a member of the Church for a short time many years ago. He showed great hatred toward Mother even though he had never actually met her.

He often accused her of being a fraud. He said that she made up the teachings she delivered and that she did not come from God. He even went so far as to try to discredit her by telling me about her sexual habits, which he claimed to know about.

They will use whatever tactic they can to destroy your image of your Guru. Joseph was extremely egotistical. He really believed he was the final word on this entire matter.

But I had been a member of the Church for over five years and had worked closely with Mother and her children. So I recognized most of his information as being inaccurate or twisted. It was obvious to me that he was misinformed.

For example, Joseph would talk about the "double standard" in effect at the Church. He said there was one standard for the co-workers and another for Mother and her family. Since I had spent a lot of time with Mother and her children, I knew that they lived by the same rules as the rest of the community.

I had seen how in some cases Mother even expects more from her own children than from the staff. But I could see what a burden this part of the deprogramming session might be upon someone who had not had much direct contact with Mother.

In looking back on my experience with the deprogrammers, I always feel the wrath of God when I think how they tried so hard to destroy my Guru/chela relationship with Mother. As we know, the path of God is a mystery. Even the disciple does not always understand the initiations and the mysteries of the Path. This is why a deprogramming can be so dangerous to the delicate soul who is new to that Path.

Imagine if Milarepa's sympathetic mother had hired deprogrammers right when he was in the throes of his initiations of building and rebuilding houses under his guru, Marpa. The deprogrammers would have had a lot to say about how terrible his teacher was and how he took advantage of Milarepa for his own gain.

They would have talked about how his teacher was just a mean old man with an alcohol problem who really didn't care about anybody. They could have spoken about Milarepa's food deprivation and the sores on his back and the way he was treated and spoken to. The deprogrammers will always think they have everything all figured out with their human minds and carnal logic.

A Battle of Mind and Heart

But what was really going on? Milarepa was gaining the victory of his soul as it applied to his karma. The process was a mystery even to him and there were times when he had doubts. So how could he have explained it to another?

How could he have explained that he was simply following his heart? From all outer appearances, he looked like a fool. What would have happened to Milarepa had a group of individuals kidnapped him and tried to tell him that what he was doing was wrong?

Fortunately, the initiations we undergo in the Teachings are not as radical as those Milarepa had to go through. Nonetheless, we still have our initiations, which enable us to be engaged in the process of battling with our karma—all with the loving care and assistance of the Guru, who has such great insight into our souls.

Our Guru El Morya, who overshadows Mother, is actually a Zen Master. Mother once told me that his disciplines are specifically calculated to defy the reasoning mind so that the chela will have to develop his heart chakra and approach the path of discipleship with the discipline of the heart and the wisdom of the heart. El Morya separates the sheep from the goats by giving his chelas disciplines that are like Zen koans. It is something like the Gordian knot. If you can't undo the knot, or the koan—if you can't figure it out with the logic of the mind—you just have to take a knife and cut right through!

Those who have the love of the Guru in their hearts thrive under this type of discipline. Those who do not leave in anger with a great sense of injustice because they believe their egos have been insulted.

This kind of training quickly brings you close to your own Holy Christ Self. And the proximity of your Holy Christ Self gives you more discrimination and discernment every day until the Path is no longer a puzzlement, because you have walked through the labyrinth of the puzzle of your own karma and finally come out the other side, where you see the Master's smiling face.

The interesting thing is that when the deprogrammers

were pounding all their information about Mother into my head—even though I knew what their intention was and even though I knew they were focusing on the negative and twisting the truth—I noticed that my mind needed to consciously deal with the information they were feeding me. I don't think it's possible to just shut it all out because it does go into the subconscious.

What I found I had to do just to keep my sanity was to process the information in my mind as it was presented. I had to sort each piece of information so that the seeds of doubt they were trying to plant could never take root and grow.

For example, if they said something that I knew for a fact was not true, then I could disregard it. If they discussed something that happened before my time in the Church, I would file it in my mind under "Unknown—can be checked out later." If they said something that was taken out of context or twisted, I could file that away under "Based on truth—blown out of proportion."

This is why the deprogramming experience is so tiring. Your mind is working all the time to process the information even though you know ahead of time that their intention is to destroy the image of the Messenger.

The deprogrammers really do try to mess with your mind. It's important to never let the "facts" they are delivering to you create any feelings of doubt because this is what they want and this is what will make you more vulnerable to them. You have to constantly battle with your own mind to stay on top of it all.

Another thing that happened on Saturday was that my mother became much more involved in the sessions. Instead of me being "deprogrammed," my mother was being "programmed"! She would listen to all the horrible things they would say about Mother and then exclaim, "That's just terrible!" The more they would feed her, the angrier she would get.

So, even if you survive the trauma of a deprogramming, your parents won't! Parents will never be the same after hearing all the negative information.

In my case, my relationship with my mother was permanently destroyed. Everything she "learned" about Mother and the Church will always block us from having any kind of a normal relationship. To this day, she has never met my children, who are now one and three years old. We never even speak, thanks to Joseph Szimhart, who claims he was trying to bring us together.

By 10 p.m. Saturday evening I was exhausted and so I just got up from one of the sessions and laid down in my room in spite of what they thought about it. Instead of moving me back to the main room, they all came in my room with the TV and VCR—making a total of eight adults in that little room. It was intrusive and disturbing, which is exactly what they were trying to be.

The worst part about it was that they acted like a bunch of juvenile delinquents at a party. As they showed more of their videos, they would laugh and carry on with each other and make fun of Mother and anything else about our church they could think of. They acted wild and drunk.

I continued to lie quietly in my bed with my eyes closed. I felt as if I were in an astral pit filled with a terrible death vibration. It was like being in a nightmare.

Finally, after about an hour and a half of this, I got up and went into the bathroom, which caused them all to scurry around to take their positions. Then I sat outside in the main room. Since they had their whole set-up in my room, they decided to call it quits for the night. They moved everything out of my room, at which point I went to bed and tried to sleep.

On Sunday morning I heard Arlene, my mother's friend, come into my room and go over to my mother, who slept in the same room. She whispered to her that the plan for that day was for the deprogrammers to come into my room and "invade my space" and then continue to pound information into my head. I decided to get up and go into the bathroom so that I wouldn't be in the room when they "invaded."

When I came out the beds had been moved out of my

room and replaced with chairs and the TV and VCR. While they were moving my bed they found my Archangel Michael Rosary cassette in the tape recorder under the covers.

My mother made some comment to the effect that she could not believe that after all this I would dare to still listen to that tape. Joseph told her that I was just getting a "fix" of the brainwashing so I could maintain my position against them. After breakfast they demanded that I go into the little room.

The session began with "Becky" (Nan Henderson) confessing that she had been a member of our church for ten years. She went into a long story of how she had gotten romantically involved with a man and all the things that happened and how she was eventually asked to leave. She told me that Becky was not her real name and that she wanted me to hear her story because she had to leave that day and she felt that this would be her final effort to convince me that I was a member of a destructive cult.

After Nan had emotionally completed her story she left the room, and Joseph and Bob began showing me a video about a guy who was psychotic. It seemed he was a member of our church but he obviously had a lot of problems. The whole video focused on Joseph interviewing this guy, whose name was David. In the video David tells Joseph that he is not really a man but a lady. He begins to tell a bizarre story about how he had gone under the world and "they" had made his body into a woman's body.

David had a harelip, which along with his sincerity and feminine way of speaking, made him appear almost humorous. According to his parents, who were also interviewed on the video, he had been a perfectly normal guy until he had come into the Teachings. He had been very masculine and was a member of the National Guard.

The point of showing me the video was to convince me that the Teachings can psychologically mess up an individual. In the five years I had been in the Teachings, not only had I never heard of David, but I had never seen the Teachings have anything but a positive effect on people.

A Battle of Mind and Heart

At 12:30 p.m. they allowed me to eat some lunch in the main room. I looked out the window and I noticed that Cathy and the other bodyguard were driving away in my mother's car. I thought to myself that this was the opportunity that I had been waiting for.

I wanted to see who was guarding me, so I walked toward the door and my mother stood in front of it. All the deprogrammers in the room were watching me. When I went in the bathroom and looked out the window, I noticed my mother standing guard. I went back in the little bedroom with the deprogrammers once again because I wanted to try my escape in a moment when I would catch everybody off guard. I decided that before I would attempt to run I would try to get permission to speak to my father.

Within ten minutes after sitting back down in that little room with the deprogrammers, I became charged with adrenaline. During those three days I always wore my jeans and tennis shoes and I had my passport, plane ticket and some money in my pocket in case I got a chance to escape. I knew the time had come.

I got out of my chair and walked into the main room, where I looked at my mother straight in the eye and said to her, "I demand to speak to my father!" She said she would think about it. I then demanded again and she said no, so I ran for the glass door.

I heard a voice in my head say: "Run for your life!" I quickly unlocked the door and ran as fast as I could down a long rocky pathway toward the river. When I reached the edge, I got into the water until it was up to my knees. As I was trying to decide if I should really swim across, I turned around and saw Joseph standing right behind me. He said, "I'm not going to let you go, baby!"

Out of desperation to get away from him, I jumped in the river and began to yell for help as loud as I could, not because I was drowning but because I wanted to get attention from someone—anyone. As I attempted to swim, I started drifting down the river.

I noticed that Joseph was running alongside the river

and I saw him turn toward the house and yell for inner tubes. Another man had appeared from a house around the bend on the same side of the river. He was running in front of Joseph alongside the river with his dog. He was shouting something to me that I could not hear.

The undercurrents of the river began to feel very strong. I was out of breath from screaming, which had taken all my energy. I was not sure if I could make it across the river but since Joseph was still running along the side of the river I knew I had to try to get to the other side. The water was very cold and I felt exhausted and afraid as I fought the powerful currents that were working against me. For a moment I was certain that I was going to drown.

I remember feeling angry at all the people involved in the kidnapping for causing me to die this way. I was afraid of what the water would feel like in my lungs. I shouted to Archangel Michael to help me. All of a sudden, it felt like the current changed. Miraculously I found myself on the other side of the river. I spent the last bit of energy I could muster to grab on to a rock. I just kept thanking God over and over again.

I was so exhausted and so cold from the water that I could not pull myself out of the river. When I looked over to the other side I saw that Joseph was being pulled out of the water by the man with the dog. At some point he must have jumped into the water. He never made it across.

I still did not feel safe from my mother and these people and I wanted to get out of sight. I was certain that they would be driving around looking for me. I finally summoned the strength to pull myself out of the river.

There was a steep hill before me and I decided to try and climb it so that I could find somebody and get help. I kept asking God to help me get up the hill. It took me about fifteen minutes to crawl up that hill but as I got to the top I could see the sun shining over the top into my face and it was an exhilarating experience. I just kept thinking, "I am free!" When I came over the top I saw a house.

I stumbled over to the house, knocked on the door and

asked the lady who answered if I could use the phone. She let me in but when I tried the phone I could not place a call. Another lady in the house told me that there had been a problem with the phones in the whole area all day.

I then told these ladies that I had been kidnapped and that I had jumped into the river to escape. I told them that the people who had kidnapped me were probably looking for me. I asked them if they could please give me a ride into town.

They told me that everything in town was closed and that I would be better off hiding at their house for a little while. I began to feel sick and my head was spinning from the cold water so I sat down to think about what to do.

Within ten minutes three police arrived at the door and I told them that I had been kidnapped by my mother and some other people and that I had jumped into the river to escape. One of the police scratched his head and told me that he was confused. He said that he had been flagged down by my mother on the road, who had been driving around looking for me but could not find me.

In desperation, she had told this officer that we had been staying in a summer home across the river. She said I was psychologically disturbed and that I had run out of the house hysterical and jumped in the river. She warned him that I would probably be violent when he found me. The officer saw that I was perfectly sane and that our stories did not match.

I asked the officer if there were any chance that he would turn me back over to my mother. He asked my age and when I told him that I was twenty-eight, he said that he could not because I was legally an adult and had the right to do what I wanted.

Shortly after I had told this officer what had happened, the deputy sheriff, Kevin Christi, walked in the house. I told him the story and he realized that I had been a victim of a crime. He immediately sent the three other officers to the house where the deprogrammers were for questioning and police reports.

While I warmed up by the fire, Christi continued questioning me. I showed him my passport for identification as well as my round-trip ticket that my mother had sent me. When my clothes were dry, Christi told me we were going to go back to the house where my mother and the deprogrammers were so that I could get my things. I was concerned about going back to the house but he assured me that there was no way he would turn me back over to them.

On our way there, we went through the little town of Willow Creek and I saw Bob Brandyberry crossing the street. I told the sheriff and he stopped the car and questioned him and then took him with us back to the house.

When we arrived at the house, there were about four police vehicles there. I told the sheriff that I did not want to see or be near the deprogrammers or my mother. He said that I could wait in the car. He got out and started talking to some of the other officers.

To this day, I wish I had gone in the house escorted by the officers just to see the look on their faces. But at the time I was still in shock and all I wanted to do was to get as far away from that group as I could.

A detective came over to the car to question me. The first thing he said he wanted to know, just for curiosity, was whether the Church I was in controlled my diet. He asked me what kind of things I could eat. He then asked me if people could come visit me and if I could date.

I answered all the questions to his satisfaction but it clued me into what the deprogrammers had been telling him. When the detective was finished asking me questions, Christi got my things from the house and we went to a station nearby, where I had to give my story one more time on tape for the record.

At the time, Mother was on the platform delivering a lecture in Minneapolis, so I called Edward Francis, Mother's husband and the Church vice president, and told him what had happened. He arranged to get me home, as I had already missed my return flight.

One of the officers said that I could stay at his house with his family about a mile away if I wanted and I gladly accepted. He said that he had to go into Eureka in the morning and that he would give me a ride to the airport. I was happy about this because my mother lives so close to the airport and I was concerned that she and the deprogrammers would try and stop me from getting on the plane. I felt safe with this officer.

The following day the officer drove me to the airport and we saw no signs of my mother or the deprogrammers. I changed planes in Salt Lake, where Edward had arranged that I meet up with Mother, who was flying home from Minneapolis.

When I saw her at the airport we ran towards each other with tears in our eyes as we gave each other a big hug, overjoyed to be reunited. At last I had made it back into the arms of my beloved Guru and friend.

It was a great moment of celebration of my victory over these dark forces. I wanted to weep for the hatred this woman bears from the anti-cult movement. I told her the whole story from beginning to end as we flew home together.

A few days later Cathy, the bodyguard, phoned me to apologize for ever being involved in my attempted deprogramming. She said that they had told her it would be a loving experience but she had realized while she was in that cabin how hateful these people really were. She said she could not believe how horrible the videos were. When she had returned to the cabin, my mother had become furious with her for leaving and blamed her for my escape.

The most interesting thing, however, was Joseph's comment that some power must have protected me—otherwise I could not have made my escape the way I did. Joseph said that he had never seen anybody take off as fast as I had and that when I moved across those rocks by the river it was as if I were flying.

Praise God for Archangel Michael, who carried me in his wings to my freedom! He had the power to intercede for me because I had given his rosary twice and had prayed to him so fervently. Archangel Michael was so present that even Joseph Szimhart realized that there was a greater power involved in my escape.

Later I tried to press charges because I really wanted to see the deprogrammers stopped. I did not want to see someone else go through what I had gone through. But the district attorney refused to prosecute the case because it was a "family matter."

Six months after the deprogramming attempt I was married and I now have two beautiful children. I am grateful I survived my ordeal so that I could enjoy these precious little ones.

I have a good relationship with my father and his wife and they are supportive of whatever path I choose for my life. But I haven't had any relationship with my mother since the deprogramming.

The last thing I wish to express is how grateful I am to Mother and the Ascended Masters, who not only provide us with the teachings to be the Christ but who also give us the keys with which we can heal our psychology and the inner child of the past.

With loving gratitude to
Lanello, Mother and the Masters,

Laurie Alexander Black

Mr. and Mrs. Frank Kennedy Black

THE SCIENCE OF THE SPOKEN WORD
Books and Tapes by Mark L. Prophet and Elizabeth Clare Prophet
(continued from page 324)

ANGELS
The angels are indispensable to solving every one of the problems in your life. This booklet of 83 prayers, decrees, mantras and affirmations will help you keep the angels by your side.
Booklet. 17 pp. 9" x 6¾" #3600 $3.95

HEART, HEAD AND HAND DECREES
A handy pocket-size booklet of 76 meditations, affirmations, mantras, prayers and decrees for increasing the power, wisdom and love of God in your heart and aura.
Booklet. 36 pp. 5¼" x 3¼" #2090 $1.00

SAVE THE WORLD WITH VIOLET FLAME! by Saint Germain
These dynamic violet flame mantras, decrees, affirmations and songs will help you transmute negative karma, heal the pain of the past, and restore the joy and light of God to your world.
Each 90-minute audiotape includes four booklets. $6.95 each.
Violet Flame 1, beginning pace. #B88019   Violet Flame 2, advanced pace. #B88034
Violet Flame 3, medium pace. #B88083   Violet Flame 4, advanced pace. #B88117

VIOLET FLAME FOR ELEMENTAL LIFE—FIRE, AIR, WATER AND EARTH
Songs, mantras and decrees you can use to invigorate the elementals (nature spirits), who serve mankind by tending the cycles of nature. By giving violet flame decrees for elemental life, you can help them restore balance to nature and bear the heavy burdens of planetary karma resulting from war, inhumanity and environmental pollution.
Each 90-minute audiotape includes four booklets. $6.95 each.
Audiotape 1, medium-advanced pace. #B91114   Audiotape 2, advanced pace. #B91115

EL MORYA, LORD OF THE FIRST RAY:
Dynamic Decrees with Prayers and Ballads for Chelas of the Will of God
This tape will help you attune with the will of God for alignment with your destiny.
Each 90-minute audiotape includes four booklets. $6.95 each.
Morya 1, medium pace. #B88125   Morya 2, medium pace. #B88126
Morya 3, advanced pace. #B88127   Morya 4, advanced pace. #B94120

LANTO, LORD OF THE SECOND RAY:
Dynamic Decrees with Prayers and New Age Songs for Chelas of the Wisdom of God
Prayers, decrees and songs to the archangel and masters of wisdom for world peace, illumined action and the guidance of the youth of the world.
90-minute audiotape includes four booklets. Medium pace. #B94084 $6.95

Prices, availability and postage are subject to change. To order call Summit University Press, Dept. 470, (800) 245-5445 in the U.S.A. or (406) 222-8300 outside the U.S.A.

25

Friendship with God
Take the Leap in Consciousness!

The sons and daughters of God shall inherit the earth! But you must lay claim to the earth and claim it for Almighty God and the God within *you* and the God within the seed of the generations of Lightbearers that yet go forth through my own heart.

I am in the presence and the mantle of Abram and Abraham. And I AM THAT I AM. Know me, then, as father. Know me, then, as the descendant of *Keter.* Know me as *Hokhmah.*

Yes, beloved, the patriarchs and the prophets and the avatars do embody the mighty Tree of Life and do deliver down through the ages even the emphasis on this and another. When you know me as the Ascended Master, you see the full complement and the great harmony, through that living Son of God that I AM, of all of the *sefirot.*

Yes, beloved, I come that you might know a profile of the testing of my soul as warrior and as patriarch, as devotee of God, as one who knew the LORD and to whom the LORD did come. And therefore, the seed of Sanat Kumara, descended through me, is yet to be seen in the fullness of its glory.

I ask you, then, to polish even the "smoking furnace and the burning lamp."[1] Let there be the time, therefore, whereby the vessels of the four lower bodies are strengthened, strengthened in the might of the LORD, that you might understand that the earth is overrun even as Canaan was overrun with those evolutions who took the way of *Din* and rebelled against the mercy of God. And the mercy of God is the Universal Christ. And therefore, it is left unto the sons and daughters of God to call forth not the judgment that is the brand of the judgment and the judging of the fallen ones but the judgment of the LORD that is meted out through the Seven Archangels.

Yes, the Seven Archangels and the eighth and the ninth and the tenth, they do also embody the mighty *sefirot*. And therefore, should you come to know which of the *sefirot* is assigned to each one, you might thereby have a greater access to the Causal Body of those mighty Archangels of the LORD.

I shall not give this teaching unto you this night. For to impart the secrets for the unlocking of the names of God in the hierarchies of Light must come to those who advance in Maitreya's Mystery School and exhibit by years of sacred trust their capacity to keep the honor flame of God and to honor the Light and to honor the garment of the Light and to see that it is not soiled.

Therefore, beloved, I am called Abraham, the Friend of God.[2] I invite you to become friends of God, to cast down your idols, even as I did cast down the idols of Terah, my father.[3] I did dare to challenge anyone who did not place himself under the one God and the one LORD.

Therefore, cast down your idols! I speak to all and every one of you who come from near and afar. The idolatry of the human person and the human self cannot stand in the day of the mighty lamp of God! Know, then, the power of the Light, sacred-fire intensity within the furnace, beloved.

Therefore the sacred fire is available, but it is not accessible to you when you are in a state of idolatry of any human person or any personality, including the personality of an Ascended Master. It is to the Light that you bow and to the Universal Light. Therefore speak not of the greatness of this one or that one, lest you find yourselves outside of this camp.

This, then, is the inner walk with God. Be stripped, then, this night of your self-attachment, self-idolatry! Be stripped and know that the shield of the LORD is your exceeding great reward[4] when you cleave unto the LORD and the LORD only. Know the effacement of self and then know the appearance of the God Self within you.

How can I speak through this vessel except the vessel be emptied and therefore I may enter?

How can I speak through the vessel if the vessel be not stern in the strength of God, fierce and terrible before Evil and uncompromising with friend or loved one or enemy?

For all receive the love of the Sacred Heart of this one [my Messenger], and therefore I can impart that love to you, multiplying the intensity of the heart that my Messenger does embody. I seek to multiply the love of your heart. Therefore, let the fat be consumed by the fire of the lamp, by the fire of the furnace, by the fire of the Mighty I AM Presence!

Oh, be willing to be the chalice of God! If the heart be not perfected, the Son cannot enter.

If *Tiferet*, then, does not enter, how shall the mighty *Keter* and the *Malkut* therefore be one?

The compassionate Christ, the compassionate Buddha, the compassionate Krishna—are not these, then, the friends of God?

I give you a moment of silence that you might contemplate whether or not you consider yourself to be a true friend of God.
[21-second pause]

Friendship with God begins with trust. My trust, then, in the LORD God became the bonding of my soul to God, wherein I put my trust in the LORD and the LORD put his trust in me and entrusted unto me, beloved, the responsibility to give birth to and to nurture your souls forever and forever and forever until you should become the stars, one with your Causal Bodies.

Now you know why I have tarried so long with this stubborn and stiff-necked generation of those who have received so much and yet have taken that "so much" unto a course of self-idolatry while denying others the same freedoms that they demand for themselves. I trust I will not find any of you in this category, yet search your hearts. For you have come to a retreat whereby your soul might enter the path of true mysticism.

I, Abraham, am a mystic of old, always pursuing in my soul that bonding unto the LORD, being willing to leave my country, my father's house, my people to venture forth, and go forth knowing not where I would end up.

The will of God is indeed good. Praise YOD HE VAU HE! Praise God that the will of God is good and that it takes you step by step across the karmic highways of a distant past that must now be fulfilled.

"Trust in the LORD and obey." These are the words of the Psalmist. Make them your own. By faith, *"by faith,"* it is written, "Abraham obeyed God."[5] By faith did the great Lights of old achieve that communion.

Therefore, bind the beast within the temple, the carnal mind and the intellect, which reasons away the directives of conscience: that mighty inner voice of the Son of God—it is unerring. Listen, deliberate that you have listened carefully and truly, and then hasten to act! For each act taken in obedience to the voice of God, whether the voice within or the voice of the LORD God who does stand in the doorway of thy tent speaking to thee—each act in obedience takes you nearer to the place of the homing and the return and the hour when God shall surely give to the seed of Abraham, numberless as the stars,[6] all of the earth itself.

But yet the horror that I witnessed in that deep sleep was the realization of the four hundred years of bondage,[7] that and much more unto the hour of the present, when yet this people do not understand the true meaning of the Inner God and the Inner Son.

I say, let the breach be healed!

And in the sacrifice that I offered, beloved, there was a separation of the parts.[8] And the separation of the parts of the animal sacrifice did signify that there was a separation in this people, a separation between the soul and the I AM THAT I AM. And therefore, there did come down in the very center the angel of the LORD.

And to bring them together and thus to wed the soul to God does necessitate the true internalization of the Son in all of the joy and the beauty of that Universal Christ personified—yes, in the Lord and Saviour Jesus Christ; personified, yes, in those who will accept that Christ as their own True Self.

So it is, beloved, that the Christ, who has become the chief cornerstone in the temple, is yet a stumbling block to many.[9] "We have no need of him. We are Sons of God also!" I am ashamed of such response to the one whom the LORD God did send into the world that the world through him might have eternal Life.[10]

Yes, there are many Sons of God. But until the Son of God be fully self-realized, that Son is yet a part of the Universal Christ and not individualized because not adored, not internalized, not surrendered to. Thus, beloved, until you determine to imitate that Christ by the mirror image of the soul, you will not be fully bonded to the Holy Christ Self. Therefore, until you pass through that initiation of Sonship and Christhood, you cannot lay claim to Sonship. For Sonship is opportunity, and if opportunity is denied, if opportunity is not taken when [it is offered by] the one who can impart and initiate that particular initiation, beloved, the cycles [without Christhood] must turn and they turn again [for those who practice the denial of Christ both within and without].

And thus, for the two-thousand-year period of the age of

I Friendship with God

Pisces, I still hear the word "We have no need of Jesus Christ— *We are Sons of God.*" And I bow my head before the LORD, who came unto me with so great a promise, and I say:

"How long, O LORD, shall I struggle with this stiff-necked generation who know all things and yet know nothing, for they have not perceived the Son of God, nor in Jesus nor in themselves nor in their contemporaries nor in the little child who shall lead them!"

Therefore, the cleavage [between the soul and the I AM THAT I AM] remains and shall remain. And how long shall the LORD God extend opportunity unto those who in their spiritual pride deny their need for the Son of God? If they have no need for the Son of God, how can they have need for God himself?

I speak not only of those who are called whether the Hebrews or the Jews. I speak of all peoples who have lived under the dispensation of Jesus Christ in the age of Pisces and that not alone, but also in the golden-age civilization of Atlantis 35,000 years ago.[11] They come again and again and again!

What is this personal quarrel they have with the living Light of the ages?

Had God sent another Son or another, had another been chosen in heaven to be the fullness of the only begotten Son of the Father, full of grace and truth,[12] would they have rejected that one also?

Indeed they would! For the Christed ones have walked the earth. They have come. They have not had the full glory of the Lord Jesus Christ but they have fulfilled the requirements for the bonding to the heart of the Holy Christ Self, hence to the heart of Jesus.

There are not a few, beloved, and they walk the earth this day. But in each and every case where that Christ is raised up in the temple of the sons and daughters of Abraham, so that Christ, and therefore that one, is persecuted and not only persecuted but crucified.

Now I say, in the celebration of the five Sacred Hearts that you have taken up on the first Friday and the first Saturday of the month,[13] you can give the work that is needed to resolve this problem [of the rejection of the Son of God in the person of Jesus Christ].

Thus, I have come as Abraham, your father, to plead with you to understand that it is the very force of Antichrist that came out of *Din* that turned judgment to become the destroyer of souls. That very force of Antichrist must be named [in your invocations and decrees] as the dweller-on-the-threshold of every fallen angel and of those who maintain the antithesis of the Tree of Life and the *sefirot*, those who have created the false, those who have created the substitution and the counterfeit. As you have been told, they live by a borrowed light, for they have no power of their own.

I ask, therefore, my sons and daughters, you whom I have shepherded in all ages and long before we came under my dispensation from Sanat Kumara in ages prior to Genesis—I ask you, then, to dedicate your services to the Sacred Heart of Jesus and the Immaculate Heart of Mary to the slaying of the worldwide force of Antichrist that allows my very own children of my very own loins to yet deny the Son of God within themselves. This does cause the holdup of the entire evolution of the planet and it will make laggards out of many who did begin as true children of the Light.

Yes, beloved, I have seen you again and again tackle the fierceness of the fallen ones arrayed against the Divine Mother in the earth in you and in the Messenger. Therefore, the hour has come when if you do not slay Antichrist that does go after the little ones full of such light who come forth from the womb, that does go after those of all ages and all levels and stations in life, there shall come a turning in the planet not toward Light but Darkness. For it is an hour when the people must choose whether Jesus Christ or Barabbas, whether the thief who has stolen the Light of the Zohar or the one who is the Saviour, who is able to bring together the bodies that have been cleaved.

Now then, beloved, I, in the person of your Guru then and now, fully intend to give you a map and an outline of what must be done systematically to deal with this force. It is a force deep in the core of the dweller-on-the-threshold. (Most of you here yet have the dweller-on-the-threshold, which does not completely dissolve until the hour of your ascension unless you have a specific attainment or have had specific intercession from me.)

Thus I say to you that at the core of the dweller-on-the-threshold within yourself is that point and it is the dot of the original beginning of the not-self. It is not the dot that produced the creation of you, the Christed being, but the dot that was the force, anti-Being.

That point, beloved, is what causes you to espouse Evil, to fall into the hands of the tempter, to deny the voice of the Inner Christ, to deny the giving of love and compassion in words of comfort when you could easily give them rather than remain silent. Therefore, each one must root out of himself that which is a force of division and separation whereby *Malkut, Tiferet* and *Keter* are not able to be as one.

It is a division in your members, which is dangerous. And all who have not come to resolution with the Son of God in heaven and the Son of God in the earth, as God has sent many, many servant-Sons through the ages, will have this point of the cleavage within, of the separation [of their souls] from God, and the profound angst, even that "angst" that is spoken of.

Yes, beloved, it is a deep nonresolution that will never come to resolution until you have made your peace [with Jesus the Christ]. You cannot make peace with the Son until you have made peace with the Father, and the reverse is the case. You cannot have peace with the Son unless you have made peace with the Mother and peace with the Holy Spirit.

Thus, the four personalities of the Godhead—the Father, Son, Holy Spirit and the Mother—must be raised up in you. This means you must come to a resolution within and without, at the level of the human consciousness and the divine consciousness, with this identity in all other persons in your life.

Do you understand what I speak of, beloved? ["Yes."]

The foundations of psychology that have been laid and taught to you under the guidance of the Ascended Master Kuthumi will take you to the place of understanding—yes, understanding. But that is where psychology stops. Psychology cannot give you the full power of that lamp and that furnace, the full sacred fire and the very smoking that does take place when there is intense, deep transmutation.

Yes, the LORD God initiated me that night that I might receive in trust the commission and go forth and never waver, even unto the present hour, in my responsibility to the seed of Light of Sanat Kumara.

Yes, beloved, there must be peace within your members. And some of you have stubbornly refused to examine the components of selfhood, have stubbornly avoided the altar, and therefore the fire could not leap to greet you!

For where were you when I came? There was an empty place at the rail, a space that you did not fill.

How can I impart the fire when you so remove yourselves?

I am with you every day!

Shall I tell you how many times I have simply withdrawn because I could not get your attention from outer focusing on the outer things of this world?

Well, I tell you, the events and personalities of the world will pass. And you will pass also. The question is: Will you come to the gates of Darjeeling full of the knowledge of this world and yet empty of the spiritual fire?

Try me. Try me! *Try me, I say!* Call for my fire if you desire a new self, for *purge you I will!* And if you dare to remain a dolt at the same level for the rest of your life, I, Abraham, will shun you. For how can you neglect so great a salvation?[14]

Salvation is the elevation of the soul through the ten *sefirot,* through the steps and stages. Acquaint now yourselves with Holy Justinius and the seraphim of God and know God as he sends his living flames of the *sefirot,* guarded and borne by the bearers, the seraphim themselves.

Every day is opportunity to receive of my fire!

How can you leave me and expect that I will follow you?

Shall I follow you to the ends of the earth?

Maybe. But, beloved, there is a timetable in your chart, and I speak of the chart of the Keeper of the Scrolls. There is a timetable. Therefore, read. Read of the wise one. So it is written: There is a time to sow and a time to reap, a time to be born and a time to die.[15] Yes, there is a time to face Morya squarely, to get straight your life, to love the will of God more than wealth and material things and indulgences and sensuality that does but waste the precious fire I give you. Come into alignment with me in this conference—ten days, ten *sefirot,* ten steps of consciousness.

I AM Abraham always and I nurture my own. But many a parent will tell you that for all the nurturing, the children did not quite make it. Thus, there must be a resiliency, a receptive chord. Do not become pillars of stone, therefore set in the gaze, the mien and the stance of the proud who think they have come far enough on the spiritual path and now can be above all others. Beloved ones, you are in your infancy, but you can quickly accelerate to be wise men and women, wise children of the Light.

And who are the wise ones?

The wise ones are those who pursue the bonding to *Tiferet, Tiferet,* the Son of God—yes, the bonding to the very center of cosmos, the very nucleus of the atom, the compassion, the fires of compassion.

I place my Electronic Presence over you so that you can feel in this very moment what it is like to surrender to God and walk with God and be happy in the greatest happiness you have ever known until joy spills from your faces as sunbeams come from your very auras and you are a sun center.

Do not fear to give up those attachments, for the will of God will lead you by the shortest distance to the very goal that you desire. Do not shun me or the will of God. Sanat Kumara has sent me to *you* personally. I have accompanied you to this *FREEDOM 1992.*

I have come here. I have come to greet my own and I desire to do so from the very heart of Father.

Some of you have not known a father or have not had a good relationship with a father in this life or another life. The child within is keenly disappointed and does suffer for want of this true and so necessary association. Beloved ones, we understand these things. But unless we demand more than an understanding of our psychology, we shall remain in that rut.

You cannot lift yourself up by your bootstraps, but I, Morya, will take you on my magic carpet. (We have used them long centuries. It is not a myth.) And I will take you to new heights of consciousness. I will show you how you can be in thirty years—if this night you determine to make your resolution with the Father, with your own father in heaven and on earth and in me—that you might make your peace with the Son. You cannot love the Son in yourself if you do not love the Father who did bring you forth.

Therefore I ask you, do you love me as your father? ["Yes!"]

I come to you with the deepest love of my heart for healing, but you must know how to erase with the violet flame, how to encircle with Astrea's sword and circle of blue flame, how to bind the very record of that dweller-on-the-threshold, how to purge yourself of the patterns and even the misuse of the Light that sometimes well-meaning and sometimes not so well-meaning parents have put upon you.

I say this day, I am freeing you from this bondage and I am freeing you by sacred fire! And those of you who have studied the causes within and studied the books recommended whereby you might become masters of your own soul's psychology will find even a greater resolution for my coming and your coming.

Let us move forward together! Let us go hand in hand! I place my Electronic Presence with each one of you as your father. I am exclusively and uniquely your own. It is a one-on-one relationship. You can have all of me to yourself, each one of you. For I AM that Son whose point of origin is the Great Central Sun, and therefore the Light that passes through me to you is the replication again and again and again of beloved Alpha. Thus, beloved, know this relationship and accept it as sufficient.

If you yet yearn for the human relationship that can never be because the father is no longer here, not accessible or available or does not have the capacity to be father, then what will you do? Will you mourn forever?

I want the very roots of the sorrow of the deepest self to be consumed, and I am coming to you nearer and nearer with the fire of the lamp and of the furnace of God. I am coming, beloved, for you have willingly placed yourselves in my presence. Therefore, I shall do with you what I will, yet you may yet reject my offering.

I wish to pick you up and put you in another place on the other side of the world, you see! I wish to take you out of that circle of your karma and your human creation and your becoming set in your ways as the years move on. But, of course, this is almost not possible without your cooperation.

As someone once told the Messenger regarding a loved one, you cannot simply transplant a little flower, for it will not grow in another soil. So, you see, beloved, if I should pick you up and place you now in the true Shamballa of the East, you might be happy there for an hour or a day or three days. But pretty soon you would say, "Take me back to the scene of the familiar, the scene of my karma, the people I know, the people I need and those who need me." So you see, beloved, for this acceleration, greater than that which is usual, there must come about in you a *leap* in consciousness.

I show you the outline of my life. And I took the leap in consciousness. Each time I felt the contact of God, knew the presence of the LORD, I took the opportunity for a giant leap and I skipped the steps in between.

Did I suffer a loss?

Was I lonely?

Well, a bit, I must admit, for the human consciousness itself is slow to adjust to abrupt changes. But, beloved, I brought up the rear of that human consciousness and I beat it into submission and I said, "We go this day! We march! We go into battle for the slaughter of the [Nephilim] kings." That victorious battle enabled me to bring the fruits of my victory as a mighty tithe to the beloved Melchizedek, king of Salem and priest of the Most High God.[16]

Yes, beloved, on and on and on we went, Sarah and I. And on and on and on we go this day. We would take you with us, but I announce to you that cycles do come to an end and you are nearing the day when you must enter and come up to the level of the Father and the fatherhood of earth's children that I have borne. For the cycles will turn. Some will move on. Some will remain. But you must step into the shoes of your God Parents, even as you take over the functions of your human parents when you reach adulthood.

It is an hour, then, when I reach the greatest proximity to your souls. May you know that I love you. May you know that there is a palace of Light where we meet and there is a retreat in Darjeeling.

As the cycles have turned this summer solstice, I am the closest that I shall ever be to my chelas. I offer you my Diamond Heart, beloved, and all that I am.

Will you have me and have all of me? ["Yes!"]

I bid you enter the next step and pursue oneness with God daily.

"The Summit Lighthouse Sheds Its Radiance O'er All the World to Manifest as Pearls of Wisdom." This dictation by the **Ascended Master El Morya as the Patriarch Abraham** was **delivered** by the Messenger of the Great White Brotherhood Elizabeth Clare Prophet on **Friday, June 26, 1992,** during the ten-day conference *FREEDOM 1992: "Joy in the Heart"* held at the **Royal Teton Ranch, Park County, Montana.** Prior to El Morya's dictation the Messenger read Genesis 15. The dictation followed the Messenger's lecture "Keys from Judaism— the Kabbalah and the Temple of Man." Some of the teaching in El Morya's dictation builds on concepts covered in the lecture. For a fuller understanding of the dictation, it is important that you hear the lecture, soon to be released on audio- and videocassette. It is also recommended that you read Genesis 14 and 15. [**N.B.** Throughout this *Pearl,* bracketed material denotes words unspoken yet implicit in the dictation, added by the Messenger under El Morya's direction for clarity in the written word.] (**1**) Gen. 15:17. (**2**) **Abraham, the Friend of God.** II Chron. 20:7; Isa. 41:8; James 2:23. (**3**) Josh. 24:2. (**4**) Gen. 15:1. (**5**) Heb. 11:8–19. (**6**) **"I will multiply thy seed as the stars of the heaven..."** Gen. 15:5; 22:17, 18; Heb. 11:11, 12. (**7**) Gen. 15:12–16. (**8**) Gen. 15:7–11, 17. (**9**) **Christ, chief cornerstone and stumbling block.** Ps. 118:22, 23; Isa. 8:13–15; 28:16; Matt. 21:42; Acts 4:10–12; Rom. 9:31–33; I Cor. 1:23; Eph. 2:20; I Pet. 2:6–8. (**10**) John 3:16, 17. (**11**) See Elizabeth Clare Prophet, **"The Golden Age of Jesus Christ on Atlantis,"** on videocassette (161 min., $33.95 plus $1.48 postage, GP91106) and on audiocassette (163 min., $13.00 plus $.98 postage, A91074). (**12**) John 1:14. (**13**) **Five Sacred Hearts.** See pp. 244–45, 248 n. 7. (**14**) Heb. 2:3. (**15**) Eccles. 3:1–8. (**16**) Gen. 14; Heb. 7:1, 2.

26

"I Am Not Done with Pisces!"
Turn Back the Adversary in Defense of the Child!

I come to you out of the heart of God—thy God and my God—for there is but one. I come to you containing in my Causal Body long ages of preparation for the age of Pisces.

From the hour of the Lord Jesus' reign 35,000 years ago on Atlantis[1] unto the hour of the betrayal of his reign by the dark forces, through the aeons that have descended, the preparation of the age of Pisces and the coming of that Son of God was ongoing.

The challenge to the hierarchy of Light was how to lead those rebellious ones back to the heart of the Sun. Thus, all parties to that civilization and to the succeeding civilizations of India and throughout the earth have reincarnated again and again and again, all being led (sometimes pulled by the very nose) to the heart of the Christic experience within their very own heart: their heart one with the Heart of God.

Oh, it has been a hard, hard generation who have resisted the coming of my Son, Immanuel! Therefore, I did reincarnate again and again. And you are not aware of my many incarnations as high priest, as scientist, alchemist, originator of dispensations of the Seventh Ray in every age to the very limit that that age could endure and that would be provided for by dispensations of the Solar Logoi.

Notably, my embodiment as the prophet Samuel did bring me to the place of the anointing of the young son, David, son of Jesse.[2]

Yes, there was the one who must be king and who should descend from his own Christhood unto the hour of his being [embodied as] the Lamb of God to hold that office of the Lamb of God, who has been, who was and is slain from the very foundation of the lower worlds. Since these lower worlds have been created and sustained in measure by fallen angels and in far greater measure by the LORD God, who would not see his evolutions lost, so that Lamb [has embodied and] has been slain.

Your Holy Christ Self is indeed the Lamb of God. And as you allow this Christ to be "formed and re-formed in you"[3] in the likeness of the Holy One of God, so you shall know the experience of the slaying of the Lamb and the attempt [of the fallen angels] to pierce to the very soul of your being in order to snuff out the candle of the living Christ in the earth.

Now I have many sons and daughters, but they began with the One. Remember there was a moment before the creation when creation was not, but only *Ein Sof*. And remember how the Light went forth and did expand and the *sefirot* came forth on a descending scale.

I speak, then, of the moment of the appearing of *Tiferet*, the Son of Righteousness, the only begotten of that God. Therefore, the hour of that coming was the hour of the descent of the living Christ midpoint [on the Tree of Life]. And therefore that Christ Presence did seek to woo the soul by the lesser *sefirot* [below *Tiferet*] to the level of the middle figure [the Son] of the Chart of your I AM Presence. This Jesus came to do [in not one but many incarnations throughout the ages].

And so I was chosen to father the Son of God [in his final incarnation] and in so doing to father the Piscean age, as I said, by long preparation beforehand. All the players in that scene of the family and all whom we met and worked with, aye, John the Baptist and great adepts of the East and those with whom we were in contact [whose names are] not recorded—all those players to the scene, including disciples and the multitudes, descended knowing that they would act out the greatest pageant of all history. And in acting it out, I say to you, beloved, they were counseled and trained to play their role of individual Christhood and to play it to its fullest.

Thus, beloved, you are also counted in this mandala of Lightbearers—the beauteous, wondrous pattern of souls coming together, each one having a precious jewel to contribute to the Piscean dispensation. For reason of the dark powers that have been unchecked, that should have been checked and could have been checked had the powers and the forces of God been directed to that end, I tell you, the Piscean age [has been an age of darkness when it] could have been an age of great light, even a golden age.

Thus, *you* have come of age! Thus, you have understood profoundly that God has placed in your hands the work of binding the force of Evil, which has no power except the power that the mass consciousness does give to it. Therefore, in every place where you raise up that Christ, where the individual son or daughter of God or child of God does give glory to that Christ and raise it up, so there is that point of challenge, that point of saying [to the hosts of Darkness]: "Thus far and no farther! Go back into your lair. You shall not spot the footprints of my Lord!"

Blessed ones, to take your stand with the will of the mind, the fire of the heart, the devotion of the soul, the power of the indwelling Spirit and the power of the YOD HE VAU HE: this is your calling! And I tell you, a new empowering is coming upon you in this conference. Therefore, to receive it and seal it, I say, be purged, be rejuvenated, be restored, be illuminated, beloved ones!

For the day must dawn, must it not?

Yes, the day must dawn when you find yourself as the mirror image of your own beloved Holy Christ Self. And therefore, the separation will be slight and as that rapprochement occurs wherein the soul no longer fears to enter into complete union, no longer fears the wedding day or the wedding garment, I say, beloved, you shall walk the earth again as Christed ones as you did in that ancient golden-age civilization on Atlantis when you had balanced 51 percent of your karma. And many did ascend who went on to balance 100 percent of their karma in that time and dispensation, while others, some among you included, did lose ground and therefore did lose the 51 percent they had gained.

And therefore, you have traversed long embodiments and a certain amount of the drudgery of dealing with returning karma as it has accelerated in this many-thousand-year cycle* that is upon you again. Yes, beloved, hours and cycles turn and you have come back to the very point of beginning. In the Beginning, the point of Light and then the midpoint, the moment when, though you had garnered Light, you lost it.

How did you lose it, beloved?

I can tell you the fallen angels known as serpents are more than cunning. They have perverted the signs and the signals of the Kabbalah and therefore used it to imprison souls of Light. Not by mere enticement or the pride of the eye or the glitter of the body did they draw you away but by the very black magic that is the

---
*The 25,800-year cycle of returning karma has come full circle with the conclusion of the age of Pisces.

misuse of the set of the *sefirot*. The counterfeit set [of the ten *sefirot*] had been created by the one *Din* in the intensity of the judgment itself, the judgment that [the fallen ones] meted out upon the children of God. And thus, Evil did gain hold in the manner described to you by the Messenger according to the teachings of the Zohar.

Now understand, beloved, as you have the knowledge of the I AM THAT I AM and as you have called upon that power, so you have called upon *Keter*. And therefore you have had that point of contact [with the first of the ten *sefirot*]. So make the point of contact with each of the *sefirot* and understand that by so placing your heart and soul and mind and will and dynamic decree in these chalices, by setting yourself at a like vibration with them, you can now turn around [the evil works of *Din* and those who carry the *Din* consciousness] and demand the judgment of the forces of Antichrist and therefore work the work of God on earth, which is the ultimate binding of the evil force. Yes, beloved, the "other side" must be tackled, as the beloved Abraham has told you.

And therefore we come, fathers both, who have nurtured you. And we come with the blessed Mother Mary. We come with other Mothers ascended and the one unascended,* that you might know that there is a nurturing spirit in the heart of the earth to nurture you to the place where you can stand face-to-face, eyeball-to-eyeball, as they say, with the adversary who did betray you at Maitreya's Mystery School, known as the Garden of Eden.

And now in this hour and in this day, with increased self-knowledge and confidence in the absolute protection of the Spirit of the living God in your I AM Presence and Archangel Michael, you can indeed challenge, turn back and bind the Adversary that he go not out again to tempt the little ones, to violate their souls, to abuse their bodies and their minds.

Beloved ones, there are the filthy ones in the earth who are engaged in the violation of the sacred chakras of life in little children. You must demand their judgment and their binding before the altar of the LORD God! Come forward, then, in defense of the child! Come forward in defense of the Mother, the Cosmic Virgin, and all of the fathers in the world, who must come now and stand by their wives and by the mothers of their children!

Let the Holy Family be restored! This is the work, beloved. It does take [your giving] the judgment calls dictated by my Son Jesus and the call for the binding of the dweller-on-the-threshold (as you

---

*The embodied Messenger Elizabeth Clare Prophet bears the mantle of the World Mother. In that office she, with other devotees of the World Mother, makes continual intercessory prayer on behalf of the world's children.

have been told) of the Antichrist in the earth and the seed of Antichrist planted in you long ago, which must be exorcised and excised by you.

Yes, I AM Saint Joseph, and I walk in the full mantle of my office as protector of Mary and of every mother and every woman and of every child in the earth. And I tell you, beloved, that I play that role. As many in the earth call to me as Saint Joseph, so I respond to that name.

Knowing who I am, therefore, I can be called by any name, any key of any name of any past incarnation. Thus, I have rolled them into one and determined to be called by you merely "Holy Brother," *Saint Germain.*

I, beloved, come to you with a heart full of love and hope and determination. I come to you in the realism of that which must be bound first in yourself before it can be bound by you, in the name of God, in others. I say, submit yourselves to the altar of God and trust my mouthpiece, for I can work with you and deal with you if you recognize that the Messenger is a personal Messenger to each one of you when you need that Messenger.

I say, beloved, it is too late, too late and far too late—if you count from the hours of 35,000 years ago (and we have returned to that cycle now in this day) when you walked away from the Son of God—[to continue your dalliance in the doings of your ego]. It is not a time to assert the human ego. It is not a time for argumentation and squabbling and a need for personal glory.

Beloved, all these things must be set aside in the perspective that has been given to you many times before, and it is this:

Whatever you think you might gain from another round in the world, whether it be the intellectual world, the psychological world, the world of art and theater, the world of music and science, beloved, you have seen it all, you have done it all before. It is in your Causal Body. You have satisfied your soul's need to do these things again and again!

But I tell you, all of your efforts in all of the fields that are open to you will come to naught if you do not put first things first, [in this case] the binding of the evil force [at work] at this level of the worlds. Understand this. Civilizations will crumble. Wars shall come to pass. Plagues shall be upon the earth, and earth changes. [Yes, unless you bind the evil force,] all these things will effectively wipe out the years of your efforts in this or that discipline.

But I tell you, if you make your first and foremost holy calling the binding of that Evil, which means, beloved, to become [day by day] the fullness of the embodiment of your Christhood so that you are indeed empowered to bind that Evil, then all these other things will fall in line. And what you put into a work of your calling and your profession will endure and it will be sealed by the violet flame. And no tempter or fallen angel will be able to come into your playroom and knock down the towers you have builded with your blocks.

Yes, beloved, civilization will stand or fall. It will stand only if you determine to bind the force of Antichrist that was in the heart of Herod whereby he sent out his henchmen to slaughter the male babies in order to be sure to destroy the living Christ Jesus. And therefore, the angels of the Seventh Ray led us in the flight into Egypt[4] and it was indeed a flight from the terror of the powers-that-be of the time.

And do not think that it was not a challenge for me and for Mary. Yes, it was indeed! For we were in the form that you are in this day, we were in the times and we knew exactly what could happen if we did not play our role.

Care for your children! Care even more for your souls and their souls! Care, beloved, and guard the sacred citadels. For Christed ones have been lost in the earth for want of parents who had the teaching and the understanding of maintaining the I-AM-the-Guard consciousness.

Trust no one with your children except those who are tried-and-true devotees, beloved. Take care. For the Devil does yet wander about seeking whom he may devour,[5] and he would devour the very souls of your children before they may come of age for the realization of their Christhood.

I say, this place is indeed the cradle of a new civilization of Lightbearers! And I, Saint Joseph, am on hand as always to inaugurate cycles and dispensations by the power of the Seventh Ray.

Therefore, I come to you in the great glory of God and I tell you that the mission of Jesus Christ was an absolute God-success for those who did receive it and who did, therefore, by the power of his mouth-to-mouth, heart-to-heart resuscitation come into their own victory in the Light. But very quickly the fallen angels, the wolves in sheep's clothing, did come along, did distort the doctrine, did destroy the works of Origen and others. And therefore the perversion of the teachings of my Son are in the earth today, entrenched in doctrine and dogma and inciting fear in the many hearts of Light who should have gathered in this tent for this convocation upon the coming of Alpha and Omega—blessed be the holy names of our Father-Mother God.

Yes, beloved, they ought to be here! And because the forces of

Antichrist attacking them through the media, through the anticult movement have not been bound, therefore there is that wall that does stand between them and this altar. I say, tear down the wall by the fiat of the LORD! Tear down the wall, beloved!

For many, many can drink at this fount. And in the twinkling of an eye, as it were, even in a ten-day cycle or a period at Summit University, they can see through all of the false teachings and see through the false teachers and know who they are and know them by their fruits,[6] or should we say by their "nonfruits"? For they produce nothing of worth from their tree of life but only turn back the children of the Sun [from their Sunward flight]. They are the gray ones, and they are becoming grayer and blacker by the hour as their karma descends.

Beloved ones, this is truly the hour of which my Son did speak. Lo, the harvest is white, yet the laborers are few.[7]

Who shall be the harvester of souls in my name?

I come to you to place my mantle and Presence of Saint Joseph over you so that you may go and do the work and be our hands and feet, our hearts and our chakras in the earth.

Blessed ones, if you will spend your life and time and hours in this endeavor, I assure you that to have my Presence over you will ultimately manifest in you as the regaining of your strength, your health, your youth.

Beloved, if I may work through you, I will raise you up. But you must give attention to me. Remember me as I walked by the child Jesus, as I walked with Mary and as I guided them until the hour of my transition. Remember, then, how Jesus did go alone, joining the caravan to the East.[8] Yes, beloved, the Son of God was overshadowed by angels and by the hierarchy of the dispensation of the Piscean age and by myself when I was no longer in embodiment.

Yes, beloved, we have work to do! We have some unfinished business with the fallen ones who have moved against my Son and against you as my sons and daughters in every age, lifetime after lifetime.

This is the day and the hour to say to them:

> Thus far and no farther! We have the Word! We have the name! We have the understanding! We shall invoke the power of God and it shall not fail us. And your day is *done!* You have no power! Your day is done and you will not seduce our souls nor our children's souls nor our children's children's souls!

We shall send forth a mighty ripple of Light that is the ribbon of our own crystal cord. And we shall send it into the future that all evolutions and Lightbearers shall know! They shall know your name, ye fallen ones, ye extraterrestrials who have come to manipulate the genetic code of the evolutions of God! *We shall see you bound!* For we know your name and we pronounce it and we say: Your judgment descends in the name of God now! [49-second standing ovation]

Now I say to you, beloved, the fallen ones have been working overtime on you and many others of your companions who are not here for one reason or another. And they have sought to move you this way and that way. They have worked hard to insert into your mind thoughts that are not your own, interpretations of life, inserting desires in the mind and in the desire body.

Yes, beloved, you must take care and be on guard and protect your aura and forcefield and give the fiats, as the Messenger has demonstrated them, with the full power of the Word, the fervor of the heart chakra, the power of that mighty threefold flame that is the very same flame that does burn in the heart of Alpha and Omega. There is no difference, beloved, except in size, intensity and balance.

Therefore, you are the issue of God: Beware, for those who are not the issue of God who wander about, as I have said, seeking whom they may devour, have played with you and with some of you they have had a heyday. You have been moved this way and that way. You have been seized with an idea that they have planted. You have followed it and it has burst as a bubble, taking with it your supply and your very lifeblood.

And then you have gone another way and a-this-way and a-that-way instead of first seating yourself in the place of the Holy of holies of your heart chakra with your Holy Christ Self and simply saying:

> *Be still and know that I AM God and that the I AM THAT I AM within me is that God! And I will not be moved from my course of service to my God.*

Any distraction will do, any stray thought, just to get you away from your own interior castle, your own inner altar and the altar of the Most High God.

I want you to know that the angels of the LORD have so moved in on planet earth that they are just waiting almost breathless for someone of any religion or walk [of life] but especially for you, beloved, since you understand the science of the spoken Word, to utter the call for the binding of this and that fallen one. [These fallen ones] are ready to be picked off, beloved ones! And the angels [of the LORD] are ready to do your bidding. Won't you take this conference, then, [as an opportunity to take your stand] in defense of the work of my Son Jesus Christ, which is the work of Him that sent him?[9]

Yes, beloved, do that work for the binding of that Antichrist and see how the world will change because you have walked in this world, you have worked in this world, you have placed the imprint of the soles of your feet and the soul of your temple in the very planet itself.

And I tell you, one day it shall be said: "Blessed are these feet and the imprints they have left that we may walk in them—[the footprints of] the saints of God who saw the oncoming Darkness and reversed it by the power of the judgment of God to defeat the judgment of the fallen angels."

Now I, Saint Joseph, give you your very first assignment and it is this: As you lay your head to rest this night, make the call to be taken to the Royal Teton Retreat at the Grand Teton. You have done the work magnificently, and the multiplication of your Ashram rituals as you come together in such numbers is a beauty to behold as the whole planet glistens with an *antahkarana* that you are establishing and strengthening every hour and day of your presence here, multiplied by the chalice of Elohim[10] in the Heart [of the Inner Retreat] and multiplied by the Western Shamballa and the heart of Lord Gautama Buddha, blessed be his name.

Therefore, from the heart of the Royal Teton Retreat you shall be escorted, then, to Yugoslavia, and you shall be accompanied by many legions of angels of the Seven Archangels and of the mighty God Surya. And you shall place your bodies in the midst of the people and you shall call at inner levels for the binding of the serpents and the fallen ones who are creating this slaughter.

Remember, beloved ones, after the flood of Noah the decree went forth that human government must be established for the defense of [human] life. When the nations and the governments of the earth cease to use their powers to defend life anywhere and everywhere upon this planet, I say the reason for being of both the nations and their governments has come to an end.

Now you have seen the great powers, and what have they done to stop this slaughter? Who has interceded?

All have turned their backs with silly sanctions and mealy-mouthed words and no action. And again and again and again the slaughter in the nation continues night and day until even you are sick of seeing it on the television.

Well, beloved, there are Lightbearers everywhere and there are Lightbearers in Yugoslavia. If this slaughter is allowed to continue, I tell you, it shall open such a depth of the bowels of hell (as it already has and which [opening] you must call for the cosmic reinforcements to seal) that this action [of the slaughter of the people] will then spread. It will be repeated in your own cities, even as you have seen the upheaval in Los Angeles. Beloved ones, these two situations are related.

Where the slaughter of the good and the evil, where the slaughter of people of any kind is allowed to continue and to go unchecked, there is a rending of the veils of the entire planet and an opening of the pits and of the astral plane. Therefore, beloved, this is a most urgent matter.

Let us seal the place where Evil dwells [in Yugoslavia and elsewhere]. Let us make the call to Astrea for the binding of the evil ones on the astral plane and in physical embodiment. And let us pray for the saving of the souls of Light.

Blessed hearts, war has been on this planet as long as there have not been Christed ones, such as yourselves and such as you are becoming, to stand up against that sinister force. War must end! Call therefore to Lord Krishna, to Karttikeya, to all the mighty ones of God who lead those armies of heaven, including the God Surya, that war may end upon this planet—and the warring within the members of the people and the warring in their souls.

Yes, beloved, you live in an age when you can triumph and triumph ultimately. And remember that you did not turn your back on Saint Germain and Portia, on Jesus Christ or Mary, his Mother, but you decided to confront that force directly, come what may, and to trust God to be your mighty shield, your buckler, your defense and your armour.

I AM Saint Joseph. And though I come as the Hierarch of Aquarius, I am not done with Pisces! For I am determined to see a victory out of it all and, through you and this Messenger, the publishing abroad of the true teachings of Jesus Christ. For they are the foundation of Aquarius *and Aquarius cannot rise without the self-knowledge of every man, woman and child upon this planet of his own Holy Christ Self and of the Son of God and of the I AM Presence and of the violet flame!*

See to it, then, ye warriors of the Spirit and of the earth! See to it, ye saints of God in the flesh! Now make your life count as it has never counted before in all past ages and graduate with glory in your ascension in the Light!

Leave, then, your children to move on in your footsteps. Do not spare the rod. I did not spare the rod with my son Jesus and therefore he grew up the disciplined one. Whether you think you have an avatar or not, recognize that the four lower bodies must be disciplined and the soul itself.

Yes, beloved, I AM Saint Joseph and I shall not relinquish my role either in the Catholic Church or anywhere where I am called. And where you call to my beloved wife, Mary, I AM there. Therefore when you sing the *Sanctissima* songs, know that I am a part of the answer and the resounding flame from the heart of the Blessed, the most blessed Cosmic Virgin, who embodied to give birth to your Saviour and my Saviour, your Lord and my Lord.

[43-second standing ovation]

"The Summit Lighthouse Sheds Its Radiance O'er All the World to Manifest as Pearls of Wisdom." This dictation by **Saint Joseph** was **delivered** by the Messenger of the Great White Brotherhood Elizabeth Clare Prophet on **Saturday, June 27, 1992,** during the ten-day conference FREEDOM 1992: "Joy in the Heart" held at the **Royal Teton Ranch, Park County, Montana.** Prior to the dictation, the Messenger delivered the first half of her lecture "Roots of Christian Mysticism" and led the congregation in giving Ashram rituals 4 and 5 — Sacred Ritual for Soul Purification and Sacred Ritual for Transport and Holy Work. Some of the teaching in Saint Joseph's dictation builds on concepts covered in the Messenger's June 26 lecture, "Keys from Judaism — the Kabbalah and the Temple of Man." For a fuller understanding of the dictation, it is important that you hear this lecture, soon to be released on audio- and videocassette. [**N.B.** Throughout this *Pearl,* bracketed material denotes words unspoken yet implicit in the dictation, added by the Messenger under Saint Joseph's direction for clarity in the written word.] Throughout these notes *PoW* is the abbreviation for *Pearls of Wisdom.* (**1**) See Elizabeth Clare Prophet, **"The Golden Age of Jesus Christ on Atlantis,"** on videocassette (161 min., $33.95 plus $1.48 postage, GP91106) and on audiocassette (163 min., $13.00 plus $.98 postage, A91074). (**2**) I Sam. 16:1–13. (**3**) Gal. 4:19. (**4**) Matt. 2:1–18. (**5**) I Pet. 5:8. (**6**) Matt. 7:15–20; 12:33; Luke 6:43–45. (**7**) John 4:35; Matt. 9:35–38; Luke 10:1, 2. (**8**) See Elizabeth Clare Prophet, ***The Lost Years of Jesus,*** available in hardbound ($19.95 plus $1.91 postage), softbound ($14.95 plus $1.48 postage), and pocket book ($5.95 plus $1.05 postage). (**9**) John 9:4. (**10**) **The chalice of Elohim.** See 1991 *PoW,* p. 552 n. 2.

Columbus Day Retreat October 8–12

Atlanta, Georgia
Castlegate Hotel

Make Your Plane and Hotel Reservations Now!

Beloved of Saint Germain's Heart,

I invite you to rediscover America as you celebrate with Saint Germain the 500th anniversary of Christopher Columbus' arrival in the West Indies. Be with me for our five-day retreat and recharge in Atlanta, Georgia, October 8 through 12, over the three-day holiday weekend. (Monday, October 12, is a national holiday.)

In his life as Columbus, Saint Germain set the stage for the rise of Western civilization with its great scientific advances and political, economic and religious freedom. I'm looking forward to discussing Columbus' life with you, including the criticisms by revisionist historians, in my lecture "Columbus: The Man and the Myth." I'm sure you'll also be interested in my lecture "Karma, Reincarnation and You," in which I examine the past lives of nine public figures.

The first dictation is Thursday, October 8, at 7 p.m.; the last is Monday night—the grand finale with dictations from Saint Germain and Jesus Christ. So don't plan on flying out till Tuesday morning or you'll miss the crowning moment.

Let's begin right now with an acceleration of violet flame decrees so we can present Saint Germain with a great big anniversary gift of oceans of violet flame.

I look forward to seeing all of you there.

Mother

Beloved Lord Lanto
FREEDOM 1992 "Joy in the Heart" III

27

Turn the World Around!
A Replica of the Great Causal Body

Welcome to my Heart! I come from the mountain of the LORD and I come to you as your tutor, beloved hearts. I will tutor your souls this night that you might receive Alpha and Omega having the maximum light focused in the crown chakra.

Therefore, the legions of the Second Ray and all who are the Buddhas and the Bodhisattvas are beginning to stream to this very Heart [of the Inner Retreat], cleansed now [and being cleansed] by the rain [for the clearing] of some ancient records that must be removed. And a little at a time they are being removed, beloved, year upon year, as the light you invoke does penetrate and as elemental life do cooperate.

It is the consideration of the Council of the Royal Teton and the Darjeeling Council that it is necessary for you to prepare more adequately to receive the Light* of Alpha and Omega and of Helios and Vesta. Therefore, we request that you concentrate on the decrees of the Second Ray and weave them in a braid with the violet flame, supporting this matrix with your judgment calls and pillars of blue flame from the heart of Hercules and Astrea, Archangel Michael and Surya.

Blessed ones, this preparation shall allow you to take and hold more Light—Light for the illumination of a world! For a new day has dawned and that new day, beloved, is the coming of age of many souls of Light, who will reach the point of the crown chakra

---
*Christ consciousness and God consciousness

as you raise up the sacred fire yourselves and hold that focus for the opening of the crown.

Jophiel and Christine contribute mightily to the dispensation of illumination. And I think, beloved ones, that you do not give them enough attention even in the singing of the hymn to Jophiel and Christine. For they do come and they do tarry, beloved, and they will saturate you in yellow fire! They will do much more if you will reconsider and reread their dictations. You will discover that they have mentioned the clearing of the planet of many conditions of ignorance and all manner of burden upon the people, but they must have your dedication to their activity.

We have therefore [had your Messenger] place on the cassette of the Archangel Michael songs[1] our songs to the beings of the yellow ray. Let them ring in your hearts and in your headsets so that you may have streams and ribbons of yellow fire coming down, imparting hope to the nations, hope to your own beating heart!

We of the Council of the Royal Teton are aware of the opening of mighty vortices of Light from the Central Sun and the opening of hearts and minds. Yet how the brains of the people of this planet need a scrubbing! How the sacred fire of the Mother must be focused and employed by you for this distillation, for this cleansing, beloved!

The yellow flame is a purifying fire. We desire to see the Christ Mind congruent with the lower mind, yet vessels must be emptied. And not only must there be a fasting from food but there must be a fasting from the entertainment of the world and the continual bombardment of the mind by the rhythms that are not rhythms at all but are arhythmic.

So, beloved, [in order that we may] use the minds of the people [constructively], we call upon you and all elemental life, and especially the body elementals of the people, to engage in that decree work whereby many may come into a true illumination of their own consciousness, their own being, their own lifestream, their own tie to God.

How can the people perceive the kingdom of God within them if that kingdom is so cluttered with the debris of the centuries?

Beloved ones, you may know this and you may have heard this before but I speak in the context of a world in transition, and unless the minds of the Lightbearers and of the children be quickened, where shall we find the planetary home?

You can see through the schemes of the politicians and those who represent you in the offices of government. This nation is in a crisis of confidence and many do not even dare to run for office again, so convinced are they that their constituents will not elect them.

Truly it is the hour of the raising up of the Feminine Ray. And may the woman who does come forth to represent the people be blessed, and let the man who does come forth be blessed. And let them both raise up the Light of the Feminine Ray, for only thereby will the true God-solution to the world's problems be found, beloved, and be known.

We come for the education of the heart as well as the mind. We come with gladness that so many students desire to study at Summit University and have answered the call of Kuan Yin to come to learn how to teach the children. Surely it is an hour when wisdom is exploding everywhere and the hunger for the knowledge of God is everywhere. And where shall they go for that water which they may drink which will give to them everlasting Life?[2]

Tell them! Tell them, I say to you! Tell them of the Christ that lives in the heart. Tell them of the soul that must rise. Tell them of the kingdom of God and of the world in transition and of the hour and the day when the mountains shall shake and the trembling of the earth shall come and there shall be the melting of the elements with a mighty fervent heat[3] and the alchemy of a world shall come about.

Let that alchemy and that quaking and shaking begin where you are! Let it begin, therefore, for the settling and the leveling and the leavening of consciousness. Let there be the repolarization of every lifestream upon this planet to the Great Central Sun Magnet! Come forth, O legions of Light!

Now behold with your inner eye how rings upon rings of angels of the yellow flame do congregate. And so the legions of Holy Justinius, Captain of Seraphic Bands, do come with their rings upon rings of white fire. And therefore we are building in this place, beloved ones, a replica of the Great Causal Body and we begin with the white fire core of the seraphim of God, who establish their fount of Light in the Great Central Sun. And the legions of the yellow ray come.

And therefore the first two spheres of the Causal Body are being established over this place and these two spheres, beloved, relate to certain evolutions, certain key lifestreams, who must make their ascension through the victory of those spheres and those worlds and those preparations that they long ago received in those quadrants of the Great Causal Body of God in the Great Central Sun.

Therefore, as we lay down this replica of the Great Central Sun Magnet during this conference, you will find that there will be an awakening within your soul of your experiences in the heart of the Great Central Sun with your twin flame in the Beginning. And therefore you will remember why you have come, what you were sent to do, what was the point of your origin and destiny. See, then, how, nestled in the white fire core of Alpha and Omega, you were born sons and daughters of God, mated to go forth to bring the full complement of the Father-Mother to the evolutions whom you would reach.

It is time to go back to that point of origin, to begin the whole round all over again and to retrace it, almost as with a computer of the Mind of God—to go through light-years of the descent of the soul finally to these octaves, to trace your footsteps and then to engage in the reverse and to return, [step by karmic step,] all the way back to that point of origin.

Thus, in going to the center, in coming out from the center and going unto it again, you are weaving the mighty cosmic daisy and you are seeing the increase and the adding unto your Being, unto the I AM THAT I AM, of these mighty rings of Light. They are vast, beloved! The rings of Light incorporate the entire cosmos, and yet you can relate to that individualized Causal Body as a mighty sphere above you.

Is not this the wondrous activity of our God, beloved?

Is it not the action whereby the living Christ does reach out to save that which is lost?

Thus, out of the fiery purity of your original blueprint, go forth into the golden yellow sphere and reactivate the Mind of God within you and allow the fat upon the brain to be removed and dissolved until the brain itself glistens like crystal and is able to coalesce the white fire of God of your Holy Christ Self.

What a worthy goal! What a joyous goal to empty the pockets of the cells of every organ of the body and every atom of those organs. What a joy, beloved, to find yourself being restored to the Adam Kadmon, yes, beloved ones, to the original matrix of perfect man and perfect womb-man.

To return to that point, beloved, will allow you to bring forth again original root races and lifestreams who also go back to that etheric blueprint and have been denied it and therefore have not entered into embodiment. I speak also of the seventh root race.

Now then, for the turning around of worlds, let the physical bodies be prepared, let the desire bodies be prepared, let the etheric body be prepared, let the mental body be prepared!

III Turn the World Around!

Beloved souls of Light, hear my call in this hour! Hear my awakening, even as I take hold of the giant sheet that does traverse a cosmos. And I shake it, beloved! And the waves go forth, the waves of illumination, the waves of white-fire purity, preceded, then, by legions of the violet flame and of the blue lightning and of the Ruby Ray, who are clearing the cosmos for the descent of the sons and daughters of God.

There are so very many who desire to descend to this level for the rescue mission of the Christs and the Bodhisattvas. They are in place, beloved. Now we come to see that you are in place and that you understand how to seek the refinement of the Spirit.

I AM Lanto, Chohan of the Second Ray. I come on behalf of the Royal Teton Council and I come on behalf of Alpha and Omega. I plead with you: Let not this nation go down in ignorance for a failure to educate the children in the true things of the Spirit and to set the geometry of the material universe in right programs of education so that [the children we send forth] might be vessels for a greater science, a greater sound of music and discoveries and dispensations that may be channeled through them because, beloved, you have laid the foundation and given them the proper teaching as well as the education of the heart.

Let there be the turning around, beloved! For you know there does come a time in the downward [spiral of] degeneration, whether of a body or an organ, when it simply fulfills itself in the death spiral. *There is a time to turn a world around and there is a time when it is no longer possible.*

I say, you have come to the point on this day and date wherein it is possible to turn the world around! And yet I say to you: Insert a mighty momentum of fervent prayer into the earth in this place to start that spiral, to make yourselves congruent with Elohim! For unless you do, beloved, there may not come another opportunity.

How long, how long can Elohim, therefore, hold back the avalanche of the descent of civilizations worldwide?

You are seeing it everywhere. Do not become ho-hum about what you see, for what you see is truly the most dangerous aspect of a world in transition. And instead of [seeing a world] going up, [you are seeing] a world going into [the spirals of] self-disintegration. Look all around you and see the bodies and minds that are disintegrating.

Know whereof I speak! And know that it is the angels of the Second Ray that must come in your name and by your call for the mighty quickening of the people! For their ears, their minds, their hearts, their eyes have waxed dull and they no longer see cause related to effect and effect related to cause.

I cry out for enlightenment and for the enlightened ones to decree for that enlightenment unto all who can potentially carry it, namely, the Christ-bearers, the children of the Light and all who will come into our camp and determine once and for all to be servants of God.

I have made a plea to you, beloved, perhaps not as great as I would have liked to. But I must speak, as I speak from my heart, and I must tell you that to burden you anymore or to burden the councils of the Brotherhood anymore would perpetuate my delivery too long.

Therefore, I cast out a flame of hope! I cast out cloven tongues of yellow fire! And they sit upon you, one and all, on the crown chakra as though it were the day of Pentecost, and yet it is not. It is the day of the coming of the Lords of the Second Ray. It is the day of the coming of the Buddhas and the Bodhisattvas. It is the day of the coming, beloved ones, of a commitment and a promise that must be on both sides.

I ask you to give attention to the yellow ray and see what you can do to *awaken* America!

I AM Lanto, always very near to you in the quietness of Wisdom's flame.

"The Summit Lighthouse Sheds Its Radiance O'er All the World to Manifest as Pearls of Wisdom." This dictation by **Lord Lanto** was **delivered** by the Messenger of the Great White Brotherhood Elizabeth Clare Prophet on **Sunday, June 28, 1992,** during the ten-day conference FREEDOM 1992: "Joy in the Heart" held at the **Royal Teton Ranch, Park County, Montana.** Preceding the dictation, the Messenger delivered the second half of her lecture "Roots of Christian Mysticism." [**N.B.** Throughout this Pearl, bracketed material denotes words unspoken yet implicit in the dictation, added by the Messenger under Lord Lanto's direction for clarity in the written word.] **(1)** *Hail Light Victorious! A Salute to Archangel Michael, Captain of the LORD's Host,* 17 songs performed by the Church Universal and Triumphant Choir conducted by Elizabeth Clare Prophet. 55 min., stereo recording, available on CD ($11.95 plus $1.05 postage, D92045) and on audiocassette ($8.95 plus $.75 postage, A92045); words to the music included in accompanying booklet. Send for your copy today and sing your devotions to the Lord—never alone but always all one with the devotees who make a joyful sound unto the Lord at the Royal Teton Ranch! **(2)** John 4:6–14. **(3)** II Pet. 3:10, 12.

I AM the Witness

"Jesus Loved the Little Children Most!"

My Dear Guru Master:

You have such a tender heart concerning children that I know this story will warm your heart. It happened only because of your devotion to your calling and your faithfulness to the Teachings of the Ascended Masters.

I now work as a volunteer in a hospital that treats children with cancer. My duty is to read to, rock, play with or hold the children—whatever seems needed at the time.

One little girl, Heather Elizabeth, was very dear to my heart. She was three years old, and I spent much extra time with her. She came from a Catholic home so knew a bit about Jesus and Mother Mary.

I would rock her and, as she lay on a contour pillow on my lap, I would tell her about Jesus and how he loved the little children and especially *her*. She never tired of hearing of Jesus and would ask over and over again for the story about the disciples telling the mothers not to bring the children to bother him. When I would get to the part where Jesus said, "Suffer the little children to come unto me and forbid them not," she would finish the story every time in her own words, saying: "Jesus loved the little children most!" I did my best to make Jesus real to her.

Sometimes she would cry when I started to leave, and I would promise her that a special angel would come and be with her. I assured her angels were all around even if we couldn't see them. Then I would say a simple prayer for the angels to watch over her and I could go.

We talked about God, Jesus, Mother Mary and the angels many times. One day I told her about Lady Master Nada, who especially loved children. I showed her Lady Master Nada's picture and, oh, how she did love her! I carefully explained that she could talk to Lady Master Nada or Jesus or Mother Mary anytime she wanted to—that they loved to have children talk to them.

She learned that she must call to the one she wanted by name. She *understood*. She was so trusting, and it was so sweet to hear her call the angels herself when it was time for me to leave her.

Last Wednesday she had a painful night, and when I saw her in the morning she looked so tired. I asked her if she called Lady Master Nada to come and help her and she said, "Yes, Lady Nada put her *cool* hands on my head and made me feel better and I went to sleep."

I believe that with all my heart. I had taught her what the word "cool" meant, so she *knew* when something cool touched her.

She had sky blue eyes. I have no idea what color hair she would have had. She had none. Such a precious little one! She would have been four on Valentine's Day.

They called me this morning to tell me that Heather Elizabeth had left in her sleep to be with the angels sometime in the early evening. I am sure Lady Master Nada welcomed her.

If it had not been for your teachings, I would never have known about Lady Master Nada or the Masters or believed too much in angels. I will thank you in my heart forever.

You have given up your dreams this entire lifetime in service to others and had to battle your way much of the time, but it may make you feel happy to know that one little girl with sky blue eyes benefited greatly from your efforts.

Life is like the highway we drive our cars on—there are lines to guide us, boundaries to drive safely within. The lines and boundaries are like your teachings. We have guided boundaries so we don't wander off the Path.

Someone must draw those lines and lay those boundaries or what a mess it would be. God chose *you* and, with the revelations from the Masters, what a great artist you are! Not one line is crooked, not one boundary off center.

My heart is full today as again I realize what my life would be without you in it.

Great love to you as a prophet and as a person,

To Become the Bride of Christ

Beloved Mother,

So amazed and thrilled was I this evening to feel the nearness of the presence of Jesus that I found myself wanting to write to you right away so that I could share with your readers this almost inexpressible blessing.

It took place during our First Friday service for Keepers of the Flame. During the service, we gave the prayers from the booklet "Devotions to the Sacred Heart of Our Lord and Saviour Jesus Christ." I meditated on the heart of Jesus as I participated in the recitations and, having recently become inspired by the writings of Saint Thérèse of Lisieux, I found myself contemplating what it means to prepare oneself to become the bride of Christ.

Knowing as little as I do of the life of Saint Thérèse and of her lifelong quest to be received by her Divine Spouse, I nonetheless was aware that this sacred calling was not an everyday occurrence. I reflected on my own lack of readiness for this bonding to Christ—my lack of surrender and sacrifice, my insufficiency of love—and yet I was at the same time aware of an even greater longing in my heart to be so received by him.

I AM the Witness

Was it really possible to become united with Jesus as Thérèse had? Or was this an experience reserved solely for the saints of old?

I recited together with the congregation: "I take you, then, O Sacred Heart, to be the sole object of my love, the protector of my life, the pledge of my salvation, the remedy of my frailty and inconstancy, the repairer of all the defects of my life, and my secure refuge in the hour of death." I then reconfirmed in my heart that through the Sacred Heart of Jesus I could transcend all outer limitations, all sin and the sense of sin and be received by him in the alchemical marriage—*if I but first gave myself to him.*

This was my first step. Jesus stands ready to receive us, but we must do our part and move closer to him. It seems such a simple concept, but then why does he seem so distant from so many? I determined with greater zeal to give my heart to Jesus and was instantaneously and profoundly comforted by an inner knowing that because I had done so, he would receive me.

The comfort and soul satisfaction of this simple realization alone would have been my sufficient reward during this evening service, and yet Jesus had not finished revealing to me the grace of his Presence. As I took Holy Communion and returned to my seat, I was immediately bathed in an indescribable essence, which I can only define as the Light and Love of Jesus. From head to toe I tingled. I felt purified and holy. I felt washed clean by his Body and Blood. For the first time I *experienced* transubstantiation, something I had only previously understood intellectually.

Never before had I felt such a nearness of Jesus' Presence in the sacrament. I wondered for a moment why I felt it so tangibly this night. The answer was impressed upon my heart: "Draw nigh unto me and I will draw nigh unto you." I realized that because I had minutes before made my determination to move closer to Jesus' Sacred Heart, Jesus in turn was able to step closer to me. I had expressed my willingness to receive him.

I looked at those around me in the Communion line and wondered, "Are they, too, experiencing this Light and the Presence of Jesus as they receive Holy Communion? Are their hearts willing to receive him tonight?"

It was hard to say. I decided that such an experience of the Presence of Jesus must be personal and individual to each one, for each in his own way and in his own measure draws nigh to Christ. I can only witness to the sacred experience when our blessed Saviour drew nigh unto me because I had opened my heart to him and bade him enter. It seems such a simple thing.

Thank you for setting the example,

Divine Love Heals the Anger of Separation from Our Source

It's been a year of psychology—psychology of self—and I'd like to share an initiation I had in the context of hope.

I was put in contact with a Keeper of the Flame whom I needed to work with. There was a problem! Every time I got around this person I became irritated and wanted to argue. My thoughts were not of a kindly nature—and I indulged! I found people who agreed with me about this person and one thing led to another. Yes, I was talking behind this person's back in a fashion that could not be deemed Christlike.

Unfortunately, I carried on like this for about two weeks, but then a sudden awakening of my consciousness made me realize my mistake. My Holy Christ Self or an Ascended Master or angel must have enlightened me. I was truly horrified at my behavior and wondered how I could ever have behaved so viciously. I knew instantly that I had to make amends but that it would not be easy for me.

I called this person on the telephone and simply apologized for any behavior on my part that was not Christlike. (I realized this person had some of the same traits as my father, with whom I had not resolved my relationship.)

Even though I felt somewhat better, I felt things were still not resolved between us. I prayed and prayed for the God-solution. Within a few days, this person came to my house and out of the blue apologized to me!

At that very moment, a wave of love descended upon me, so encompassing that it instantly dissolved all my negative feelings towards this person. I emphatically knew that from that moment on, no matter what this person did or said, I would forever love the Christ within and never again be upset or disturbed by the human consciousness. This grace of God was so powerful and moving that I just sat there, unable to speak.

As God is my witness, I have not to this day been agitated in any way by this person's behavior. I truly consider us friends on the Path.

I cannot express enough gratitude to Mother and the Masters for the Teachings and the Path. For with this knowledge, though I may stumble and fall, I can pick myself up and run through the obstacle courses of life. The Teachings of the Ascended Masters inspire you to deal with your karma—rather than run away from it.

I have learned that the fear of facing our trials cannot compare with the Love God blesses us with when we face and conquer them.

God loves us, each and every one—but how much more can be given to us when we but give to him!

In loving gratitude,

N.B. Testimonies of disciples of Jesus Christ and the Ascended Masters stating their witness to the power of Truth in their lives will regularly appear in this column in the *Pearls of Wisdom*. If you would like to witness to the power of Truth in your life brought about through the Ascended Masters and their Messengers, we welcome your testimony for publication. Your letter will be kept on file in our archives but your name will be withheld from this page to protect your privacy and your progress on the Path.

28

Break the Spell of Non-Victory!
A Moment when All Could Be Won and All Could Be Lost

Ho, legions of the Great Central Sun!
Ho, legions of the Great Central Sun!
I AM Victory! And I AM *here* to break the spell of non-Victory in the lives of the Lightbearers of earth!
[47-second standing ovation]
Ho, I AM come! And I am here to put down these fallen ones who have determined to pervert the very life-force, the lifeblood and the beings of the servants of God.
I AM here, beloved ones, for the spirals of Victory descend!
I respond to Alpha and Omega. I respond to all the legions of the Second Ray. I am responding to and representing the mighty Bodhisattvas who dwell on the inner planes of the etheric octave and desire to take embodiment. I come to you brimming with a joy that we can meet together the expectations and even the demands of Lord Lanto and all who serve with him, who read as we do the handwriting on the wall.
Therefore, beloved sons and daughters, be drenched in the flame of Victory! Be drenched in the flame of Justina! And know that we are one and that we add the momentum of our twin flames to those cloven tongues of golden fire that descend upon your crown chakras now. And they are meeting a certain amount of density and therefore we feed them our fire as the Light does penetrate through the etheric sheath, through

the mental, through the desire, through the physical.

O beloved ones, help us with right diet. Help us with pure thought. Help us with meditation. Help us with doing your *pranayama*. Yes, beloved, we will remake you in the image and likeness of God if you will cooperate. *Therefore, will you cooperate?*

["Yes!" (22-second standing ovation)]

I speak quickly and with a mighty fire, that I might inject in you the sense of acceleration. You have been on other worlds and systems of worlds and in higher octaves where you would think more easily and more quickly, your motions would be more direct and mercurial and you would accomplish so much more of the penetration of the Mind of God and the drawing forth even of the engineering and the design and the architecture of the golden cities of Light in the etheric octave.

Yes, you have lived in those levels, you have known a greater communication and now, I say, the forces of anti-Victory, the forces of non-Victory have heaped upon you a momentum and a burden and a weight, beloved ones. *And you must listen to me!* You must know that it must be challenged by you and you alone!

And the fire of you is the fire of God in you, for you are God-Victory in manifestation! And I see you as manifestations of ourselves, of Victory and Justina, in the God Flame of Victory. And I see you in your mighty golden robes and golden winged sandals of Victory. And you are that Victory and I affirm it now!

And therefore I say: Take the fire of Victory in your souls! Take the fire of God-Victory that is the God-Victory of your own Mighty I AM Presence and *jump* out of those snakeskins, *jump* out of that density and go forward enjoying the vastness of the universe. For your own mind can tap it because you have chosen to develop your heart and meditate in your heart, and therefore the rings of fire grow—and therefore the Bodhisattvas may come to you, they may touch you, they may quicken you!

Beloved ones, come into balance. Come into balance, I say! And cherish nothing in this world more than your own individual equilibrium—your equilibrium in your own Tree of Life, in your own Mighty I AM Presence.

Let us say that everything that detracts from that equilibrium south, north, east, west, beloved ones, does detract from your mighty Victory. And I say, a mighty Victory you must have! And you should not make it [merely] by the skin of your teeth in the hour when your name is called at roll call at Luxor. Yes, beloved, [you] should [graduate] with flying colors and the highest honors! You should be ready for your ascension *tomorrow*, if necessary,

IV Break the Spell of Non-Victory! 389

or the next tomorrow or the next year or the next five. Yes, beloved, be ready now, and then walk the earth as that example that others may see and follow.

This *is* an hour of cycles turning. Whether we can turn them around depends on the response of every Lightbearer on this planet to my message given this day! And therefore I ask you to communicate [your response] through prayer, through decree, through [the dissemination of] information, through giving to individuals the *Pearl of Wisdom* that shall be printed of my dictation and [telling them] of the work and of the calls of the legions of the Second Ray.

It is a moment, beloved, when all could be won and all could be lost. Do not discount your Godhood! One individual who is God, and knows it, is the pillar of fire, the rod in the earth that shall be the focus of the Great Central Sun Magnet. And many coming together in this place, even once a year, beloved, does produce that concentration of fire whereby we may penetrate and probe in the earth and place our probes, allowing the Light you invoke to penetrate more deeply and more deeply.

Therefore I say, prepare for coming here again next year, starting the day that the conference has concluded. Make your plans, determine to have the funds and the means and decree for the absolute God-Victory of souls.

Now I will tell you what we did with these earthquakes this day. We have taken the opportunity of your holding the balance for the earth in this place to allow these earthquakes to happen (as they would have inevitably happened) but with the least amount of loss of life and damage because *you* have kept the Flame, because you have tarried these days, because you determined to go and you did go to the Royal Teton Retreat last night.

And therefore you did journey with legions of Light and you did perform a mighty spiritual work over Yugoslavia.[1] And it did come to pass that you established a coordinate in that nation and other coordinates upon the planet with other servants of God whereby these earthquakes might be for a mitigation [of world karma], a balancing [of planetary forces] and a release of pent-up [misqualified] energies in the earth.

Therefore, understand how much we can do when we have a body of Lightbearers who can remain at the same place for a period of ten days or even more, but for any amount of time we are grateful—even if you determine to do a twenty-four-hour marathon in your Study Groups and Teaching Centers, where you can hold the flame of harmony and make of that flame one of God-illumination with the violet flame and all the calls that you give.

I will tell you, beloved, the [volcanic] release in Alaska has the same [portents]. And some of you who are "old-timers" have seen earthquakes of this dimension (yet not of this magnitude) happen from time to time during conferences and it has always been because the student body has been able to hold the balance for a release. And without that holding of the balance, there could have been far greater calamity and destruction to life.

You know that earth changes are in the planetary plan, but how and where they shall manifest and what degree of burden or loss of life shall be upon the people surely rests upon the individual decision that shall be made each and every day by the servants of God on earth.

I say, become fiery electrodes! Love the wisdom teachings, pursue the path of the mystics, be together in the Light and therefore convey a spiritual teaching and a spiritual consciousness. Read the books and the foundations of these mystical paths of the world's religions and thereby understand all people. And when you give your Ashram rituals, beloved, you will be able to contact in a deeper way so many souls of Light because now you will understand their path. And when you understand their path you understand their vibration.

(Therefore, be comfortable by being seated.)

Beloved ones, in order for me to speak to you I must have a dispensation from the Lords of Karma, from the Four and Twenty Elders and beyond that the Solar Logoi. Therefore, I deem it a great privilege to be with you in this hour.

It has been weighed time and again preceding conferences and it has been decided that I should not speak. For the power of Victory is great and the power of Victory can unleash such tremendous enthusiasm and fire of purpose that when it does descend on the unenlightened evolutions of a planet it can stir up the urge to go out and do those things that are not the will of God.

Therefore we have created a trusted chalice, as you are that chalice and as you have placed your trust in God and made yourselves available to Lord Krishna and the hosts of the LORD. I desire, then, to continue to release this night the Power, the Wisdom, the Love of Victory! And to do so I need your cooperation in harmony. I need it, beloved, because if the Light I release is so easily misqualified by those who are among the most advanced in the outer world today, then, you see, I will make that karma and I will again be limited in coming.

Consider, then, all those areas of your life in which you desire

IV Break the Spell of Non-Victory!

to be victorious. You would do well after this session or in the morning to write down each point of your personal lifestream and activities where you desire *victory*. You can chart it on a map, beloved, a map of your life, and you can put those golden ribbons at that place where you are determined to have your victory—*victory* over self and every condition, *victory* in this Church, *victory* in the dissemination of the Teachings, *victory* in the nations, *victory* in the governments, *victory* in education, *victory* in every area of life!

Beloved ones, look all around you in this hour, and what do you see? You see *defeat,* beloved hearts. Everywhere people are being defeated by their own ignorance, by their own absence of the fiery coil of the Divine Mother, of the sacred fire rising up within them. They are being defeated on every hand—in the economy and in business and in life. There is a world depression that is not as apparent as it might be. For if the world could know the state of world depression that is upon the people, perhaps they would determine to do something about it.

Well, I will tell you, your violet flame marathons in this conference, sprinkled with the intensity of the yellow fire, will awaken and quicken some. They will awake as from a deep slumber and they will begin the quest and they will search.

And when they search, *who* will they find?

They will find *you* as myself and Justina, and we will be there with you and we will be there to bring home the Victory!

Let America awake! Let Americans awake! And let the fire of the entire Spirit of the Great White Brotherhood go forth from your hearts.

I, Victory, with my beloved consort, greet you in this hour! And we are transferring to you increment by increment that which you can spiritually assimilate of Victory. Therefore continue your calls and affirmations to me this night and see what we will do together!

There are other events in the planet in store during this conference. We desire to see a mighty action for the right, for the feeding of the hungry and the liberation of souls and the exposure of the dark forces that are yet intent upon global warfare. These must be bound on the astral plane, and those in embodiment [must be bound] as well, by legions of Victory, legions of Jophiel and Christine!

We come in anticipation of Alpha and Omega. Now, precious hearts of Light, so rise to that mighty occasion.

For notes, see *Pearls of Wisdom*, vol. 35, no. 29, p. 398.

Earthquakes and Volcanic Eruptions

June 28, 1992 (Associated Press and Reuters):

Two powerful earthquakes rocked southern California today, killing one child and injuring dozens of people. The first quake occurred at 4:58 a.m. (PDT) and registered 7.4 on the Richter scale. The epicenter was about 6 miles north of Yucca Valley and about 80 miles east of Los Angeles. The quake was felt as far away as Denver. It was the third most powerful earthquake in the United States in this century. There were more than 20 aftershocks in the two and a half hours after the earthquake, including one that measured 6.0 on the Richter scale.

The second quake occurred at 8:07 a.m. and lasted about 45 seconds. It was centered near Big Bear Lake in the San Bernardino Mountains, about 20 miles west of the first quake. Its magnitude was about 7.0 on the Richter scale. According to Kate Hutton, a seismologist at the California Institute of Technology in Pasadena, scientists were considering whether the two might portend an even larger shock on the San Andreas Fault itself.

The first earthquake was 25 miles from the San Andreas Fault and the second 5 to 10 miles away from it. The most serious damage appeared to be concentrated in desert communities east of Los Angeles near the earthquake epicenter.

The quakes were described as "gentle giants" by local radio stations because they did not cause major damage in heavily populated cities like Los Angeles, Las Vegas and Palm Springs.

Yesterday, June 27, Mount Spurr Volcano, which is 80 miles west of Anchorage, Alaska, erupted for the first time in 39 years. The eruption was large enough to throw steam and ash 5 miles into the atmosphere. So far, scientists haven't made a correlation between the two events.

Updates

July 5. The Yucca Valley region was jolted by an aftershock of magnitude 5.5. No injuries or damage were reported. The quake was felt in Los Angeles and as far away as Las Vegas.

July 11. A 5.1-magnitude earthquake occurred 12 miles northeast of Mojave, California, causing slight damage and minor injuries to one person. It was felt 90 miles to the south in downtown Los Angeles.

July 15. The Yucca Valley June 28 quake was upgraded in magnitude from 7.4 to 7.5 on the Richter scale by the National Earthquake Information Center, tying it with the May 17 quake in the Philippines for the strongest earthquake of the year. The Big Bear June 28 quake was downgraded from 7.0 to 6.6.

July 20. A score of minor earthquakes shook the Lake-Fishing Bridge area of Yellowstone National Park. No damage or injuries were reported. The largest quake, centered about 1.5 miles northwest of Fishing Bridge, measured 4.4 on the Richter scale.

Huge Quake Risk in the Pacific Northwest

Recent scientific studies indicate that giant earthquakes, more powerful than any to strike North America in this century, have reshaped the Pacific Northwest in the past—and are likely to do so again. The last major earthquake struck the region about 300 years ago. The massive temblors have occurred at intervals from 90 to 560 years.

Geologists Samuel H. Clarke, Jr., and Gary A. Carver reported in the January 10, 1992 issue of *Science* that over the past 1,700 years at least three powerful earthquakes have shoved the ground 15 to 20 feet upward in places and suddenly slumped it in others. The giant quakes have been caused by the movement of the earth's plates along the coast from Vancouver, British Columbia, to Mendocino, California. Two smaller plates are inching under the North American plate in a process called subduction. The entire region is known as the Cascadia subduction zone.

Until recently, scientists believed that the Juan de Fuca plate was grinding smoothly under the vast North American plate. The evidence now shows that the plates are locked. When this happens, the strain builds until a massive earthquake suddenly relieves the pressure. According to Dr. Carver, these quakes, often lasting many minutes, "can be so monstrous that they deform the earth over tens of thousands of square miles." Such subduction processes, which can produce deadly volcanic eruptions as well as earthquakes, are also occurring off the coasts of Alaska, Japan and South America.

Geologists James C. Savage and Michael Lisowski reported on their study of land deformation in Washington's Olympic Peninsula in the April 5, 1991 issue of *Science*. Their findings showed that the mountains along the Olympic Peninsula are moving closer together at the rate of one-eighth inch per year and that the coastal land is also inching up—two clear signs that major earthquake stresses are building in the region.

The scientists noted that these stresses could generate a temblor of magnitude 9.5, causing coastal areas to slump 6 feet in minutes and creating giant waves along the fault line. A quake of this magnitude, expected to last about three minutes, would collapse most of the buildings in a city such as Portland, Oregon. The majority of structures in the region are not built to withstand a major earthquake.

Dr. Thomas Heaton, a seismologist at the U.S. Geological Survey, says that an earthquake measuring 9.5 or above would be generated if the fault breaks as a unit. If it breaks in segments, it could generate three or four magnitude-8 earthquakes within years or decades of each other, only partially relieving the stress. Such quakes could be thousands of times more damaging than the one that struck San Francisco in 1989.

Although Clarke and Carver do not project when the next massive quake might occur, they note in their report that "great subduction-related earthquakes have occurred in this region in the recent past and presumably will recur in the future." (See Sandra Blakeslee, "Geologists See Huge Quake Risk in the Northwest," *New York Times*, 5 April 1991, National edition; and David Perlman, "New Evidence of Huge Quakes in Humboldt Area, Northwest," *San Francisco Chronicle*, 10 January 1992.)

Ascended Master Prophecies

Alaska. In a dictation given Holy Thursday, March 26, 1964, God Harmony released a "mighty tide of cosmic energy" over the Atlantic and Pacific oceans. He explained that had the energy been released upon the landed areas, cataclysmic action would have ensued. God Harmony charged the angelic hosts to distribute the release over the continents. The Alaskan earthquake occurred the following day during the dictation of God Tabor. El Morya later explained that "certain karmic conditions having to do with aspects of human greed recorded on the Aleutian Islands and the Alaskan mainland during the eras of the gold rush had to be expiated."

Nicaragua. On November 19, 1972, Helios pronounced: "I will bring a great earthquake to pass upon this world.... Behold, the wickedness of mankind today is as the wickedness of Sodoma and Gomorrah. And behold, I shall shake the pillars of the earth! And surely, saith the LORD, an earthquake shall come and no man shall be able to stop it or to stay it!" On December 23, 1972, 70 percent of the city of Managua, Nicaragua, was destroyed by earthquakes. An estimated 10,000 people were killed, 10,000 to 15,000 injured and at least 200,000 left homeless.

Guatemala, Arizona, Mexico. On February 1, 1976, following a dictation by Sanat Kumara in which he released an increment of fire, the Messenger spoke of the accompanying potential for cataclysm. She said: "According to the ability of Keepers of the Flame to keep the flame, so will the disturbance in the elemental kingdom and in the four lower bodies be held at a minimum." Three days later, there was an earthquake in Guatemala and another in Arizona. Two more earthquakes struck Guatemala on February 6, bringing the death toll there to more than 22,000. Another earthquake occurred off the coast of Mexico on February 9.

Mount St. Helens. On April 6, 1980, Virgo and Pelleur, hierarchs of the gnomes, delivered a warning of planetary upheaval and implored Keepers of the Flame to increase and intensify their invocations to the violet flame to transmute the burdens on elemental life. On May 18, Mount St. Helens erupted with a force approximately 500 times that of the atomic bomb dropped on Hiroshima. Saint Germain told us on June 1, 1980, that the amount of violet flame invoked had not been sufficient to stay the hand of this catastrophe.

San Francisco. On October 17, 1989, at 5:04 p.m., 17 days after Cuzco stated that it is "the hour of earth changes," an earthquake measuring 7.1 on the Richter scale struck the San Francisco Bay area. Sixty-five people were killed, over 3,000 injured and at least 44,000 sought refuge in shelters. On October 18 and 19, 1989, a series of earthquakes jolted northeastern China west of Beijing. Twenty-nine people were killed and an estimated 60,000 left homeless.

29

See What You Can Do!

For the Acceleration of Earth without the Destruction of Earth

Ho, legions of seraphim from the Great Central Sun! March, then, to the Heart of the Inner Retreat! March, then, and establish now with legions of the Second Ray that platform for the coming of our beloved Alpha and Omega!

So the legions come, beloved, and I salute you in their name. I salute you in the name of the God Flame in your hearts! Visualize now the seraphim who form the concentric rings round the Central Sun making their way to this place to assist you in holding the balance in the earth for the coming of Alpha and Omega. [21-second standing ovation]

These seraphim are your very best friends and probably the friends you ignore the most. I shall remind you, therefore, that they are of the order of Serapis, that they attend your ascension and that they have attended [the degrees of] your ascension in every embodiment since you have left the Great Central Sun.

When they place their mighty wings [upon you], these four-winged creatures therefore superimpose themselves upon your bodies. And with one command from you, made by the authority of the Christ in your heart, you can watch how the seraphim bring you into alignment—[how they] bring all the functions of all of the levels of your being into alignment. Miracles, *seeming* miracles, take place in the very auras of the seraphim of God!

Do not neglect, fathers and mothers, health-care practitioners, physicians, healers, *do not neglect* the call to the seraphim of God when you are dealing with even the slightest out-of-alignment state. For the seraphim are the greatest physicians of all. They are the greatest healers, ranking with the highest legions of Raphael and Mother Mary.

And therefore, because they have in their auras the mighty power of the Central Sun and the white fire core of being and do always carry the vibration of your Father-Mother God (who have given you life and divine plan and matrix and their attention to every detail of your life), [the seraphim] can restore [you] by the energies of the Great Central Sun. And there is no greater restorative power than that of the Great Central Sun as it is transmitted and stepped down by and through the seraphim of God.

I say, one and all, reread the *Dossier on the Ascension*.[1] And now enter into the highest conception of the point of the Beginning beyond the Beginning, the point of *Ein Sof*. This you can achieve through the mind of the seraphim as in no other way.

Why, to look upon you and your neglect of the seraphim, one would almost think that you really want to be sick and have your ailments! For if you really did want to get rid of them, beloved ones, would you not call upon [the seraphim], I say? ["Yes!"]

Well, then, as they say on this planet, examine your psychology and determine why you want to enter into a codependency between yourself and your ailments!

Beloved ones, it is time to have done with those ailments. It is time for the resurrection. It is time for the ascension flame! Now be drenched in these fires as they are tempered to your present condition and know that some of you have truly not prepared for our coming, but you may do so even in these few days [by way of] preparing yourselves to contain more Light.

It is a wondrous occasion when the Solar Logoi will authorize so many legions of seraphim to come to earth. Now, beloved ones, consider this, for you are wise ones. Consider that since with the coming of Alpha and Omega so many hosts of Light come in attendance, there shall ultimately be in this conference an extraordinary gathering of the hosts of the LORD for those dictations.

Therefore say to yourself: "With so many in such proximity, why should we not request some labors from our beloved El Morya? Why should we not go to work, when we have such reinforcement of one another, to go after that force of Antichrist in the world?" And see and prove here, now, if the LORD God himself and if we will not defeat that force through you, and how

V See What You Can Do!

mighty numbers and even the number of the 666² will go down!

See what you can do, beloved! And be impressed with the fact that your journeying in the inner octaves and your presence here has already, even in the third day of this conference, allowed earth changes to take place without further calamity.

Blessed ones, it is a delicate matter for elemental life and the attending angels, who must tend a planet in transition, a planet which must be saved, a planet which must be healed, a planet which must be purged all at once—*this is a delicate operation.* And some of you know that this is directed from the retreat of Cuzco and by the mighty power of Surya as he maintains his focus in the God Star, Sirius.

Therefore, I assure you that thousands upon thousands of Ascended Masters who are experts in the sciences of geology at all levels of the earth are working now at a very intense level. And they request your support. And they are Ascended Masters, beloved! You simply do not realize the conditions of the earth and the horrendous weight of untransmuted karma that weighs down the earth and elemental life, not to mention the pollutions and the toxins [that weigh down] the bodies of the people themselves.

This earth has been raped, as you know, [by extraterrestrials]. It has been abused. And yet you have found a pristine place, fairly untouched, to consecrate the work of the Great White Brotherhood. And that place, as you know, has been dedicated long, long time for its connection to the Grand Teton.

So, beloved, when I tell you that Ascended Masters and Archangels and Elohim are working very hard to produce the acceleration of earth without the destruction of earth, I know whereof I speak! And you can think of the individual on the operating table whose life hangs in the balance. And if such and such a procedure is tried, perhaps the patient will not recover and therefore the decision [must be made] by physicians and surgeons: "Shall we try it or not?"

Blessed hearts, earth is a sick planet and many divine physicians are attending. We bid you join us. Join the seraphim of God! Join the legions of the Fifth Ray! And make this experience in the very mountains of the LORD one that counts for all evolutions of the planet!

I AM Justinius, Captain of Seraphic Bands! And I announce to you the day and the hour when the opportunity shall be open to you to take your ascension *if* you prepare for it from this moment on. Yes, beloved, it is only an opportunity if you exercise it. It is only an open door if you will walk through it and if you will have the courage to take every step that is necessary to make it. Then you will know how it feels to walk the earth as an Ascended Master moving among those who are the Lightbearers, quickening them! You will know what it is to place your Electronic Presence everywhere over the Lightbearers.

Therefore, take care that you leave in embodiment many fine souls and well-trained ones so that the continuity of the spiritual life of the true mystics of all ages may survive on planet earth and that thereby the earth herself may survive!

Into your hands I give you the planet, beloved ones. It belongs to *you*. This is your day and your hour. See what you can do to bring her Home, with her evolutions cut free!

I AM your servant, Justinius. [31-second standing ovation]

"The Summit Lighthouse Sheds Its Radiance O'er All the World to Manifest as Pearls of Wisdom."
This dictation by **Holy Justinius** was **delivered** by the Messenger of the Great White Brotherhood Elizabeth Clare Prophet on **Sunday, June 28, 1992,** during the ten-day conference FREEDOM 1992: "Joy in the Heart" held at the **Royal Teton Ranch, Park County, Montana.** [N.B. Throughout this *Pearl,* bracketed material denotes words unspoken yet implicit in the dictation, added by the Messenger under Holy Justinius' direction for clarity in the written word.] **(1)** Serapis Bey, *Dossier on the Ascension,* $5.95 (add $1.05 for postage). **(2)** Rev. 13:18.

Notes from *Pearl* no. 28 by Mighty Victory with Justina:
This dictation by **Mighty Victory with Justina** was **delivered** by the Messenger of the Great White Brotherhood Elizabeth Clare Prophet on **Sunday, June 28, 1992,** during the ten-day conference FREEDOM 1992: "Joy in the Heart" held at the **Royal Teton Ranch, Park County, Montana.** [N.B. Throughout this *Pearl,* bracketed material denotes words unspoken yet implicit in the dictation, added by the Messenger under Mighty Victory's direction for clarity in the written word.] **(1) Spiritual work over Yugoslavia.** In his dictation given June 27, 1992, Saint Joseph asked that we make the call that night to be taken to the Royal Teton Retreat and from there angels would escort us to Yugoslavia (see pp. 373–74). Prior to the dictation, the Messenger and congregation had given Ashram rituals 4 and 5 — Sacred Ritual for Soul Purification and Sacred Ritual for Transport and Holy Work. These two rituals assist the soul in performing world service while out of the body during the hours of rest. The rituals are published in *Ashram Notes* by El Morya, pp. 37–42, 46–59, $19.95 (add $1.48 for postage), and *Ashram Rituals,* 64-page booklet, pp. 33–52, $4.95 (add $.98 for postage). They are also available on two audiocassettes (total time: 2 hr., $11.90 plus $.98 postage, A90028).

30

Become Shiva!

Tonight we are going to do whatever it takes to get you to become Shiva! And since nobody was even moved to leap up in the presence of Shiva while we were singing to him,* we've got a little work to do. I'm going to give you some background on Shiva now so we can get on with the bhajans until you become "jumping Shivas."

Shiva is very personal to me, a very personal friend, a very personal being who defies being circumscribed by any concept of him. Yet he is always there.

Shiva means "auspicious" or "kindly." He is indeed both. He is known as the Destroyer, and we welcome the Destroyer because we want everything that is not like God where we are to be transmuted by the all-consuming sacred fire. As the Third Person of the Hindu Trinity, he destroys the universe at the end of each world age so that it can be created all over again.

The Hindu Trinity is defined in the Hindu scriptures, the Puranas, as consisting of Brahma (the Creator), Vishnu (the Preserver) and Shiva (the Destroyer and Regenerator). All three are manifestations of Brahman.

Brahman is God in the Beginning—God in the Beginning with the Word. And by the Word did Brahman create and without the Word was nothing made that was made.¹ Do not confuse Brahma with Brahman. Brahma is Father; Vishnu, Son; Shiva, Holy Spirit—the Trinity who serve under Brahman and the Word.

─────────
*The Messenger and congregation sang the bhajan "Śiva Śambhu" (number 654) prior to this lecture.

As I mentioned in my lecture "The Inner Path of Hinduism," devotion to the Trinity is not widespread among the Hindu people, but I teach that the Hindu Trinity is parallel to the Christian Trinity. Shiva represents the stripping action of the Holy Spirit, whose love consumes the forces of ignorance and anti-Love. Shiva is not only the destroyer of the universe: he is the destroyer of evil, hatred, disease, worldliness, evildoers and demons. And, as Anjani Srivastava writes, Shiva is also "a nourisher who bestows long life."[2] But he will not give that nourishment until he has cleansed the vessel.

When you call to Shiva, you must be prepared for a purging by the holy fire of Love. And if you desire to receive that purging, when it comes you will be filled with such Light and God-Power as to not know where to turn to direct your service to life.

Shiva is known as Shambhu (benign), Shankara (beneficent), and Pashupati, which means "lord of cattle." Actually, it means the lord of souls in the sense of the shepherd who tends the sheep. He is also known as Mahadeva (great god).

Shiva is associated with death. He dances on battlefields and cremation grounds, and what he is doing is extracting the light that was once held in the cells of the body. He is withdrawing it and sending it back to the Godhead, back to the Great Central Sun.

He is first and foremost the destroyer of the human ego. He destroys the ties that bind us to human existence. You may think you do not want him to destroy those bonds and yet, I tell you, when he does you will find that you have a much stronger binding to God. You will have bonds that come from God and the whole universe that bind you to the soul and the heart of all people in the world, that bind you more tightly to loved ones, to children, to those in your immediate family. When the selfish, self-centered human bonds are not there, the God bonds become much stronger.

We are in a period of transition where we fear to let go of what is really not worth hanging on to, because we don't understand the unknown. The unknown is what is real. What we have today is unreality. Reality is more rich, more intense in color, in vibration, in thought, in feeling.

Everything you experience today that is ephemeral will pass away. Nothing lasts in the human condition. You can experience the same things at a higher level and they will never pass away. Love never passes away. Wisdom doesn't pass away. Caring doesn't pass away. The true love of soul to soul becomes immortalized through Shiva—it becomes immortalized through Vishnu and through Brahma.

VI Become Shiva!

Hindu scholar Margaret Stutley writes that Shiva "is also the death of Death, the bestower of immortality on his devotees."[3] If you are not willing to have your mortality destroyed, then Shiva cannot give to you your immortality.

There is somewhat of an attachment to that human skeleton and that human body. Even the highest yogis have had moments of great burden and sorrow in leaving their body in their final *samadhi*, when the soul passes on and does not return. This is called the *mahasamadhi*.[4]

Stutley says Shiva is "the embodiment of yogic power that destroys the bonds binding the individual spirit to the world and so gives liberation."[5] What I have been telling you in this conference is that you can have God and the whole universe and yet not lose the levels of human experience that are necessary to your evolution and to your working through your psychology. It's not as if suddenly you were to embrace God as a totality and as your total being, and as a result you wouldn't know yourself and no one else would know you.

I can tell you, the people who count will know you. The people who don't count and shouldn't be your companions in the first place will somehow not be around anymore. You have to expect to make new friends and to make the Ascended Masters, the angelic hosts and the Archangels your friends. And when you do, you'll meet millions of people upon earth who also move in those circles.

After all, there are some things that are worth making a transition for. There are some things that are worth going up the steps for and leaving behind some of the old landmarks. If you really love your friends and companions, even though they may have led you astray here and there, and you really feel for their souls, the only way you can ever help them is to go up a couple of stairs. Then you can step down and reach out that powerful arm you will have acquired through your devotion to Archangel Michael and pull them up and transfer to them the Light you have gained.

And that doesn't come overnight. You can't be a student and a teacher all at once. You need to be working on that path until you come into a true strength where you can help those whom you never could help when you were on an equal footing with them at a lower level of consciousness.

Shiva often appears as a yogi with snow-white face and matted hair, dressed in a tiger skin. He is the friend of yogis who helps them to attain their goal of God-realization.

You are yogis whether or not you practice any kind of physical yoga. You need to remember that. You may be a bhakti yogi, you may be a jnana yogi, a karma yogi or a raja yogi.

So we are all yogis because we are taking upon us the yoke of Jesus Christ, which is Light and which is easy. "Come unto me, all ye that labor and are heavy laden, and I will give you rest. Take my yoke upon you and learn of me, for I am meek and lowly in heart and ye shall find rest unto your souls. For my yoke is easy and my burden is Light."[6] We are yogis under the Ascended Masters. We are yogis as we perfect the science of the spoken Word.

So Shiva, dressed up as a yogi, is a true friend of all yogis. We see him in this role in the Vedic myth of the winning of the waters. In the myth, the Vedic god Indra slays the serpentine monster Vritra, thereby releasing the waters to flow to the sea. As I mentioned in my lecture on Hinduism, this myth is symbolic of the practice of yoga. Indra represents the Self and the waters represent the light released from the chakras to flow upward to the crown.

In one version of the story, Indra cannot succeed without Shiva. Shiva lends him the strength he needs to conquer Vritra. This tells us that it is Shiva who will give us the strength we need to overcome the serpent of the not-self so that we can attain enlightenment.

Shiva is also known as the distributor of the seven holy rivers. This means that he is the one who distributes the light to our chakras and will help us control the light in our chakras and balance the light at each of the levels.

You will notice that I have a statue of the wonderful dancing Shiva in front of me on the altar. I have carried this Shiva with me all over the world in my Stumps and wherever I speak. Shiva stands between me and the dweller-on-the-threshold of anyone in the audience or anyone in the world or any force on the astral plane that would attack the delivery of the Word from the altar.

If you would like to have a Shiva of this size and presence and strength, please let us know and we'll see if we can get one for you. I think it's one of the most important statues of our Church and Shiva works through it for you in an absolutely fantastic way.

Shiva's consort, or Shakti, appears in three primary forms. *Shakti* means "power." It is the Feminine Principle of the Godhead, the Divine Mother who went forth out of the Divine Whole. Shiva's main Shaktis are Parvati, daughter of the god Himalaya, a benevolent goddess and devoted wife; Durga, "the unfathomable one," known as the destroyer of demons; and Kali, "the power of time." Kali is a symbol of destruction, who appears with black skin wearing a necklace of skulls. Yet she bestows blessings upon those who seek knowledge of God and is revered by her devotees as

VI Become Shiva!

the Divine Mother. As you know, she was the chosen deity of Ramakrishna.

Lord Shiva lives on the summit of the sacred Mount Kailasa in Tibet. He is pictured there both as a solitary ascetic and with his Shakti, Parvati. John Snelling, in his book *The Sacred Mountain*, recounts how Parvati contributed to the origin of Shiva's third eye:

> Legend describes [Parvati] playfully covering her Lord's eyes as he sat in meditation on a peak of Himalaya. Instantly all light and life were extinguished in the universe until, out of compassion for all beings, the god opened his third eye, which blazed like a new sun. So intense was its blazing that it scorched the mountains and forests of [the Himalayas] to oblivion. Only when he saw that the daughter of the mountain was properly contrite did he relent and restore her father [who is the mountain] to his former estate.[7]

This legend shows Shiva as the Destroyer. The opening of his third eye represents the opening of the eye of knowledge that destroys ignorance. Swami Karapatri explains: "The frontal eye, the eye of fire, is the eye of higher perception. It looks mainly inward. When directed outward, it burns all that appears before it. It is from a glance of this third eye that...the gods and all created beings are destroyed at each of the periodical destructions of the universe."[8]

Shiva is also known as the Lord of the Dance, Nataraja. His dance destroys the fetters that bind the soul. He dances triumphantly on the demon who personifies ignorance and illusion.

As scholar Veronica Ions writes, "When dancing, Shiva represents cosmic truth."[9] In his upper right hand, Shiva holds a drum, which represents the sound from which the universe was created. His upper left hand holds a tongue of flame. His left foot is raised, telling us that we can raise ourselves and attain salvation.

Ananda Coomaraswamy writes, "[The] deepest significance [of Shiva's dance] is felt when it is realized that it takes place within the heart and the self. Everywhere is God: that Everywhere is the heart."[10]

Shiva is the great Guru who comes to save us from ignorance, from forgetfulness and our human ego. His kindly love is a fierce love that strips us of all that separates us from oneness with him. Shaivites repeat the mantra *Om Namah Shivaya*—"I bow down to thee, Lord Shiva"—in order to attain union with Shiva. Let's give it together now:

Om Namah Shivaya (given 69 times, clapping)
Ommmmmmmmmmmmmmmmmmmmm

We're going to give some other Shiva mantras so I would like you to visualize Shiva all around you. See his Electronic Presence larger than life, larger than you, and you inside of him. (This is if you desire, if you have the will to do so.) And as you give the mantra, bow to Shiva before you.

You can follow the exercise linearly by seeing him first before you as you give your adoration to him through the bhajan. Then, as he comes toward you, feel the union of the Divine One with your soul—the Divine Lover of your soul with your soul. And finally, see Shiva superimposed over you and you inside of him.

Now, I would like you to give these bhajans in great devotion to the Holy Spirit—if you feel comfortable doing so. If you don't feel comfortable with Shiva, that is your right. But if you do and you do the meditation, I ask you to notice when you spontaneously feel that presence of Shiva around you to such an extent that you can no longer remain in your seat but must literally stand up. Then notice when you can no longer stand up without jumping in the air by the very power and force of the Shakti of Shiva, of the sacred fire of his being. And just let yourself do it!

So all who wish to participate in this may do so.*

Messenger's Invocation:

O infinite Light sealed in our hearts, we adore by thy Holy Spirit, *Shiva!* By the infinite Light of God, so manifest thy rings upon rings of Light in this place. *Shiva!* ["Shiva!"]

O mighty one of God, come forth! Dispeller of Darkness, destroyer of Death and Hell, *descend, descend* to the depths of planet earth. Come now! Multiply your Presence a billion times. Stand in the aura. Dance in the aura! Sit in the heart of every lifestream upon earth. *Shiva!* ["Shiva!"]

O living Light, penetrate now! Penetrate now, Mahadeva. Penetrate now! Let us be drawn up in the fire of the Ruby Ray, in the planes of the Dhyani Buddhas and the planes of the Bodhisattvas and the planes of the Buddha of the Ruby Ray.

Lord Gautama, Sanat Kumara, Seven Holy Kumaras, Lord Maitreya, Jesus Christ, all hosts of the LORD's Spirit of the Great White Brotherhood, invoke now *Shiva!* ["Shiva!"]

O living Light, draw the line now. Draw the line now! *Draw the line now!* As thou didst assist Indra, so release and free now our geothermal waters! Release and free now our geothermal waters!

*At this juncture, the Messenger and congregation sang the bhajans "He Śiva Śaṅkara" (number 655) and "Mānasa Bhajore" (number 656), followed by the mantra *Tat Tvam Asi*.

VI Become Shiva!

[Congregation affirms with the Messenger:]
Release and free now our geothermal waters!
Shiva! ["Shiva!"]

Come forth, O Divine Mother! Come forth, Parvati. Come forth, Durga. Come forth, Great Kali. O thou Divine Mother, secure the earth unto the very core of the earth. Secure the Grand Teton and the Royal Teton Ranch. Secure the earth for the Lightbearers all!

I call unto the Lord Shiva in this hour for the binding of Death and Hell. All hosts of Shiva, all manifestations of Shiva, mighty Electronic Presence of Shiva, be everywhere in the earth this night, in every bush and flower, in every heart of every deer, every elk, all that roam these lands. O God in all levels of creation, let there be now, we pray, the liberating power of *Shiva!* ["Shiva!"]

I call forth the Light. I call forth the living presence, Brahman. *Brahman, Brahman, Brahman,* come forth! Release through thy Word the glory of creation, the victory of the Great White Brotherhood in the earth, the victory of all Ascended Masters and their chelas. Blaze the power of the Godhead now, O Lord!

Come forth, Brahma, Vishnu, Shiva! Come forth, Vak, Divine Mother! We greet thee in our hearts, in our temples. Within, without, thou art *Shiva!* ["Shiva!"]*

*Following the invocation and in preparation for the dictation of Lord Shiva, the Messenger and congregation sang the bhajan "Hara Mahādeva" (number 653).

Elizabeth Clare Prophet delivered the profile "Become Shiva!" on June 30, 1992, prior to the dictation of Lord Shiva. It was the concluding section of her lecture "The Inner Path of Hinduism" and has been edited for publication. The major portion of "The Inner Path of Hinduism" was delivered June 29. The lecture and dictation were part of the ten-day conference FREEDOM 1992: "Joy in the Heart" held at the Royal Teton Ranch, Park County, Montana. (1) John 1:1–3. (2) Anjani Kr. Srivastava, "Lord Shiva—the Master of Life and Death," in R. S. Nathan, comp., *Symbolism in Hinduism* (Bombay: Central Chinmaya Mission Trust, 1989), p. 180. (3) Margaret Stutley, *Hinduism: The Eternal Law* (1985; reprint, Wellingborough, Northamptonshire: Aquarian Press, Crucible, 1989), p. 107. (4) **You and your body elemental: emotional attachment to the body.** Almost everyone (with the exception of those who suffer severe psychological detachment from self and body) forms an emotional attachment to the body. After all, this is the body we have worn and worked through, the body that has provided the temple for our soul and the means by which we experience pleasure and pain on this plane, balance our karma and do good deeds. So we say, "Blest be the tie that binds us to earth when we need to be earthbound to fulfill our reason for being and blest be the liberating power of Shiva! when it's time 'to shuffle off this mortal coil.'" Emotions connected with our attachment to the body are natural, and you should be aware that your body elemental has a consciousness and its consciousness permeates the physical body. But you are the master of your body elemental. As you give him positive input instead of those complaining negatives, you will be much happier, more healthy and more holy—and so will your body elemental. And, of course, body elementals cannot do the best job, even though they would like to, when you don't give them the best food and exercise, spiritual teaching and practices. Don't mistake your body elemental's fears for your own. Your body elemental is also attached to the body, because that's his job. He takes care of the body. No more body, no more job! So he's wondering where he's going and what he's going to do when you lay that body aside in your final embodiment. You have to comfort your body elemental as you would a little child and promise him that you are taking him with you to the next octave because he has been a very faithful servant. Tell him he can still be your aide-de-camp after you've ascended and he'll have plenty of assignments. (**5**) Stutley, *Hinduism,* p. 107. (**6**) Matt. 11:28–30. (**7**) John Snelling, *The Sacred Mountain,* rev. and enl. ed. (London: East-West Publications, 1990), p. 11. (**8**) Swami Karapatri, "Śrī Śiva tattva," *Siddhanta,* II, 1941–42, 116, quoted in Alain Daniélou, *The Gods of India: Hindu Polytheism* (New York: Inner Traditions International, 1985), p. 214. (**9**) Veronica Ions, *Indian Mythology* (London: Paul Hamlyn, 1967), p. 44. (**10**) Ananda K. Coomaraswamy, *The Dance of Shiva,* rev. ed. (New York: Farrar, Straus and Company, Noonday Press, 1957), p. 72.

Sing your devotions to Lord Shiva
with the
Messenger and devotees who gathered at
FREEDOM 1992: *"Joy in the Heart"!*

Available after August 31 on audiocassette:

The Messenger's lecture "Become Shiva!"
Lord Shiva's dictation *Only Make the Call "Shiva!"*
—and four bhajans led by the Messenger:

Śiva Śambhu
He Śiva Śaṅkara
Mānasa Bhajore
Hara Mahādeva

On two 90-minute audiocassettes, $15 plus $.98 for postage.

Order your copy now and invoke the Presence of Shiva!

I AM the Witness

A Terrible Accident Proves God's Deliverance

Dearest Mother,

I would like to witness to the tremendous intercessory powers of the Archangels.

On a Wednesday night not too long ago a group of teenagers, whose schedules were packed with high school activities, found time to come together. Their purpose this night was to listen to my friend Mary Ellen speak about her religion. Mary Ellen is a Keeper of the Flame and a member of Church Universal and Triumphant. The teens found her message new and interesting.

Mary Ellen taught them about Archangel Michael and his "Traveling Protection" decree. She also told them that in an emergency they could simply call out: "Archangel Michael, help me, help me, help me!" — and Archangel Michael would instantly intervene.

Little did anyone realize the importance and the preciseness of this gem of wisdom given that night.

The following Saturday night, four of the teenagers got into a car. Before they left the curb, they asked God to protect them and the car they were in. Within hours they were in a terrible accident. An 18-wheel truck, fully loaded with someone's household goods, hit them broadside. The thrust of the impact was so great that the truck stalled out, rolled up over the car and dragged the car under its wheels for 500 feet before stopping.

The scene outside the car: the truck wheel was on top of the car. On the side of the impact, the car was reduced to approximately 30 inches from top to bottom. The smell of gas permeated the air. People gathered. The truck driver and others tried in vain to start the truck.

I happened to pass by the accident, not knowing who was in the car. I thought to myself, "It will be a miracle and the grace of God if anyone survives that impact."

The condition of the four teenagers inside the car: three of the occupants had relatively light injuries. They sustained cuts, bruises, a slight head injury and one broken bone. The fourth passenger, Kelly, was pinned in the crushed metal from the bottom of her feet to mid-chest. One wheel of the truck was directly above her lower body and she was not able to breathe. She knew time was short and that she would probably not survive the accident.

As her best friend crawled out of what remained of the back window, she turned around and realized that Kelly was not able to breathe. She called out to her, "Kelly, call to Archangel Michael! Decree! Do something!"

People were frantically trying to start the truck. They knew there was not much time left. (Four minutes' grace, then insufficient oxygen would cause brain damage and death.) Nothing worked. The truck would not turn over... Time moved on!

Kelly heard the words of her friend, "Call to Archangel Michael!" With all the strength she had left, in the silence of her heart she called out for help. *Instantly the truck lifted. She had time to twist the upper part of her little body free.* She was able to breathe!

Then the weight of the truck descended again. Kelly received a crushed pelvis, her leg was snapped in half and she had internal injuries. Although she was in extreme pain, none of this mattered—she was alive!

It took another hour for her to be cut free from the wreckage. During this time she was at peace knowing that a mighty Archangel had come to her rescue. Through the grace of God, Archangel Michael heard her silent call and came as he had promised.

Those who witnessed this event could not explain what happened. They only knew that a miracle had taken place and that a life had been spared.

There is a happy ending to the story. Through the grace of God and after three surgeries, Kelly's body has been repaired. She is a senior in college and will be a teacher—a teacher who knows and is willing to share the story of an Archangel.

I witness to you, as the mother of Kelly, that Archangel Michael is always at our side. He simply awaits our call, for he may not intercede unless asked.

God bless you, beloved Mother, for your service in delivering the teaching whereby we are no longer in ignorance of the Law.

Always Victory!

By God's grace,
I AM a grateful chela on the Path,

N.B. Testimonies of disciples of Jesus Christ and the Ascended Masters stating their witness to the power of Truth in their lives will regularly appear in this column in the *Pearls of Wisdom*. If you would like to witness to the power of Truth in your life brought about through the Ascended Masters and their Messengers, we welcome your testimony for publication. Your letter will be kept on file in our archives but your name will be withheld from this page to protect your privacy and your progress on the Path.

31

Only Make the Call, "Shiva!"

Ho! *Shiva* is come—come to you, each one!
I AM come. I AM here. I intensify the fire: Shiva!

I intensify it first and foremost in your heart. Open your heart now to receive the infinite God that I AM, that you are, that we are. For I, Shiva, desire to enter.

Open your heart! I knock at the door.

Will you receive me, my loves? ["Yes!"]

Thus, I come. I come as the great regulator of life and the flow of life—oh, the mighty flow of life in your being! I come to cleanse and purify your heart from the physical level to the very heart of the Inner Atman unto the Inner God—not that the Atman requires purification but that your perception of the Atman requires purification.

O my beloved ones, won't you be this night my Parvati, my Durga, my Kali and be seated as brides, one and all?

With great anticipation mighty yogis of the East have seen me fly to this place and they are joyous as they hear with the inner ear the devotions to Shiva.

Shiva I AM. Shiva you are. Will you not be now the negative polarity of my being forever and forever and forever so that we may purge the earth of Death and Hell so that earth may go through her purgation and the souls of the earth and the dead, and the deader than dead, might be consumed by the power of Divine Love?

Lo, I AM that Shiva! Lo, *I AM intensifying that fire!* Now I send forth my Light through all the arteries and the veins and the capillaries. I send my Light now!

Take a mighty inbreath with me. Now over the mighty breath that you inbreathe, which is my own breath, I am sending Light and reinvigoration and eternal youth and regeneration.

Lo, I AM THAT I AM. *Lo, I AM THAT I AM!* And I may be seated in your physical body! I may be seated in your desire body! I may be seated in your mental body! I may be seated in your etheric body! Now then, if you will invite me, I will do so promptly.

[Congregation gives forth fiats and clapping *Shivas* for 39 seconds.]

I enter for a solemn purpose, beloved. I enter because I desire to give myself this night to the mighty warriors of Light, whom you are, to the blessed devotees, to the blessed mothers and sisters and daughters and knights and heroes all over the world. I desire to give you a boost! I desire to give you that much of myself which the law of your being allows.

Each day the law of your being is read to you by your Holy Christ Self. The law changes almost like the readings on the stock market, beloved, for there is the coming and the going and the rising and the falling as you make negative karma, as you balance the negative by the positive and as you continue and continue and continue.

Now then, beloved ones, I am desiring to give you more Light for prolonged incarnation. I can give this to you, beloved, today but the one sure way for you to sustain it and maintain it is to recite [or sing] one of these bhajans to me daily.

In the power of the sound you have generated and will generate again and again, may you have a recording of this assembly in this place in the Heart, in this place that is purged physically and at inner levels by the mighty rain of Alpha, by the mighty rain of Omega. (The clearing of the earth is one of the points on the agenda of this conference for the Darjeeling Council and for others of our bands.)

So, beloved, if you will take the recording of the sound that is echoed in this tabernacle of the congregation, resounding amongst the hills and the mountains, you will know that I will surely *jump* inside of you again each day for the giving of one, a single one, of these bhajans.

I look to your longevity, *for I look for pillars of fire in the earth!* I look for those who shall walk with the walking stick

VII Only Make the Call, "Shiva!"

of Shiva, who will walk with my flame and in the honor of God and who will be a focus of that white fire, dispersing Death and Hell where'er they walk.

Yes, beloved ones, I look for Western Shaivites who will follow me, who will be myself that I might be their self—and that is the key! If you will allow me to be yourself for moments of the day, *I will repolarize you.*

Take care, then, that you observe the rules of the Great White Brotherhood, that you let not the sun go down upon your wrath,[1] that you resolve all things by the fire of *Shiva*, by the fire of the violet flame, by the blessed heart of the great avatar Saint Germain.

Yes, beloved ones, we rejoice that the Western yogis and yoginis are pursuing the path of the violet flame. It is an action ray which, when coupled with the ruby fire that I bear and the white light, will bring immense change in the earth!

Now, change needs to come quickly, yet not so quickly as to be a scorching fire that destroys in the process of the change. The violet flame will bring it about gently.

It is worth all lifetimes and many lifetimes to stay at the Heart of the Inner Retreat, to stay near the Royal Teton Ranch where you can have some livelihood for yourselves and your families. [It is worth it] just to be able to come together in such numbers at least one day a week that is set aside for this mighty action of the sacred fire's invocation. It will not take much more for the hierarchies of the Himalayas and the Great White Brotherhood to do much for the earth.

I can tell you, in these days deep changes are taking place gently by transmutation. Oh, thank you for the violet flame you have invoked this day! All elemental life blesses you, honors you and bows before the Light of God within you.

You need these servants of God and man in nature, beloved ones. And when they see your auras blazing and your dedication in their behalf, there is a ripple of mighty hope going forth through the mountains, the forests, the hills of all the hemispheres!

And they desire to see this entire body [of students] transported here and there over the earth! So we shall accommodate them, shall we not? ["Yes!"] Therefore we shall go this night.

You have made your certain connection with the Great White Brotherhood. Make the call and seal yourself in that Sacred Ritual for Transport and Holy Work.[2] So do it, beloved, without the necessity of going through again all of the words; but accept and affirm in your inner being before you retire that you shall therefore journey with Shiva.

You will journey to the places in the earth where earth is violated, elemental life is violated, the resources are violated and the toxins and the poisons are violating the bodies of all people but most especially those of the Lightbearers.

Let there be a cleansing in the earth without major cataclysm! *This is our goal.* To this we call you!

Saint Germain has called you in the past and many of you have responded, giving day after day your calls to the violet flame. I ask you to consider again, as the cycles are turning in this decade, [how you will] multiply the mantras of the violet flame by the Ruby Ray, and the Ruby Ray by the power of the mantras to Shiva, to Lord Krishna, and see what you can do to *clear* the minds, *clear* the opposition, *clear* those conditions that you hear about [in the media].

Beloved ones, I ask you to be seated as my brides. If you will remain seated and be still in the posture of your preference, you will find that I am able now to build along the spinal altar a certain conductor of light and a certain [action of the] healing of your central nervous system and brain. This is essential, beloved ones. You are hearts to be cherished and I indeed cherish you!

Blessed ones, there are many actions being taken in the earth, none more diabolical in this moment than the decree by the justices of the Supreme Court of the United States of America, five in number, who have agreed to uphold *Roe v. Wade* and the right, which is now called a "constitutional" right of woman, to abort her own Life becoming Life, her own child in the womb, her own *God* in the making, for that is *God* that is being aborted!

It is the abortion of the Atman! It is the abortion of a mission! And therefore it becomes, in some respect, *the abortion of an age* each time an individual is denied entrance into this world!

Can you believe, beloved ones, as I have seen with my own eye, that abortion actually being shown on television last night? Blessed ones, how can there be such low, low levels of descending into the Darkness and dragging woman and her child to that level?

O beloved ones, these members of this Court are examples of those who followed the way of *Din* in the betrayal of the LORD God's judgment and therefore took upon themselves the right to judge [life], the right to condemn life, the right to criticize [life], the right to purge and destroy [life].

Yes, beloved ones, they shall come to naught. The living Christ Jesus under Sanat Kumara has given to you the individual judgment calls and the judgment call for the binding of the dweller-on-the-threshold.

VII Only Make the Call, "Shiva!"

These individuals who have upheld a law that should never have been made a law, these individuals who have neglected the Holy Child now find upon their own heads the ultimate burden of karma for every child who is aborted hence, following their decision.

Beloved ones, this is an hour of great, great Darkness in the land, for we had hoped that there would be one individual who could be moved. Well, I AM *Shiva* and I tell you, I went to each one of them at inner levels and I attempted to move them. And they did defy and reject me and they would not be moved from their position to guarantee the right to kill the child who is God in the womb. *For shame! for shame! for shame* upon this civilization!

Therefore, I say, what shall we do?

We shall call the judgment upon those who know what they do! And these five *know* what they do. And all those who have led woman astray, those who know what they do and pronounce their judgment [upon the unborn] and provide the [milieu for] abortion and the abortion tools and the abortion clinics and the abortion doctors—all those who know what they do, *they* shall receive unmitigated judgment from my heart!

For I AM the destroyer of Death and they are Death incarnate, and they are seeking to lead the children of the Light into their death camp and to take them from embodiment.

Oh, shame! oh, shame! oh, shame! beloved, that that very abortion you saw on television was the abortion of a mighty Lightbearer!

I enlist those who fear me not, who know that there are few resources directly available to them through which the [spiritual] fire can be directed. Blessed ones, remember the scorching power of my third eye, remember the whirling of my being and my aura as I dance in the heart of the sun—and my own aura of [the sun-]manifestation.

Therefore, you see that an Ascended Master, an Archangel, a God or Goddess may go to those in embodiment and attempt to move them, attempt to convince them, even show them the akashic records of where they will end up by the folly of their decision. But, beloved ones, we do not interfere with free will. This is the law of all those who are beyond this level of embodiment.

You have free will in the earth. These justices represent you. Therefore, you can call to God and through your call, through your presence and through your life the judgment may descend upon them for their actions, for their deeds and even for their rejection of Shiva! Understand, therefore, what lies in your hand.

All you needed to understand was the mighty power of the

Ein Sof and of the *sefirot* and then you could see the mighty Tree of Life superimposed upon you as the Mighty I AM Presence. You could see the powers of God waiting to be invoked—*waiting, waiting!*

When you say, "How long, O Lord, how long, O Lord, wilt thou allow such suffering in the earth and the murder of the child?" the LORD God says back to you, "How long, O ye sons and daughters, how long, O ye brides of Shiva, will you wait to make the call and call for the judgment and the binding of the dweller-on-the-threshold of the entire consciousness, *the diabolical consciousness of abortion* that comes directly out of the pit of Death and Hell?"

How can you stand it any longer when you have the tools, the sponsorship and you must only say the word to see the turning of the cycles and the turning of the Darkness and the dark ones until they shall no longer be able to inhabit the earth?

For the vibration of earth shall accelerate through your call! And as it accelerates, beloved ones, therefore it will *spin off* those who are not of the Light, who will refuse to rise in vibration. And they must go to another place that they created long ago.

And these very ones who complain, these "environmentalists" who complain about the pollutions of the earth, they will go to the very place that they themselves have polluted in the past and they will truly have to deal with an environment that they themselves did destroy!

And I speak not only of the physical environment, I speak of the astral plane and the mental belt. And the mental belt is highly polluted. So is the etheric octave!

And therefore, beloved ones, when *you* increase in Light, when *you*, the sons and daughters of God, understand that the earth is the LORD's and you are the LORD's and you are his caretakers here below, you are going to go forth to keep the [flame for] planet earth.

And when you keep the Light in your body and you keep the Light in the temple, then *you* will dominate [the Darkness and the dark ones by the Light]: *you*, [the Lightbearers,] will be the dominant power, as the fallen ones are now the dominant power.

Therefore, we are able to help the individual, but how can we help the multitudes, beloved ones, when they are beset by and do embody the mass consciousness that is perpetrated upon them by the Nephilim gods and the fallen ones?

But I say to you, *you* have the power in your Mighty I AM Presence! *You* have the power in God and *not* in your human self, *not* in your carnal mind, *not* in the dweller-on-the-threshold but in God and God alone, who lives in you, to call for the binding of

VII   Only Make the Call, "Shiva!"

the destroyers in the earth—*not* the destroyer who is Shiva: [rather call to] Shiva, who will destroy the destroyers! For I AM *Shiva!*
   [*"Shiva!"* (22-second standing ovation)]
   Only make the call, *"Shiva!"* Only make the call, *"Shiva!"*
   Only make the call, *"Shiva!"* Only make the call, *"Shiva!"*
   [Congregation gives Shiva's fiat, clapping:]
   Only make the call, "Shiva!" Only make the call, "Shiva!"
   Only make the call, "Shiva!" Only make the call, "Shiva!"
   Only make the call, "Shiva!" Only make the call, "Shiva!"
   Only make the call, "Shiva!" Only make the call, "Shiva!"
   Only make the call, "Shiva!" Only make the call, "Shiva!"
   Only make the call, "Shiva!" Only make the call, "Shiva!"
   Only make the call, "Shiva!" Only make the call, "Shiva!"
   I have given you this mantra. I have burned it into the cells of your being and into your very bones lest you forget to only make the call, *"Shiva!"* [Congregation joins Shiva, clapping:]
   to only make the call, "Shiva!" to only make the call, "Shiva!"
   to only make the call, "Shiva!" to only make the call, "Shiva!"
   to only make the call, "Shiva!" to only make the call, "Shiva!"
   Beloved ones, I have stood and stood through a certain adept, who shall not be unveiled to you this night. I have stood through and around and in a certain adept and I have pierced my eye through the eye of that adept in physical embodiment and I have shown that one that a certain individual in a certain place, a total stranger standing there, was an immediate manifestation in physical embodiment of [an alien from a] UFO. And that individual was there and was identified. And I did put through the eye of the adept the power of my own eye, and that individual quickly moved from that place and, out of the sight of the adept, was bound and was removed.
   Blessed ones, I say to you: Work for your adeptship! *Work* for it and cherish it. Cherish it as though your adeptship were the very necessity [for you] to be the presence in the earth that must be there for the denying of abortion, for the sparing of those souls who must enter. Think of it as working for your knighthood or your ladyhood.
   Yes, beloved ones, think of the necessity to rise to the degrees of self-mastery because in that self-mastery I can work through you and know that you—as I knew with that one—will not in any level or degree misqualify the Light or the manifestation of my presence, for you, like that one, will have proven yourself [trustworthy] many, many times.
   I will take no chances. I will not make karma for your indiscretions, for your misuses of the Light. Therefore, *see* who I will

work through, who has the inner peace and the balance of the four lower bodies, who has followed the Messenger in using the diet of the Eastern adepts as a means to that God-control of all the physical levels of the body and then the emotions and then the mind and then the memory.

Beloved ones, the discipline is total, but look at what is before you! If suddenly this place were removed and all of a sudden you were in a large arena and in that arena were men of war, men of largeness, and they were slaughtering thousands and thousands of babies, you would leap to the center, you would bind them, you would rescue those whom you could rescue.

The situation of abortion is out of sight, out of mind. You are heroes and heroines every day of your lives as you serve, but *do not blind yourselves* to these events taking place daily—the murder of the child. Do not close your ears to the screams of the child, for they are heard across the planet. And these screams coming from every state and nation are reverberating such a sound, such a sound, beloved ones!

What Lightbearers could possibly be attracted to embody here when the very sounds of the earth rise up, whether as the agony of the child aborted or as the anger of the fallen ones as they go through the horrors of untimely death by all of the plagues coming upon the race?

Yes, there is great pain in the earth, but there is no pain so great to my heart, to your heart or to the heart of the Divine Mother as that pain of a soul that is dying, the soul that is being lost, the soul that is fading away, whether from weakness or from the anger and rebellion against God that in turn has also become a passivity.

The death of the soul, beloved, even far exceeds the pain of the abortion of a child. For a child may come again and be born again if parents can be found but when there is the death of the soul, the potential to realize God is permanently removed from that particular individuality in God that had opportunity to make that individuality permanent.

I think you agree with me that the infamy of planet earth has reached a high watermark. ["Yes."] And I think you know in the depth of your souls and in the marrow of your bones that things cannot get much worse without some reaction from the Great Tao, from the Great *Ein Sof,* from the Great God, the unmanifest God who chooses to manifest himself through us.

Yes, beloved, it is an hour of such opportunity for the binding of the forces of Antichrist. I solemnly speak to you. *May you not forget my word and my message.* May you fulfill all things necessary, and I say *necessary,* in your life. But may you not heap, and stack upon heap, obligations and activities that are actually not necessary to your livelihood, to your divine plan, to your good karma of caring for those in your care and for doing to others as you know God would have you do unto them, whoever is at the door.

There are things you must do in life, but won't you all admit once and for all there are many things you do that are not a necessity at all, whether to your health, to your ongoing edification or even to the opening of the flower of love of the heart.

I ask you, please, please make a list of those things that you can put aside and say, "I have done these things long enough, for many lifetimes. I can set them aside. For God in every child on planet earth is crying out to me and I cannot deafen my ears to those cries. I must help the little children. For once I was a little child, too, and I was helpless. And I took the hand of my mother and I took the hand of my father and others in whose care I was, and I went where they took me. I had no power of my own to do this or that. And I waited the long years till I came to that point of maturity when I could say, 'I am an adult. I am free at last! I am my own person. I shall do what I must do.'"

Blessed ones, being a child in the earth of whatever age is truly an unenviable position today, for child abuse is on the rise [and there are] the toxic chemicals in the body, in the water, in the food, in the substances they partake of, in the toys they play with.

What is fed to the [child] mind through the television is nothing but Death and Hell itself! I place my image over the television—between it and children—but, beloved ones, they and their parents have free will and I can only screen out so much.

Remember, you were once a child and helpless. And remember, when you are in your final days you may also be helpless. But *today* you have the strength and the vigor of life for all that you would acquire by following the right formulas for existence on earth. You have my offer of my presence.

I believe that deep down in your heart there is not one of you who is present at this conference who cannot say, because you are true chelas of the Light, that you are not satisfied with your present condition of spirituality and that you are here because you are *compelled* by your inner soul and your Inner Atman to rise another level and then another level and then another level!

You have reached a certain plateau in certain areas and you have finally said, *"I cannot rest here!* I am not breathing enough of the breath of eternal Life! I am not imbibing enough of the Light of the Eternal God and I am not doing enough for my people. I will find out how! I will *do something* and I will see change in my life, that I might give a better self to my Lord Brahman."

Blessed ones, in the flame, I AM Shiva. *Shiva,* yes. ["Shiva!"] *Shiva,* yes. ["Shiva!"] *Shiva,* yes! ["Shiva, yes!"]

I AM that flame. I AM that Shiva where you are. I want you to feel this with a great God-Reality. I AM here now as the slayer of illusion! And for this very moment I take the mighty sword and *I slay illusion all around you!* And I ask you to take the remainder of this class to see just [how much more] you can see for the illusions that I will now take. [Shiva does his sword work through the Messenger.]

As you might say, "You could cut it with a sword!" The illusions are as thick as the densest cheese you would find. Can you imagine living with such illusions? Yet you do, beloved ones. But the sacred fire raised up and the violet flame will clear them.

My beloved brides, I take you to my chamber, the chamber of my heart, this night. We shall go and minister to elemental life from the gathering place of the Royal Teton Retreat, where millions of other Lightbearers who are receiving this instruction at inner levels will be happy to join you. Our final stop will be, once again, Yugoslavia.[3]

You have made profound progress at deep inner levels. Let us keep it up, [journeying to Yugoslavia] for thirty-three days, beginning from the moment of our going forth and then our return.

In the name of the Divine Mother, in whose body I serve, Above and below, *I AM Shiva!*

And who are you? ["Shiva! Shiva! Shiva!..."]

[Congregation gives forth clapping *Shivas* for 45 seconds.]

"The Summit Lighthouse Sheds Its Radiance O'er All the World to Manifest as Pearls of Wisdom." This dictation by **Lord Shiva** was **delivered** by the Messenger of the Great White Brotherhood Elizabeth Clare Prophet on **Tuesday, June 30, 1992,** during the ten-day conference *FREEDOM 1992: "Joy in the Heart"* held at the **Royal Teton Ranch, Park County, Montana.** The Messenger delivered the major portion of her lecture "The Inner Path of Hinduism" on June 29. Prior to the dictation, she gave the concluding section, "Become Shiva!"—a profile on Lord Shiva—and led the congregation in singing bhajans. "Become Shiva!" has been edited for print and is published in *Pearls of Wisdom,* vol. 35, no. 30. [**N.B.** Throughout this *Pearl,* bracketed material denotes words unspoken yet implicit in the dictation, added by the Messenger under Lord Shiva's direction for clarity in the written word.] **(1)** Eph. 4:26. **(2)** The congregation gave the Sacred Ritual for Transport and Holy Work (Ashram Ritual 5) on the night of June 27. **(3)** See pp. 373–74, 398 n. 1.

I AM the Witness

Pray for Visualizations!

Dear Mother,

It is with great joy that I write this letter to you. I am fairly new to the Teachings of the Ascended Masters, having traveled over many paths to find them. Your being resonates with such clarity and truth that I am sure you are real!

I want to tell you about an experience I had several months ago while doing the violet flame decrees. I had been doing the decrees for a few months and reading the dictations and Teachings of the Masters. I was beginning to build a strong momentum but was at times frustrated because I felt I didn't have the proper visualizations. So I began to pray that I be shown visualizations that would be helpful. What I received was beyond all expectations!

One day I was about thirty minutes or so into my decrees and was giving decree 70.11:

> I AM the Violet Flame
>   In action in me now
> I AM the Violet Flame
>   To Light alone I bow
> I AM the Violet Flame
>   In mighty Cosmic Power
> I AM the Light of God
>   Shining every hour
> I AM the Violet Flame
>   Blazing like a sun
> I AM God's sacred power
>   Freeing every one

As I closed my eyes, I realized I was seeing something besides the blank screen of my inner eyelids. Something was moving, and it was as real as anything I had ever seen with my eyes open.

I continued giving the decree as a feeling of peace and love swept through my being and was anchored. After a few minutes, I realized that what I was witnessing was the violet flame! The flame moved slowly and gently and lovingly. I also heard the most beautiful music. (Is there a "third ear"?) It was not an image that I could control—it moved gently and freely in a beautiful and deep shade of violet. Truly, it was the most beautiful spiritual experience that I have had while fully conscious.

After a few minutes, I noticed a white light in the flame that would intensify and become brighter. Surrounded in violet, it would then move behind the flame. I stopped the decrees and just "watched" for several minutes. After a few more minutes, I opened my eyes. When I closed them again the flame was gone.

Since that day, I have seen the violet flame many times, though I have noticed it requires a strong decree momentum. The more I call forth the violet flame, the easier it is to see and watch this flame as it transmutes karma. What a wonderful gift Saint Germain has given to us all!

Thank you, Mother, for all you have done for me and your service to the chelas of the will of God. I look forward to seeing you at the October Class.

In Light, I AM,

The Tangible Tube of Light

Dear Mother and Lanello,

I witness with joy to the reality of the tube of light and to the power of visualization.

The day before Thanksgiving 1986, I went to a grocery store to pick up some last-minute items for the holiday dinner. The parking lot and store were jammed full of shoppers. I felt the urge to spiritually protect myself before joining the crowd.

I wasn't yet studying the Teachings, but a friend of mine had taught me a short call for the tube of light and told me to visualize it as I called it forth. I sat in my car and invoked the tube of light, concentrating on a mental picture of myself sealed in an impenetrable cylinder of light with a radius of about six feet. I continued until I could feel the light surrounding me.

Holding the visualization of the tube of light, I walked into the store. A three- or four-year-old boy was running straight toward me, or rather, toward the automatic sliding doors just behind me. He gazed at the floor a few feet in front of him as he ran, joyously unaware that we were on a collision course. Then he halted sharply about six or seven feet away from me, as if to avoid crashing into something. After an odd glance at me, he ran around me in a perfect semicircle about six feet from where I stood. He was running around my tube of light! Once he had cleared it, he continued on his original course toward the doors.

What a wonderful demonstration! By God's grace, what we call forth is as real as we allow it to be.

Thank you, Mother and Lanello, for your unwavering service to the Light and to the Light in each of God's children. Thank you for your loving service in bringing forth the Teachings of the Ascended Masters and their precise decrees.

All glory to God!

32

Do Not Doubt God!
Love God and Love One Another

Our Most Beloved Sons and Daughters:
    We come surrounded by legions of angels whose acquaintance you have met in ages past. Be at home, then, for we place over this place, so consecrated by your hearts and the heart of Lord Gautama Buddha, even the replica of our Home, your Home in the Great Central Sun. So long, so long—as time is reckoned and as cycles of coming and going are reckoned—has been your absence from our Home.
    Now you have said the Om. You have sounded it from within. Now experience it in this moment that will be for you, we trust, a springboard to a new thrust for your Victory and for the ultimate Victory of the Lightbearers of the earth. Therefore, be at rest.
    Our gratitude to servants of the Light, helpers, angels, elementals, all who have come to prepare this place. In a single year you have made it once again our cradle—the cradle where we do give birth to souls of Light annually.
    Oh, it is a coming together! Oh, it is a sun center, this very place! And thus, beloved, a planetary and a personal purging is ongoing. Welcome, then, the rain, for it is a special rain of our beloved Alpha.

I, then, Omega, greet you, and I greet you in the love of such tender understanding of your innermost thoughts and needs and desires and questionings and doubts.

It is not easy to be in this octave, beloved. But I would remind you that the divine spark within, which is called by a number of names by the various ones who have experienced the divine spark, even the Atman itself, truly does have a name and that name is Alpha/Omega. We are the Divine Presence in your heart. Brahman is the Divine Presence. The Universal Christ is that Presence.

Therefore, as we can understand even the dilemma of living in this octave, so will you not understand that there is also the very present possibility for you to live in that holy aura, truly that universe of Light that is the secret chamber of the heart?

This place of our Home of Alpha and Omega with which we surround you in this hour is available to you, each one, as you will retire to the secret chamber of your heart each day.

Beloved, just as all of Death and Hell move against your going in consciousness to the Great Central Sun, so do not underestimate the opposition to your soul each and every day of your life—that opposition which would deny the soul her entering in, as the great ritual of the conclusion of the day, entering in to the secret chamber of the heart.

This you do in the name of your Mighty I AM Presence and Holy Christ Self, in the name of Archangel Michael. For you do understand that there are boulders and mountains of karma that stand between you, as the soul seated in the seat-of-the-soul chakra, and that secret chamber that is the replica of our Home and of all universes within and without.

Therefore, under the old dispensation, you could not have lawfully risen to such a holy place without having balanced that karma, but in this day and hour the Archangel Michael does place his Presence over you. And therefore, in the presence of that God-free, wondrous manifestation of I AM THAT I AM, your soul may rise to that level (as she has not done in many centuries) and be tutored, beloved ones.

Is this not the mighty grace of the Lord, who weeps for you, who loves you, who desires you not to be absent but with him, with him in the very heart of Brahman?

Therefore, grace and mercy abound—and the grace of the Word, the Shekinah, beloved ones, the mighty power of Mother Flame and of Shakti of God. By that grace and mercy, then, you are able to come to the secret place of your God and to do so regularly and daily. To so do will strike in you a new tenderness, a tenderness so rare, whereby you can hardly find a harsh feeling or a harsh word thereafter—so wondrous, so loving [is the Presence and] so much love do you find in that [secret] place [where the threefold flame does burn].

Let the rituals of the heart not take hours, beloved. There is no time and space in this. There is being the caretaker of your thoughts and feelings, the body, the heart and the mind, so that by a thought at the end of the day you can give the fiat to Archangel Michael, you can call to us as Father-Mother and you can mount the spiral staircase [from the seat-of-the-soul chakra to the secret chamber of the heart] and be one.

And then when day breaks and you must go and pick up your karma again after you have journeyed through the night to the etheric octaves, you return through that point of the secret chamber of the heart to your lawful place in the seat-of-the-soul chakra and you work the works of God. And you have such love that you pour into each work! And you retain the memory of the exercises of the guarding of the throat chakra, of the silence of the bliss of God that you can maintain no matter what is the requirement of the hour.

You, then, compress the fire of being and concentrate it, using it not for many, many idle words but saving it for the peace-commanding presence, raising it up to the point of the third eye, whereby you may see and know and make, without error, your decisions and take your steps and live in the cycles of the hours as though you were living, and indeed you are, in the spheres of the Great Causal Body of your I AM Presence.

I AM your Divine Mother, beloved ones, and I desire to make you comfortable in the earth. (Yes, I know there are many who attempt to take from you that comfort.) Comfort comes first from the twin flames of the Holy Spirit, Alpha and Omega. It comes also as these flames may manifest the basic necessities of life and that which does establish the circle of hearth and home and family and community of brothers and sisters who are keeping the Flame with seraphim at the altar of God day and night.

Yes, beloved, I understand the burdens that are upon you and I understand, all too well, those who place them upon you.

Receive from my heart, O Mother of the Flame, in this hour the empowerment to call on behalf of the sons and daughters of God for the binding of the oppressor and the oppression. Receive it now, O Mother, and exercise it in behalf of thine own, whom thou doest love so profoundly!

O beloved hearts, in your Holy Christ Flame is the intensity of Light which can be multiplied by you to accomplish so much more than you accomplish *for your nonbelief.* Yes, beloved, it is a matter of believing.

Those who believe in God and in the God-identification of one and another and another in embodiment, beloved, may therefore have that tie [of God-identification] established through that One to the Great Central Sun and know many miracles. Those of nonbelief can receive nothing—I say *nothing*—whether from Alpha and Omega or from our Messenger.

Therefore, go after with the vengeance of Kali the very momentum of nonbelief, unbelief, doubt, self-doubt and doubt of God which torments you and causes you to doubt anyone and everyone whom you may meet!

Blessed hearts, self-doubt is self-denial and it is the denial of God. It is a most dangerous state of consciousness. You must wage war against it! For unless you remove it, how shall we enter in and how shall you enter in?

You see, doubt breaks the cord of Light you build with your decrees. Each cutting doubt is a cutting of the rope you have built and raised unto the sky as a yogi with yogic powers.

Yes, beloved, do not doubt the Law! Do not doubt God! Recognize God in yourself and do not doubt his Spirit in you as the Atman. This is the most precious advice I could give you for a lifetime and many lifetimes.

When you are sure of the self that is God within you (and there is absolutely no reason why you should not be, because God is faithful unto you even when you have been faithless), when you are absolutely faithful to that God and trust that God, beloved, there is therefore established a tie that cannot be broken, neither by yourself nor by Death and Hell—except you yourself by free will should once again entertain doubt and break it.

This, then, is the portion that you must give to God. If you will but give faith and trust and build upon it wisdom and illumination, wisdom and understanding, and build upon it a true and profound knowledge of the will of God, then you will find through your study not one or five or ten but many, many reasons why you ought to have faith and not doubt.

O beloved, if the Lord Jesus Christ when he journeyed into the cities "did not many mighty works there for their unbelief,"[1] do you think the father and the mother of Jesus Christ or the son, the daughter of God in the earth who is the bearer of the mantle may do any more?

VIII Do Not Doubt God!

I tell you no! And therefore, we witness to the work of the Messenger unto those who believe and have faith and see beyond the veil the shining of the God Presence that is able to reach out to them and raise them. Thus, they are raised. Thus, they are healed.

We see [that that work cannot manifest] in those who have inner conflict, inner compromise, who violate the laws of Alpha and Omega, do not confess, atone, receive penance, do not determine to work upright in the face of their God or even, God forbid, have in their conversations the criticism of the Messenger or our servants.

Beloved ones, what we offer you today is a very direct and living contact to us through the Messenger and through the mantle of Guru that is upon her solidly and sealed. Thus, know it. Understand it. The Path and the relationship are open to *you* as long as you will maintain the single foundational quality, which is love.

Love contains all others! Love balances all others! Love consumes all others! In the center of God's love and your love for him, you may approach such a close nestling to the heart of myself, your Divine Mother.

I will tell you that the Messenger will never pursue you, beloved. You yourselves must make the request to be a known and counted and sponsored direct chela of the Messenger and, through the Messenger, to be [a chela of] the heart of El Morya and the entire hierarchy of Light unto our hearts.

Yes, beloved, let the ties become tighter! Let them not become bondage but let them become a mighty soul liberation unto all who are a part of the great *antahkarana* of Life!

I, Omega, bring you the greetings of untold billions of points of Light and angels and sons and daughters—points of Light, who after all are simply the One.

Their love be upon you this day and forever. May you receive it this day and forever because you vow to yourself and your God Self never to leave off loving God and loving God in one another.

How can you go wrong with this formula?

I myself do not know.

"The Summit Lighthouse Sheds Its Radiance O'er All the World to Manifest as Pearls of Wisdom." This dictation by **beloved Omega** was **delivered** by the Messenger of the Great White Brotherhood Elizabeth Clare Prophet on **Wednesday, July 1, 1992,** during the ten-day conference FREEDOM 1992: "Joy in the Heart" held at the **Royal Teton Ranch, Park County, Montana.** Before the dictation, the Messenger led the congregation in the Sacred Ritual for Oneness (Ashram Ritual 6), devotional songs to the Father-Mother God in the Great Central Sun, and the sounding of the Om.   (1) Matt. 13:58.

I AM the Witness

The Burning Flame of the Son of God in My Heart

I, Elizabeth Clare Prophet, Messenger for the Great White Brotherhood, do witness to the chelas and the world to the presence in my heart of my Lord and Saviour Jesus Christ. I witness to his Sacred Heart, one with my heart. I witness to his all-consuming love and mercy and grace upon my soul and the souls of all true Lightbearers, all true chelas of the will of God.

I witness to the sacred fire he has placed in my heart. It is a burning fire that kindles my soul, my chakras, all of my house. This fire I often feel as a physical fire. And whenever I give concentrated devotion, decrees and meditation to Jesus' Heart within my heart and my heart in his, the burning fire increases until it becomes such an all-consuming passion, and compassion, that I must leave off from this ecstasy lest I be transported from the realm of daily practicalities.

In this *Pearl*, our beloved Omega speaks to us of our Home in the Great Central Sun. Our Divine Mother and Alpha have placed a replica of it on the etheric plane over the Heart of the Inner Retreat and it is available to us as we go to the secret chamber of the heart each day.

This is a permanent focus. Before you retire at night you can ask to be taken to the etheric Retreat of the Divine Mother at the Royal Teton Ranch and the Western Shamballa at the Heart of the Inner Retreat. And while you are there, you can be "at Home away from home" in the forcefield of our Home in the Great Central Sun that Alpha and Omega have established over the entire area of the conference site.

Please note that beloved Omega tells us on page 422 that "there is also the very present possibility for you to live in that holy aura, truly that universe of Light that is the secret chamber of the heart." Now please reread page 422 of this *Pearl*.

In sealing my witness to you of the burning flame of the Son of God in my heart, I quote from *How to Know God: The Yoga Aphorisms of Patanjali:*[1]

> 36. **Concentration may also be attained by fixing the mind upon the Inner Light, which is beyond sorrow.**

The ancient yogis believed that there was an actual center of spiritual consciousness, called "the lotus of the heart," situated between the abdomen and the thorax, which could be revealed in deep meditation. They claimed that it had the form of a lotus and that it shone with an inner light. It was said to be "beyond sorrow," since those who saw it were filled with an extraordinary sense of peace and joy.

From the very earliest times, the masters of yoga emphasized the importance of meditating upon this lotus. "The supreme heaven shines in the lotus of the heart," says the Kaivalya Upanishad. "Those who struggle and aspire may enter there. Retire into solitude. Seat yourself on a clean spot in an erect posture, with the head and neck in a straight line. Control all sense-organs. Bow down in devotion to your teacher. Then enter the lotus of the heart and meditate there on the presence of Brahman—the pure, the infinite, the blissful."

And in the Chandogya Upanishad we read:

> Within the city of Brahman, which is the body, there is the heart, and within the heart there is a little house. This house has the shape of a lotus, and within it dwells that which is to be sought after, inquired about, and realized.
>
> What, then, is that which dwells within this little house, this lotus of the heart? What is it that must be sought after, inquired about, and realized?
>
> Even so large as the universe outside is the universe within the lotus of the heart. Within it are heaven and earth, the sun, the moon, the lightning and all the stars. Whatever is in the macrocosm is in this microcosm also.
>
> All things that exist, all beings and all desires, are in the city of Brahman; what, then, becomes of them when old age approaches and the body dissolves in death?
>
> Though old age comes to the body, the lotus of the heart does not grow old. It does not die with the death of the body. The lotus of the heart, where Brahman resides in all his glory— that, and not the body, is the true city of Brahman. Brahman, dwelling therein, is untouched by any deed, ageless, deathless, free from grief, free from hunger and from thirst. His desires are right desires, and his desires are fulfilled.

And in the Mundaka Upanishad: "Within the lotus of the heart he dwells, where the nerves meet like the spokes of a wheel. Meditate upon him as OM, and you may easily cross the ocean of darkness. In the effulgent lotus of the heart dwells Brahman, passionless and indivisible. He is pure. He is the light of all lights. The knowers of Brahman attain him."

This method of meditation is helpful, because it localizes our image of the spiritual consciousness toward which we are struggling. If the body is thought of as a busy and noisy city, then we can imagine that, in the middle of this city, there is a little shrine, and that, within this shrine, the Atman, our real nature, is present. No matter what is going on in the streets outside, we can always enter that shrine and worship. It is always open.

37. Or by meditating on the heart of an illumined soul, that is free from passion.

Let your mind dwell on some holy personality—a Buddha, a Christ, a Ramakrishna. Then concentrate upon his heart. Try to imagine how it must *feel* to be a great saint; pure and untroubled by sense-objects, a knower of Brahman. Try to feel that the saint's heart has become your heart, within your own body. Here, again, the localization of the image will be found very helpful. Both Hindus and Christians practice this form of meditation—concentrating not only upon the heart but also, sometimes, upon the hands and the feet and the whole form [of a personality of the Godhead, i.e., an Ascended Master, or a saint].

---

(1) *How to Know God: The Yoga Aphorisms of Patanjali*, translated with a new commentary by Swami Prabhavananda and Christopher Isherwood (New York: New American Library, Mentor Books, 1969), pp. 49–51. Reprinted from a hardcover edition published by Vedanta Press (1953).

If you would like to have your very own personal copy of *How to Know God*, send $4.50 plus $1.25 postage to Summit University Press, Dept. 434, Box 5000, Livingston, MT 59047-5000, and we will mail it to you posthaste.

33

The Fourth Woe

"I Will Become the Example!"

Hail, O Alpha's Sons and Daughters!
    I AM come. I AM Alpha here and in you. And I deliver unto you this day *my Love, my Love, my Love!* [43-second standing ovation]
    Again the heathen rage and the people imagine a vain thing. But I, the Lord, do hold them in derision. Therefore, let us laugh today, let us laugh tomorrow and let us laugh again![1]

I Bring You an Elixir of the Waters of Everlasting Life

    For though they seek to take from you the geothermal waters of the Divine Mother in the earth, I tell you, they shall never take from you the waters of everlasting Life, which I bring this day and which my angelic hosts now offer you as the cup of cold water in Christ's name, and more—as the elixir that you might quaff and know that I am urging on the points of light and cells in your body to move toward the ascension in the Light! [27-second standing ovation]
    Now stand very still and receive the beloved seraph who loves you, who knows you, who attended your birth in the Great Central Sun. Can you imagine [that there is] such a seraph who has known you since first you opened your eyes and saw the Beloved and saw your God?
    So that one, that precious one, now hands to you each one this cup of the elixir. Drink, then, beloved ones. It is sparkling and ready. [22-second pause] Every Lightbearer in embodiment upon earth

who has raised himself or herself to a certain level, with or without this Teaching, shall also be served this drink during the hours of rest. Now then, beloved, be seated for the assimilation of the elixir and my word.

The Keeper of the Scrolls Stands before You: Know Your Weaknesses and Your Strengths

There are some things that are to be endured in the earth and there are some things that cannot be tolerated, nor by God nor by his sons and daughters. Therefore I am grateful that you are in the earth in this hour. I have placed you here, beloved, but that which I could never do is to force your free will or your hand to become devotees and disciples of Alpha and Omega in this life.

You were surely God-taught. You were surely received before our altars in the retreats of the Great White Brotherhood. You were shown the possibilities and the karmas and the pitfalls and your weaknesses and your strengths and the actions of past lives that did take you apart from the way, the straight and narrow way, and how you would confront them again [and that] you would be tested, you would be initiated.

Now then, the angel of the Keeper of the Scrolls[2] stands before you. And in a moment and in a flash you can already review this life and see how you came upon or, I should say, *how there came upon you* fallen angels, cunning. And they have purveyed their drugs and all manner of illusory experiences, drawing you into the byways of the misuse of the light of your seven chakras.

That which they most desired to pervert in you, beloved, was and *is* the chakra of the Divine Mother. For it is the fount of life on earth and the fount of eternal Life that rises from the base-of-the-spine chakra to the crown and is activated and crystallized and sealed by the descending Light of your I AM Presence.

Because, therefore, you call to your Mighty I AM Presence daily and hourly, and some of you even awaken realizing you have been making the call in your dreams—beloved ones, because of this, we have not stressed to you Kundalini yoga. For you are accomplishing the goal by the merging of the Light of the descending action of your Mighty I AM Presence and the rising action of the Omega flame within you. And by the force of the descent of the Alpha flame in you, the Alpha flame does magnetize and draw up the Omega. And therefore, you find that there is a regulating and there is a balancing, there is a strengthening of the chakras.

And if you follow the diet of the Messenger, [which is the diet] of the Eastern adepts [adapted to your needs and life-style], beloved ones, you will know the strengthening of the corresponding organs and you will know that I, Alpha, with Omega, will place more and more of our flame in each part of the body and especially those parts that have the greatest strength.

Therefore know your strengths always, beloved. They are a chalice for our coming. And I speak not only of physical strengths but character strengths—the strengths of the mind, the will and the heart. And also know your weaknesses and determine what is your greatest weakness, beloved. Then go after it and remember that it will also be related to the weakest of your organs.

Thus, you must bring up the whole manifestation of the four lower bodies. This we seek. Each one must become his own pyramid of Life. Each one must raise up that coil of the ascension flame depicted in the book of Djwal Kul.[3]

Learning from Experience, Karma and the World

Yes, beloved, come now and understand where you have faced the fallen ones and where they outdid you because your teachers were not in embodiment and at your side from your earliest birth and from your childhood. And then again, when you have had teachers, you have chosen to ignore them at a certain stage of your life and you would learn your lessons by experimentation and experience.

Beloved ones, it is understandable that there are some things that must be learned by experience. Otherwise, we should all be placed in a box. We should place *you* in a box and open it up when you are twenty-one years old!

Well, beloved, that experiment of Skinner never did work, never would work, but the fallen ones attempted it as one more means to drive the children of the Light crazy. Yes, beloved ones.

Therefore, I tell you, you have chosen the world to be your guru. And I ask you: How many here this day are through with having the world as your guru? ["I am!"]

Well, it is a wise choice, beloved ones, for you have seen the world long enough and in long embodiments. But even in this one a certain amount of pain has been necessary to wean you from the temporary pleasures of the world. And, of course, you have had to be weaned from placing your trust in other individuals, who would suddenly abandon you, taking with them the members of your family, your children, your belongings, and never be seen again! And you in dismay have said, "How can this be?"

Well, it is because you have trusted in the flesh and you have not first trusted in God. Had you trusted in God, beloved ones, things might have turned out better. And that is the lesson you should have learned.

There are some karmas that you must balance personally and that cannot be balanced in any other way. If you come upon such a karma, go for it, *drive into it.* Use your mighty sword! Be diligent, give it your all! If necessary, lay down your life and take it again. Give all of your strength each day. Be restrengthened in the night and go for it again and again until you hear the mighty holy angel of God: "Blessed one, you have accomplished this karma. It is fulfilled. It is concluded. You may now step [out of this situation] and move on with your life, if it is your choice."

Learning from a Guru-Chela Relationship with the Messenger

So, beloved, we recruit you where you are and we say, if you truly desire to receive the training of the Gurus of Maitreya's Mystery School, we shall give it to you as never before. You must understand that neither the Masters nor the Messenger shall interfere with your life one iota unless you request it, unless you implore us and determine that you would like the direct contact and the direct disciplining and the direct love whereby you can be quickly delivered of certain elements of your lifestream that perhaps you are not even aware of yourself.

Therefore, beloved, if you will address your letters in writing in the physical octave to me and to my beloved Omega and to the Messenger, stating what level of chelaship you would desire wherever you might live on earth, or whether you enter this Community as a chela, so, then, we shall begin our course. Whether at inner levels or on the outer simply depends on how much the Messenger is able to give on a one-to-one basis.

You can understand this, beloved, for there are thousands upon thousands upon earth who are yearning for this relationship. And we, Alpha and Omega, bring you the message this day that in consideration of the Messenger and of yourselves, we shall place ourselves in position through the Messenger that she might tend to the many, not necessarily physically, personally, but by a mighty action of the heart and the mind and by a certain [soul] tutoring [at inner levels]. For, beloved ones, there are certain elements [of karma/psychology] in everyone that must be dealt with. And therefore, you can do this as tens of thousands [of chelas] and come up another step. Thus, there are gradations and grades for all.

Beloved ones, you may have wondered why the Messenger has not spoken to you directly about many things. It is because you have not made that commitment in physical writing that

IX The Fourth Woe

you desire that Guru-chela relationship. Therefore, I can tell you, when you desire to have this, the Messenger will not spare the rod *or* the love to bring you to that very centeredness in the heart of your own God Presence.

One thing I will tell you: the Messenger has no desire whatsoever to possess you but to bring your soul to us. Therefore, you may accept my word and place your trust in me that *you can rely on your Messenger to assist you all the way Home!* [39-second standing ovation]

Please be seated.

Matters of Global Consequence

Beloved ones, I address you now on matters of global concern, matters that must be dealt with by the hierarchy of Light and by yourselves. Your success in dealing with these matters does depend on the Guru-chela relationship that you keep. And, of course, you know that the beloved El Morya, the beloved Lanello are the ones closest to you in this octave through the Messenger.

Therefore, I speak of my coming on the occasion when I pronounced the three woes—*Woe! Woe! Woe!*—and I told you, beloved, that these are the woes of karma and that these woes that descended are the woes of the violation of the Light of the Father and of the Son and of the Holy Spirit. And I did state to you, beloved, that one day, *one day* (and that day known only to me) I would release the fourth woe.[4]

And the fourth woe, beloved, is the woe of the descent of the karma of the misuse of the Light of the Divine Mother and her seed. The hour has come, therefore, for those violators of the body of woman and of her children to receive their judgment.

Blessed hearts, all have had opportunity abundant to come to the defense of woman, to come to the defense of *soul*—*soul* who is the feminine principle and the potential to realize the fullness of God. Yes, this opportunity of ministering unto the souls of male and female and child, of son and daughter of God and every level of evolution upon the planet has been given. And I say, beloved, of all things in the earth, that which is most neglected by all is the individual soul.

Then there is the persecution of the child, the abuse of the very Christ in the body of the child and therefore the defilement, or attempted defilement, of that Christ being formed and descending into that temple.

I speak, then, of this portent of the fourth woe, but I would first speak to you now of certain things in the earth that have changed.

You have seen the receding of World Communism. Blessed ones, the trees of World Communism have been topped. But the trunk of the tree and the root of the tree has not changed, has not lost its vitality. Therefore beware, for your representatives in the West desire to believe all lies of the Liar and even to accept all murderings of the Murderer.

Be it known, then, that though the outer colorations may change, the beast of World Communism is far from dead in the earth. It is a mentality. It is a vibration and a state of consciousness that has been long on the earth, far antedating its present manifestation in this century. Thus, though Lenin unfurled it and though Stalin intensified it, yet there are those, many in embodiment today, who at heart still maintain that focus of World Communism.

There has been major change in the earth. Do not think that it has not been by the action of the invocation of the Light, for it has! And since my prior coming, you have accomplished many labors by long hours of giving of decrees here and in your Teaching Centers and, therefore, much has been cleared in the earth of the fallen ones.

Yet, on the other hand, those in positions of power who enjoy that power, who know that their day is through have not in any way responded to the Light nor to the Seven Archangels nor to the message proclaimed to them by the Seven Archangels of the consequences of their deeds.

Neither the president of the United States nor the Congress has seen fit to put in place the necessary defense of this nation. And therefore, beloved, there is a vulnerability that continues, and it continues for the breaking down of defense itself and the continuing trust [on the part of the people] of those who are not yet Christ-identified and far from it.

Trust No Man: Trust the God in Each One

The byword of the brothers and sisters in white, beloved, is "Trust no man, trust no woman." Therefore, whom do you trust?

You trust the divine spark and *the God within each one.* And to that God [you bow] and with that God you make contact, beloved. When you come upon individuals who have long ago snuffed out the divine spark, who have long ago squandered the Light, who have denied the soul potential to be and therefore draw their energies from the masses of the people whom they control, what is there to trust in them?

I speak of the leadership of East and West and of every nation! And I speak of those in the leadership at all echelons and

IX The Fourth Woe

compartments of society. There is no nation that has a corner on these Nephilim gods, beloved ones.

And you see in this hour the great mistrust of the Congress of the United States by the people. Well, beloved ones, when the new recruits come in, as they will be elected, I remind you: Trust no man, trust no woman, but trust in God *and invoke that God!*

And if you want to see real God-action through your representatives in every nation upon earth, then I say, do not fail to exercise the decree for the binding of the dweller-on-the-threshold. For that carnal mind, that not-self, must be bound that the Great Tao may act through them, that the *sefirot* may act through them, that the I AM THAT I AM may act through them, that the Lord Christ, the Lord Krishna and the Inner Buddha might act through them!

There is no assurance of the Light acting through anyone who is not a devotee or through anyone who is. It is not guaranteed unless either that one who knows of the decree [gives the decree] or others give that decree for him or her. The binding of the not-self provides the greatest freedom of choice to the soul, to the heart and to the very goodwill of many servants of God in government.

One day they promise this and the next day they take it away, and that is because of the influence of the lower levels of being. Therefore, this call for the binding of the dweller-on-the-threshold accomplished by yourself on yourself and loved ones and all Lightbearers of the earth is the single greatest, most effective call you can make for world change and for the putting of the brake on the downward course of civilization. Therefore, I tell it to you.

And I say to you, you must know who your representatives are on every issue. You must know *who* will be making decisions for you and *when*. It then becomes your spiritual responsibility in this octave, in our name and in the name of the Seven Archangels, to call for the binding of all forces of Darkness that would interfere with [your representatives in their] bringing about the manifestation of the will of God.

It is not that you wish to interfere with their free will, beloved. It is that you desire to liberate their mind and heart and soul to receive the will of God and to act upon it.

Let not your prayers, then, be prayers of malintent, of manipulation—not that they are, for you are dispassionate and objective in your calls—but understand that where the individual [representative of the people] is, [through ignorance,] not free to affirm the rightness of the law of God and man and how it is to be interpreted, that individual is [subject to] making karma.

You as angels in embodiment, and many of you are, and you

as sons and daughters of God must stand in the defense of life and attempt to uphold those individuals who could be making good karma, who have a good soul and a good fire within them yet do not have the sure and certain understanding of what they must do, nor the vision nor the inner knowledge. Therefore, knowledge above all, as you have been told, is *the key* to the saving of a planet.

Become the Example: You Can Make the Difference

Now therefore, beloved ones, it is indeed a time of great transition. It is a time when, more than ever, people cannot find leaders. They have no confidence in those whom they see. They take the one that is the least evil, not finding one who is God-good.

I understand this, beloved hearts, and I tell you, if you cannot find that person whom you seek, then you must become that person yourself! Is not that what the whole world is telling you in this hour? [So you must say to yourself:]

"There are no examples. Therefore I will not look here or there. *I* will become the example by the grace of God and in true humility of Alpha. *I will become the example!"*

Blessed ones, there are not sufficient role models. Become them! I urge you to consider that calling and to remember, though you think no one sees your good deeds or your bad, when you are a soul tied to the Great White Brotherhood your soul is seen by every other individual on planet earth and everyone on planet earth does take his step and his stride from your step and stride.

All the earth watches the devotees of Light. So do the forces of Death and Hell. You are indeed seen, beloved! And where you are a Light that lightens your home and your town, people know it, even though they may not know you or see you. They sense your presence and know that in your town there is a soul putting on her Christhood. And therefore, they sleep easier at night because you are there.

I say, beloved, and I implore you as your Father: *Do not let the people down.* Do not let the people of earth down and do not let us, your parents, down. For you can make the difference! Yes, beloved, *you can make the difference but you must do it!* It is not enough that I tell you you can. You must do it!

And doing it somehow becomes a fuzzy proposition and you allow the forces to stop the physical actions, to stop the conclusion of projects that have come forth as a gift from my mind to your own. And you see the project, [and perhaps you start it,] but you do not

IX The Fourth Woe

bring it to completion; and therefore it is aborted, it is stillborn.

Blessed hearts, if it is a right idea, then see it through and give your decrees and, come what may, do not give up! The key here is to determine that it is a right idea. And this you must do by your meditation and decrees to the Great Divine Director, to Cyclopea, to El Morya, to the entire Spirit of the Great White Brotherhood.

The Release of the Fourth Woe: the Judgment of the Persecutors of the Divine Mother and Her Seed

Angels of God, take your positions now at all points in the earth! Cosmic reinforcements, rings of seraphim, legions who have come, you have surveyed the earth. You have received unto your bodies of light the photographs, the recordings on film and sound tape of all that is taking place where you stand. We, therefore, have for our archives in the sun of Helios and Vesta and in the Great Central Sun recordings of all that is taking place on planet earth at all levels.

This is a necessary reading taken by us when we are, as you would say, physically present in the earth. We take our readings also from the higher spheres. But this is a specific reading, beloved, where we shall be able to view, as you would view in your motion picture theaters, the sound, the aura, the intent, the mind and the record of all that has been recorded.

Blessed ones, understand that when such a thorough review of a planetary home and system is taken, cycles are indeed turning, and in this hour we are seeking what is the greatest mitigation that can come and what is the judgment that will not be turned back. Therefore, beloved ones, I ask you to stand. Please keep silent.

Urrrrrrrrrrrrrrrrrrrrrrrrrrrrrrrrrrrrrrrrrrrrrr
Urrrrrrrrrrrrrrrrrrrrrrrrrrrrrrrrrrrrrrrrrrrrrr
Ehmmmmmmmmmmmmmmmmmmmmmm

Powers of the octaves, *powers of the octaves,* powers of the octaves, release now the fourth *woe!*

Woe! Woe! Woe! Woe!

Therefore, there is the descent into the earth in this hour of the judgment of the persecutors of the Divine Mother and her seed and of the souls of Light and of the children of the Light—the persecutors of the Divine One in every temple on earth, the persecutors of Atman and of the living Christ and of the Inner Buddha.

Therefore, you who have embodied this persecution of the Divine Mother, I declare to you as I place my Electronic Presence before every one of you on planet earth—on the astral plane, the etheric plane and in the mental belt—I declare before you:

Your judgment has descended! It is sealed in your four lower bodies. It is sealed in your record. It is descending now and in this hour as I speak. Mark and note it well!

Therefore, the judgment has descended. And you who have again given liberty to woman to murder her child, you who represent millions upon earth who agree with you—you stand guilty before mankind and all aborted souls on the etheric plane. You, therefore, shall come to judgment, for *you* have committed the murder of God and *it shall not stand!*

Therefore, it is done. And I, Alpha, seal this judgment. And you will not remove it! You will not dodge it! You will not displace it! You will not in any way extricate yourself from the hold of Alpha's judgment!

Woe! Woe! Woe! Woe!

In the four quadrants of the earth, I release the Light of the Dhyani Buddhas for the fixing of the judgment:

Woe! Woe! Woe! Woe! Woe!

Therefore know, beloved, that when the buildings fall all around you and the avalanches descend and the continents shake, *you* must stand fast in the very pillar of your God! And as I said in my former address, when the fourth woe descends it is time to get thee up into the mountain of God.[5]

I AM Alpha. Those who bear my Light are sealed, protected, nurtured, tutored. There is *no* ongoing dispensation for those who are not servants of Light. But unto those who become servants of Light there is the grace complete, necessary to their victory in this life or a succeeding life, where their karma does not allow [it in this one].

This is the pledge of Alpha. Do not doubt it but take advantage of it. For I AM here. I AM Brahman. I AM the Atman. As Above, so below, *I AM your Self.*

"The Summit Lighthouse Sheds Its Radiance O'er All the World to Manifest as Pearls of Wisdom." This dictation by **beloved Alpha** was **delivered** by the Messenger of the Great White Brotherhood Elizabeth Clare Prophet following the dictation by Omega on **Wednesday, July 1, 1992,** during the ten-day conference *FREEDOM 1992: "Joy in the Heart"* held at the **Royal Teton Ranch, Park County, Montana.** The fourth woe was released by Alpha at 6:47 p.m. MDT. [**N.B.** Throughout this *Pearl,* bracketed material denotes words unspoken yet implicit in the dictation, added by the Messenger under Alpha's direction for clarity in the written word.] (1) Pss. 2:1–4; 59:8. Notes are continued on p. 477.

Mother Mary's Ascension Day Address 1992

34

"Be Careful!"

Hold Fast to Me

Sons and Daughters, Hear Me Well!

I come in an hour when devotion to my Immaculate Heart ought to be a perpetual prayer vigil in this Community. If but one heart, [heart after heart,] should continue the rosaries unbroken, then you will know the strengthening of the cord—the cord of life from the Heart of Mother Omega through my own Heart to the hearts of those on earth whose flames flicker, whose flames have gone out.

There are many changes happening behind the scenes. There are many things hidden. The political situation in this nation is a cause of great grief to my Heart, as it is to the members of the Darjeeling Council. Pray, then, and invoke the Spirit of the Cosmic Christ and the Holy Christ Self of the sons and daughters of God to be in the positions of leadership in this nation. The gravity of the hour is not clear [to you] through the sources of communication that you have.

Beloved ones, who is equipped to lead the nation to new levels of righteousness? Who will understand the world equation and the forces of Darkness that are not spent and those that come from the levels of Death and Hell to torment the Lightbearers?

Today you entered the sign of the Mother, Virgo.[1] Know, then, that in this earth sign you must defend yourselves by the sword of Archangel Michael from the attacks upon the body of the Mother—your body, the bodies of children and of all Lightbearers.

Know well, precious hearts, that I am in this court, as my Electronic Presence is over my statue, and that you have recourse to me. This recourse will increase as you make the mantra of the Hail Mary one that sings in your heart and as you pray, "My Lord Jesus Christ, have mercy upon my soul!" O the mantras of perpetual prayer! These are what establish and reinforce the ties of your heart to the intimacy of the secret chamber of my Heart.

I come, then, with a sword and with the strength of a mighty rope to tie you ever more tightly to my Heart. Beloved, you must sustain [this rope]. And therefore you must be willing to look at the corners of darkness and to bring that to the light which must be examined and considered, perhaps reconsidered, and either passed into the flame for transmutation or be fired with permanency.

Look at "this" and look at "that" within yourself and do not tarry to decide "Yes" or "No." Keep it or do not keep it, but do not allow misqualified substance of the gray areas or extremes of darkness to idle there wherein you do not let go yet you do not transmute it, or you do not let go and you do not hang on to it[—you simply refuse to deal with it].

It is a time to clean house, yes, to clean your house and the House of Representatives and the political bodies of the nations. It is a time to demand justice, and it is a time for a stripping and exposing of those who would represent *what?* Truth? Justice? God? Perhaps by some feeble attempt and with lip service, but they represent their own agenda and the agenda of the powers-that-be who have sent them to seek the highest offices in the land.

I ask for this perpetual novena to my Immaculate Heart to be unbroken at least through the November elections in this nation. For, beloved, it is surely, *surely* an hour of the coming of the Great Darkness as pertains to those who shall lead, make policy, enact laws and legislation.

Yes, beloved, what shall be done with a people of Light of this planet who have allowed themselves to be put down and to be under those who have not Light? Has not this been the challenge of all ages that we all have had to meet as we have been on the road of life?

Indeed, it has. And the challenge unto you is as great as it has ever been in all ages. For where there is the appearance of freedom, there there is the greatest bondage.

Individuals do not understand that they are in bondage to their own states of consciousness, their own limitations, their own ambitions, their own desires. And, alas, even Keepers of the Flame are not tidy to divide the Real from the Unreal and to stay on their tippy-toes in order to be certain that they do not harbor darkness.

Blessed ones, let the smugness depart. Let those who have entered states of spiritual pride or self-idolatry strip these from themselves and be stripped while they are yet here at the altar of God.

I am come to tell you that I bring and encapsulate in my Immaculate Heart in this hour all that has been said by the ascended hosts at the recent conference in the Heart. I energize it. I multiply it by the strength of the Cosmic Virgin, who I AM. I multiply it, beloved, to strengthen you, your bodies and your souls.

Prepare for the morrow and transmute your yesterdays lest they besmirch your tomorrows with those footprints of a past karma that will trip your soul and even shorten your life span if you are not careful. I say to you, Be careful! This is the sign of this dictation that I bring to you. Be careful, beloved, of that which lurks beneath the surface of world events and of your own consciousness. Establish a profound peace in God. Be not moved whatever is the next turn of events in your life. Hold fast to me.

I am a Mother of the seas and of the land and of the air. I am a Mother in the fire and the heart of the nucleus of the atom. I stand guard for the defense of freedom and I give my very Heart to forestall those certain conditions of karma that could descend.

They have been mitigated; and where they have not been mitigated, they have been simply held back. This has been because there are still those in the earth who decree, there are still those who invoke the violet flame, who listen with sincerity and rapt attention to our dictations and attempt with all in their power to implement them, to realize them and to increase the spheres of Light through the Ashram rituals.

Do not be asleep, beloved. Do not be asleep, but rather make hay while the sun shines. For you see how quickly the summer can retreat and the darkness may come and that darkness in which, it is said, "no man can work."[2] There is a darkness of the soul and the dark night of the soul. There is a darkness of karma and then there is a world darkness.

It is well that you light a candle and see that it is the increase of light in your threefold flame or the capturing again of that flame by such determined devotion to the Sacred Heart of Jesus and such an intense tie established to my Heart. If you would remember this—that the candle must be tended in this octave and that our Twin Hearts[3] do stand for your victory—you would have far less problems, far less vacillation: this way, that way, which way shall I go?

Being centered in our Hearts, as we have offered [you] this [refuge] for many a century, beloved, even before the Christian dispensation, will find you in a position of wholeness, equanimity of mind, peace in the midst of turmoil or war or sudden changes. I say, Be not moved by anything that comes suddenly upon your house but instead be prime movers who continue to move and hold steady, yes, hold steady the flame of God, the flame of the ark of the covenant.

When all else fails, beloved, it is the fire of the heart that will see you through. Therefore increase it while there is peace in the world, while you have a nation where you are not besieged either by famine or by war or the brutalities that you are seeing in Sarajevo. Blessed ones, these conditions in the earth are only a foreshadowing of the prophecies I have given, the prophecies my Son gave two thousand years ago and continuing through the Messengers.

[Speaking to Summit University students in attendance at the summer session:] Yes, beloved, it is good you have come this summer for a great preparation. Take every morsel and make it your own as you assimilate the Word and day by day realize more of your Christhood. Have compassion on the poor in spirit. Have compassion on the sick. Above all, have divine pity upon those who have no desire whatsoever for God or to be rekindled in his name—yes, beloved, divine pity upon those who have turned their backs on the Son of God and the Great Central Sun and continue to walk away from the center of Being.

These are hours of testing. These are hours when the fallen ones have attempted to turn your heads this way and that way to lure you here and there. I say, of all things that you could pray for [for yourselves], I would have you pray for that great divine gift of the discernment of spirits,[4] of the discernment of your own heart and mind and what is influencing you that does not come from God.

The discrimination of the Christ Flame requires that you invoke the shield of Christ, the shield that is held unto you by your Holy Christ Self, who, one and all among you, is dressed this night as a knight of the flame. Even the Holy Christ Self of those of feminine incarnation is in the armour of the whiteness of those who join the Faithful and True.[5]

Some of you, then, who are the feminine incarnation appear as prototypes of Joan of Arc, as your gaze is upon God and upon the Son of God and your ear is inclined to Archangel Michael; and that mighty sword Excalibur, wielded by you as sons and daughters of the Spirit, does yet protect a space and a time for souls who must be born and must move on.

The hours pass, then, and the days pass. Do not fail to endow them as cups of opportunity, to do things well, to keep the mind at its point of yangness, to keep the mind, as you say, as a steel trap, alert, and the listening ear attuned to the Mind of God so that when your Holy Christ Self speaks, you hear, when your soul speaks, you hear—because in the recesses of your being you have established a sanctuary where you meet God daily and you become wise men and women of the Spirit and warriors joining with the legions of Sirius.

These are days and hours when I increase my appearances. Remember, then, you are under the dispensation of bearing your own karma, as my Son has given it to you to bear[6] that you might have the better resurrection and the great God-mastery and access to the portals of Luxor and the ascension flame.

Remember that I do not weep in this place, for it is the one place on earth where I can still know happiness.[7] And my happiness is in the flame that you keep. It is in your diligence as you tend to the chores of being the keepers of a planet and a people, even as you apprentice under the Mother of the Flame and Lanello.

So you must do the chores, beloved! And in this hour when all depends upon you, I say, do not let that candle grow dim. Do not leave off from your calling in this court. For you have saved many a day for another opportunity of serving and living and rejoicing in the progress [of your] souls. You have saved many a day by your decree sessions.

Therefore, where I weep, I weep for many reasons. I weep for ignorance. I weep for hardness of heart. I weep for the decadence of some priests and other religious. Yes, beloved, I weep for conditions within and without the Church, for I bear the Immaculate Heart for all religions and for all peoples. I weep for the souls that will be lost. I weep for those who do not even have the enlightenment or the love to give the rosary in the understanding of the mighty grid of light that is formed [around them and the planet] by [the giving of the rosary—and that is reinforced each time they give it].

I say, if you are looking for a place to take a vacation, then why not go to one of the places of my appearances, where so many thousands come? Why not, then, go bearing my cassettes of the songs that you sing that will tie them to this altar and this particular statue of myself? Why not go, then, with the rosaries of the New Age that they might understand these and feel the tie to the heart of the Two Witnesses?

Be not troubled, beloved ones, for the passage concerning the Two Witnesses that has been recited in the rosary.[8] Understand that the Witnesses have passed through these trials, and yet one is taken and one is left. Therefore, by sponsorship of the Great White Brotherhood, by perseverance and determination, all of these things have already come to pass and we move on to the era of the Woman clothed with the Sun,[9] of my appearing and of the representatives of myself appearing.

Be representatives of my Immaculate Heart, beloved. Call, then, for the Electronic Presence of Mother Omega and of myself and rejoice in the coming of the era of your defense of the children of God and of the Divine Manchild aborning within you.

As you take your inner child and rear that inner child and bring that inner child to the point of union with your Holy Christ Self, lo, beloved, that inner child becomes the Divine Manchild! And what is the Divine Manchild? It is one who has the Holy Spirit in his mother's womb. You, then, are in the womb of Omega, in a sense of the word, putting on the fullness of that inner child until the soul rises so gently and is evermore one with the Holy Christ Self.

Thus, beloved, it is perfectly in order for you to bring those [song and rosary] tapes to areas of pilgrimages around the world and to sell them, necessarily, to cover your expenses. It is perfectly in order to see where you can give [them away], where you can place them [in religious stores], where you can sell them so that there is a net of light of *antahkarana** of my Heart through your hearts. For your hearts are converging with your Christ Self and tying in to many devotees upon earth whose profound devotion to my Heart has caused them to accelerate on the Path. I desire to see you also attain that acceleration. Measure for measure as you give, I give of myself [to you and to millions whom I can reach through your heart when you regularly give the rosary].

Let there then be the turning to my Heart in this hour. For I would have you know, beloved ones, that although the Roman Church has chosen to designate my ascension as the "assumption"[10] into heaven, I announce to you in this hour that I did indeed make the "physical" ascension.[11]

Know this to be true and therefore follow in the wake of my garment. Nestle your little footprints in my own and walk closely behind me that you might be carried up in the garments of my ascension flame and you might also aspire to this event in your life—not that it is an absolute necessity, but by your call to the resurrection flame and your balancing of the yin and yang forces in your four lower bodies, this may indeed come to you.

Do not seek it out of pride. Do not seek it for any other reason

---

*antahkarana [Sanskrit, "internal sense organ"]: the web of life; the net of light spanning Spirit and Matter connecting and sensitizing the whole of creation within itself and to the heart of God.

except to fulfill the Law of Love. There is a path to the physical ascension, as Enoch has told you, as Rex and Nada and Bob and Pearl have explained.¹² So it is true that some have taken that ascension and therefore marked a mighty cross of white fire in the earth that others might achieve the same.

I AM, then, [and I come to you in this hour] in the fullness of my mantle [as I bore it in] the hour of my ascension, in the moment when there was a release from my Causal Body unto all those who had the same tie to me as Elisha had to Elijah. [Therefore,] if you see me when I am taken up, you shall have that which you ask— a double portion of my Spirit.*

Let your celebration of the rosaries, then, in coming days and weeks and months be for the protection of this nation under God and your [respective] nations. All know that should America go down, beloved, [the nations will ask:] "Where shall any other nation appear?" Therefore, wherever you come from, from wherever you hail, beloved, remember that America must not be allowed to fail or to go down.

And fail she will and go down she will if the majority of the people have their way with abortion on demand. This, then, remains the Achilles' heel of America today.

See, then, that you pray with all of your heart and your might that those who have this in their hearts and those who would make it a universal law and availability for all womankind on the planet are barred from positions of leadership. [For these] should be occupied by those who come bearing some portion of the mantle of their Holy Christ Self, some portion of the mantle of my Son.

In the hours and weeks ahead, then, I want you to remember that I am at your side, assisting you in resolving all things and doing so as quickly as you are able—[that is,] as quickly as you are able to surrender and enter in to the largess of heart of that burning fire of the flame of Jesus, as quickly as you are able to pass your fingers over the notes (and especially the wrong notes) of your own psychology and play the right notes and then to seal that chord of harmony in your being, to seal it, protect it and not allow it again to be violated anywhere, anytime by any person.

Hold fast what thou hast received!¹³ Keep your eyes open. Keep your heart in the secret love star of Venus, where many of you have come from. Preserve the Teaching, first by assimilating it and [then by] radiating it to an entire world.

I speak to those who come from the Southern Hemisphere.

---

*"'And it came to pass... that Elijah said unto Elisha, 'Ask what I shall do for thee, before I be taken away from thee.' And Elisha said, 'I pray thee, let a double portion of thy Spirit be upon me.' And he said, 'Thou hast asked a hard thing: nevertheless, if thou see me when I am taken from thee, it shall be so unto thee; but if not, it shall not be so.'" (See II Kings 2:1, 9–15.)

I speak to those of Central and South America. You have a mighty work before you and many souls to contact. Keep steady at the point of your humility. Be self-emptied and filled with the presence of Jesus and of myself, overshadowed by the Two Witnesses, your Messengers. Do not shortchange yourself regarding decrees; for when you decree for yourself, you decree for all to whom you are tied karmically and in the dharma of the seventh root race. Hasten, then, the spread of the Teachings but always keep the vigil of my Heart.

I speak to you who come from all over the world. As long as you make your devotions to my Immaculate Heart and to the Sacred Heart of Jesus the primary action of your day and the very first priority, you will always know strength. You will have warning from our angels of times of trouble descending, you will be kept out of harm's way, and you will be graced by the blessedness of the Holy Spirit to prosper and multiply this Church Universal and Triumphant.

Become the white stone in that Church. Be foundations. Let balance be remembered. For though you may not accomplish so many physical things, you shall begin to pluck the *antahkarana* you build each day by the rosaries and by the Ashram rituals. And when you pluck [its strings] and your heart itself is as a fine-tuned stringed instrument, you will know that your prayers have reached millions because of the momentum of the daily use of the rosary.

Strengthen your heart by letting it be tied in to that universal *antahkarana* of Light and also strengthen [the *antahkarana*]. This contact with souls of Light through devotions transcends karmic ties. It allows you to balance karma with almost, and I say almost, anyone by universal service and by universally contacting every Lightbearer each day who does become a part of that *antahkarana* because he or she does give some devotion to God.

I rejoice in the little children. I rejoice in the child of your own heart, whom I cradle in this moment to heal the hurts, to transmute the records, to remind you that I have always cradled you. There were some experiences that were necessary, even some burdens grievous to be borne that seemed so unjust at the time.

You are clean but not wholly clean, pure but not wholly pure.* And in yesteryears you have had to bear adversities, injuries, insults and abuses. Accept these whether they are of karma or of a soul testing or of your very own soul's volunteering to bear these burdens in the body and these persecutions that some of you have borne as little children.

I want you to feel better about yourself and who you are, knowing that some of that which you did bear you did so voluntarily

---

*"Jesus saith to [Simon Peter], 'He that is washed needeth not save to wash his feet, but is clean every whit: and ye are clean, but not all.'" (See John 13:2–20.)

in Christ's name for your love of him, your love of me and your desire to bear some weight of planetary burden.

Yes, beloved, some of you were Christ children. Some of you had such a Light and such a deep understanding in your hearts. Now that you are adults, do not lose that sense of yourself as the Christ Child. Put back together again the innocence of your early beginnings and the great wisdom that presaged your own coming. For you yourself had the wisdom to know that which you would be and you were told what you would bear, which would thereby enable you to enter the Path and move on and help others.

Let these rings in your tree of life grow! Let them now begin to grow symmetrically as rings of fire and as by the Heart of Kuan Yin, the Heart of Jesus, you know grace and mercy, you know these abounding, and you can finally let go of that sense of injustice because you yourself have been the embodiment of Divine Justice, as well as of human injustice—and you have wanted, you have willed, you have determined and accepted this life as the time when you would balance all things.

The desire for balance in some of you is an all-consuming desire. You want to balance your debts, balance your four lower bodies, your threefold flame, your chakras, your relationships. The sign of the great scales, beloved, is something to look upon and visualize, for how easily they are tipped! And this, of course, is the coming trap when you enter the sign of Libra.

Balance, then, the mind and the heart, the feeling body and the mental body. Learn not to be moved but to rejoice: to stand guard, to defend the little ones and to recognize that the prayer that you leave unspoken may mean a heart that is broken. A comfort that is not said might be forfeited, for the dead move on and they no longer hear what might have been said.

Therefore take each day's opportunity to comfort life and use the power of the word to increase the joy to the world, the joy that comes because you are an obedient disciple of my Son and because you do not fear that Master-disciple relationship as it is offered to you.

Come Home, my sons and daughters! Come gather round me, my children, for I would heal your wounds. And they would indeed be healed but you do not let go at some level of your being.

Now then, keep always the sense of co-measurement of world events and which way they are moving even as you watch the weather. Do not allow yourself to not be aware of the shadings of turns or the sudden plummeting of the stock market or of nations or of politicians who no longer represent what they used to represent.

Keep your co-measurement with an eye on yourself and your soul, with a true self-knowledge of what it takes to place one foot after the other as you climb the highest mountain.

You climb the mountain: You climb the mountain of karma. You climb the mountain that leads to the abode of Lord Himalaya. You climb the mountain of success. Seeing that it takes you nowhere, you come back down that mountain and begin to go up, up and up the mount of Maitreya. Each step gained is a level of initiation corresponding to the level in the etheric octave that you might enter at the conclusion of your victorious battle over Darkness in this life.

I AM the Queen of Angels and in that office I may accord you a special grace or dispensation. I ask you to think about this for seven days and then come to a conclusion as to what special grace you might ask of me. Seven days hence I shall return. I shall return for such a grace and the giving of it and such a dispensation and the giving of it.

Thus, as you pursue the rosaries, I ask you for the first fourteen days to give the long rosary on one day and the Surrender Rosary on the next—every other day the Surrender Rosary, every other day the long rosary. And thereby when you come to knock on the door of my Heart for a grace, you shall ask for a grace, I trust, that shall enable you to become who you are, to fulfill your mission and to serve others.

May you appeal to me, beloved, for you are the strong workers in the vineyard of my Father and, as the Son has said, "Truly, the fields are white to the harvest but the laborers are few."[14] May you go forth, then. May you harvest souls and bring them home to my Heart.

If you will enlist yourself [in the ranks of] my legions, my army of Light, I promise you blessings and graces not only in the hereafter but every day of your life. I shall come as the Divine Mother leading great armies of heaven, which you may join as you serve the Divine Mother in this calling even as Joan of Arc responded, even as you yourselves as the knights of old did go forth to slay dragons and demons, to rescue children and mothers.

Oh yes, beloved, there is much to be done! Tighten up, then, the concentration of the good servants of this Community and of its [outer] rings that span the planet. Tighten your service, your chelaship. Yes, tighten your belt. Yes, finish all things, bring all things to fruition. For the hour and the time of the change in planetary cycles is coming.

I seal you, then, in my Immaculate Heart. May you accept

this sealing and confirm it by affirming it each day.

Bless you, my children. Bless you, my strong sons and daughters. You are myself in the earth. *Yes, you are myself.* And the recitation of the Hail Mary reestablishes that reality of my Electronic Presence over you every day and hour of your life.

"The Summit Lighthouse Sheds Its Radiance O'er All the World to Manifest as Pearls of Wisdom." This dictation by **Mother Mary** was **delivered** by the Messenger of the Great White Brotherhood Elizabeth Clare Prophet at the conclusion of the **August 22, 1992** Saturday evening service held at the **Royal Teton Ranch, Park County, Montana,** in celebration of Mother Mary's Ascension Day (August 15) and the feast of the Queenship of Mary (August 22). In a candlelight vigil begun prior to the dictation, the Messenger and congregation gave Mother Mary's Scriptural Rosary for the New Age: The Healing Mysteries (the Fifth Ray). [**N.B.** Throughout this *Pearl,* bracketed material denotes words unspoken yet implicit in the dictation, added by the Messenger under Mother Mary's direction for clarity in the written word.] Throughout these notes *PoW* is the abbreviation for *Pearls of Wisdom.* (**1**) The sun entered the **sign of Virgo** at 3:10 p.m. MDT. (**2**) John 9:4. (**3**) **Twin Hearts.** The Sacred Heart of Jesus and the Immaculate Heart of Mary are sometimes referred to as the Twin Hearts. Some Catholics use this term specifically in connection with parallel devotions to the Sacred Heart of Jesus and the Immaculate Heart of Mary given on First Fridays and First Saturdays of the month. The tradition of veneration to the Sacred Heart of Jesus and the Immaculate Heart of Mary has come down to us through many saints of the Church, including Saint Bernard of Clairvaux, Saint Gertrude the Great, Saint Mechtilde, Saint John Eudes, Saint Margaret Mary—and through the messages of Mary to the children of Fátima. (**4**) I Cor. 12:10. (**5**) Rev. 19:11–16. (**6**) **Jesus' request that we take back the karma he has borne for us.** In his Christmas Day Address, December 25, 1989, Jesus Christ said: "You are my own, and any number of you are the one for whom I have gone after, leaving the ninety and nine.... I have brought you through many lifetimes to this moment when you could see and know and understand.... I have also paid the price. For in order that your spiritual senses might be quickened I, Jesus, have taken upon myself some of the stripes of your karma. Now I say to you, beloved, you are securely here. You have made the contact. You have tied yourself to my Sacred Heart.... If you will take back that [karma] which I have borne [for you these two thousand years], for which I have paid the price, and balance it yourself and thereby grow in the stature of your Christhood, freely asking Hercules' assistance, when needed, then, you see, I may leave you as the ninety and nine and I may now go after [those] other [ones], even as many as a thousand other souls who need [me to] bear their burden.... So you see, beloved, in the process of [doing] this so little a thing that I ask you, [for you also have the violet flame,] you are also becoming world saviours; for in a sense you are allowing me to bear another's karma. Thus you yourself do bear it, do you see?" (See 1989 *PoW,* pp. 814–15.) (**7**) **The one place where Mother Mary still knows** happiness. In her December 29, 1991 dictation, given at *The Rapture of Divine Love* at the Royal Teton Ranch, Mother Mary told us: "When I come to this place, beloved, it is the place of my rest and repose from going out and appearing to the many, who understand my visage as the tears flow and even the blood. They understand through that image not only the sorrow of the Mother but that the body of the Mother in the earth is desecrated and is also martyred, even as the child within her body is aborted. So, my beloved, I know surcease from pain, for how can I do aught else but rejoice at such a company of devotees—you who ceaselessly pray about all of the conditions that Saint Germain and the Darjeeling Council have called to your attention. Know, then, beloved, that this altar is for me, as well as for you, a haven, [a holy place for] a coming apart, a surcease from the burdens and the sorrows of the world." (See p. 32, this volume.) **(8)** The Fifth Healing Mystery, **"The Two Witnesses"** (Rev. 11:3–13), in the Healing Mysteries (the Fifth Ray), given prior to the dictation. **(9)** Rev. 12. **(10) The Assumption.** Belief in the assumption of Mary has been a centuries-long tradition in the Catholic Church. The word is derived from the Latin *assumere* 'to take up'. In 1950, Pope Pius XII officially defined the doctrine of the Assumption in his apostolic constitution *Munificenitissimus Deus.* He wrote: "The Immaculate Mother of God, the ever-Virgin Mary, having completed the course of her earthly life, was assumed body and soul into heavenly glory." The *Practical Catholic Encyclopedia* (Pegis, 1956) states: "The body of the Blessed Virgin Mary, who was free from original sin and so was not subject to death in the same way that creatures are, was taken into Heaven and united to her soul." The Church teaches that because of her purity, Mary did not have to wait until the Second Coming of Christ for her bodily resurrection. They believe her physical body was glorified and perfected into an immortal spiritual body in the same manner that all the faithful will experience it in the resurrection at the end of time. The reason for the difference in terminology between Jesus' "ascension" and Mary's "assumption" is that Catholics believe Jesus was a divine being and Mary merely human. Jesus thus ascended into heaven "by his own power" whereas Mary was "taken" into heaven. Hence, they see Mary's assumption as a "hopeful doctrine" because what has been promised to all faithful Christians has already been realized by one. **(11) The physical ascension.** The Ascended Masters teach that in the ritual of the ascension, the soul is united with the white-fire body of the I AM Presence. This does not require the raising of the physical body; the soul itself may take flight from the mortal coil and be translated through the ascension process. In order to ascend, the candidate must have balanced at least 51 percent of his karma. In order to make a *physical* ascension, he must have balanced between 95 and 100 percent of his karma. When a physical ascension takes place, the physical body is transformed by and superseded by the Ascended-Master Light Body. During the ascension ritual, the soul becomes permanently clothed with this Body, also called the "wedding garment," or the Deathless Solar Body. Serapis Bey describes the process in his *Dossier on the Ascension:* "The flame above (in the heart of the Presence) magnetizes the flame below (the threefold flame within the heart) and the wedding garment descends around the silver cord to envelop the lifestream of the individual in those tangible and vital essence currents of the ascension. Tremendous changes then take place in the form below, and the four lower bodies of man are cleansed of all impurities. Lighter and lighter grows the physical form, and with the weightlessness of helium the body begins to rise into the atmosphere, the gravitational pull being loosened and the form enveloped by the light of the externalized glory which man knew with the Father 'in the beginning'.... The individual ascends, then, not in an earthly body but in a glorified spiritual body into which the physical form is changed on the instant by total immersion in the great God flame" (see *Dossier on the Ascension,* pp. 157–59, 175–77). In a dictation given October 2, 1989, the Ascended Master Rex told us that those who are called to the physical ascension must have had many thousands of years of preparation. Today most people whose souls qualify for the ritual of the ascension ascend from inner levels after the soul has departed the physical body. The soul attains union with the Mighty I AM Presence to become a permanent atom in the Body of God just as she does in a physical ascension.

The Catholic doctrine on the "assumption" of Mary and the ascension of Jesus parallels the teachings of the Ascended Masters on the physical ascension. The Catholic Church teaches that the bodies worn by Mary and Jesus on earth were translated and perfected into the incorruptible spiritual bodies they now wear in heaven. This is analogous to what the Ascended Masters teach happens in a physical ascension. The Ascended Masters' Teachings illumine us further, however, as to how this divine alchemy actually occurs, as described by Serapis Bey above. Some points where Catholic theology and Ascended Master teaching differ are as follows: According to Catholic doctrine, Mary and Jesus were unique because they were "conceived without sin" and remained perfectly sinless throughout their lives. Hence, it would not be meet that their physical bodies should be corrupted in a grave. In the Catholic perspective, Jesus would naturally ascend at the end of his mission because, although he had an earthly body, he also had a full divine nature. Catholic doctrine holds that because Mary was human like us, she is an "exception to the rule" in that she did not have to wait until the Second Coming of Christ for her bodily resurrection. The Ascended Masters set before each of us the goal of balancing at least 51 percent of our karma and ascending at the end of this life. They teach that it is possible—if we balance 95 to 100 percent of our karma—to ascend physically. However, we have each lived many times before. The Ascended Masters teach that the path of karma-balancing and spiritual progress leading to the ascension is not accomplished in one lifetime but through many incarnations. The many bodies worn during the soul's earthly sojourn are not resurrected at the end of time; but all souls who ascend, whether in a physical ascension or not, are permanently clothed at the hour of their ascension in their Ascended-Master Light Body. Jesus and Mary set the example for all to follow. They are joined in heaven by countless saints who have also attained their soul's victory through the divinely ordained ritual of the ascension. **(12)** Rex with Pearl, Bob and Nada, October 2, 1989, **"The Physical Ascension,"** in Keepers of the Flame Lesson 31, pp. 70–74. **(13)** Rev. 2:25; 3:3; 3:11. **(14)** John 4:35; Matt. 9:37; Luke 10:2.

I AM the Witness

The Blessed Mother Wanted Me to Go to Summit University

Beloved Mother,

I wanted to share with you a story of Mother Mary's intercession in my life that I have always treasured as very precious.

After I attended my first Summit Lighthouse conference in November 1975, I began to feel strongly that God was calling me to Summit University. I was 21 years old and in college at the time but felt that it was important that I attend Winter Quarter—only a month away. I knew that, financially, the only way I could do this would be to borrow the necessary funds. So I decided to appeal to my father, who was then a staunch Catholic and very devoted to the Blessed Mother.

I met him for lunch at work one day and shared with him my heart's desire to go to Summit University. He expressed his apprehension and uncertainty about my plans and about lending me the money but said he would pray about it. He feared that Summit University would only be a detour from my studies and what God wanted me to do with my life.

That evening after dinner, he told my mother that he was going out to take a walk and give the rosary. He said he would pray to the Blessed Mother that he might somehow know God's will in this situation. I went to my room and fell asleep and was awakened by a telephone ringing.

Soon after, my mother ran in and excitedly told me that an old friend had just called, offering "out of the blue" to buy a small piece of property that my father had been trying to sell for quite some time. The friend had asked if it was still for sale and offered the exact amount of money I had asked to borrow from my father!

My mother's eyes sparkled as she told me of the phone call. She took my hands and said that although she did not understand it, there could be no doubt that the Blessed Mother wanted me to go to Summit University. When my father returned from his walk, she told him what had happened and that surely the Blessed Mary had heard his prayers and sent this special sign and blessing. My father was so moved that he decided to give me the entire amount of money needed, without any obligation to pay it back! He said he would have to learn to place his trust in God and surrender me unto his care.

Since that time my father has fallen away from the Catholic Church and from devotion to Mary. But recently I sent him the *Sanctissima* album for his birthday and he wrote me back saying how beautiful it was and how much he enjoyed it and that he plays it in the car wherever he goes! I pray that beloved Mary will draw him back to her heart.

I am ever grateful for your and Mother Mary's sweet presence in my life—and for the special miracle that brought me to Summit University and then to Staff.

With love,

35

The Light of Persia—
Mystical Experiences with Zarathustra

        In the name of my Mighty I AM Presence
I bow to the Light of the Ascended Master Zarathustra.

    The teachings of one man have influenced Judaism, Christianity, Islam, Taoism, Mahayana Buddhism, Christian and Jewish Gnosticism, Pythagoras, Plato, the Essenes and all of us who are gathered here. Yet very little is known about him.

    His name was Zarathustra, he was the founder of Zoroastrianism, and he started a revolution of Light against Darkness that is ongoing today. And *we* are a part of that revolution!

    Mary Boyce, Emeritus Professor of Iranian Studies at the University of London, points out: "Zoroastrianism is the oldest of the revealed world-religions, and it has probably had more influence on mankind, directly and indirectly, than any other single faith."[1]

    Who was Zarathustra?

    According to R. C. Zaehner, former Spalding Professor of Eastern Religions and Ethics at Oxford University, Zarathustra was "one of the greatest religious geniuses of all time.... [He] was a prophet, or at least conceived himself to be such; he spoke to his God face to face.... [Yet] about the Prophet himself we know almost nothing that is authentic."[2]

    Zarathustra lived in a nonliterate society, whose people did not keep records. His teachings were passed down by oral tradition, and much of what was later written down about his life and teachings has been lost or destroyed.

What scholars have been able to piece together about him comes from three sources—the study of the historical milieu prior to and during the time Zarathustra is believed to have lived, tradition, and seventeen sacred hymns called Gathas. Scholars concur that Zarathustra composed these hymns. The Gathas are recorded in the Avesta, the sacred scriptures of Zoroastrianism.

It is not clear where or when Zarathustra was born. It is believed he was born in what is now east central Iran, but that is not certain. Zarathustra's date of birth is even more difficult to establish. Scholars place it sometime between 1700 B.C. and 600 B.C. The consensus is that he lived around 1000 B.C. or earlier.

The Gathas are the key to determining Zarathustra's approximate year of birth. They are linguistically similar to the Rigveda, one of the sacred texts of the Hindus. According to Boyce:

> The language of the Gathas is archaic, and close to that of the Rigveda (whose composition has been assigned to about 1700 B.C. onwards); and the picture of the world to be gained from [the Gathas] is correspondingly ancient, that of a Stone Age society.... It is only possible therefore to hazard a reasoned conjecture that [Zarathustra] lived some time between 1700 and 1500 B.C.[3]

Other scholars working with the same evidence place his birth between 1400 and 1200 B.C.

The Gathas say that Zarathustra was of the Spitama family, a family of knights. One school of thought says the name Zarathustra means "owner of old camels." Well, if that is the real meaning, Zarathustra, we are your camels!

Dr. H. Michael Simmons of the Center for Zoroastrian Research says this meaning comes from *Zarath*, meaning "old," and *Ushtra*, meaning "camel." But the Greek name for Zarathustra is Zoroaster, which Simmons says means "Golden Star," or "Golden Light."[4] So, happily we are saved!

Zarathustra, will you have us as your golden stars?

Let's look at Zarathustra's life before he received his calling. In the Gathas, Zarathustra referred to himself as a priest. There were different categories of priests. The specific group Zarathustra belonged to wrote elaborate religious poetry.[5]

Zarathustra also referred to himself as a *manthran*. Can anybody guess what that is? A *manthran* is one who is able to formulate mantras. You just about got that, didn't you?

Zarathustra was also an initiate. According to Boyce, "He...

describes himself [in the Gathas] as a 'vaedemna' or 'one who knows,' an initiate possessed of divinely inspired wisdom."[6] But first and foremost, Zarathustra was a prophet, and *he is* a prophet and he lives today among us as an Ascended Master.

The Gathas depict him as talking to God. They say, "He is 'the Prophet who raises his voice in veneration, the friend of Truth,' God's friend, a 'true enemy to the followers of the Lie and a powerful support to the followers of the Truth.'"[7]

Zarathustra was an outspoken enemy of the followers of the Lie. I like that kind of a guy, don't you? [7-second applause] All of us count ourselves, I think, as true enemies of liars, but how many of us often go up to them and tell them about it? That's what's special about Zarathustra.

Tradition holds that at the age of twenty Zarathustra left his father, mother and wife to wander in search of Truth. Ten years later he had the first of many visions. See how long God tries your soul. So keep on allowing him to try you.

Boyce writes: "According to tradition Zoroaster was thirty, the time of ripe wisdom, when revelation finally came to him. This great happening is alluded to in one of the Gathas and is tersely described in a Pahlavi [Middle Persian] work. Here it is said that Zoroaster, being at a gathering [called] to celebrate a spring festival, went at dawn to a river to fetch water."[8]

Now, at dawn tomorrow be sure you're at the Mol Heron Creek! Wait till you hear what happened to Zarathustra:

> He waded in to draw [the water] from midstream; and when he returned to the bank...he had a vision. He saw on the bank a shining Being, who revealed himself as Vohu Manah 'Good [Mind]'; and this Being led Zoroaster into the presence of Ahura Mazda and five other radiant figures, before whom 'he did not see his own shadow upon the earth, owing to their great light'. And it was then, from this great heptad [or group of seven beings], that he received his revelation.[9]

We can conjecture that the seven beings of this great heptad were none other than the Seven Holy Kumaras.

Ahura Mazda means "Wise Lord." Zarathustra recognized Ahura Mazda as the one true God, the creator of the universe. The significance of this cannot be overstated. Zarathustra may have been the first monotheist in recorded history. Zaehner points out, "The great achievement of the Iranian Prophet [was] that he eliminated all the ancient gods of the Iranian pantheon, leaving only Ahura Mazdah, the 'Wise Lord', as the One True God."[10]

Some scholars assert that Zarathustra was not a strict monotheist but a henotheist, that is, one who worships one God but does not deny the existence of others. This is a technical distinction. As David Bradley, author of *A Guide to the World's Religions*, notes, "[Zarathustra] was a practicing monotheist in the same way that Moses was."[11] Bradley thinks that Moses knew of the existence of lesser gods but insisted on the necessity of siding with the true God against all other gods.[12]

Shortly after his first vision, Zarathustra became a spokesman for Ahura Mazda and began to proclaim his message. According to Simmons, Zarathustra instituted a religious reform that was more far-reaching and more radical than Martin Luther's challenge of the Roman Catholic Church.[13]

Zarathustra's reform had a number of facets. His main objective was to stamp out Evil. He began to condemn the religious doctrines of his countrymen.

The old religion, as best we can tell, had two classes of deities—the *ahuras*, or "lords," and the *daevas*, or "demons." According to Zaehner:

> It is...the *daevas* specifically whom Zoroaster attacks, not the *ahuras* whom he prefers to ignore.... In all probability he considered them to be God's creatures and as fighters on his side. In any case he concentrated the full weight of his attack on the *daevas* and their worshippers who practised a gory sacrificial ritual and were the enemies of the settled pastoral community to which the Prophet himself belonged.[14]

At first Zarathustra had little success in spreading his message. Zaehner observes, "It is obvious from the *Gathas* that Zoroaster met with very stiff opposition from the civil and ecclesiastical authorities when once he had proclaimed his mission."[15] He was persecuted by the priests and followers of the *daevas*. According to tradition, they tried to kill him a number of times.

It took ten years for Zarathustra to make his first convert, his cousin. (That's what you get for attacking everybody else's gods!) He was then divinely led to the court of King Vishtaspa and Queen Hutaosa.

Vishtaspa was an honest, simple monarch but was surrounded by the *Karpans*, a group of self-seeking, manipulative priests. They convened a council to challenge the revelations of the new prophet and successfully conspired to have him thrown in jail. As the story goes, Zarathustra won his freedom by miraculously curing the king's favorite black horse.

Vishtaspa granted him permission to teach the new faith to his consort, Queen Hutaosa. The beautiful Hutaosa became one of Zarathustra's greatest supporters and assisted him in converting Vishtaspa.

After two long years, the monarch was finally converted. But Vishtaspa required one final sign before he would totally embrace the faith. He asked to be shown what role he would play in the heaven-world.

In response, Ahura Mazda sent three Archangels to the court of Vishtaspa and Hutaosa. They appeared as effulgent knights in full armour, riding on horseback. According to one text, they arrived in such glory that "their radiance in that lofty residence seemed...a heaven of complete light, owing to their great power and triumph;...when he thus looked upon [them], the exalted king Vishtaspa trembled, all his courtiers trembled, all his chieftains were confused."[16]

Radiating a blinding light and the sound of thunder, they announced that they had come on behalf of Ahura Mazda in order that the king might receive the fullness of the message of Zarathustra. They promised Vishtaspa a life span of 150 years and that he and Hutaosa would have an immortal son. The Archangels warned, however, that if Vishtaspa should decide not to take up the religion, his end would not be far away. The king embraced the faith and the entire court followed suit. The scriptures record that the Archangels then took up their abode with Vishtaspa.

In a dictation given January 1, 1981, the Ascended Master Zarathustra spoke of King Vishtaspa and Queen Hutaosa, and this is what he said:

> I AM come to deliver the sacred fire of the Sun behind the sun to raise you up and to establish in you the original teaching of Ahura Mazda, Sanat Kumara, delivered long ago in the land of ancient Persia unto me and unto the king and queen who received the conversion of Archangels and of the sacred fire and of holy angels by the descent of Light. Thus, by their lifestreams' acceptance of my prophecy, there came to pass the multiplication of the bread of Life from the heart of Sanat Kumara, whose messenger I was, whose messenger I remain....
>
> The teaching of the hosts of the LORD and the coming of the great avatar of Light, the teaching of betrayal and the consequent warfare of his hosts against the evil ones, was

understood and propagated. The law of karma, the law of reincarnation, and even the vision of the last days when Evil and the Evil One would be vanquished—all of this went forth by the conversion of the king and the queen and the reaching out of the faith to all of the subjects of the land.

Thus, the tests were given by the Archangels through my office unto these two chosen ones. Thereby passing the tests, they became blessed as secondary emissaries of Sanat Kumara. And therefore, I the prophet and they holding the balance in the earth manifested a trinity of Light and the figure-eight flow.

Realize the necessary ingredients for the propagation of the faith throughout the earth.

The Archangels send their Messenger with a gift of prophecy that is the Word of Sanat Kumara to every culture and in every age. Thus, the prophet comes forth with the vision, with the anointing and with the sacred fire. But unless the prophet find the fertile field of hearts aflame and receptive, the authority of the Word does not pass unto the people.[17]

Thus, we hear that Ahura Mazda is none other than Sanat Kumara.

Let's take a closer look at Zarathustra's teaching. Zarathustra recognized Ahura Mazda, the Wise Lord, as the creator of all, but he did not see him as a solitary figure. In Zoroastrianism, Ahura Mazda is the father of Spenta Mainyu, the Holy Spirit. *Spenta* means "holy" or "bountiful." *Mainyu* means "spirit" or "mentality." The Holy Spirit is one with, yet distinct from, Ahura Mazda. Ahura Mazda expresses his will through Spenta Mainyu.

Boyce explains: "For Zarathushtra God was Ahura Mazda, who . . . had created the world and all that is good in it through his Holy Spirit, Spenta Mainyu, who is both his active agent and yet one with him, indivisible and yet distinct."[18] Simply put, the Spirit is always the Spirit of the LORD. When we speak of the Holy Spirit, it is the Spirit of God.

Ahura Mazda is also the father of the Amesha Spentas, or six "Holy" or "Bountiful Immortals." Boyce says that the term *spenta* is one of the most important in Zarathustra's theology. To him, it meant "possessing power." When used in connection with the beneficent deities, it meant "possessing power to aid" and hence "furthering, supporting, benefiting."[19]

Zarathustra taught that Ahura Mazda created the world in

seven stages. He did so with the help of the six great Holy Immortals and his Holy Spirit. The term *Amesha Spenta* can refer to any one of the divinities created by Ahura Mazda but refers especially to the six who helped create the world.[20] According to Boyce:

> These divinities formed a heptad with Ahura Mazda himself.... Ahura Mazda is said either to be their 'father', or to have 'mingled' himself with them, and in one... text his creation of them is compared with the lighting of torches from a torch.
>
> The six great Beings then in their turn, Zoroaster taught, evoked other beneficent divinities, who are in fact the beneficent gods of the pagan Iranian pantheon.... All these divine beings, who are... either directly or indirectly the emanations of Ahura Mazda, strive under him, according to their various appointed tasks, to further good and to defeat evil.[21]

The six Holy or Bountiful Immortals also represent attributes of Ahura Mazda. The Holy Immortals are as follows:

Vohu Manah, whose name means "Good Mind," "Good Thought" or "Good Purpose." According to Boyce, "For every individual, as for the prophet himself," Vohu Manah is "the Immortal who leads the way to all the rest." Asha Vahishta, whose name means "Best Righteousness," "Truth" or "Order," is the closest confederate of Vohu Manah.[22]

Spenta Armaiti, "Right-mindedness" or "Holy Devotion," Boyce says, embodies the dedication to what is good and just. Khshathra Vairya, "Desirable Dominion," represents the power that each person should exert for righteousness as well as the power and the kingdom of God.[23]

The final two are a pair. They are Haurvatat, whose name means "Wholeness" or "Health," and Ameretat, whose name means "Long Life" or "Immortality." Boyce says these two enhance earthly existence and confer eternal well-being and life, which may be obtained by the righteous in the presence of Ahura Mazda.[24]

"The doctrine of the Heptad," she says, "is at the heart of Zoroastrian theology. Together with [the concept of Good and Evil] it provides the basis for Zoroastrian spirituality and ethics, and shapes the characteristic Zoroastrian attitude of responsible stewardship for this world."[25] In later tradition, the six Holy Immortals were considered to be Archangels.

When it came to Good and Evil, Zarathustra tended to see

things in terms of black and white. According to Zaehner, "The Prophet knew no spirit of compromise."[26]

There is no prophet who ever knows any spirit of compromise. I will tell you why. The prophet of God embodies the Mighty I AM Presence. He is not the mediator. He is the one who embodies God as Law and Lawgiver. And so he walks the earth with a great intensity of fire, seeking to separate people from their relativities that suck them into the maya and glamour of the illusionary existence.

So this was true of the prophets of Israel. They had such an intensity of oneness with the Mighty I AM Presence and they delivered that intensity. That "stuff" of the Mighty I AM Presence is the stuff that prophets are made of.

Zaehner says: "On the one hand stood Asha—Truth and Righteousness—[and] on the other the Druj—the Lie, Wickedness, and Disorder. This was not a matter on which compromise was possible [as far as Zarathustra was concerned].... The Prophet [forbade] his followers to have any contact with the 'followers of the Lie'."[27]

The origin of the conflict between Truth and the Lie is described in the Gathas. It is presented as a myth about two Spirits, called twins, who must make a choice between Good and Evil at the beginning of time. One of the two is the Holy Spirit, the son of Ahura Mazda. The other is the Evil Mind or the Evil Spirit, Angra Mainyu.

Zarathustra introduced the myth with the following words, which underscore the all-important concept of free will and that every man must choose the Truth or the Lie: "Hear with your ears, behold with mind all clear the two choices between which you must decide, each man [deciding] for his own self, [each man] knowing how it will appear to us at the [time of] great crisis."[28] Then he proceeded to recount the myth:

> In the beginning those two Spirits who are the well-endowed twins were known as the one good and the other evil, in thought, word, and deed. Between them the wise chose rightly, not so the fools. And when these Spirits met they established in the beginning life and death that in the end the followers of the Lie should meet with the worst existence, but the followers of Truth with the Best Mind.
>
> Of these two Spirits he who was of the Lie chose to do the worst things; but the Most Holy Spirit, clothed in rugged heaven, [chose] Truth as did [all] who sought with zeal to do the pleasure of the Wise Lord by [doing] good works.

X The Light of Persia—Mystical Experiences with Zarathustra

Clothed in rugged heaven, he came! Isn't that an apt description of the character of the Holy Spirit as he appears to us?

Between the two the *daevas* [the demons] did not choose rightly; for, as they deliberated, delusion overcame them so that they chose the most Evil Mind. Then did they, with one accord, rush headlong unto Fury that they might thereby extinguish the existence of mortal men.[29]

The Holy Spirit and the Evil Spirit are, as Zaehner puts it, "irreconcilably opposed to each other."[30] Zarathustra said, "I will speak out concerning the two Spirits of whom, at the beginning of existence, the Holier thus spoke to him who is Evil: 'Neither our thoughts, nor our teachings, nor our wills, nor our choices, nor our words, nor our deeds, nor our consciences, nor yet our souls agree.' "[31]

Zaehner notes that this state of conflict affected every sphere of activity human or divine. In the social sphere, the conflict took place between the pastoral communities of peaceful cattle breeders, who were "followers of Truth or Righteousness," and the bands of predatory nomads, who raided the cattle breeders. Zarathustra called these predatory nomads the "followers of the Lie."[32]

On the religious plane, the conflict took place between Zarathustra and his followers and those who were followers of the traditional Iranian religion and worshiped the *daevas*. The adherents of this ancient religion said it was founded by Yima, the child of the Sun. Zarathustra attacked Yima and the ritual of animal sacrifice he had introduced.[33]

He also condemned the rite associated with drinking *haoma*, the fermented juice of a plant that caused "filthy drunkenness."[34] Scholars are not sure what *haoma* was, but they conclude from the description of the effects it had on those who drank it that it probably contained a hallucinogen. Zaehner writes: "For Zoroaster the whole cult with its bloody sacrifice and ritual drunkenness is anathema—a rite offered to false gods and therefore a 'lie'."[35]

Zarathustra said "the followers of the Lie" destroyed life and strove to "sever the followers of Truth from the Good Mind."[36] The followers of the Lie knew who Zarathustra was, recognized the danger he represented and did everything they could to destroy him. To this end, they continued to sacrifice bulls and participate in the *haoma* rite.

According to Zaehner, "There would seem to be little doubt that an actual state of war existed between the two parties, Zoroaster and his patron Vishtaspa standing on the one side and the so-called followers of the Lie, many of whom he mentions by name, on the other."[37]

Finally, the battle went on right within man. John Noss, author of *Man's Religions,* observes that "it was perhaps Zoroaster's cardinal moral principle, that each man's soul is the seat of a war between good and evil."[38]

One of the principal weapons used to attack demons and evil men was the prayer written by Zarathustra, the Ahuna Vairya. This short prayer is the most sacred of Zoroastrian prayers. I will read it to you:

> As the Master, so is the Judge to be chosen in accord with Truth. Establish the power of acts arising from a life lived with good purpose, for Mazda and for the lord whom they made pastor for the poor.[39]

The lord in the last line of this prayer is thought to be Zarathustra himself. The prayer is ancient. It is written in the style of the Rigveda. According to Simmons, this prayer is a mantra. Simmons says that Zoroastrians believe that "pronouncing words in Zoroastrian ritual has an effect on the external world." They believe that if a particular mantra is pronounced correctly, it will affect outer circumstances.[40]

A mantra is always effective when properly recited, whether it is given in the form of our decrees or as Hindu mantras or other legitimate mantras handed down to us from the heirs of Sanat Kumara. All true living Gurus on this planet have descended from Sanat Kumara. He is the Great Guru and the one who sponsors the earth and the Great White Brotherhood in the earth. He is the one who has released the mantras through them. Descending from his lineage are the Buddhas, the Bodhisattvas, Jesus Christ, and so forth—all of the great Lights that have come down.

When we give their mantras and give them correctly, the entire four lower bodies of the earth and her people are affected. And that means that we ourselves must be a chalice for the mantra and hold the balance for the mantra as it penetrates the sheaths of the earth.

Zaehner sums up:

> For Zoroaster there is only one God, Creator of heaven and earth and of all things. In his relations with the world God acts through his main "faculties" which are sometimes spoken of as being engendered by him—his Holy Spirit, [his] Righteousness, [his] Good Mind, and Right-mindedness.

Further he is master of the Kingdom, Wholeness, and Immortality, which also form aspects of himself.

Righteousness or Truth is the objective standard of right behaviour which God chooses.... Wickedness or disorder... is the objective standard of all that strives against God, the standard which the Evil Spirit chooses at the beginning of existence. Evil imitates the good creation: and so we find the Evil Spirit operating against the Holy Spirit, the Evil Mind against the Good Mind, the Lie or wickedness against Truth or Righteousness, and Pride against Right-mindedness.

Evil derives from the wrong choice of a free being who must in some sense derive from God, but for whose wickedness God cannot be held responsible. Angra Mainyu or Ahriman, [names for] the Devil, is not yet co-eternal with God as he was to become in the later system: he is the Adversary of the Holy Spirit only, not of God himself.[41]

But in the end, according to Zoroastrian doctrine, Good will triumph over Evil.

These concepts about the birth of Evil very closely parallel the concept of the birth of Evil that we studied in the Kabbalah. It would be well for you to compare the two when you are able to study both of these lectures or do your own research on the subject.

Another important point we have here is that Evil imitates the Good. In order to win good souls to its cause, it must appear to be good.

This is where we find that disciples on the Path under the Ascended Masters are most often fooled. They look at people and, without the discernment of the Holy Spirit, they think that because people are parroting good they must be good. They go through the footsteps and the motions of good, they are outwardly personable, they appear to be good human beings. But when you study the parrots, you will see that at subtle levels they often do have evil motives and so they put a patine of good over an evil core. That is why the scriptures say that we must "try the spirits" to see whether they be of God.[42] And, "By their fruits ye shall know them."[43]

Remember, Evil has nothing original of its own. It's a copycat. Everything it does and everything it has it has to first copy from God and then slightly distort—introducing an inharmonious chord, a sour note, a kind of a downward spiral that is interesting, enticing, enjoyable, pleasurable, et cetera, but very subtly it takes you down by degrees.

The force works on souls not for a day or a decade but for centuries. Century upon century upon century the Lightbearer, the potential Lightbearer, the potential Christ, will be worked on by evil forces presenting themselves as good.

How many evil people have you ever met who said to you, "Hi! I'm evil and I want you to know it"? Even a black magician will not reveal himself to you until he has, as Mark Prophet always used to say, "chewed you up and spat you out."

So beware. Beware and test the spirits and don't make hasty judgments or hasty alliances—or hasty decisions to part with your money. This is one of the biggest problems we see. People part with their money because within themselves they have a desire to multiply that money, to invest it, to gain by it. And so they will trust almost anyone who comes along and will, without even examining or thinking or scrutinizing, enter into some business deal that is ludicrous on the surface.

So please understand that people are not willfully evil unless they are tied to Absolute Evil. But they may have taken on themselves, through many lifetimes, the ways of the Evil One. They may have compromised Truth, compromised their speech, compromised their actions, all the while actually believing that they are very good people. And deep down inside, they probably *are* very good people, but at the moment they are in a position to influence you on the downward spiral.

So, this is about the old story of the rabbi who sits his son on the wall and tells his son to jump off the wall. And he says, "I'll catch you." So his son jumps off the high wall, but the rabbi doesn't catch him and he falls and hurts himself. So he says, "Dad, why didn't you catch me?" And his dad says, "Because I don't want you to ever trust anybody."

Trust God and wait and see. Pray about things and sleep on them and be careful where you commit your life and your energy.

Now here are a few final concepts from Zarathustra's teaching. His concept of morality can be summed up with the words "good thoughts, good words, good deeds."[44] This is the threefold ethic of Zorastrianism. Boyce writes:

> All Zoroastrians, men and women alike, wear [a] cord as a girdle, passed three times round the waist and knotted at back and front. Initiation took place at the age of fifteen; and thereafter, every day for the rest of his life, the believer must himself untie and retie the cord repeatedly when praying. The symbolism of the girdle (called in Persian the

'kusti') was elaborated down the centuries; but it is likely that from the beginning the three coils were intended to symbolize the threefold ethic of Zoroastrianism, and so to concentrate the wearer's thoughts on the practice of his faith.

Further, the kusti is tied over an inner shirt of pure white, the 'sudra,' which has a little purse sewn into the throat; and this is to remind the believer that he should be continually filling its emptiness with the merit of good thoughts, words and deeds, and so be laying up treasure for himself in heaven.[45]

Fire, of course, also plays a central role in Zarathustra's religion. Fire was a symbol of Ahura Mazda. It was also a symbol of Truth because of its power to destroy darkness.[46] Bernard Springett writes in his book *Zoroaster, the Great Teacher:*

> Fire, the great object of reverence of Zoroaster's disciples,... has ever been looked upon as a symbol of Spirit, and of Deity, representing the ever-living and ever-active light—essence of the Supreme Being. The perpetual preservation of fire is the first of the five things consecrated by Zoroaster.... The perpetual preservation of fire typifies the essential truth that every man should in like manner make it his constant object to preserve the divine principle in himself which it symbolises.[47]

According to tradition, when Zarathustra was seventy-seven he was assassinated by a priest of the old Iranian religion. Springett writes that "fabulous accounts of Zoroaster's death are given by the Greek and Latin patristic writers, who assert that he perished by lightning, or a flame from heaven."[48]

Much of what happened after Zarathustra's death is shrouded in mystery. Scholars say that his successors reintroduced the old gods that he had dethroned back into his system. They also condoned the *haoma* ritual. (Today Zoroastrians use a non-hallucinogenic substance in this ritual.)

By the time the Medes came to power in the seventh century B.C., Zoroastrianism was a major force in Persia. But when Alexander the Great conquered Persia in 331 B.C., he killed the priests and burned down the royal palace, destroying whatever may have been recorded of Zoroastrian tradition.

As Boyce describes it, "The Zoroastrians sustained irreparable loss through the death of so many of their priests. In those days, when all religious works were handed down orally, the priests were the living books of the faith, and with mass slaughters many ancient works (the tradition holds) were lost, or only haltingly preserved."[49]

About A.D. 225, Zoroastrianism reemerged in Persia and was the state religion until around 651, when the Moslems conquered Persia. Although Zoroastrianism was officially tolerated, the Arab conquerors encouraged conversion to Islam through societal pressures, economic incentives or force. Many Zoroastrians converted or went into exile. Loyal Zoroastrians who remained in Persia were taxed for the privilege of practicing their faith. In later centuries, persecution of Zoroastrians escalated. As of 1976, there were only 129,000 Zoroastrians in the world.[50]

According to Zaehner:

> Zoroastrianism has practically vanished from the world today, but much of what the Iranian Prophet taught lives on in no less than three great religions—Judaism, Christianity and Islam. It seems fairly certain that the main teachings of Zoroaster were known to the Jews in the Babylonian captivity, and so it was that in those vital but obscure centuries that preceded the coming of Jesus Christ Judaism had absorbed into its bloodstream more of the Iranian Prophet's teaching than it could well admit.
>
> It seems probable that it was from him and from his immediate followers that the Jews derived the idea of the immortality of the soul, of the resurrection of the body, of a Devil who works not as a servant of God but as his Adversary, and perhaps too of an eschatological Saviour who was to appear at the end of time. All these ideas, in one form or another, have passed into both Christianity and Islam.[51]

Some modern-day Zoroastrians say that Zarathustra taught a path of mystical union with God. Dr. Farhang Mehr, a founder of the World Zoroastrian Organization, says that the Zoroastrian mystic seeks union with God but retains his identity. In his book *The Zoroastrian Tradition,* he writes: "In uniting with God, man does not vanish as a drop in the ocean."[52]

Mehr says that Zarathustra was "the greatest mystic" and that the path of mysticism is rooted in the Gathas. According to Mehr, the path of mysticism in Zoroastrianism is called the path of Asha, or the path of Truth or Righteousness.[53]

Mehr delineates six stages in this path, which he correlates to the attributes of the six Holy Immortals. In the first stage the

X The Light of Persia—Mystical Experiences with Zarathustra

mystic strengthens the good mind and discards the evil mind. In the second stage he embodies righteousness. In the third he acquires divine courage and power. This enables him to selflessly serve his fellowman.

In the fourth stage the mystic acquires universal love. This allows him to replace self-love with a universal love—God's love for all. In the fifth stage he achieves perfection, which is synonymous with self-realization. And in the sixth and final stage, he achieves immortality, communion (or union) with God.[54]

Now let us take another look at Ahura Mazda. We have seen that Ahura Mazda is none other than Sanat Kumara, the Ancient of Days spoken of in the Book of Daniel. Sanat Kumara is the hierarch of Venus and Great Guru of the seed of Christ. The name Sanat Kumara comes from the Sanskrit, meaning "always a youth."

Aeons ago all Light had gone out in the evolutions of earth. So great was their departure from cosmic law that the Cosmic Council decreed the dissolution of the planet. Sanat Kumara volunteered to come to earth to keep the threefold flame of Life on behalf of her people. The Solar Lords granted him a dispensation to do so. One hundred and forty-four thousand souls from Venus volunteered to come with him to support his mission. They vowed to keep the Flame with him until the children of God would once again serve their Mighty I AM Presence.

Many of you were among that 144,000, also spoken of in the Book of Revelation.[55] You volunteered to come here with Sanat Kumara, and you knew that you would remain until the people you were responsible for had the teaching of the Mighty I AM Presence and once again had found the way back to God.

That day is dawning in this age, and thereby we know that finally we do have an opportunity to take our leave of planet earth, if we so choose, in the ritual of the ascension. And so the twentieth century has been a wondrous century, and it is a wondrous century of opportunity that is coming upon us as the fulfillment of the ancient teachings is made known publicly in the marts of the world.

So, Sanat Kumara established his retreat called Shamballa on an island in the Gobi Sea, now the Gobi Desert. Four hundred, who formed the avant-garde, preceded Sanat Kumara to earth and built this most beautiful palace of Light and retreat on that spot.

The first to respond to his flame was Gautama Buddha, followed by Lord Maitreya and Jesus Christ. Sanat Kumara held the position of Lord of the World until his disciple Gautama Buddha reached sufficient attainment to hold that office. On January 1, 1956, Gautama Buddha was crowned Lord of the World. Sanat Kumara retained the title Regent Lord of the World and returned to Venus and to his twin flame, the Lady Master Venus.

What we learn from the records and the history of Zarathustra is nothing compared to what we learn when we stand in his aura. Being in the presence of Zarathustra is like being in the presence of the physical sun itself. The mastery that he has of spiritual fire and physical fire is, if not the highest, among the highest of any adept ascended from this planet.

If you want to keep the flame of Zarathustra, you must visualize him keeping the flame, the divine spark, in your own heart. He is the greatest "fire-tender" of them all, if you will.

And when you call to him, remember that when you are engaged in the battle of Light and Darkness and you give our call for the binding of the forces of Antichrist, there is no greater devourer of the dark forces than Zarathustra himself. And he does it with his ten thousand flames. And to think of him having had this zeal for thousands upon thousands of years (and, who knows, perhaps as far back as Atlantis and Lemuria) as he came again in the dawn of history to Persia to bring the knowledge of the religion of fire—it is truly awesome.

This is why Zoroastrianism and Mighty Zarathustra are placed on the Eighth Ray chakra, the secret chamber of the heart. It is the Eighth Ray chakra and the eight-petaled chakra. In order to enter there, you must first be able to stand in the twelve-petaled heart chakra. The threefold flame burns on the altar of the secret chamber of the heart. Your high priest, who is your Holy Christ Self, retires to that secret chamber to keep that flame. Zarathustra and other Ascended Masters can and do visit you there and they tutor your soul.

Since we are Keepers of the Flame, we are fire-tenders. We are surely initiates of Zarathustra if we desire to be and, more than that, initiates of the priesthood of Melchizedek.

It is very important that we are acquainted with this religious tradition of Persia and that we have and feel in our hearts this tremendous zeal of this Zarathustra, who is alive and more alive than ever today! Just remember, Ascended Masters are never static. They increase and add rings upon rings to their Tree of Life. And in Zarathustra's case, he is most certainly adding rings upon rings of fire to his aura and Causal Body.

I will say, if you dare, call him to stand where you are tonight and feel what it feels like to have that substance melted that is hard as rock, as rock can be—substance that has been in your subconscious and your unconscious for aeons. That is the experience we anticipate as we prepare now for the dictation of the Mighty Zarathustra. Thank you. [21-second standing ovation]

Messenger's Invocation before the Lecture:

Light descending from Ahura Mazda, penetrate all elements of being. Let Light be reflected in Light.

O Thou Fiery One, Mighty Zarathustra, we welcome you to the chamber of our heart! O Thou Great Master of the Eighth Ray chakra, burn brightly tonight! Burn brightly thy flame on the altar of our hearts.

O Holy One of God, thou who hast shown us the way of the sacred fire consuming all Evil, evil ones and the energy veil, mighty pioneer in the separating of Light from Darkness, enter this company of souls who love you, who adore the sacred fire that you are. Take us, then, tier upon tier, to the planes of heaven. Part the way by sacred fire!

We gladly submit to thy flame, O Blessed One, whilst thou dost hold for us the mighty balance for all substance not of the Light, all sticky substance of the human consciousness.

Blaze, O fire! *Blaze,* O fire! *Blaze,* O fire of Zarathustra!

In the name Ahura Mazda, in the name of the Father, the Son, the Holy Spirit and the Divine Mother, Amen.

"**The Summit Lighthouse Sheds Its Radiance O'er All the World to Manifest as Pearls of Wisdom.**"
"The Light of Persia—Mystical Experiences with Zarathustra" was delivered by the Messenger Elizabeth Clare Prophet prior to the dictation of beloved Zarathustra on Wednesday, July 1, 1992, during the ten-day conference FREEDOM 1992: "Joy in the Heart" held at the Royal Teton Ranch, Park County, Montana. It has been edited for publication. (**1**) Mary Boyce, *Zoroastrians, Their Religious Beliefs and Practices* (London: Routledge and Kegan Paul, 1979), p. 1. (**2**) R. C. Zaehner, "Zoroastrianism," in *The Concise Encyclopaedia of Living Faiths,* ed. R. C. Zaehner (1959; reprint, Boston: Beacon Press, 1967), pp. 222, 209. (**3**) Boyce, *Zoroastrians,* p. 18. (**4**) Telephone interviews with H. Michael Simmons, Center for Zoroastrian Research, 28 June 1992, 17 August 1992. (**5**) Mircea Eliade, ed., *The Encyclopedia of Religion* (New York: Macmillan Publishing Co., 1987), 15:557. (**6**) Boyce, *Zoroastrians,* p. 19. (**7**) Gathas: Yasnas 50.6, 46.2, 43.8, quoted in Zaehner, "Zoroastrianism," p. 210. (**8**) Boyce, *Zoroastrians,* p. 19. (**9**) Ibid. (**10**) Zaehner, "Zoroastrianism," p. 210. (**11**) David G. Bradley, *A Guide to the World's Religions* (Englewood Cliffs, N.J.: Prentice-Hall, 1963), p. 40. (**12**) Ibid. (**13**) Simmons, telephone interview, 28 June 1992. (**14**) Zaehner, "Zoroastrianism," p. 210. (**15**) R. C. Zaehner, *The Dawn and Twilight of Zoroastrianism* (London: Weidenfeld and Nicolson, 1961), p. 35. (**16**) Dinkart 7.4.75–76, quoted in Bernard H. Springett, *Zoroaster, the Great Teacher* (London: William Rider and Son, 1923), p. 25. (**17**) Zarathustra, January 1, 1981, in *Where the Eagles Gather,* Book I (1981 Pearls of Wisdom, vol. 24) (Livingston, Mont.: Summit University Press, 1982), pp. 143–44. (**18**) Mary Boyce, ed. and trans., *Textual Sources for the Study of Zoroastrianism* (1984; reprint, Chicago: University of Chicago Press, 1990), p. 12. (**19**) Boyce, *Zoroastrians,* p. 22. (**20**) Ibid. (**21**) Ibid., p. 21. (**22**) Ibid., p. 22; Boyce, *Textual Sources,* p. 13. (**23**) Boyce, *Zoroastrians,* p. 22. (**24**) Ibid. (**25**) Boyce, *Textual Sources,* p. 14. (**26**) Zaehner, *Dawn,* p. 36. (**27**) Ibid. (**28**) Gatha: Yasna 30, quoted in Zaehner, *Dawn,* p. 42. (**29**) Ibid. (**30**) Zaehner, *Dawn,* pp. 42–43. (**31**) Gatha: Yasna 45.2, quoted in Zaehner, *Dawn,* p. 43. (**32**) Zaehner, "Zoroastrianism," pp. 211, 210. (**33**) Ibid., p. 211. (**34**) Gatha: Yasna 48.10, quoted in Zaehner, "Zoroastrianism," p. 211. (**35**) Zaehner, "Zoroastrianism," p. 211. (**36**) Gatha: Yasna 32.11, quoted in Zaehner, "Zoroastrianism," p. 211. (**37**) Zaehner, *Dawn,* p. 36. (**38**) John B. Noss, *Man's Religions,* 5th ed. (New York: Macmillan Publishing Co., 1974), p. 443. (**39**) Ahuna Vairya, in Boyce, *Textual Sources,* p. 56. (**40**) Simmons, telephone interview, 28 June 1992. (**41**) Zaehner, "Zoroastrianism," p. 213. (**42**) I John 4:1. (**43**) Matt. 7:15–20; 12:33; Luke 6:43, 44. (**44**) Zaehner, "Zoroastrianism," p. 221. (**45**) Boyce, *Zoroastrians,* pp. 31–32. (**46**) Zaehner, *Dawn,* pp. 47–48. (**47**) Springett, *Zoroaster,* p. 60. (**48**) Ibid., p. 32. (**49**) Boyce, *Zoroastrians,* p. 79. (**50**) Ibid., p. 226. (**51**) Zaehner, "Zoroastrianism," p. 222. (**52**) Farhang Mehr, *The Zoroastrian Tradition: An Introduction to the Ancient Wisdom of Zarathustra* (Rockport, Mass.: Element, 1991), p. 93. (**53**) Ibid., pp. 94, 93, 70; telephone interview with Farhang Mehr, 1 July 1992. (**54**) Mehr, *Zoroastrian Tradition,* pp. 94–96. (**55**) Rev. 7:4; 14:1–5.

36

Thou Purging Fire!
Do Not Quench the Flame

Lo! Lo! Lo! Let the full fire of your Mighty I AM Presence descend. *Descend* now! O come forth, thou purging fire! After the purging rain, so let there be the purging fire and the purging wind for the purging of the mind and the soul and the heart!

Wherefore did you come to the mount of Zarathustra if you did not reckon to receive the fire?

Therefore, welcome my fire, beloved, and thereby open your heart to me. For I come to perform a service unto your soul and unto your spirit, Atman, yet imprisoned in your temple.

I smile, beloved, for no one welcomes me.

[36-second standing ovation. Congregation gives the salutation:]

Hail, Zarathustra! Hail, Zarathustra! Hail, Zarathustra! Hail, Zarathustra! Hail, Zarathustra! Hail, Zarathustra! Hail, Zarathustra! Hail, Zarathustra! Hail, Zarathustra! Hail, Zarathustra! Hail, Zarathustra! Hail, Zarathustra! Hail, Zarathustra! Hail, Zarathustra!...

Ho! Ho! Ho! Now, beloved, by your welcome I gain necessary entrée to your heart. And truly I come from the heart of Helios and Vesta that I might give you fire for fire. And even if you have so little or none, yet I shall deliver the fire. Thus, be still in your seats now.

I ask you to meditate upon the chakras and to know that the all-consuming fire of God is just that: it is all-consuming. It is like the mighty sculptor. It does chisel away only that portion that was never real in the first place.

Oh, how I love the fire! Be fearless before the fire, beloved ones. Oh, be fearless! For in the day and in the night the gentle caressing of the flame of God and the rainbow rays—this is a great protection, this is a point for acceleration, this is Life's all-transfiguring, all-resurrecting flame. The flame *is* Life! Extinguish the flame: no God, no manifestation.

Fire is central to the worship of all peoples of all time, for it is, after all, the gift of Ahura Mazda. Yes, beloved, it was the gift of Sanat Kumara when all the fires of all the hearts of all the people who had so degenerated on planet earth were self-extinguished.

Therefore, hollowed-out man we found when we came from his home star. Hollowed-out man we found, hollowed-out woman, hollowed-out child. It was a day and an hour when, as you know, the Cosmic Council had decided to cancel [opportunity for earth's evolutions], to extinguish the planet itself as a failed experiment. But who [of the Council] could turn down the beloved Sanat Kumara, who did come offering his flame, offering to kindle the hearts of earth one by one?

Therefore none [of his devotees from Venus, his home star,] would allow him to go alone. Many did volunteer [to go with him][1] and many of those volunteers [who reincarnated in this era] do gather [today] on the mountain here in this place.

You have been pursuing the fire and the fiery ones for aeons upon aeons. Now you know so much about the flame. You know the workings of the violet flame. You know the Dhyani Buddhas and that they do deliver the flames of the five secret rays. Yes, beloved, the flame, its coloration, its vibration, the level that it is native to—all these things you have become sensitized to and you are becoming more sensitive to daily.

You understand the harmonies of the flames, the rays of the flames, their acceleration and how they bless the body and the body cells, and this (which you know at inner levels and somewhat on the outer far more than many upon earth) does make you candidates to come to my retreat, to come to that place prepared that is a mighty retreat that is a replica of the secret chamber of the heart, your very own heart.[2]

I look forward to welcoming you there, beloved ones, yet I have not released the whereabouts of this retreat, nor shall I. For when you make attunement with your own heart, beloved ones, and when you are in that heart as the devotee of the God within your heart, then so know and so understand: you shall not be able

XI Thou Purging Fire!

to avoid reaching that retreat of mine that is the [replica of the] secret chamber of the heart. Thus, I will tell you one thing. It is deep within the mountains. But which mountains, beloved, you will have to discover for yourselves.

Now I come for the preparation of your beings to be, oh, so sensitized to the Maha Chohan, to the Holy Spirit, to many who are unknown to you who are in the higher octaves as Buddhas and Bodhisattvas. They have not come, beloved, because you have not yet mastered even the threefold flame of your heart and the uses of the sacred fire. For that fire can work much good but it can also be misused for ill.

Therefore, you may enter the path of initiation with me, and that path will involve your willingness and ability to be trusted with the flame and entrusted with it. So, beloved, it is the greatest element of all. And without it, no other elements would have integration, for the fire is the nucleus of all life in all octaves and the very center of a cosmos.

Thus, I am speaking to you as you are being gently warmed by the angels of fire who come with me and by the fiery salamanders. And therefore, though it may be cool, you may begin to feel a warmth that is comfortable. But by and by it will not be comfortable, beloved ones, for I bring you a heat that you can stand and withstand, whereby you can be purged within the pores and cells and molecules of being.

This, then, is an offering that can be given. For listen to the silence! Listen to the love! Listen to your heartbeats one—one with the Central Sun, one in desiring to love and be loved and once and for all to end the separation between yourselves and God.

Oh, such a holy place! Oh, such a cradle, as we call it, for the coming together of souls who can "rub souls" with one another and therefore polish one another's auras and also know the meaning of the oneness of God in so many manifestations.

I AM THAT I AM. I AM in the heart of the flame. Ho! I AM Zarathustra and I choose to come gently in this moment, gently intensifying. Thus, I am causing the fiery salamanders to intensify the pressure: first of the light, then of the warmth, then of the fire itself.

Thus, beloved, I give what Alpha and Omega have called me to give. For they have prepared you, even as the preceding ones have prepared your auras, to assimilate absolutely the most fire that can possibly be given and received. Thus, for the moment be still and contemplate the rainbow flames all about you. [20-second pause]

Your body elemental is enjoying a fire bath. The body

elementals love the fire bath of the multicolored flames. They delight in this! They are scientists beyond your ken, beloved. They know the science of the body, they know what the flames heal and how to apply them. They not only enjoy the bath but are busy directing specific rays of the flames into specific needs of the body. They produce a well-beingness and a relaxation. They produce the harmony of the spheres.

And now the flame forms the cosmic egg around you, an ovoid of Light. You can sustain the pattern of the flames, beloved, and magnetize them to yourself at will by using the mantra I have given you to the Mighty Threefold Flame of Life. This mantra, beloved, will call my Electronic Presence around you. It is not short, because through your giving of the mantra, whilst you are giving it, I am realigning your chakras, assisting you to balance the threefold flame at all costs and to bring God-control to every aspect of your life.

Thus, some mantras work well as a line or two of affirmation. But when I wish to activate in you the spirals of the rainbow rays of God, then I must have this mantra. And while you give it, beloved, I can sustain the Presence. Thus, if it become a perpetual mantra in your heart, see where the increase of fire will bring you—closer to all of my chelas at inner levels and on the outer, closer indeed to the members of the priesthood of beloved Melchizedek. Thus, the mighty threefold flame of Life is the gift of God so pure!

Into the flame now comes your own beloved seraphim, the same, the very one who was with you in the hour of your birth in the Great Central Sun. Beloved ones, this seraphim has an attachment to you and to your twin flame and desires to bring you together. This seraphim has an attachment to bringing your body and mind and soul into the health of God, the health enjoyed by seraphim.

I would suggest you woo your seraphim and woo him to your side that he may not return to the Central Sun except according to the regular rotations and cyclings and recyclings of the seraphim from the Great Central Sun to the outer rings they form in the outermost universes [and back again].

So, beloved, seraphim are personally devoted, as they should be, to whomever God appoints them. Inasmuch as the seraphim, as you have been told, are great healers, they use these rainbow rays now for that healing purpose.

I AM in the white fire core of the flame. I AM in the pulsation of resurrection's flame. I AM in the action of the point of your Holy Christ Self.

In this moment of our meditation, beloved, I AM one with your Holy Christ Self. Now look upon your Holy Christ Self and see the smiling face of Zarathustra. In this moment I am not in my fiercest mode but when you see me turn upon the forces of Antichrist, then you may tremble by the fury of the elements and the wind and the vortex of the fire, beloved. But remember, in all of this it is directed. It is directed, beloved ones, and under the God-control of myself and legions of Light.

Therefore, while you are in this hour of assimilation of the flame, I shall perform the service now of dealing with those forces of Antichrist.

Bind the Forces of Antichrist in the Earth!

Ho! Mighty legions of the Light, descend!
Ho! Mighty legions of the Light, descend!
Ho! Mighty legions of the Light, descend!

Take up your positions in the quadrants of the earth now. By the mighty sword of the Divine Mother, therefore bind the forces of Antichrist in the earth and in the sea, *in the earth, in the earth, in the earth,* in the air, in the mental plane, in the etheric octave!

Blaze the full power of the Great Central Sun!

Mighty legions arrayed and circles of seraphim of God, legions of the mighty fire beings of the Ruby Ray and all of the secret-ray Dhyani Buddhas, come forth now for the binding of the forces of Antichrist in the earth!

Let all of heaven now unleash that full-gathered momentum of Elohim! *ELOHIM ELOHIM ELOHIM*

Let the full power of God descend for the displacing in the earth, for the consuming in the earth, for the binding in the earth, for the judgment in the earth of those who are the force of Antichrist, known or unknown, embodied or disembodied!

Let it descend now, O God! Let the fire descend as you have accorded it, as you have decreed it, as you have sent it and sent me into this very midst!

Therefore, let the fire descend! And let the all-consuming fire deal with that consciousness and that manifestation whose time is up. And therefore, let it be bound, let it be dissolved and let it be taken now into the very heart of the Central Sun for that action of the sacred fire which is meet!

Now the rain of fire-snow descends. ("Fire-snow," a misnomer, but fire-snow it is.) Descend, O fire-snow! Goddess of

Purity, Goddess of Light, Queen of Light, all hosts of the Fourth Ray, Astrea and Purity and all legions of Zarathustra, *go forth, then!*

They are bound by the hosts of the LORD and the hosts of the LORD shall continue the binding!

And therefore, I *seal* the action of the binding in the name Ahura Mazda! And I seal your temples in the flame that will not be quenched by God, will not be quenched by the Lord Christ or the Lord Buddha, will not be quenched, beloved, by your Holy Christ Self. The only one who can quench the flame is you.

See thou do it not! *See* thou do it not! *See* thou do it not! Salutations from all legions of *Zarathustra!*

[37-second standing ovation]

"The Summit Lighthouse Sheds Its Radiance O'er All the World to Manifest as Pearls of Wisdom." This dictation by **beloved Zarathustra** was **delivered** by the Messenger of the Great White Brotherhood Elizabeth Clare Prophet on **Wednesday, July 1, 1992,** during the ten-day conference *FREEDOM 1992: "Joy in the Heart"* held at the **Royal Teton Ranch, Park County, Montana.** Prior to the dictation, the Messenger delivered her lecture "The Light of Persia—Mystical Experiences with Zarathustra" (see *Pearls of Wisdom,* vol. 35, no. 35). [**N.B.** Throughout this *Pearl,* bracketed material denotes words unspoken yet implicit in the dictation, added by the Messenger under Zarathustra's direction for clarity in the written word.] (**1**) For the story of **Sanat Kumara and the devotees from Venus who accompanied him to earth,** see 1979 *PoW,* Book I, pp. 82–86. (**2**) Lord Maitreya has also told us that he has such a place. Any number of Ascended Masters maintain a room in their retreats that is a **focus of the secret chamber of the heart.**

XI Thou Purging Fire!

Notes from *Pearl* no. 33 by Alpha continued:
(2) The Keeper of the Scrolls is the custodian of the archives containing each man's book of life. He is the head of the band of angels known as the angels of record, or recording angels. Each soul evolving in time and space is assigned a recording angel, who records every action, word, deed, thought and feeling. At the end of each day, the recording angel submits the record of that day to the Keeper of the Scrolls. It is the responsibility of the Keeper of the Scrolls to provide the Ascended Masters and the Lords of Karma with the life record of any or all incarnations of any individual about whom they may inquire. On October 13, 1972, Mother Mary told us that we could apply to the Keeper of the Scrolls to see the records that would assist us in overcoming the human consciousness and attaining our victory. Mother Mary said: "The Keeper of the Scrolls...will draw forth from the Book of Life in your behalf, if you will call to him and to the Lords of Karma, those pages that require seeing and examination if you are to make the proper calls." **(3) Coil of the ascension flame.** See Djwal Kul, *Intermediate Studies of the Human Aura,* pp. 68, 100, plates 20, 23, 24, $9.95 plus $1.05 postage (also published in Kuthumi and Djwal Kul, *The Human Aura,* pocket book, pp. 140, 180, plates following pp. 140, 182, $4.95 plus $1.05 postage). **(4)** See **"A Proclamation" by Alpha,** delivered during Gautama Buddha's May 13, 1987 Wesak address, in 1987 *PoW,* pp. 242–43. **(5)** See "A Proclamation" by Alpha, p. 242.

O Mighty Threefold Flame of Life
by Zarathustra

O Mighty Threefold Flame of Life,
Thou gift of God so pure,
Take my thoughts and energy
And make them all secure.

Under bond of Brotherhood
And understanding fair,
Send thee forth unto my soul
The gift of holy prayer.

Communication's strands of love,
How they woo by heaven's law
A tender blessing for the good,
Releasing holy awe

That draws me near the throne of grace
To now behold thy sacred face
And without fear dispense aright
The passions of pure God-delight
Which set me free from all that's been
The sinful nature of all men.

Christ, raise me to self-mastery,
The living passion of the free.
Determination, now arise
And lift me ever to the skies!

I AM, I AM, I AM
Enfolding life and being all
With the God-command
"Amen!" that shatters human pall.

I AM, I AM, I AM
The free—no bondage holds me back;
I AM the fullness of Love's law
Supplying every lack,
And consecration in full measure
Is my will and God's own pleasure.

Saint Germain and Jesus dear,
Hold my hand with Morya's here
And let the love of Mary then
Be the wings to raise all men.

Until they all unite in Love
To serve that purpose from above
That comes to earth at any hour
Responding to the call of Power;
Send thy shining Wisdom then
That is God's love
Expanded for all men.

I thank thee and I accept this done right now with full power. I AM this done right now with full power. This is the full manifestation of **the Law of Love** that raises me to my eternal Victory, now and forever!

Taken from *Prayers, Meditations and Dynamic Decrees for the Coming Revolution in Higher Consciousness,* Section I, $2.95 plus $1.05 postage. *Heart, Head and Hand Decrees* booklet, $1.00 plus $.52 postage.

I AM the Witness

The Power of Shiva's Third Eye

Dear Devotees of Light,

I'd like to share something with you regarding the dictation Shiva gave at the *FREEDOM 1992* conference. I first began to invoke the name of Shiva back in 1984 after attending Level I at Summit University. I have learned from experience how incredibly powerful the single word *Shiva* is. And I just have to tell you about a dream I had before this summer class that parallels what Shiva told us in his dictation.

In my dream I was in a room that was all white with no furniture. This room was connected to many other white rooms. I was in an intense battle with an individual whom I will call "the evil one." He was good-looking (a Nephilim type), tall and blonde, and had a sinister grin and malicious laugh.

I thought he might be a "UFO guy" or a black magician. In any case, he was trying to destroy me. The only way I could keep him from destroying me was to keep my attention (i.e., my third eye) on him. My attention became the barrier that protected me from his power. However, he kept dematerializing and then reappearing quickly behind me so that I would have to turn instantly to keep my eye on him.

He kept repeating this sequence over and over again, always dematerializing and then reappearing somewhere else to catch me off guard. I was beginning to weary and knew I had to do something before I lost the battle. It was then that I thought of Shiva and I invoked his presence right when the evil one was reappearing again, this time in an adjacent room.

I shouted *"Shiva!"* and the most amazing thing happened! Shiva appeared before me instantly just as the evil one was reappearing. The look on the evil one's face turned from glee to overwhelming fear as he recognized Shiva. He tried desperately to get away but Shiva was too quick and released a golden emerald ray out of his third eye. He directed it at the third-eye area of the evil one, who was instantly annihilated.

Then Shiva disappeared and I was left standing in the white room simply awed by the experience. I woke up and praised the name of Shiva, who had once again delivered me!

I cannot fail to witness to the power of a single word: *Shiva!* It is absolutely awesome what one word can do. Praise God, praise the name of Shiva!

Gratefully, I remain

A Poem to Archangel Michael

Beloved Mother and All Keepers of the Flame,

I would like to share with you a poem I wrote regarding the angelic sponsorship of the police. I wrote it in October of 1990 and, by God's grace, was fortunate to have had it printed in the January 1991 issue of a police publication that goes out to all the law-enforcement personnel of the Los Angeles area.

Interestingly, as cycles of opportunity would have it, the very police officers who were exposed on the now-famous videotape of the Rodney King beating (Los Angeles, March 1991) had had an opportunity to read my (or Archangel Michael's) words just two or three months earlier. The Rodney King incident sparked such an outcry across the nation regarding police brutality that things will never be the same. I feel it has precipitated a certain judgment upon all law enforcement, and praise God for it!

One nearly shudders at the thought that it is possible for violent, bully types to dress up in uniform, hiding behind a badge, and commit crimes under color of law. I can see now that Archangel Michael and the cosmic councils must have decided that they were going to have no more of it!

What I want to say to my brothers and sisters on the Path who have not yet tested that "still small voice within" that prompts them to do, say or write something is: Do it! If you feel you have a particular attunement with an Ascended Master or Archangel who may have a message for the people of earth, I encourage you to write it down and do something with it. Remember, you are God's instrument where you are, and when you feel that inspiration that you know comes from on high, write it down right away and follow up on it.

Don't listen to the carnal mind that says, "Oh, I'll remember this. How could I ever forget it? I'll write it down later when I get home and I'm at my desk." Many a poet and songwriter can relate stories of the lyrics or poetic phrases that just slipped away and disappeared back into the ethers because they were not captured with pen and paper at the exact time of inspiration. And any good student of the science of Mother Mary's Cosmic Clock knows that the particular moment is the moment because it is the moment!

Be diligent and always have close at hand wherever you are a pad of paper and two pens—one to back up the other one that will always seem to run out on you right in the middle of your greatest inspiration!

So, if, by God's grace, I have been fortunate enough to inscribe the poetic thoughts of our dearly beloved Archangel Michael, I'd like to share them with my brothers and sisters on the Path who may then in turn share them with more of our brothers and sisters "in blue." These know at the "reality level" of their soul that Archangel Michael is their true sponsor, that he knows who they are and that he loves them and stands beside them (and around and over them) as they work.

Imagine how much additional protection the police would have

I AM the Witness 481

if they actually began praying to Archangel Michael!

Thank you, Mother, for being the example as you stand immovable at your intersection of Light in the mandala of the Great White Brotherhood, standing and still standing with your message of Truth, regardless of how popular or unpopular that message may be. May we all learn by your example.

And praise God for the "I AM the Witness" section of the *Pearls of Wisdom*, for I am grateful to be able to stand as a witness to the reality of the presence of Archangel Michael in the earth.

With all my love, Mother, to you and your family and staff, I remain your friend and chela, in service to our beloved El Morya.

Here is the poem:

Your Sponsor in Blue

You ride with your sponsor, an angel of blue,
With knowledge or not of his presence with you;
It's more than symbolic, that shield that you wear,
That covers your heart, protecting you there.

The children can see him accompanying you;
They wave and they smile—it's the reason they do!
Perhaps they can see the blue sword from the sun
That's standing behind your badge and your gun.

The mission is sure: "To Protect and to Serve";
No room in the ranks for those lacking in nerve,
Who would compromise truth and would further the cause
Of dishonoring the ranks and eroding the laws.

Your power, remember, is only on loan;
'Tis a most fearful master and not yours to own.
The people've entrusted it, angels have, too,
From the ranks of the many to only the few.

Have you noticed that mantle descend upon you
As you glance in the mirror for one final view
Before hitting the streets, as you straighten your tie?
Your sponsor is looking you straight in the eye!

This angel, remember, is always on call,
Should ever you need him, should ever you fall.
Decked out in khaki or your shade of blue,
He's instantly there in service to you.

On duty or off, you are never alone,
If enforcing the law is the interest you've shown
That has led you through training, now sealed by an oath;
The things that you do now reflect on you both.

Through service you may now return to this one
Your payment, of sorts, for all that he's done.
Defending the faithful and noble's his game;
And for those who would know, Archangel Michael's his name!

(Copyright 1990 Saint Adrian & Co., P.O. Box 824, Glendale, CA 91209. All rights reserved. Printed in the U.S.A.)

Is Your Electric Blanket Sapping Your Strength?

Dear Mother,

I used an electric blanket for a few months about twenty years ago. During the time I used the blanket, I felt agitated. I stopped using it because I was convinced—although I didn't have any proof except my feelings—that it was not healthy. Since then I've met several others who have had similar experiences with electric blankets.

In December 1991 I read Dr. Bruckheim's "Family Doctor" column in the *Billings Gazette*. A reader had written in with concerns about electric blankets. Dr. Bruckheim's discussion on the possible health risks associated with their use showed me that my suspicions were well founded. I think it's important to spread the word about the potential hazards of electric-blanket use. Fortunately, in this case, avoidance is a simple matter.

I am enclosing Dr. Bruckheim's column in the hope that you will share it with others.

Are Electric Blankets Safe?
by Dr. Allen Bruckheim

Recently my sister came to spend a few days with us to enjoy the holidays. While giving her a tour of our new home, she noticed the cord from our electric blanket on our bed. She rattled off a list of horrors that left me gasping and shaking. I'd like to know what the dangers are. I don't think she meant I could be electrocuted. What was she talking about?

It wasn't electrocution she feared, but the effects of the electrical current that runs through the wires of the blanket to generate the heat. It's a controversial topic, but I can afford you a bit of insight and a suggestion or two.

When common house current, which is a 60-hertz, alternating current (AC) flows through a wire it generates an electromagnetic field. This is true of power lines, video display terminals and some household appliances as well as electric blankets. This type of field is called an "extremely low frequency" (or ELF) electromagnetic field.

Ongoing research investigating the possible negative effects of such ELF fields has been conducted since 1979. That's when some studies suggested that the higher-than-expected frequency of cancer and birth defects was linked to the presence of these fields. The

Environmental Protection Agency issued a preliminary statement of its findings last year, and called ELF fields "a possible but not proven cause of cancer in humans." The EPA's final report is expected to be released shortly.

However, the Food and Drug Administration, basing its actions on the preliminary EPA report, recommended that the electromagnetic fields produced by electric blankets be reduced. Since that time, the manufacturers of these blankets have made blankets with the electromagnetic fields reduced by as much as 95 percent. These are the type of blankets available today in most stores. Some of these newer blankets are even labeled as being newly engineered.

Even though many electrical appliances generate similar fields, the danger with an electric blanket results from its many hours (about eight hours on average) of contact with the body during a night's sleep as well as the close proximity of contact with the user.

ELF fields are strongest next to the electrical source of the field. So the closer you are to the current the greater the exposure will be. Since blankets lie directly on the sleeping user, the exposure is high. Thus the U.S. Office of Technology Assessment has recommended "prudent avoidance" in the use of such blankets.

Let me underscore that the type of research used to develop these recommendations was based upon epidemiological studies rather than laboratory experiments. They represent a statistical analysis that attempts to link a cause with an effect and can be mere coincidence. Still there's probably enough evidence to validate the concern.

You still can gain some advantage from your blanket, should you choose to continue to use it. Turn the blanket on before you retire. Get the bed warm and comfortable; however, turn the blanket off before sliding into bed. You can achieve all of the benefits with none of the possible risks.

Pregnant women and children are best advised to forgo the use of such blankets completely.

I disagree with certain of Dr. Bruckheim's conclusions. Let's say you forget to turn off the blanket that you intended to use just to warm your bed on that cold winter night. Then again, if it's not OK for pregnant women and children, it may not be OK for anyone. I was neither pregnant nor a child when I felt the bombardment of my body during the period of time I used an electric blanket.

Finally, until our scientists can tell us precisely what the association is between the use of electric blankets and the higher incidence of cancer and birth defects, how can we know for certain that an electric field alone—

which may still be produced unless the blanket is unplugged—is not of itself harmful to our health?

For anyone interested in reading in more detail about the potential risks associated with extremely low frequency electromagnetic fields, one highly readable brochure I've found on the subject is "Electric and Magnetic Fields from 60 Hertz Electric Power: What do we know about possible health risks?" written by Professor M. Granger Morgan. It is available for $3.50 from the Department of Engineering and Public Policy, Carnegie Mellon University, Pittsburgh, PA 15213. Another good article, "Are Electric Blankets Safe?" was published in the November 1989 issue of *Consumer Reports* and is available in the reference section of most public libraries.

Sincerely,

My Heart Is the Heart of Christ

While I was a part-time staff member at Camelot in California I had an experience that unfortunately has never been repeated but has been an important inspiration to me. I was an usher at the time and was asked to sit in the Chapel of the Holy Grail while Mother was giving baptisms. Jesus was present and I could feel his and Mother's love for each child as they came forward. My heart was also filled with love as I looked at the children's innocence and purity and watched Mother baptize them.

The line was very long and after some time something happened to my heart chakra that I had never felt before. It is hard to describe but it felt like my heart was continuously leaping for joy or leaping with love. My heart felt like it was overflowing, and it was a very blissful and beautiful feeling. In the past my heart had often burned with love but this was quite different. The feeling continued for several hours after the baptisms and then slowly faded away.

I have been profoundly grateful ever since because I believe that we can continually be in such a state of bliss if we diligently follow the path given to us by the Ascended Masters. But it would have been hard for me to imagine what such bliss is like if I had not had this experience.

Sincerely,

N.B. Testimonies of disciples of Jesus Christ and the Ascended Masters stating their witness to the power of Truth in their lives will regularly appear in this column in the *Pearls of Wisdom*. If you would like to witness to the power of Truth in your life brought about through the Ascended Masters and their Messengers, we welcome your testimony for publication. Your letter will be kept on file in our archives but your name will be withheld from this page to protect your privacy and your progress on the Path.

Royal Teton Ranch

Box 5000, Corwin Springs, Montana 59030-5000 406/848-7441

September 12, 1992

Dear Friends of Saint Germain,

On August 30 Saint Germain delivered a soul-stirring message to the Montana community, to Summit University students—and to the world! Saint Germain had already delivered two dictations at our summer conference, one on June 27 in the mantle of Saint Joseph and the other draped in Old Glory as he took the platform to deliver his Fourth of July address.

You have read and perhaps already heard and seen Saint Germain say, "I am not done with Pisces!" These were his immortal words:

> I say, this place is indeed the cradle of a new civilization of Lightbearers! And I, Saint Joseph, am on hand as always to inaugurate cycles and dispensations by the power of the Seventh Ray....
>
> I come to you to place my mantle and Presence of Saint Joseph over you so that you may go and do the work and be our hands and feet, our hearts and our chakras in the earth....
>
> Yes, beloved, we have work to do! We have some unfinished business with the

fallen ones who have moved against my Son and against you as my sons and daughters in every age, lifetime after lifetime....

I AM Saint Joseph. And though I come as the Hierarch of Aquarius, I am not done with Pisces! For I am determined to see a victory out of it all and, through you and this Messenger, the publishing abroad of the true teachings of Jesus Christ. For they are the foundation of Aquarius and Aquarius cannot rise without the self-knowledge of every man, woman and child upon this planet of his own Holy Christ Self and of the Son of God and of the I AM Presence and of the violet flame!

See to it, then, ye warriors of the Spirit and of the earth! See to it, ye saints of God in the flesh! Now make your life count as it has never counted before in all past ages and graduate with glory in your ascension in the Light!

Now you are impatiently waiting to both read and hear and see his cry to the nations on the Fourth. This is a sample:

Hail, Keepers of the Flame! I AM come for the victory, for there is nothing else to come for!...

You **must** not fail! You **will** not fail! For I am told by the cosmic hierarchy and the Lords of Karma, unless we do it this time and do it well, there will not be another opportunity that we have in this interval of cosmic space and cosmic silence to turn the whole Dark Cycle around.

You must wake up! So, I plead with you. Others have pleaded with you. Yet you must know that every moment you can spend before your altar and with your decrees you are buying time for Saint Germain. I want to be with you. I <u>can</u> be with you. I can place my Electronic Presence with you. But give that call to the living flame of cosmic freedom....

I will tell you how much time you have to turn the world around. Measured in cosmic time, beloved, it is seconds. Yes, beloved, it is seconds....

As far as we are concerned and the Seven Holy Kumaras and all of our bands who have come together and come together in this hour after so many thousands of years, we will accept nothing else but a golden age of Aquarius! We will not accept a downward-spiraling age, building downward upon the downward spiral of the Piscean. We will have our golden age or we will not have an age at all!

His third dictation in his summer series was truly the capstone. On August 30 Saint Germain sealed

all who are of merit who have been a part of me for ages with an amethyst heart which I place over your heart chakra as a shield, aye, as a crystal and as a transformer that the love that you give... might be multiplied even by this focus of my heart and that the love that you receive might also be multiplied for a more swift transmutation of every force of anti-Love within and without your being.

The experience of delivering this dictation was surely one of the highlights of my thirty-one-year career in the service of Saint Germain. It brought me back to the moment when he had quickened my heart at age eighteen when I was about to leave home for college. It took me through, dot by dot on the map of the years, those very special moments when he has taken me up into his mighty Presence to teach and comfort me, to give direction for our Church and his world revolution—the Coming Revolution in Higher Consciousness.

It brought me back to the moment when El Morya called me to "stump" and I said, "What?" and he said, "Stump! Stump the nations. Deliver the message of the Teachings of the Ascended Masters." That call took me across North America to Africa, Europe, the Philippines, India, Australia; all of that was preceded by our 1973 tour to Mexico City and South America.

And so Saint Germain said on August 30:

I have told you I am not finished with Pisces, I have not yet done with it.

Therefore you can expect me to appear in various places when least expected, for I intend to send my Messenger in the year ahead and I intend to send her where she must be myself in physical action and can therefore provide you with my Electronic Presence and you may be in polarity with that Presence and therefore work seeming wonders. But there are no real wonders for the Wonderman of Europe but only the scientific principle of the alchemy of God, the all-chemistry of your own Causal Body that we may use to make all the difference....

Yes, beloved, I am yet in the business of securing grants from the Karmic Board and the Cosmic Council and I have secured a grant, beloved. Therefore I am very, very happy this day. [31-second standing ovation]

You have been told that grants do not come easy to the Ascended Masters in this hour. And therefore it is considered a great boon by all of the Darjeeling Council, who are looking over my shoulder now, wondering what I will do with this grant. [laughter]

Well, I can assure you, beloved ones, from our experience in recent and past history, that I shall not so liberally dispense the energies and the backing that comes with the grant. But I want you to know that it is here and it is here for those selected chelas who themselves select to walk the Path in an extraordinary devotion and who would seek, having had the disciplines of El Morya and desiring to continue his disciplines, their own chelaship with me.

Yes, beloved ones, I desire to take certain of you on as my own chelas and this shall be, of course, by that merit.

If I were to draw a profile around Saint Germain's aura as he placed his Presence over me to deliver his August 30 dictation, I would say that in that moment I was standing in the aura and the mantle of none other than Christopher Columbus. It was as though Saint Germain was about to rediscover the world 500 years later, was going to bring to that New World the lost teachings of the Saviour and an enlightenment of a magnitude not measured since the last golden age of Atlantis.

My being thrilled as I felt myself magnetized and repolarized to the polestar of the blessed Master. And I said to myself, "If Saint Germain is not done with Pisces, then

I am not done with Pisces either! Wherever he goes, I go!"

The following letter from Christopher Columbus to the king and queen of Spain, who had given him the title Admiral of the Ocean Sea, gives us that profile of Saint Germain as Christopher Columbus:

Most Christian and noble rulers:

The following is a statement of my proposal for the restoration of the House of God to the Holy Church Militant.

Most eminent rulers: At a very early age I began to navigate upon the seas, which I have continued to this day. Mine is a calling that inclines those who pursue it to desire to understand the world's secrets. Such has been my interest for more than forty years, and I have sailed all that can be sailed in our day. I have had business and conversation with learned men among both laity and clergy, Latins and Greeks, Jews and Moslems, and many others of different religions. I prayed to the most merciful Lord concerning my desire, and he gave me the spirit and the intelligence for it. He gave me abundant skill in the mariner's arts, an adequate understanding of the stars, and of geometry and arithmetic. He gave me the mental capacity and the manual skill to draft spherical maps, and to draw the cities, rivers, mountains, islands and ports, all in their proper places.

During this time, I have searched out and studied all kinds of texts: geographies, histories, chronologies, philosophies and other subjects. With a hand that could be felt, the Lord opened my mind to the fact that it would be possible to sail from here to the Indies, and he opened my will to desire to accomplish the project. This was the fire that burned within me when I came to visit Your Highnesses. All who found out about my project denounced it with laughter and ridiculed me. All the sciences which I mentioned above were of no use to me. Quotations of learned opinions were no help. Only Your Majesties had faith and perseverance. Who can doubt that this fire was not merely mine, but also of the Holy Spirit who encouraged me with a radiance of marvelous illumination from his sacred Holy Scriptures, by a most clear and powerful testimony from the forty-four books of the Old Testament, from the four Gospels, from the twenty-three Epistles of the blessed Apostles—urging me to press forward? Continually, without a moment's hesitation, the Scriptures urge me to press forward with great haste.[1]

"The Admiral was the first to open the gates of that ocean which had been closed for so many thousands of years before. He it was who gave the light by which all others might see how to discover." (Bartolomé de Las Casas)[2]

It is clear to me that the 500th-year anniversary of Christopher Columbus' discovery of America will mark the release on October 12 in Atlanta of a tremendous dispensation from the Causal Body of Saint Germain. I believe that release will be comparable to nothing less than the magnitude of a supernova, which in its exploding will release the light of spheres of Saint Germain's Causal Body that have remained inaccessible to his students for many thousands of years.

Therefore I anticipate October 12 in Atlanta as an hour of destiny for Saint Germain and his Keepers of the Flame throughout the world. I expect that it will return each one of us to the moment when we knew Saint Germain in one or another of his incarnations, when we stood at his side to behold the wonder of this soul, this Son of God, this man of the centuries and of the ages whose presence on earth has been the opening of continents and thereby the mind of the whole human race.

His work in age after age has initiated science and invention and engineered civilizations. As Francis Bacon, he captured the essence of life in the hearts and minds of the good and the evil in his 'bible' written for the godly and the ungodly—the Shakespearean plays. Saint Germain is not only the Wonderman of Europe, he is the Wonderman of the Americas, of ancient Atlantis and the civilizations of Lemuria.

Saint Germain has called me in many lifetimes and he has also called you. Every Keeper of the Flame in the world is a Keeper of the Flame because he or she knows the heart of Saint Germain, knows the Master and identifies his or her own destiny with his.

Saint Germain has given us purpose in living. From the rising to the setting of the sun, we chart our course by his compass. What meaning would there be to life on earth without his flame of freedom that he ignited in the hearts of our founding fathers, that assembled the twelve tribes and the thirteenth, the tribe of the Christed ones, the thirteen colonies, who took their stand against tyranny one more time and declared "that these United Colonies are and of Right ought to be Free and Independent States."

There is not a heart of a starving child in Somalia, of the persecuted in South Africa, of the poor whites and blacks of America, of the students in Tiananmen Square, or of the high and the mighty who control the power and the wealth of nations that does not resonate with that spark of freedom, that spark of divinity. Whether those who perform the blackest of deeds or those who labor selflessly to nurture the poor, the suffering, the sick and the dying, all do so in the name of free choice, free will and in the inner knowing that America is the land of the prophet Samuel, of Saint Joseph, the true father of our Lord, of Saint Alban, of Merlin, of Roger Bacon, of Francis Bacon and the immortal Count Saint Germain. Why, thinking about what the world would be like without Saint Germain is like imagining the world in twilight having the bleak and lifeless terrain of the Moon or Mars or a thousand dead asteroids.

Yes, I want to be there in Atlanta with you, my dearest friends, for Saint Germain's dictation, for his love, and to give him once again—in honor of his discovery and his dedication of this entire continent to the Saviour of the world—the chalice of my heart, even as you give him yours, that, combined, these might serve him yet many a year that he might finally seal all of his Piscean projects and have done with them so that he might get on with the great business of Aquarius.

The fact that beloved Jesus will speak following Saint Germain tells me that our Masters are coming in an hour of great portent to tell us those things that the politicians are not telling because they cannot: what is the divine and the practical solution to the economy, to Yugoslavia, to drugs, to abortion, to the pollution of the earth and of the souls of her people.

Side by side with the sick and sinful politicians that bore us nightly on the evening news with name-calling and accusations when a platform for world change ought to be presented by true statesmen in the tradition of the world's great leaders, we behold with love and awe and hope the figures of our guiding lights: Jesus Christ and Saint Germain.

Every dictation at the October conference will be a voyage of soul discovery—from Listening Angel, who opens the conference, to Mary the Mother of Jesus, whose recent appearances in Marlborough, New Jersey, are not far from my hometown, to Saint Teresa of Avila, whose soul ascended in the 1970s, to the Buddha of the Ruby Ray, the incomparable one who ensouls the momentums of all other Buddhas, to beloved Omri-Tas, Ruler of the Violet Planet, who has given not only to ourselves but to Saint Germain a new hope for world transmutation in the dispensation of his violet flame sea, to Sanat Kumara, who will be present as one of the Seven Holy Kumaras. We will receive a royal welcome as they include us in their councils and speak to us of what we must do to implement the dispensations of FREEDOM 1992 and to make our voice count in this decade.

Beloved Saint Germain has called us to Atlanta. And, as usual, his agenda is manifold. Saint Germain says that there are hearts of Light who "<u>must</u> be contacted." He says: "I am interested in connecting your hearts by a strong cable to the hearts [of those]...who must be the called-out ones, who must have the knowledge of the I AM THAT I AM before the year 2002 rolls around."

But let us not forget the tribulation, the trial and testing of Christopher Columbus. Although he was not a perfect man by twentieth-century standards, we see in him the reflection of the Christ and a reminder that in our darkest hour the angel of the Lord is nigh. This excerpt from the Admiral's journal tells of his darkest night and the opening of the heavens in approbation upon a very special Son of God. Read it and take heart:

> I was outside and all alone on this very dangerous coast, with a high fever and greatly exhausted. There was no hope of rescue. In this state, I climbed in pain to the highest point of the ship and called, in tears and trembling, to Your Highnesses' mighty men of war, in all the four corners of the earth, for succour, but none of them answered me.
>
> At length, groaning with exhaustion, I fell asleep, and I heard a most merciful voice saying: "O fool, so slow to believe and to serve thy God, the God of all! What more did He do for Moses or for His servant David? He has had thee in His care from thy mother's womb. When He saw thee a grown man, He caused thy name to resound most greatly over the earth.
>
> "He gave thee the Indies, which are so rich a part of the world, and thou hast divided them according to thy desire. He gave thee the keys to the gates of the Ocean, which were held with such great chains. Thou wast obeyed in many lands, and thou hast won a mighty name among Christians. What more did He do for the people of Israel when He led them out of Egypt, or for David, that shepherd boy whom He made a king in Jewry. Turn thyself to Him, and acknowledge thy sins. His mercy is infinite.
>
> "Thine old age shall not prevent thee from achieving great things, for many and

vast are His domains. Abraham was more than a hundred years old when he begat Isaac; and Sarah, was she a girl? Thou criest for help, with doubt in thy heart. Ask thyself who has afflicted thee so grievously and so often: God or the world? The privileges and covenants which God giveth are not taken back by Him. Nor does He say to them that have served Him that He meant it otherwise, or that it should be taken in another sense; nor does He inflict torments to show His power. Whatever He promises He fulfills with increase; for such are His ways.

"Thus have I told thee what thy Creator has done for thee, and for all men. He has now revealed to me some of those rewards which await thee for the many toils and dangers which thou hast endured in the service of others."

I heard all this as if in a trance, but I could find no reply to give to so sure a message, and all I could do was to weep over my transgressions. Whoever it was that had spoken, ended by saying: "Fear not, but have faith. All these tribulations are written upon tablets of marble, and there is reason for them."[3]

Last October we were in New Orleans, this October Atlanta. Let us do our part and place our bodies where the Body of Christ is, for truly those who will speak to us and transfer to us their great Light in this momentous occasion are the saints of the Mystical Body of God. Let us gather together, then, as eagles and continue the mission begun long ago, which we are not done with—the mission of the Christ, of Pisces and his Love, and the mission of Saint Germain who has never ceased to move heaven and earth that the Saviour's comfort, love and teaching might be a light to lighten the world that never grows dim.

When Saint Germain gave his dictation on August 30, the Goddess of Freedom and beloved Portia, the Divine Mother of Justice, flanked him. Saint Germain called upon us, as did the Ascended Master El Morya, to perform a labor for the judgment of the forces of the fallen ones who perverted God's justice and his true and righteous judgment and who, ever since, have embodied this force known as <u>Din</u>. (For an understanding of this profound and vital teaching on the origin of evil, please order your audio- or videotapes of the lecture "Keys from Judaism: The Kabbalah and the Temple of Man," which I delivered at the July conference.)

Saint Germain said on August 30 that Portia herself had "earned her own dispensation" for the putting down of these forces. Thus, the Hierarchs of the age of Aquarius, Saint Germain and Portia, only need our labor to accomplish this task. Saint Germain said: "When these forces [of the fallen angels] are bound and put down, then you will see that there will be no stopping the Lightbearers, and the security of those of us in higher octaves and you here shall be sealed! I promise you this and I come to secure your promise that you will receive the labors on this and you will act to perform them well."

Keepers of the Flame in attendance gave their assent to Saint Germain's request in a standing ovation. And he gave the send-off to all who had been here for the summer: "Go be the pillar of fire in your town and city and home and turn this old world around for Saint Germain!"

Truly, beloved, in the purple fiery heart of Saint Germain we find the greatest exponent of the message and the love of our Saviour

Jesus Christ. May we come to his aid and love him in this era of the turning of worlds.

We have an appointment in Atlanta! Be there and make your statement by your presence that you are with Saint Germain all the way to the victory of planet earth and your own victorious ascension in the Light.

All my Love,

Mother

P.S. I recently saw the movie <u>Christopher Columbus</u> and found myself tying in to the Presence of Saint Germain as Columbus, and Saint Germain as Saint Germain. Though this movie could have been better, it provided an opening for a precious contact. I hope you and your families will see it before the class. Because there is more to Columbus than meets the eye—much, much more.

P.P.S. If you're in or near New York, please join me Sunday, October 4, for my lecture on "How to Contact Angels" and a dictation by Archangel Chamuel—at the Hilton at Rockefeller Center, 11:30 a.m. to 2:30 p.m. Then we will move to the Marriott Marquis on Broadway, from 7:30 p.m. to 11:30 p.m. Join me there as I give you essential keys on "How You Can Contact God" and deliver a dictation by El Morya. This will be followed by questions and answers. The event will be held at the Marriott Marquis Westside Ballroom, 1535 Broadway. (To preregister, call 800-245-5445. For more information, call 406-222-8300.)

(1) The *"Libro de las profecías" of Christopher Columbus: an en face edition*, translation and commentary by Delno C. West and August Kling (Gainesville, Fla.: University of Florida Press, 1991), p. 105. (2) Bartolomé de Las Casas, quoted in John Noble Wilford, "Discovering Columbus," *New York Times Magazine*, 11 August 1991, pp. 27–28.
(3) Christopher Columbus, quoted in Björn Landström, *Columbus* (New York: Macmillan Company, 1966), pp. 172–73.

―――― A SPOKESMAN FOR THE DELEGATION ――――
OF THE PRIESTHOOD OF MELCHIZEDEK IN ATTENDANCE
FREEDOM 1992 *"Joy in the Heart"* XII

37

The Great Mystery of the Violet Flame
Give a Cup of Cool Violet Flame in Christ's Name

Salutations to all sons and daughters of God present and not present and to all children of the Light! I bring these salutations, as I represent the delegation of the order of the priesthood of Melchizedek.

I am chosen as a nameless one to speak to you that you might know that as aspiring candidates to this priesthood you have begun well and run well. Therefore, finish your course and do not weary. For the requirement for studying under the Master Melchizedek is your mastery of some level of the fire [element], and you are given this opportunity each time you invoke the violet flame.

Let us speak of the mastery of this flame since you are familiar with it and it does not strike a certain fear, as the physical flames of earth's fire [sometimes] do. Therefore, beloved, be seated in the violet flame, for soon the day will be upon you, on July 3, wherein you will have the great joy of communing for twenty-four hours in the mighty aura of Omri-Tas, Ruler of the Violet Planet.*

[Each month] we look forward to and anticipate his coming with great joy. And we prepare all the days of the month unto the third [of the next month] that we might bring a greater concentration

―――――――――――
*See "Omri-Tas' Violet Flame Day," p. 84 n. 1.

[of violet flame] and also be initiated by Omri-Tas. For with the blessing he extends to you and all Keepers of the Flame, he does also stop by at Zadkiel's retreat to offer us some portion of that mighty flame which we have earned in the previous cycle. Therefore, what is true for us is true for you, beloved. Look forward to this opportunity as nothing else.

Visualization of the violet flame begins your concentration and results in your God-mastery. Visualize the fire in the heart, then, and let the violet flame burn in the heart, surround the heart.

And when you know your mantras by heart, as many of you do, then sit in deep meditation and let the violet flame increase in size, beginning within and then encompassing the physical heart and the heart chakra. [Let the action of the violet flame] remain intense by your visualization and by the intensity of your call. Then let it expand slowly so that the intensity is such that you cannot see through the flame; for it has become a dense manifestation of the [violet] ray of light [as it has] descended from the sun and then sprung up as a flame at your point of invocation.

Your point of invocation is your throat chakra. [It can also be defined as the plane of your soul's incarnation.] Therefore I say, invoke the flame through the throat chakra and add to [your invocation] the instrument of the heart chakra, thereby pouring love to the flame and drawing love from the flame. Use the third eye to invoke the violet flame by intense visualization, drawing the flame into the third eye and giving to the flame the momentum of the sacred fire of that chakra. So use each of the chakras to meditate upon the flame, to focus the flame and then to give [devotion] unto the flame even as you receive [the devotion of the flame].

The more creative you are in the use of the violet flame, the more you understand that the violet flame is a ritual, has a consciousness of ritual and looks forward to the hours of the day that you have consecrated to invoking a mantra of the violet flame—or, should I say, invoking the violet flame through a mantra?

Well, the mantra is the flame and the flame is God and so is the mantra! The question is: Are *you* all three? Are you the flame, the mantra and the manifestation of God?

This is the attainment you look forward to as you visualize the violet flame rising up from beneath your feet, rising and pulsating and purifying every level of your being. Then when the concentration is complete in the physical body and you see and feel it, let it slowly extend [out from you] as an aura having the magnetism of the violet flame and let it increase and intensify.

XII The Great Mystery of the Violet Flame

And so, beloved, as you go through the world, [remember to] put on your tube of light to protect your momentum of the violet flame. But also be ready when you see the eyes of a Lightbearer and the child in need and the soul who looks to God for help. Do not fear to be the instrument to transfer a cup of cool violet flame in Christ's name.

To have a reservoir of the violet flame means that when you invoke the violet flame, you are using the action of the mighty sea of violet flame in the heart of the earth, you are using the mighty action of Saint Germain's Maltese cross[1] and you are establishing that pillar of fire where you are[—multiplied by your own reservoir].

After all, it is the seventh age and the seventh dispensation, beloved ones. It is that age and hour when you can all become priests and priestesses under the Order of Lord Zadkiel, under Melchizedek, under Saint Germain, [under Zarathustra and even Oromasis and Diana]. It is that moment in an entire [twelve-tiered] cycle when you have come all the way around the Cosmic Clock of the ages back to the place of the Aquarius sign—the sign of the liberation of the soul through the violet flame.

In no other past age since the last [age of Aquarius], twelve cycles ago, has there been such an opportunity for world transmutation, soul transmutation, the balancing of karma and [your soul's] restoration through the Lord and Saviour Jesus Christ to your own inner Christ-potential. So, beloved, the opportunity is vast. It is increased by the dispensation of Omri-Tas, who has brought to you an [unprecedented dispensation (given the present level of earth's evolutions) to reduce your karmic cycles] by light-years.

Therefore know what a boon all students in the retreats of the Ascended Masters on the etheric octave who are not in embodiment consider this one day a month to be to them! Why, all the retreats of the entire planet are simply pulsating with the joy of the violet flame!

And we do keep that flame and we do conserve it and we preserve it in the urns upon our altars. And therefore, when world crisis breaks out or the planetary [hierarchs] and the Solar Logoi give the word that there must be earth changes, we have upon the altars of all of the retreats of the Great White Brotherhood on earth the wherewithal to apportion that violet flame that we have carefully invoked and garnered so that there might be a smooth transition [when the Great Law decrees] the balancing of that karma which is [weighing heavily] in the earth body [and being borne by] so many billions of souls who live thereon.

So you see, beloved, you can do the same! You can bank the

fires of the violet flame in all of your chakras and in all of the levels of your being, as tier upon tier your chakras represent the seven planes of heaven. You can rise up those tiers, beloved ones! And you can rise up the *sefirot* unto the point of the I AM THAT I AM, and one day you may go beyond the I AM THAT I AM to the point of the *Ein Sof*. So understand the meaning of the cycles of the degrees [as you walk the Path a true initiate of the Great White Brotherhood].

Now understand, beloved, the great mystery of the violet flame. The violet flame is an action that can be stepped [up or down] and tuned to any level of the seven [chakras]. Therefore the violet flame that you keep in the heart will have a different frequency than the violet flame that you keep in the solar-plexus chakra, and so on. And as you are stepping up the grades of the violet flame [from the base-of-the-spine chakra] to the crown chakra, there is an acceleration of the violet flame affecting all of those levels in the earth body. So when you begin at the base chakra [and proceed], rising to the crown, you are experiencing God in the seven levels of heaven *right in your very own being!*

Therefore I say to you, value the chakras in your body. Value them well, beloved, for they are chalices. And in the day and the hour when sudden calamity or terminal disease or plague of any kind comes upon your house or upon your body, you will have vials filled with violet flame as a precious medicine, as a precious unguent that you may use spiritually and physically.

Understand therefore, beloved, that he who does not collect his pots from all of his town and townspeople and bring them into one place on the third of the month and fill them with the violet flame surely does not anticipate that the day may come when there will be no violet flame rain anymore. And therefore, [in that day] the pots will be dry if you do not fill them now and they will be full if you do fill them now!

So, beloved ones, this is not hoarding. For the violet flame is infinite—infinite out of your own Causal Body of Light, infinite from the Violet Planet and from Omri-Tas. But I can tell you, we, the brothers and the sisters who study under our beloved priest Melchizedek, who was indeed king of Jerusalem and priest of the Most High God,[2] know the value of garnering the violet flame. And we are asking you to do the same, beloved, in your octave.

For where there are pockets of concentration of the violet flame and you in your joy and love for beloved Saint Germain and Portia and all they have ever done for you do keep that violet flame, well, you see, you are as points igniting a whole world with the violet flame. You are practically as a tinderbox! And someone

XII The Great Mystery of the Violet Flame

may come along and invoke a single violet flame and catch the whole momentum that you carry. And therefore the violet flame will be contagious! And it will *leap* from heart to heart, from continent to continent, from village to village!

Do you understand, beloved? Our goal is to see planet earth become, as she should be, a Violet Planet herself! And thus, Omri-Tas and all of the mighty beings of the Violet Planet are rooting for you. And that is why Alpha has come with the fourth woe. For that woe does descend for the binding of the forces of Antichrist who defile the Divine Mother in her children and in her sons and daughters.[3]

This judgment must come, for we cannot have the fallen ones misusing the violet flame. For every flame can be abused by black magicians on the left-handed path, and they take it not to liberate but to imprison. Thus, know this, beloved ones. And therefore, the time may come when there is a limit to the violet flame that the earth can be given [unless and] until these fallen ones are bound.

Happy are ye who understand the concept of the mighty labors of the Elohim of God so that you can make light work and fast work of the binding of those forces of Evil who would abuse the very gifts of Saint Germain that he has [so lovingly] given [to his own; for the forces of Evil] are already abusing them, as they have abused science and technology in all manner of manifestations from the last days of Atlantis. [And, as you know, these] manifestations of the abuses of science were actually one of the major causes of the sinking of Atlantis.

Beloved ones, have I expanded your horizons a bit? ["Yes!"]

Happy are ye when ye have illumination! You may think I have brought to you the violet flame but I have brought to you the violet flame of illumination's flame!

Now hear this. There is the violet flame of the blue ray. There is the violet flame of the yellow ray. There is the violet flame of the pink ray. There is the violet flame of the white ray. There is the violet flame of the green ray. There is the violet flame of the purple and gold ray flecked with ruby. And there is the violet flame of the Seventh Ray of the violet flame!

Now therefore, beloved, see how the violet flame can clarify in the mind, the heart, the body and the being all of the understanding, all of the knowledge, all of the perception, all of the senses, all of the functions of the chakras. [This can happen] when they are cleansed and revivified and purified by the elixir of the violet flame. Why, you see every color more brilliantly! You see the crystal and the white fire core of each ray more brilliantly!

So the violet flame has an aspect on each of the seven rays. And as [you invoke it and allow] it to complement the seven rays, beloved ones, you will learn more about those rays than you have ever learned by just concentrating upon those rays alone.

The violet flame is surely the universal aura of the planet in this hour, for many angels and elementals and Keepers of the Flame have invoked it. I say, continue to invoke it! For the greatest miracles of all will come to you through this flame and through this flame combined with others.

We have emphasized illumination, beloved, because, of course, without illumination there is simply utter darkness and the dark night of the soul and the Dark Night of the Spirit, where there is no candle.

I bring to you—and all of the priesthood of Melchizedek who are here with me this night bring to you—candles, candles of the violet flame. The wax, or substance like it, is of the violet flame color and the flame is the violet flame color.

Now take your candle, beloved ones. Hold it before you! Be at peace! *Be* a Keeper of the Flame! *And go set the world on fire with violet flame!*

I bow to the violet flame within you and I bid you adieu.
[39-second standing ovation]

"The Summit Lighthouse Sheds Its Radiance O'er All the World to Manifest as Pearls of Wisdom." This dictation by a **Spokesman for the Delegation of the Priesthood of Melchizedek in Attendance** was **delivered** by the Messenger of the Great White Brotherhood Elizabeth Clare Prophet on **Wednesday, July 1, 1992,** during the ten-day conference FREEDOM 1992: "Joy in the Heart" held at the **Royal Teton Ranch, Park County, Montana.** [N.B. Throughout this Pearl, bracketed material denotes words unspoken yet implicit in the dictation, added by the Messenger under the direction of Melchizedek's Spokesman for clarity in the written word.] Throughout these notes PoW is the abbreviation for Pearls of Wisdom. **(1) Omri-Tas' violet flame sea and Saint Germain's Maltese cross.** See 1991 PoW, pp. 348–49, 355–56, 742. **(2)** Gen. 14:18; Heb. 7:1–3. **(3)** Rev. 12:17.

I AM the Witness

For a Safe and Swift Delivery
Call upon the Messengers

Dear Mother,

I am writing to thank you and to witness to the intercession of you and Lanello in the recent birth of my son.

My wife and I had chosen to have a home birth with a certified nurse midwife in attendance. After having a normal pregnancy, my wife's labor began and continued many hours with little progress being made. At this point, the advice of our midwife was to check into the hospital for consultation and monitoring. She called the ranch and left a message with your secretary that because of the difficult labor we would be transferring to the hospital.

We had been at the hospital for an hour and still no progress (due to what was later diagnosed as a dysfunctional labor pattern that prevented dilation from occurring). The doctor said he would wait another hour for any change in the labor. The papers authorizing a cesarean section had been prepared by the hospital staff and signed by myself.

The doctor and the nurses left the room and my wife and I were alone. All along I had been making calls and praying to the Masters for intercession during the labor and delivery and I was now pondering what call would be the most needed at this critical time. I suddenly remembered one that I had overlooked. The thought flashed into my mind: "Call to Lanello and Mother for intercession!" I remembered the teaching that because of your mantles as Messengers, you are the ones who can intercede most quickly in the physical octave.

Then I recalled Lanello's 1992 Ascension Day Address. He said that he could do so much more for us if we would only call to him. I remembered his words:

> Don't forget to call to me, for Lanello is my name. Don't forget my little ones, all of the children in this Community and beyond and those who are coming and those who must be on this path. There are so many that I hold in my arms. Don't forget to teach them to call to me and to tell them that Lanello is my name.

I remembered how loving and soft his voice was. It seemed he wanted so much to be a more intimate part of our lives. I made a very heartfelt call to him and to you, Mother, to please intercede swiftly on behalf of my wife and the delivery of the baby.

The nurses came back in and suggested that I get something to eat since I hadn't eaten in a long time. I left for about twenty minutes and was in the hospital lobby speaking with my parents when the midwife came running in to tell me that suddenly total dilation had occurred and the labor was now proceeding quickly. I hurried to be with my wife and in another five minutes you telephoned the delivery room to offer her encouragement and to make calls and prayers over the phone for her and the baby.

Our son was born about one-half hour later to the great joy of everyone in the room. I just knew that Lanello's intercession was the prime reason for the swift birth. This was confirmed a couple of weeks later when you spoke with my wife. You told her that right before you telephoned the hospital Lanello had told you to "Call now!"

In the past week as I was contemplating the miracle of my son's birth, I felt compelled to reread a dictation from beloved Rose of Light, published in the 1989 *Pearls of Wisdom*. In this *Pearl,* Rose of Light states:

> Therefore know that the office and mantle of Mother of the World is one that is offered gladly by your Messenger as a means of intercession in all manner of burden and tribulation. Whereas you can well understand that the Messenger in embodiment may not have hours and minutes in the day to [personally] answer in this octave all of the calls that are sent to her (although she does answer many), you can be absolutely certain that at inner levels the simple call to the Christ Self [and] the I AM Presence of the Messenger and to Lanello ascended will bring you immediate intercession.

Rose of Light goes on to say:

> Do not hesitate, therefore. For when you have one in physical embodiment [such as the Messenger to intercede in your behalf], sometimes you can make the connection to our octaves much more swiftly than when you call to us directly; [for she has the direct contact whereas, due to planetary effluvia or your emotions of the moment, often you do not.] Such is the meaning of Hierarchy. And you yourselves are a part of this Hierarchy and may also be instruments, through your own path of Christhood, to transmit to those in need a quantity of Light from above.

Our family is so very grateful to you and Lanello for being the spiritual "midwives" in the safe delivery of our beautiful son. God bless and thank you for your service to life.

In deepest gratitude,

N.B. Testimonies of disciples of Jesus Christ and the Ascended Masters stating their witness to the power of Truth in their lives will regularly appear in this column in the *Pearls of Wisdom*. If you would like to witness to the power of Truth in your life brought about through the Ascended Masters and their Messengers, we welcome your testimony for publication. Your letter will be kept on file in our archives but your name will be withheld from this page to protect your privacy and your progress on the Path.

38
The Worship of the Goddess—
The Path of the Divine Mother

And now some notes on the Divine Mother:

The Divine Mother in her manifestation as Sarasvati is the Shakti of Brahma. Brahma is known as the Creator in the Hindu Trinity. The Ascended Masters teach us that Brahma is parallel to God the Father in the Western Trinity. He is the Divine Lawgiver, the source of all knowledge. Together, Brahma and Sarasvati are the embodiment of cosmic force.

Sarasvati is known as the Goddess of the Word. She is identified with Vac, the Word. She represents eloquence and articulates the wisdom of the Law. She is the Mother/Teacher to those of us who love the Law, revealed by Brahma. And she is the power of volition, the will and motivation to be the Law in action. Sarasvati represents the union of power and intelligence from which organized creation arises.

In the book *Symbolism in Hinduism*, A. Parthasarathy notes that the name Sarasvati literally means "the one who gives the essence of our own Self." Sarasvati is sometimes represented with four hands, sitting on a lotus. She holds the sacred scriptures in one hand and a lotus in another. With the remaining two hands, she plays the Indian lute (veena).[1]

Parthasarathy writes: "The Goddess, therefore, represents the ideal guru.... 'Sitting on the lotus' symbolises that the teacher is well established in the subjective experience of the Truth. 'Holding the Scriptures in her hand' indicates that she upholds that the knowledge of the Scriptures alone can take us to the Truth." Parthasarathy says that Sarasvati's playing of the lute suggests "that a truly qualified teacher tunes up the mind and intellect of the seeker and draws out of him the music and melody of life."[2]

According to scholar David Frawley, in an esoteric sense Sarasvati "represents the stream of wisdom, the free flow of the knowledge of consciousness."[3] She is called the Flowing One, the source of creation by the Word.

Sarasvati also represents purity and wears white. David Kinsley, Professor of Religious Studies at McMaster University in Ontario, Canada, explains:

> The predominant themes in Sarasvati's appearance are purity and transcendence. She is almost always said to be pure white like snow, the moon, or the *kunda* flower.... Her garments are said to be fiery in their purity....
>
> Sarasvati's transcendent nature...is also suggested in her vehicle, the swan. The swan is a symbol of spiritual transcendence and perfection in Hinduism.... Sarasvati, astride her swan, suggests a dimension of human existence that rises above the physical, natural world. Her realm is one of beauty, perfection, and grace; it is a realm created by artistic inspiration, philosophic insight, and accumulated knowledge, which have enabled human beings to so refine their natural world that they have been able to transcend its limitations. Sarasvati astride her swan beckons human beings to continued cultural creation and civilized perfection.... She not only underlies the world and is its creator but is the [very] means to transcend the world.[4]

Sarasvati is associated with speech, poetry, music and culture and is known as the Goddess of Learning and the patroness of the arts and music. She is revered by both Hindus and Buddhists. To Buddhists she is the consort of Manjushri, the Bodhisattva of Wisdom.

Buddhists appeal to Manjushri for intelligence, wisdom, mastery of the Teaching, the power of exposition, eloquence and memory. He works with Lord Maitreya. The two are sometimes depicted in a triad with Gautama Buddha in which Manjushri

XIII The Corona of Sarasvati and Lakshmi

represents the wisdom aspect and Maitreya the compassion aspect of Buddhist teaching.

I am holding before you a very precious statue of Manjushri that I keep on the altar. You can feel his powerfully comforting presence as he places a focus of his light body over his likeness. In his right hand he wields a flaming sword of wisdom to vanquish all ignorance. His sword has been called a "sword of quick detachment" and the "symbol of enlightened will." Like Sarasvati, Manjushri brings the gift of illumination.

In the earliest Hindu texts, the Vedas, Sarasvati is a river goddess. The Vedas say that Sarasvati was the greatest river in India. For years the Sarasvati was believed to have been a myth, but an archaeological survey in 1985 found an ancient riverbed that matched the description of the Sarasvati. It was a great river, four to six miles wide for much of its length. It flowed westward from the Himalayas into the sea. Frawley believes that the Sarasvati was the main site of habitation at the time the Vedas were composed thousands of years ago.[5]

Frawley says that the Sarasvati, "like the later Ganges, symbolizes the Sushumna, the river of spiritual knowledge, the current that flows [through the spinal canal] through the seven chakras of the subtle body. She is not only the Milky Way or river of Heaven, inwardly she is the river of true consciousness that flows into this world."[6]

The Rigveda calls Sarasvati "the best mother, the best river, [and] the best Goddess." It also says, "Sarasvati like a great ocean appears with her ray, she rules all inspirations."[7]

Her sacred "seed syllable," or bija, is *Aim*. A bija mantra encapsules the essence of a Cosmic Being, of a principle or a chakra. Sarasvati's mantra is *Om Aim Sarasvatye Namaha*.

The Divine Mother in her manifestation as Lakshmi is the Shakti of Vishnu. Lakshmi is known as the Goddess of Fortune and Beauty. In earlier texts she is known as Sri, which means "splendor," "beauty," "prosperity," "wealth." Vishnu holds the office of Preserver in the Hindu Trinity. The Preserver is parallel to the principle of the Son in the Western Trinity. As the Son, Vishnu embodies Cosmic Christ wisdom. He is also the mediator, or bridge, between the human consciousness and Brahman, Absolute Reality.

According to the teachings of Hinduism, Vishnu was incarnated nine times, most notably as Rama and Krishna. Lakshmi took human form to serve as his consort in each of his incarnations.

Lakshmi's incarnations included: Sita, the faithful wife of Rama; the cow girl Radha, beloved of Krishna; and Rukmini, the princess whom Krishna later married.

As the Preserver, Vishnu preserves divine design conceived in Wisdom's flame. He restores the universe by Wisdom's all-healing Light. Lakshmi shares his role as Preserver. Her wisdom is revealed in blessings of prosperity and the precipitation of the abundant life. She bears the cornucopia of good fortune by "eye magic," the eye magic of the All-Seeing Eye of her Beloved. She embodies divine compassion and intercedes on our behalf before her consort. She is the mediator of the Mediator!

Lakshmi is described as being "as radiant as gold" and "illustrious like the moon." She is said to "shine like the sun" and "to be lustrous like fire."[8] She teaches multiplicity and beauty and is called "She of the Hundred Thousands." Whatever matrix is in her hand, whatever you hold in your heart, Lakshmi can multiply by the millions, for one idea can be reproduced infinitely. Lakshmi also teaches us mastery of karmic cycles on the Cosmic Clock.

At the beginning of the commercial year in India, Hindus give special prayers to Lakshmi to bring success in their endeavors. She is worshiped in every home on all important occasions.

But Lakshmi has a deeper, esoteric significance in that she is associated with immortality and the essence of life. In Hindu lore, she was created when the gods and demons churned a primordial ocean of milk. Their goal was to produce the elixir of immortality. Along with the elixir, they also produced the Goddess Lakshmi.

Lakshmi is seen as the one who personifies royal power and conveys it upon kings. She is often depicted with a lotus and an elephant. The lotus represents purity and spiritual power; the elephant, royal authority.

Kinsley says, "To be seated upon, or to be otherwise associated with, the lotus suggests that the being in question...has transcended the limitations of the finite world.... She is associated not only with royal authority but with spiritual authority as well, and she therefore combines royal and priestly powers."[9]

Remember the phrase in the Book of Revelation "kings and priests unto God."[10] The mantle and the office of that kingship and that priesthood unto God are the bestowal that God would make upon all Lightbearers of the world. Such are the crowns and scepters that are there to be bestowed. It is as though your mantle and your royal or priestly robes (or both) were hanging on a hanger in a retreat, waiting to drop upon you when you fulfill your reason for being.

XIII The Corona of Sarasvati and Lakshmi

So know, O my beloved children, that it is the Divine Mother who will carefully take your robes from the hanger and put them on your shoulders when you will have proven without a shadow of a doubt that you are a trusted servant of the Light—trustworthy to the end. This is the ceremony of entitlement.

In ancient times Sri-Lakshmi was considered to be the source of the power of kings. Carl Olson writes: "The relationship of the goddess to the king is so intimate that she is described as residing in the sovereign.... Thus Sri is the source of the king's power. And she is very concerned about the exercise of royal virtues like truth, generosity, austerity, strength, and [the] *dharma*."[11] The Mahabharata states that when one ancient king fell from power, "he lost his royal *sri*."[12]

Kinsley points out that several Hindu myths tell of "[the god] Indra's losing, acquiring, or being restored to Sri-Lakshmi's presence." He says, "In these myths, it is clear that what is lost, acquired, or restored in the person of Sri is royal authority and power."[13]

Please note that I said in my lecture on Hinduism that Indra represents the Self. So, in the process of realizing your Real Self, if you depart from the 'royal' virtues, you may temporarily lose the sponsorship of the Divine Mother until you value your embodiment of those virtues more than you value your freedom to embody either vices or a vacuum.

Lakshmi is the one who anoints us with the Christ Light, the Light of Vishnu. This is the Light that makes every son of God royal, every son of God a king or a priest unto God. The office of *king,* remember, defines "the one who holds the *k*ey to the *in*carnation of *G*od"—k-i-n-g. The office of *priest* defines "the one who holds the *p*ower of the *R*a and the *R*ai and who *i*ncarnates the *e*nergy of the *s*acred *T*au and *T*ao"—p-r-i-e-s-t.[14]

Lakshmi is often shown with an elephant on either side showering her with water from their trunks. Kinsley tells us that these images are "probably meant to portray the act of royal consecration."[15] And I would say "the consecration of the mind," because it is out of the memory of God that we are able to properly rule ourselves and all who may be with us or under us. The elephant-god Ganesha has the infinite memory of the Mind of God. Without that memory we cannot really progress on the Path.

Kinsley writes that this concept of royal consecration by elephants resonates with the Vedic royal consecration ceremony, "in which the king was consecrated by having auspicious waters poured over him."[16]

Has anyone seen any auspicious waters these days?*

The Hindus believe that these auspicious waters bestowed authority and vigor on the king. So claim your authority and vigor when the rain rains upon your tent! Nothing happens by accident or without certain purpose.

The king can be seen as representing the Christed one who has gained enlightenment. Author Adrian Snodgrass interprets the sprinkling of water as a spiritual initiation of the soul in which one is "washed free of mortality."[17]

So, we see the Goddess Lakshmi as an embodiment of the Divine Mother. We see her in her role as consort of Vishnu, the Second Person of the Trinity, as very much a part of the ceremony of the marriage of your soul to your Holy Christ Self. When you are wed and bonded to that Christ Self, that is when you become royal in the godly sense of the word. Each one of us can receive this "royal" initiation when we have earned the grace of the bountiful Lakshmi. Lakshmi restores us to our original estate of oneness with God.

In one Tantric text, Lakshmi says of herself: "Like the fat that keeps a lamp burning I lubricate the senses of living beings with my own sap of consciousness."[18] Lakshmi bestows upon us the nectar of God consciousness when we gain her favor. Vishnu is the Christ Light and Lakshmi is the bestower of that Light. The riches she brings are spiritual riches and admission to the kingdom of heaven.

Lakshmi's seed syllable, or bija, is *Srim*. Her mantra is *Om Srim Lakshmye Namaha*.

---

*reference to the special cleansing, purifying rain in the Heart of the Inner Retreat at the ten-day FREEDOM 1992 conference that brought transmutation of local and planetary records in preparation for the coming of Alpha and Omega.

XIII The Corona of Sarasvati and Lakshmi

Messenger's Invocation before the Lecture:

O sweet flame of Divine Love burning in our hearts, expand now and glow! Let the glow of Divine Love in our bodies and in our souls, O God, which you have placed there provide a new emanation of the aura of the Lightbearers of the earth. Let this Light accelerate by all of the Causal Bodies of all of the beings of Light who are one with us in this hour in the Divine Mother.

O thou greatness of Divine Love that we share, let the full power of the Godhead through the mighty Shakti so multiply and multiply and multiply again, O God, for the victory of every soul of Light on planet earth. Encircle them now! Lakshmi, Durga, Sarasvati, Kali, Parvati, come forth!

O mighty ones of God, O Divine Mother in concentration in manifestation throughout all cosmos, be one with your chelas in this hour! Be one with us. Oh, magnify the Lord as Mother within us! And let us mother all life, succor all life, O God, that they might be free, free from fear and want and doubt, free to stand with thee in the heart of creation.

O beloved Father, because thou art, so we have our Mother with us, as Above, so below. We are grateful, O God! Our gratitude overflows beyond this cosmos unto thy throne. Receive us now, O God.

CHANT THE BIJA MANTRAS TO THE FEMININE DEITIES

1. SARASVATI: AIM
   OM AIM SARASVATYE NAMAHA
2. LAKSHMI: SRIM
   OM SRIM LAKSHMYE NAMAHA
3. KALI: KRIM
   OM KRIM KALIKAYE NAMAHA
4. DURGA: DUM
   OM DUM DURGAYE NAMAHA
5. AIM HRIM KLIM CHAMUNDAYE VICHE

Elizabeth Clare Prophet delivered the profile "The Corona of the Brilliant Sarasvati and the Bountiful Lakshmi" on July 2, 1992, prior to the dictations of Sarasvati and Lakshmi. It was the concluding section of her lecture "The Worship of the Goddess—The Path of the Divine Mother" and has been edited for publication. The lecture and dictations were part of the ten-day conference FREEDOM 1992: "Joy in the Heart" held at the Royal Teton Ranch, Park County, Montana. (1) A. Parthasarathy, "Consorts of the Three Gods," in R. S. Nathan, comp., Symbolism in Hinduism (Bombay: Central Chinmaya Mission Trust, 1989), p. 157. (2) Ibid., pp. 157–58. (3) David Frawley, From the River of Heaven: Hindu and Vedic Knowledge for the Modern Age (Sandy, Utah: Morson Publishing, 1990), p. 126. (4) David Kinsley, Hindu Goddesses: Visions of the Divine Feminine in the Hindu Religious Tradition (Berkeley, Calif.: University of California Press, 1986), pp. 62, 141. (5) David Frawley, Gods, Sages and Kings: Vedic Secrets of Ancient Civilization (Salt Lake City, Utah: Passage Press, 1991), pp. 72–76, 354–57 nn. d–g. (6) Ibid., p. 219. (7) Rigveda 2.41.16, 1.3.12, quoted in Frawley, Gods, Sages and Kings, pp. 70, 71. (8) Sri-sukta 1, 6, 13, 4, in Rigveda, cited by David Kinsley, The Goddesses' Mirror: Visions of the Divine from East and West (Albany, N.Y.: State University of New York Press, 1989), p. 55. (9) Kinsley, The Goddesses' Mirror, pp. 56–57. (10) Rev. 1:6; 5:10. (11) Carl Olson, "Sri Lakshmi and Radha: The Obsequious Wife and the Lustful Lover," in The Book of the Goddess Past and Present: An Introduction to Her Religion, Carl Olson, ed. (New York: Crossroad Publishing Company, 1983), p. 136. (12) Mahabharata 9.18.14, cited by Olson, "Sri Lakshmi and Radha," p. 136. (13) Kinsley, The Goddesses' Mirror, p. 58. (14) **Ra** was the ancient Egyptian sun-god, the official god of the pharaohs. The Egyptian pharaohs were looked upon as both the son of Ra and Ra himself incarnate. In his March 5, 1967 Pearl of Wisdom, Lord Maitreya defined the power of Ra as "the power of the Son of God, the power of Light itself" (1967 PoW, no. 10, p. 2). In the days of Atlantis, **Rai** was a title used for the emperor or monarch. **Tau** is the twenty-second and final letter of the Hebrew alphabet ("t" or "th"); it signifies "cross." In the film A Mystical Journey through the Hebrew Alphabet, Dr. Edward Hoffman explains: "[The letter Tau] symbolizes that our universe is marked by cycles in all things and the ultimate end of this human cycle in joyful, complete redemption. Tau begins the word Torah, an infinite realm, and also the word tikkun, our soul's task or mission here on earth." As noted in The Universal Jewish Encyclopedia: "The written word was always regarded as sacred, particularly by the Jews.... Abraham knew the secrets of the wisdom of the alphabet. God tied the twenty-two letters to his tongue and revealed to him all the mysteries of the universe" (s.v. "Alphabet in Mysticism"). The word **Tao,** which literally means "Way," is the animating principle of life that sustains all creation and is in all creation. According to the teachings of Taoism, it is the transcendental First Cause, the Absolute, the Ultimate Reality. (15) Kinsley, The Goddesses' Mirror, p. 57. (16) Ibid. (17) Adrian Snodgrass, The Symbolism of the Stupa (Ithaca, N.Y.: Cornell Southeast Asia Program, 1985), p. 317. (18) Lakshmi-tantra 50.110, quoted in Kinsley, The Goddesses' Mirror, p. 66.

39

We Do Work!

Illumination—the Only Cure for Earth

I am sent to you by my Lord Brahma, who has said:

O Sarasvati, now is the hour for the appearing of dazzling knowledge, the power of the might of purity multiplying illumination's flame.

Go forth, then! Go forth, then, with Lakshmi and multiply thy powers and the powers of the Divine Mother Durga and Kali.

And therefore penetrate the sheaths of the four lower bodies of the earth with knowledge, with Light, with brightness of the spiritual cosmos.

I AM Sarasvati. I come to you, beloved, for the only cure for the earth in this hour is illumination—illumination that comes from the light of the Word and the delivery of the Word by right speech preceded by right mindfulness.

O the Mind of God! O let it descend! Let it descend everywhere. Legions of the Divine Mother, legions of the Divine Mother, come forth! Come forth now and reveal to these inner eyes the shafts of golden yellow light, crystallized as glass, as crystal itself, penetrating the layers of density.

O my God, I *plead* for the removal from the eyes of the young and all people of that which is utterly a nonessential in this earth—and that is 95 percent of that which passes through the television sets everywhere upon the planet. This is the destroying not only of the third-eye development but of the development of the crown chakra.

I AM Sarasvati! I am ready to pursue with you the opening of the crown. I am ready to assist you in the raising of the Light of the Goddess Kundalini. But I must have [in you] a nucleus of golden-yellow white fire. I must have [in you] an intensity of desire for the knowledge of God and for the knowledge of what is truly transpiring in the earth and all of the trespasses that are made against the children of the Light.

O ye sons and daughters of Brahman, now hear me! Hear my call! I am very present in this Community, for I have an affinity with the work of the Messenger and the Messenger has an affinity with my work; and therefore, we do work! And you work also and you share in the veils of my garments that I extend.

So, yes, I wear the white, beloved, but I also wear all of the rays as I bring that fiery white core of knowledge into all manifestations in the outer and the inner traditions. This earth must have knowledge! Woman must have self-knowledge, man must have self-knowledge and the child must know the Inner Christ as the Holy Christ Self and the Inner Buddha as the I AM THAT I AM. This is the teaching, and so much more.

We rejoice, therefore, to offer the mantle of our office, "Sarasvati," to all who teach children. And if you would have the mantle, then I say, take an hour or two or three here and there to teach children something of your own expertise in this Community.

What is life without having a child for a true friend?

Go into our schools and give of your talent that your talent may not die. For it is the requirement of every disciple of the Divine Mother to pass on his talent to the next generation ere he take his leave from this octave.

So, beloved, before the day and the hour of your transitioning to other planes, remember to deposit in many hearts your skill, your creativity, your art, your science, the melody of your soul, the preciousness of your heart. And do not think for one moment that you do not have anything to teach! If you have nothing you have learned, beloved, then teach compassion, teach love, teach joy, teach gratitude, teach all children of all ages how to magnify the Lord in their hearts.

Thus, I come to you and I come in the great Spirit of God. I come in the hour, then, when I will contribute the great river of illumination to your endeavor. Unless illumination cleanse the

XIV We Do Work!

earth, inundate the earth, take over the earth, beloved, where will the people go? How will they recognize the Truth?

Let them recognize it within you, I say!

Sarasvati is both Person and Principle. Sarasvati is in the heart of every one of you. Each one of the four principles, [the four seed syllables that the four Goddesses embody,] is a part of the threefold flame. For we are in the sphere of the white fire that is the source of the fount of the Trinity.

So you see, beloved, I AM an Ascended Lady Master. I AM a Goddess. I AM a Principle. I AM the Counterpart of Brahma. Therefore, where Father is, there AM I, the other side of Father.

Know, then, that as you meditate upon the Trinity in your heart and you say the names Father, Son and Holy Spirit—Brahma, Vishnu and Shiva—you are automatically saying and affirming our names: Sarasvati, Lakshmi, Durga. Yes, beloved, and then you have Kali and then you have Parvati.[1] And then you have the wondrous Presence of the Divine Mother all in one, as the mantra makes us one divine manifestation.[2]

The mantras that descend in Hinduism—and, I should say, the principle of the mantra as it has been applied by your beloved Saint Germain to you in this time—are the key and the means to the turning around of the age. [Therefore] I pour forth illumination and you invoke the violet flame to clear the way for its absorption by all people of earth.

I come to you, then, with the fierceness of self-knowledge. I expose to you your True Self in glory! I expose to you your unreal self and I say: Choose this day whom you will serve and be about your Father's business, your Father Brahma, the mighty one who sits on the twelve o'clock line of the north, who is represented by the Great Divine Director and all beings of Light who serve in that quadrant.

Yes, beloved, come to know us as we walk and talk with you, as God of gods and Lord of lords and Goddess of goddesses. Come to know us intimately and personally and you will find the great key to bhakti yoga and devotion to God, the key to jnana yoga and knowledge of God. You will find the key to raja yoga and royal integration with God. You will find the key to karma yoga and the path of your soul's resolution in God by the flame of transmutation.

I am with you because I am kindling a flame! I am speaking with you, and while I am speaking I am transferring a phenomenal manifestation of filigree of illumination's flame. And Lakshmi and I have, in fact, consorted together and we have determined that we shall press through by the fire of Kali, by the power of the deep blue of the cosmos, by the Ruby Ray, by the power of the purple and the violet flame—we shall press through in this hour such a desire for true illumination of a spiritual nature as to produce, if you will be our instruments, a worldwide awakening to the spiritual path of the entire Spirit of the Great White Brotherhood.

This illumination, beloved, can come through all of the mystical paths of the world's religions that are being revealed to you. But I tell you, orthodoxy in every world religion and a priest class who are not servants of the Light and not Sons of the Solitude do block the true revelation of the indwelling God. Therefore, expand the paths of mysticism. Renew them, intensify them, review them so that you may understand how it is that a soul [journeying] on one of these [mystical] paths will more clearly understand union with God [through her religion].

Helios and Vesta radiate tremendous light of the golden pink glow-ray for the intensification of knowledge. So the mighty ones have told you, so we reiterate it: Teach the Teachings, clear the levels of ignorance and the poisons of ignorance, and replace them by the binding power of wisdom that binds all that is unreal, for thereby you will come to the feet of your Inner God.

Pass on true knowledge. Do not hide it under a bushel! There is no time to waste. Pass on the Teaching to those who are interested and pass by those who are not. You are looking for those eyes! You are looking for those chelas! You are looking for those souls! *Go and find them.* And keep on going until you know you have found one, for, beloved, sometimes they are few and far between.

You have a lifetime, or the remainder of a lifetime, at your disposal. Therefore, consecrate your days and hours to the Lightbearers who are searching and waiting for the Truth. And call to me—call to me, beloved, for I will connect you to those who must be contacted by you in this life for your karma does dictate it.

For your karma is that from time to time you have denied the light and the wisdom of the Divine Mother; now you must balance that karma and I will help you! *I will help you.* Feel the strength of the Shakti of the power of God, beloved, and know of a certainty that I will not fail you in your mission. And I ask *you* not to fail *me*.

I AM Sarasvati. I will stay close to you and I will not leave you until you ask me to leave and dismiss me. But, beloved ones, do not neglect me. At least give my seed-syllable mantra daily that you might know the wavelength of my office and share in it:

Om Aim Sarasvatye Namaha

Lo, I give you what I AM and I guard what I AM in you.

XIV We Do Work!

I AM Sarasvati, profoundly concerned for the future of earth and her evolutions. Teach the children! Teach them by example. Teach them by love. Teach them by the will of God. Teach them by the power of his Presence.

Love them and I shall love them through you.

"The Summit Lighthouse Sheds Its Radiance O'er All the World to Manifest as Pearls of Wisdom." This dictation by the **Goddess Sarasvati** was **delivered** by the Messenger of the Great White Brotherhood Elizabeth Clare Prophet on **Thursday, July 2, 1992,** during the ten-day conference *FREEDOM 1992: "Joy in the Heart"* held at the **Royal Teton Ranch, Park County, Montana.** The dictations of Sarasvati and Lakshmi were the culminating events of an evening devoted to the Divine Mother. The Messenger began the evening by delivering the major portion of her lecture "The Worship of the Goddess—The Path of the Divine Mother." She gave the concluding section—"The Corona of the Brilliant Sarasvati and the Bountiful Lakshmi"—prior to the dictations. This profile of the two goddesses has been edited for print and is published in *Pearls of Wisdom,* vol. 35, no. 38. [**N.B.** Throughout this *Pearl,* bracketed material denotes words unspoken yet implicit in the dictation, added by the Messenger under Sarasvati's direction for clarity in the written word.] **(1)** For more on **Shiva's consorts**—Durga, Kali and Parvati—see pp. 402–3. **(2)** This could be a reference to the fifth bija mantra to the feminine deities—**Aim Hrim Klim Chamundaye Viche** (see p. 499). This mantra is known as the Navarna Mantra and, according to one translation, means "Praise be to Sarasvati, Lakshmi, Kali, to Durga: Shattering the knot of ignorance that binds my heart, release me!"

I AM the Witness

El Morya Takes Students on a Field Trip to See God

Dear Mother,

I am writing to share a dream my daughter had on May 15, 1992. My daughter dreamed she was in Thomas More School on the etheric plane. I was the teacher, she and her friends were the students and El Morya was the principal. El Morya came wearing a gold turban and yellow robe, which was lined in a pink, blue and violet swirled fabric. He announced that the class was going on a field trip to see God. The students cheered and then climbed into a boat with their teacher and floated down a river.

Soon God met them and got into the boat too. He was wearing a gold turban and a ruby robe trimmed in gold. When he walked, rainbows seemed to swirl off behind him. As they traveled, God taught the children stories from the Bible. When my daughter was telling me about this dream, she said, "You know, Mom, God has the whole Bible memorized! You can ask him anything and he can tell you!"

The boat floated to a place where a beautiful waterfall fell into a deep blue pool. As the students gazed into the pool, they looked down upon the earth and saw all the little sheep. "But they weren't really sheep," my daughter explained. "They were the children that God said we had to teach!"

As the students looked into the pool, they also saw the present Thomas More School on earth. They knew that they had to expand it in heaven so it could then be on earth. So they busily began building the school, using clouds and crystals to form the marble buildings. The marble was pink and gold and would change color according to the ray of the day of the week. On Tuesday, the marble would be blue and gold; on Wednesday, green and gold; on Thursday, purple and gold, and so on.

When my daughter finished telling me of this dream, she said emphatically, with eyes shining, "Mom, I just *know* that if we decree enough we will have that etheric school here on earth!"

Love,

N.B. Testimonies of disciples of Jesus Christ and the Ascended Masters stating their witness to the power of Truth in their lives will regularly appear in this column in the *Pearls of Wisdom*. If you would like to witness to the power of Truth in your life brought about through the Ascended Masters and their Messengers, we welcome your testimony for publication. Your letter will be kept on file in our archives but your name will be withheld from this page to protect your privacy and your progress on the Path.

40

Let the Egos Fall!
The Torch Must Be Passed to the Children

Lakshmi I AM. Lakshmi I AM! Oh yes, beloved, I come to mediate. I come representing Vishnu, Lord Krishna. I AM the representative of the ones who are the shining Sons of all of cosmos and the One who is the Son, Lord Vishnu, in so many manifestations.

Right within you now is Vishnu in the person of your Holy Christ Self. You are familiar with the term *Christ Self.* How does it feel to say, "My beloved Vishnu, descend into my temple *now!*"

Blessed ones, it feels good, does it not? ["Yes!"]

So understand that we go before our consorts. As you receive us, so you receive them. They enter because we have first entered. Thus, the Divine Mother is always the [one] closest to her children.

And so in this hour, let the egos fall! And let the fallen ones who have fallen by the ego *fall!* Let them fall under the line of Helios and Vesta and the great cosmic hierarchy of Aries. This is the hour of the judgment. So let them be judged!

So let there come the dawn of a new day of a people who have the inner strength because they have self-emptied themselves of that ego and the Divine is indwelling. No need to prance about and strut the ego when the whole of the Divine Ego lives within you!

It is such an awesome experience that it makes you be quiet and sense a hush all about you that God walks where you walk, that God is in your temple, that Vishnu is firmly centered on the throne in the secret chamber of your heart. Understand, beloved, that when you know that God is in you, when you know that you are that God-manifestation and that he who is one with God is God, you have no need to sing your praises or to make certain that someone is aware of your talents and abilities.

Beloved ones, be in awe of the indwelling Presence of God. Go often to the altar of the inner Light and thank your God and your Great Guru, Sanat Kumara, who has saved you for this hour.

Yes, I plead with you to also be the Saviouress and the consort of the Saviouress. I plead with you, beloved, for there will be no new day and no golden age if there is not a passing of the mighty torch of the ancient ones of thousands of years and tens of thousands of years and of past golden ages and histories of a planet unchronicled [in this era].

The torch must be passed and it is not being passed. Look at the true gap between generations—[the gap between] the knowledge that you have had and the knowledge that your children and children's children do not have, [the gap between] what you were taught and what they have not been taught. It is frightening to you and it is frightening to us.

You must close this gap. You must transfer to those generations coming after you what they have missed in the schools. You must turn off the television set, as Sarasvati has said. Throw it out the window! Get rid of it! And commune with the Child of your child—commune with the inner person! Otherwise you will find your children growing up as lonely ones, as ones who seek the company not of Lightbearers but of the role models they have seen on the television, yes, beloved, the antiheroes and -heroines.

Blessed hearts, there is no place for you to be except with the little children for a portion of your life. And extend that! Be not content just to be near those in the circle of your family. Extend your love! Open your home! Teach the children! Welcome them in! Feed them what their souls need and what their bodies need. Give them love, not a mechanical TV set and mechanical people and mechanical gods and scripts written for their minds and advertising for their [desire bodies].

Yes, you have heard it before, but you have not heard it from Lakshmi! And I tell you, beloved, *this is an hour to make the difference, to turn the world around or to lose the children of the Light and all children of planet earth.* I say this as a most urgent message of this Fourth of July conference here in the [dwelling] place of the beloved Gautama Buddha.

Yes, beloved, we are mothers and fathers all. Now let us not go back to the former level of neglect and of not tuning in to what is the need of the hour.

I AM Lakshmi. Remember me in the morning and remember me in the night. Remember me when you take your soul journeys, and invoke us, [Vishnu and me,] as you take your leave of your body at night to go and serve those individuals who need your care.

Yes, continue to set your mark on Yugoslavia, for the judgment must descend and the Lightbearers must be protected. But you can multiply this by transferring to the map of the world the concentration that you have placed there [in Yugoslavia]. And when you return to the Royal Teton Retreat after your night's work, you can transfer that entire momentum [of your inner work] to other areas of the earth and not dilute the concentration of [that work]. This is the multiplication of God's power. This is the multiplication and maximizing of your effort.

Call to us and we will teach you to multiply your Presence, your Electronic Presence. We will use our Presence as mediators to assist you that you might place yourselves in many places through your own Christ Self wedded to the Divine Mothers. Yes, beloved, you can increase your effectiveness and your work. And watch how the newspapers do reflect that which is going on at inner levels.

I, then, go with Sarasvati this night to the Retreat of the Divine Mother that is over the Royal Teton Ranch. Come, then, to that retreat and meet others who wait for you, for the representatives of the Divine Mother hold a reception for all of you this night. Bring your children and make the call for all Lightbearers of the world to gather.

For we must have our convention! We must have our meeting of the minds! We must determine at inner levels to take our assignments and meet in committee and go in full force with an organized plan into the towns and cities and the nations for the illumination of the children and for the giving to those children who have a spiritual light and a desire to know the Truth that cup of wisdom, that cup of knowledge, that cup of Christ consciousness, that cup of the Inner Buddha.

We *are* your friends. Come, take our hands—hands of all of us who represent the mighty ones. Come! Come! Come! *We* are the Shakti!

Will you be the Shakti with us? ["Yes!"]

Will you make it happen? ["Yes!"]

Yes, beloved, say yes! Lay the plan and the blueprint, and do it! And call for our strength, for *you will need it* and *we will give it!*
[35-second standing ovation]

"The Summit Lighthouse Sheds Its Radiance O'er All the World to Manifest as Pearls of Wisdom." This dictation by the **Goddess Lakshmi** was **delivered** by the Messenger of the Great White Brotherhood Elizabeth Clare Prophet on **Thursday, July 2, 1992,** during the ten-day conference FREEDOM 1992: "Joy in the Heart" held at the **Royal Teton Ranch, Park County, Montana.** [N.B. Throughout this Pearl, bracketed material denotes words unspoken yet implicit in the dictation, added by the Messenger under Lakshmi's direction for clarity in the written word.]

I AM the Witness

I Shall Not Be Moved by Earthquakes

I would like to witness to the power of the Teachings of the Ascended Masters in a moment of an emergency.

It happened in the city of Guayaquil, Ecuador, where my husband was working. I had an apartment in the same building where the main offices of the company were, and I had just come from seeing the craftsman who was remodeling my living-room furniture.

I had one hand on the closet door and the other on a hanger, ready to hang my dress in the closet, when the whole room started to move. I said, "Oh, my God! It is an earthquake!" I then took a big breath, centered myself in my heart in the white fire core of being, and visualized the tube of light covering the whole apartment.

The next thing I remember was the earthquake passing. The building was still trembling a little, but I went out of the apartment and into the corridor that led to the stairs where the main offices of the company were. I saw all the people that worked there gathered at the main entrance door, some crying and screaming. Big books and binders had fallen off the shelves and were scattered on the floor. The whole office was a mess. The rest of the buildings in that complex had all been damaged, as well as many others all over the city.

The people from the company were surprised that nothing had happened in my apartment. I had three shelves of parcels from all over the world and souvenirs and gifts of all sizes—but none were harmed. Nothing was damaged in my apartment.

Always a Keeper of the Flame,

My Dream of the Blue Room

Dearest Mother,

I have always wanted to tell you this story. Now I am grateful that I can share it with all through the "I AM the Witness" column in the *Pearls of Wisdom*.

I was about five or six years old when I first had a certain dream. It was a beautiful dream in which I was lost after a storm. Alone I wandered and came upon a single house. When I knocked on the door, a lady opened it. She was in her golden years with silvered hair. She was very gracious and kind.

Welcoming me, the lady laid out a cloth covered with necklaces of precious gems—emeralds, sapphires, rubies and diamonds. She offered me my choice and invited me to come inside. I took an emerald one and went in.

As I explored the house, I found a room that had many seats in rows and a sloping aisle leading toward a platform. The room seemed larger inside than the house had looked outside. And, amazingly, the air was blue—not smokey, but clear, with every molecule softly shimmering in royal blue light.

Then I woke up.

I really enjoyed this dream and it came again a couple of times a year over the next few years. Sometimes there were minor variations in it, but the lady, the jewels and the room were always the same. I loved the necklace but what really intrigued me was the room.

Then the dream didn't come as often, but I found that I could ask to experience it again and I would. As I matured, however, I forgot all about it.

In the fall of 1976, I attended my second Summit Lighthouse conference. It was in Pasadena, the first there since the purchase of the campus. The auditorium was newly decorated and full-length blue curtains formed the backdrop for the altar and covered the walls.

As the lights dimmed and the meditation music swelled for the first dictation, I looked around and all I saw was blue. My heart began to beat faster and I took a quick breath. I looked again—even the air seemed blue!... BLUE?! Tears welled up in my eyes. I perceived the room of my dreams!

I am so grateful to you, dear God, for giving me that dream so many times over so that I wouldn't pass up the precious gems of the Ascended Masters' Teachings when I found them!

And a special thanks to Ascended Lady Master Clara Louise, the first Mother of the Flame. In her recent dictation (1991 *Pearls of Wisdom*, p. 385), she said:

> When I was in my final embodiment I had many hours to pray and I developed an intense white fire to direct into problems at a world level, those involving children and individuals for whom I would pray. That momentum came with many years of fierce, undivided attention for hours of [keeping my] morning vigil on behalf of the babies and youth.
>
> I see so many among you for whom I did pray in this my final incarnation, and I would tell you that it is clear in the record that my prayers did make the difference in your entering the Path.

And it is true. You see, she was the lady in my dream.

Oh, let us also pray for the children and youth of the world that they may find the Teachings and come all the way Home!

All my love,

"Your Heart Is Fine"

Dear Mother,

The tender care and love that Mother Mary has for each one of us was recently so clearly demonstrated to me that I would like to share the experience with you.

During the month of May I increased my devotions to Mother Mary, as we were especially consecrating that month to her flame. In mid-June it was my turn for night-shift duty in my department. Each night after everyone else had gone, I would play the *Sanctissima* album. The songs of this "Musical Mass for World Peace" helped sustain a forcefield of Light in the office. Then came our July conference, *Joy in the Heart*.

One day during the conference I noticed that I did not feel right. I was short of breath, somewhat light-headed and felt pressure in my chest. I later learned that doctors interpret pressure as pain. I also found the following passage in the *American Red Cross Community CPR Workbook:*

> The most significant signal of a heart attack is chest discomfort or pain. A victim may describe it as uncomfortable pressure, squeezing, a fullness or tightness, or as an aching, crushing, constricting, oppressive, or heavy feeling. The pain is described as being in the center of the chest behind the breastbone. The pain may spread to one or both shoulders or arms, or to the neck, jaw, or back. In addition to chest pain, there may be other signals, including sweating, nausea, shortness of breath.

After I consulted with our staff doctor, it was decided that I should have my heart checked out. So, I was taken to the hospital emergency room. Even though an electrocardiogram did not indicate a problem, the emergency-room doctor thought it best to keep me overnight and do some further testing the next morning.

There I was that night, lying in bed, hooked up to a heart monitor, possibly having had damage to my heart. Needless to say, I was not feeling very pleased especially since I had not quite reached the age of fifty. It was then that I remembered a dream I had had about a week before, which I had described to two other staff members.

In the dream I was sitting up in a bed similar to the hospital bed in which I was now lying. A woman, another staff member, had her arm around my shoulders and was comforting me. I knew that in the dream this woman represented the Mother Flame and Mother Mary. She told me, "Your heart is fine."

At the time, I thought the dream might have spiritual significance. Even so, I had made calls for the protection of my heart and the hearts of everyone around me.

As I lay in the hospital bed remembering the dream, I was again comforted. I knew that no matter what had occurred earlier that day, my heart was fine. I marveled that such comfort had been given even before it was needed. I am grateful to Mother Mary and Kuan Yin for such a blessing. They are truly so very close to each one of us.

After further tests the next morning, including a jog on a treadmill and a checkup two weeks later, there was no evidence that a heart attack had occurred. I decided that even though I had not had a heart attack, I would take the event as a warning and get my body in better shape. Exercise is now tops on my list and "rebounding" has become part of my daily routine.

Another interesting thing is that the day I had the symptoms was my fifteenth anniversary on staff. What a wonderful anniversary gift of comfort Mother Mary gave to me—ahead of time!

In gratitude for the presence of the Mother Flame, I send my love to you and all of our other Mothers above.

N.B. Testimonies of disciples of Jesus Christ and the Ascended Masters stating their witness to the power of Truth in their lives will regularly appear in this column in the *Pearls of Wisdom*. If you would like to witness to the power of Truth in your life brought about through the Ascended Masters and their Messengers, we welcome your testimony for publication. Your letter will be kept on file in our archives but your name will be withheld from this page to protect your privacy and your progress on the Path.

INDEX

This is an index of the 1992 *Pearls of Wisdom*. It does not include material from *Kabbalah: Key to Your Hidden Power* or the "I AM the Witness" column. For the definitions of many of the philosophical and esoteric terms used in the *Pearls of Wisdom*, see the comprehensive glossary, "The Alchemy of the Word: Stones for the Wise Masterbuilders," in *Saint Germain On Alchemy* published by Summit University Press.

Abortion: and America, 445; denying of, 415; do not blind yourselves to, 416; Lord Shiva on, 412–14

Abraham: El Morya on his embodiment as, 362; and Isaac, *following* p. 484 (p. 12 *in Sept. 12, 1992 letter*); a mystic of old, 355; seed of, 356; a strong heart-tie to, *following* p. 304 (p. 1 *in June 1, 1992 letter*)

Acceleration: on the Path, 444; sense of, 388

Activities, that are not necessary, 417

Adam Kadmon, 380

Adept, shown an alien, 415

Adeptship, work for and cherish your, 415

Adversary, who did betray you at Maitreya's Mystery School, 368

Adversities, that you have had to bear in yesteryears, 446–47

Advertising, 508

Age: the key to the turning around of the, 503; opportunity in the seventh, 487. *See also* Aquarius; Piscean age; Pisces

Ahriman, 463

Ahuna Vairya, 462

Ahura Mazda: fire was a symbol of, 465; is Sanat Kumara, 457, 458, 467; sent Archangels to the court in ancient Persia, 457; and Zarathustra, 455, 456; in Zoroastrianism, 458–59

Ahuras, 456

Ailments, your, 396. *See also* Disease

Akasha, defined and explained, 303n.24

Alaska: volcanic eruption in, 392; volcanic release in, 390

Alaskan earthquake, in 1964, 394

Alban, Saint, *following* p. 484 (p. 9 *in Sept. 12, 1992 letter*)

Alchemist(s): of the Holy Spirit, 274; you are, 268

Alexander the Great, and Zoroastrianism, 465
Alien, shown to an adept, 415. *See also* Extraterrestrials
Alpha: Alpha/Omega is the name of the divine spark, 422; has called you to pray for the Lightbearers, 258
Alpha and Omega: coming of, 395, 396; Guru-chela relationship with, 432–33; prepare more adequately to receive the Light of, 377
Alpha flame, does magnetize and draw up the Omega, 430
Altar: altar call, 300; submit yourselves to the, 369; that is a haven for Mother Mary, 450n.7
Ameretat, 459
America: and abortion, 445; anniversary of Columbus' discovery of, *following* p. 484 (p. 7 *in Sept. 12, 1992 letter*); must not be allowed to go down, 445; and Saint Germain, *following* p. 484 (pp. 8–9 *in Sept. 12, 1992 letter*). *See also* Nation(s)
American dream, 259
Amesha Spentas, 458
Amethyst heart, placed over your heart chakra, *following* p. 484 (p. 3 *in Sept. 12, 1992 letter*)
Analogies, of life, 255
Anchor(s): can be symbols, 263; cast into the bedrock of God-Reality, 259; cast into the heart of the Christ Self, 258; of desire, 249; Gautama Buddha on the thoughtform of the, 255–56, 257; of Love to multiply God-qualities, 263–64; and the mother ship, 265–66; and the quality of hope, 268–69; that you must heave into the highest octaves, 250; in the thoughtform for 1985, 264–65, 266; two qualities of the, 251–52; at the United States Naval Academy, 263; used by Maitreya in his clipper ship, 264; your insights as you ponder the thoughtform of the, 270
Anchorite, 256; defined, 269
Angel(s): of the Keeper of the Scrolls, 430; recording, 477n.2; of the Seventh Ray and the flight into Egypt, 370; waiting breathless for someone to utter the call, 372–73; warning from, 446; of the yellow flame, 379. *See also* Archangels; Fallen angel(s); Seraph; Seraphim
Anger, against God, 416. *See also* Wrath
Angra Mainyu, 460, 463
Angst, 359
Animal sacrifice, 461; separation of the parts of the, 356
Antahkarana: defined, 444n; of hearts, 444; of Life, 425; universal, 446
Antichrist: binding of, 370, 373, 416, 475–76; force(s) of, 357–58, 371, 396; the fourth woe for the binding of the forces of, 489; judgment of the forces of, 368; seed of, 369. *See also* Fallen ones
Anti-cult movement, 371
"Aquarian Age Child" seminar, *following* p. 304 (p. 2 *in June 2, 1992 letter*)
Aquarius: age of, 487; foundation of, 374, *following* p. 484 (p. 2 *in Sept. 12, 1992 letter*); golden age of, *following* p. 484 (p. 3 *in Sept. 12, 1992 letter*). *See also* Age
Archangels: embody the *sefirot*, 354; sent to the court in ancient Persia, 457, 458; in Zoroastrian

theology, 459. *See also* Jophiel and Christine; Michael, Archangel; Zadkiel, Archangel
Architecture, of the cities in the etheric octave, 388
Aries, hierarchy of, 507
Arizona, earthquake in, 394
Armies: of heaven led by the Divine Mother, 448; many who are helpless before oncoming, 259
Arts, patroness of the, 494
Ascended Master(s): are never static, 468; direct contact with, 260, *following* p. 304 (p. 8 *in June 1, 1992 letter*); do not interfere with free will, 413; do not reincarnate, 293; establishing your heart-tie to, *following* p. 304 (p. 6 *in June 1, 1992 letter*); idolatry of the personality of an, 354; walking the earth as an, 398; who are experts in geology, 397. *See also* Masters
Ascended-Master Light Body, 293, 450n.11, 451n.11; Elijah and Moses appeared to Jesus in, 296
Ascension: be ready for your, 388–89; coil of the, flame, 431; described and explained, 450–51n.11; and the dispensation of the 51 percent, 263; and the dweller-on-the-threshold, 358; from inner levels, 293–94; of Jesus, 451n.11; key lifestreams who must make their, 379; Mother Mary made the physical ascension, 444; Mother Mary on the physical ascension, 444–45; opportunity to take your, 397–98; physical, 293, 450–51n.11; seraphim attend the degrees of your, 395; translation of a soul to heaven in the, 292–93
Asha, 460

Asha Vahishta, 459
Ashram rituals, 373, 390; *antahkarana* you build by the, 446; increase the spheres of Light through the, 441
Assumption, of Mother Mary, 444, 450n.10, 451n.11
Astral body, when deeper levels of it come to the surface, 274. *See also* Four lower bodies
Astral plane: great agitation in the, 257; opening of the pits of the, 374; withdraw yourself from the, 250
Astral sea: do not be anchored in or to the, 249; Gautama on the, 250; things brewing beneath the, 257
Astrea, the call to, 279. *See also* Elohim
Atlantis, *following* p. 484 (p. 8 *in Sept. 12, 1992 letter*); golden-age civilization of, 357; Jesus' reign 35,000 years ago on, 365; one of the major causes of the sinking of, 489; when you had balanced 51 percent of your karma, 367
Atman, 409, 424
Attachments, do not fear to give up, 360
Avatars: choose the hour when they reveal their mission, 289; embody the Tree of Life, 353. *See also* Christed ones
Avesta, 454

Bacon, Francis, *following* p. 484 (p. 9 *in Sept. 12, 1992 letter*); Saint Germain as, *following* p. 484 (p. 8 *in Sept. 12, 1992 letter*)
Bacon, Roger, *following* p. 484 (p. 9 *in Sept. 12, 1992 letter*)
Balance, 388; an all-consuming desire for, 447; holding of the, 390;

scales signifying, 264–65
Barabbas, people must choose Jesus or, 358
Base-of-the-spine chakra: fount of eternal life that rises from the, 430; and the violet flame, 488. *See also* Chakra(s)
Beauty: contemplation of, 255; Goddess of, 495
Beggars, law of feeding the, 258
Believing, 424
Bhajans, daily, 410
Bija mantra(s): to the feminine deities, 499; Lakshmi's, 498; of Sarasvati, 495
Bird, in Maitreya's heart, 265
Black magician(s): "chewed you up and spat you out," 464; every flame can be abused by, 489. *See also* Fallen ones
Blindness, spiritual, 299
Blueprint, etheric, 380
Bodhisattvas, 388; who desire to take embodiment, 387
Bodies: Paul's teaching on mutable and immutable, 294–95; prepared, 380. *See also* Four lower bodies
Body: Ascended-Master Light Body, 293, 296, 450n.11, 451n.11; attachment to the, 401, 405n.4; attacks upon the, 439–40; of the Blessed Virgin Mary assumed into heaven, 450n.10; as a city, 427; of the Mother desecrated and martyred, 450n.7; old patterns of the physical, 273; and the ritual of the ascension, 450–51n.11; the soul does not retain a physical, 294. *See also* Four lower bodies
Body elemental(s), 378, 405n.4; and the fire bath of the multicolored flames, 473–74

Bondage: four hundred years of, 356; greatest, 440
Book of Life, each man's, 477n.2
Brahma, 399; Counterpart of, 503; parallel to God the Father, 493; Shakti of, 493
Brahman, 399; in the lotus of the heart, 427
Brain(s): fat upon the, 380; healing of your, 412; need a scrubbing, 378. *See also* Mind(s)
Breathing exercises, for more than meets the eye, 275
Buddha: consciousness of the, 260; Inner, *following* p. 304 (p. 5 *in June 1, 1992 letter*), 502. *See also* Gautama Buddha
Buddhist text, 249
Burden(s): "every man shall bear his own karmic burden," 301; surcease from, 450n.7; that some of you have borne as little children, 446–47
Business deal, that is ludicrous, 464

Caduceus, children of Israel looked upon the, 266
Cage, a little white bird in a golden, 265
California, earthquakes in, 392
Call(s): on abortion, 414; and each man's Book of Life, 477n.2; to play on autoreverse tape recorders, 279; that may be answered, 258. *See also* Decree(s); Fiats; Invocation; Judgment call(s); Mantra(s)
Canaan, overrun with evolutions who rebelled against the mercy of God, 354
Candles, of the violet flame, 490
Carnal mind, reasons away the directives of conscience, 355–56. *See*

also Dweller-on-the-threshold
Cassettes, of the songs that you sing, 443. *See also* Tapes
Cataclysm. *See* Earth changes; Earthquake(s)
Catholic Church, and Saint Joseph, 375. *See also* Church
Catholic doctrine, on the assumption of Mary and the ascension of Jesus, 451n.11
Causal Body: and the Dharmakaya, 271n.3; of Gautama Buddha, 267; living in the spheres of the Great, 423; of Maitreya, 271n.8; a release from Mother Mary's, 445; replica of the Great, 379–80; Saint Germain's, *following* p. 484 (p. 7 *in Sept. 12, 1992 letter*); sea of Light that is the, 249; star of your, 279; vast and individualized, 380; your, *following* p. 484 (p. 4 *in Sept. 12, 1992 letter*)
Ceiling, cracks in the, 277
Central America, Mother Mary speaks to those of, 446
Central nervous system, healing of your, 412
Chakra(s): Eighth Ray, 468; realigning your, 474; regulating and balancing and strengthening of the, 430; represent the seven planes of heaven, 488; twelve-petaled, 279; and the violet flame, 486, 488, 489; which the fallen angels most desired to pervert in you, 430. *See also* Base-of-the-spine chakra; Crown chakra: Heart(s); Heart chakra; Seat-of-the-soul chakra; Third eye; Third-eye chakra; Throat chakra
Chalice: of Elohim, 373; of God, 355
Challenge, of all ages, 440
Changes: sudden, 442; taking place gently by transmutation, 411

Chart of Your Divine Self: and the Dharmakaya, Sambhogakaya and Nirmanakaya, 271n.3; middle figure of the, 366
Chela: with a capital C, 267; in moments of despair, 256; true, 261; who approaches the altar of initiation in Maitreya's heart, 265; who says, "I cannot understand this intensity. I will depart," 277; you must make the request to be a, 425. *See also* Chelaship; Disciple; Guru-chela relationship; Initiate; Students; Yogin
Chelaship: with Saint Germain, *following* p. 484 (p. 5 *in Sept. 12, 1992 letter*); tighten your, 448. *See also* Chela
Child, 369; aborted, 450n.7; discipline of the, 276; inner, 444; murder of the, 416; persecution of the, 433; remember you were once a, 417; within, 361. *See also* Children
Child abuse, is on the rise, 417
Children: balancing karma by caring for and educating, 258; burdens you have borne as, 446–47; caring for your, 370; and discipline, 375; educating, 381; Lakshmi on, 508; Lord Shiva on, 417; organized plan for the illumination of the, 509; some of you were Christ children, 447; teach, 505; teaching, *following* p. 304 (pp. 2, 3 *in June 2, 1992 letter*), 502; violation of, 368; violators of, 433. *See also* Child
China, earthquakes in, 394
Christ: attempted defilement of the, 433; denial of, 356–57; of every man, 258; Inner, *following* p. 304 (p. 5 *in June 1, 1992 letter*); persecuted and crucified, 357; point

of challenge where you raise up, 367; as the *Tiferet,* 366; Universal and individualized, 356; Vishnu is the Christ Light, 498. *See also* Christ Self; Christed ones; Christhood; Jesus; Son; Son of God

Christ Child, yourself as the, 447

Christ Self: bonding to the heart of the, 357; dressed as a knight, 442; each day the law of your being read to you by your, 410; the Inner Christ as the, 502; is the Lamb of God, 366; knowledge of the, *following* p. 484 (p. 2 *in Sept. 12, 1992 letter);* leading authority in your life, 265; and the Messenger, 277; must speak sternly to you, 276; not being fully bonded to the, 356; and the Sambhogakaya, 271n.3; in the secret chamber of the heart, 468; that might be far above the evildoer, 258; Vishnu in the person of your, 507; when you are bonded to the, 498; your inner child's union with your, 444; your Real Self and Inner Teacher, *following* p. 304 (p. 3 *in June 1, 1992 letter);* Zarathustra one with your, 475. *See also* Christ; Son; Son of God

Christed ones: choose the hour when they reveal their mission, 289; have been lost in the earth, 370; not a few have walked the earth, 357. *See also* Avatars; Christ

Christhood: becoming the fullness of the embodiment of your, 369–70; initiation of, 356; those counseled and trained to play their role of, 366. *See also* Christ

Christianity, and Zoroastrianism, 466

Church, Mother Mary weeps for conditions within and without the, 443. *See also* Catholic Church; Theologians

Church Universal and Triumphant, to prosper and multiply this, 446

Cities, agitation in your, 257

City Foursquare: and the Inner Retreat in the thoughtform for 1985, 264–65; is the Retreat of the Divine Mother, 265

Civilization(s): cradle of a new, 370; descent of, 381; will stand or fall, 370

Cloud, "cloud of knowing," 256

Cloven tongues, of yellow fire, 382

Codependency, between yourself and your ailments, 396

Colonies, thirteen, *following* p. 484 (p. 8 *in Sept. 12, 1992 letter)*

Columbus, Christopher: his letter to the king and queen of Spain, *following* p. 484 (pp. 6–7 *in Sept. 12, 1992 letter);* the movie about, *following* p. 484 (p. 14 *in Sept. 12, 1992 letter);* Saint Germain as, *following* p. 484 (pp. 5, 6 *in Sept. 12, 1992 letter);* trial and testing of, *following* p. 484 (pp. 10–12 *in Sept. 12, 1992 letter)*

Comfort: of the Holy Spirit, 423; that is not said, 447

Comfortability, 276–77

Communication, you have known a greater, 388

Community: of the Holy Spirit, 264; teach children something of your own expertise in this, 502

Conference(s): agenda of this, 410; earthquakes during, 390; events in the planet during this, 391; make your plans to come here next year for the, 389; that is the greatest opportunity in this century, 279. *See also* FREEDOM 1992

Confidence, crisis of, 379

Confucius, a strong heart-tie to, *following* p. 304 (p. 1 *in June 1, 1992 letter*)

Conscience: directives of, 356; some have silenced the voice of, 260. *See also* Voice

Consciousness, old encrustations of, 273. *See also* Human consciousness

Correction, that you will not take, 276

Cosmic Clock: an entire cycle around the, 487; karmic cycles on the, 496

Creation: the key to, 255; and progress, *following* p. 304 (p. 6 *in June 1, 1992 letter*)

Cremation, 293

Crimes, justice for, 258

Criminal tendencies, 258

Crown chakra(s): cloven tongues of yellow fire on, 382; golden fire upon your, 387; souls of Light who will reach the point of the, 377–78; and that which passes through television sets, 502; and the violet flame, 488. *See also* Chakra(s)

Crystals, and the twelve gates, 257

Cuzco: a delicate operation directed from the retreat of, 397; and the San Francisco earthquake, 394

Cycle(s): change in planetary, 448; of the degrees, 488; karmic, 496; turning, 389; twelve, 487; 25,800-year cycle of returning karma, 367n

Daevas, 456, 461

Daisy, cosmic, 380

Dance, Shiva as Lord of the, 403

Darjeeling Council, looking over Saint Germain's shoulder, *following* p. 484 (p. 5 *in Sept. 12, 1992 letter*)

Dark Cycle, opportunity to turn it around, *following* p. 484 (p. 2 *in Sept. 12, 1992 letter*)

Dark night, of the soul, 263

Dark powers, and the Piscean age, 366–67. *See also* Evil force(s); Fallen ones

Darkness: look at the corners of, 440; Mother Mary on, 441; and those who shall lead, 440; turning in the planet toward, 358. *See also* Evil; Evil force(s)

Darshan, *following* p. 304 (p. 5 *in June 1, 1992 letter*)

David, Saint Germain on, 365–66

Death, *following* p. 304 (pp. 7–8 *in June 1, 1992 letter);* death spiral, 381; Shiva is associated with, 400

Death and Hell, descent into, 263. *See also* Hell

Deathless Solar Body, 293, 450n.11

Decisions, unwise, 275

Decree(s): and all to whom you are tied karmically, 446; doubt breaks the cord of Light you build with, 424; to more adequately prepare for the Light of Alpha and Omega, 377; a single "Heart, Head and Hand" decree, 268; whereby many may come into a true illumination, 378; you have saved many a day by your, 443. *See also* Call(s); Fiats; Judgment call(s); Mantra(s)

Defeat, all around you, 391

Degeneration, spiral of, 381

Deities, bija mantra(s) to feminine, 499, 505n.2

Deliverance, whilst living, *following* p. 304 (p. 7 *in June 1, 1992 letter*)

Density, jump out of, 388
Depression, world, 391
Desire(s): fallen ones inserting, 372; old, 273; that is pulling you down, 250
Destroyer(s): in the earth, 415; Shiva as the, 400. *See also* Fallen ones
Destruction, where it will increase, 258
Devil: and his angels, 298; in Zoroastrian theology, 463. *See also* Fallen ones
Devotions, and the universal *antahkarana*, 446
Dharmakaya: defined, 271n.3; invoking Gautama Buddha's, 255
Diamond Heart, of El Morya, 363
Dictation(s): Jophiel and Christine's, 378; response to Mighty Victory's, 389; those who listen to and attempt to implement our, 441
Diet: of the Eastern adepts, 416, 430–31; right, 388
Dignity, bringing life to a level of, 258
Din: evolutions who took the way of, 354; force known as, *following* p. 484 (p. 13 *in Sept. 12, 1992 letter);* force of Antichrist that came out of, 357; those who followed the way of, 412; turning around the evil works of, 368
Discernment, divine gift of, 442
Disciple: required to pass his talent to the next generation, 502; the true, 260. *See also* Chela; Yogin
Discipline(s): and love, 276; of our retreat, 278
Discrimination: Christ-discrimination, 274–75; of the Christ Flame, 442; two-edged sword of, 276
Disease, terminal, 488. *See also* Ailments
Disenfranchised, millions of, 259

Dispensation: from Mother Mary, 448; to reduce your karmic cycles by light-years, 487; required for Mighty Victory to speak to you, 390. *See also* Grant
Distraction, to get you away from the altar, 372
Divine plan, activities that are not necessary to your, 417
Divine spark, does have a name, 422. *See also* Threefold flame
Division, in your members, 358–59
Doctrinal disputes, *following* p. 304 (p. 6 *in June 1, 1992 letter). See also* Doctrine
Doctrine: of Divine Love, *following* p. 304 (p. 4 *in June 1, 1992 letter);* Jesus' teachings entrenched in, 370; a means to an end, *following* p. 304 (p. 7 *in June 1, 1992 letter). See also* Doctrinal disputes
Dossier on the Ascension, reread the, 396
Dot, of the original beginning of the not-self, 358
Doubt, Beloved Omega on, 424
Downtrodden, all have been, 259
Druj, 460
Drunkenness, ritual, 461
Durga, 503; Shiva's Shakti, 402
Dweller-on-the-threshold: the call for the binding of the, 368–69; core of the, 358; of every fallen angel, 357–58. *See also* Carnal mind

Ear, inner, 270
Earth: cleansing it without major cataclysm, 412; clearing of the, 410; the Cosmic Council had decided to extinguish, 472; is a sick planet with many divine physicians attending, 397; Sanat Kumara's mission to,

467–68; shall accelerate through your call, 414; should be a Violet Planet, 489; sounds of the, 416. *See also* Planet

Earth changes: how and where they shall manifest, 390; and violet flame, 487; without further calamity, 397. *See also* Earthquake(s)

Earthquake(s): in Alaska in 1964, 394; in California and Yellowstone Park, 392; in China, 394; during conferences, 390; in Guatemala, Arizona and Mexico, 394; for a mitigation of world karma, 389; in Nicaragua in 1972, 394; in the Pacific Northwest, 393; in San Francisco, 394. *See also* Earth changes

Education: foundations of true, *following* p. 304 (p. 3 *in June 2, 1992 letter);* Lord Lanto on, 381; Montessori Education Workshops, *following* p. 304 (pp. 1–3 *in June 2, 1992 letter);* and Montessori International, *following* p. 304 (p. 4 *in June 2, 1992 letter)*

Effort, multiplication and maximizing of, 509

Ego: destroyer of the human, 400; it is not a time to assert the human, 369; Lakshmi on, 507; Shiva comes to save us from our human, 403

Egoless existence, 267

Egypt, flight into, 370

Eighth Ray chakra, 468. *See also* Secret chamber

Ein Sof, 396, 414, 488; before the creation, 366; reaction from, 416

El Morya: called the messenger to "stump," *following* p. 484 (p. 4 *in Sept. 12, 1992 letter);* the closest he shall ever be to his chelas, 363; closest to you, 433; did pick up the Messenger as an orphan in the astral plane, 259; Electronic Presence of, 360, 361; and the 1964 Alaskan earthquake, 394; a one-on-one relationship with, 361; a personal teaching for your life from, 268; a profile of the testing of his soul, 353; Sanat Kumara has sent him to you personally, 360; teaching which he has given to you directly, 270; a time to face him squarely, 360; why he has tarried so long with this stubborn generation, 355; will take you on his magic carpet, 361; with you every day, 359

Elections, November, 440

Electronic Presence: of El Morya, 360, 361; the Hail Mary reestablishes Mother Mary's, 449; of Mother Mary over her statue, 440; of Mother Omega and Mother Mary, 444; multiplying your, 509; of Saint Germain, *following* p. 484 (pp. 3, 4 *in Sept. 12, 1992 letter);* of Shiva, 404; your, 398; of Zarathustra, 474

Elemental life, 411; burdens on, 394; a delicate matter for, 397. *See also* Body elemental(s); Salamanders

Elephant, and Lakshmi, 496

Elijah: and Elisha, 293, 445, 445n; John the Baptist was, 285–99; on the Mount of Transfiguration, 294–96; a "wilderness prophet," 302n.2

Elisha, and Elijah, 293, 445, 445n

Elixir, of the waters of everlasting Life, 429–30

Elohim, chalice of, 373. *See also* Astrea; Hercules

Empowering, coming upon you, 367

Energy, misqualification of, 279.

See also Substance

Enlightenment, decree for, 382. See also Illumination

Enoch, was translated, 292, 293

Entertainment, of the world, 378

Environmentalists, 414

Equilibrium, your, 388

Etheric octave: becomes physical, 265; polluted, 414

Everlasting Life, elixir of the waters of, 429

Evil: binding of, 367, 369–70; and Good in Zoroastrian theology, 459–60, 462, 463; has nothing original of its own, 463; how it did gain hold, 368; seal the place where, dwells, 374; what causes you to espouse, 358; Zarathustra's main objective was to stamp out, 456. See also Darkness; Evil force(s); Infamy

Evil force(s): binding of the, 368, 369; presenting themselves as good, 464. See also Dark powers; Devil; Fallen ones

Example, that others may see and follow, 389

Experience, there are some things that must be learned by, 431

Extraterrestrials, 397. See also Alien

Eye magic, 496

Faith: and communion with God, 355; ingredients for the propagation of the, 458; and trust in God, 424

Faithfulness, in all things, 257

Faiths, merge in Divine Love, *following* p. 304 (p. 6 *in June 1, 1992 letter*). See also Religion(s)

Fallen angel(s): attempt to snuff out the Christ, 366; did distort doctrine, 370; dweller-on-the-threshold of every, 357–58; perverted the signs of the Kabbalah to imprison souls, 367–68; that came upon you, 430; who perverted God's justice and judgment, *following* p. 484 (p. 13 *in Sept. 12, 1992 letter*). See also Fallen ones

Fallen ones: anger of the, 416; have attempted to lure you here and there, 442; have been working overtime, 372; and the mass consciousness, 414; ready to be picked off, 373; what to say to them, 371–72; where they outdid you, 431. See also Antichrist; Black magician(s); Dark powers; Destroyer(s); Devil; Evil force(s); Fallen angel(s); Laggards; Oppressor

Family, Holy, 368

Famines, 259

Fasting, from food and the entertainment of the world, 378

Fat, hardened in the heart, 276

Father: come up to the level of the, 362; El Morya on, 361; peace with the, 359; and Sarasvati, 503; on the twelve o'clock line, 503; violation of the Light of the, 433. See also God

Fears, your body elemental's, 406n.4

Feminine principle, that is the soul, 433

Feminine Ray, hour of the raising up of the, 379

Fiats, as the Messenger has demonstrated them, 372. See also Call(s); Decree(s); Mantra(s)

Fire: compressing the, 423; concentration of, 389; fire-snow, 475; golden fire, 387; of the heart will see you through, 442; of Hierarchy, 278; mastery of, 485; in

Matter, 265; no creation without the heat of, 274; religion of, 468; spiritual, 359; of Victory, 388; of your I AM Presence you can draw down, 278; Zarathustra on, 471–72, 473; in Zoroastrianism, 465. *See also* Flame(s); Sacred fire; White fire; Yellow fire

Flame(s): fire bath of the multicolored, 473–74; the ray of light has descended and sprung up as a, 486; Zarathustra on the, 472, 473. *See also* Fire; Yellow flame

Forgetfulness, Shiva comes to save us from, 403

Forgiveness, extend it to life, 260

Form, Gautama Buddha on the contemplation of, 255

Fortune, Goddess of, 495

Founding fathers, and Saint Germain, *following* p. 484 (p. 8 *in Sept. 12, 1992 letter*)

Four lower bodies: balance of the, 416; discipline of the, 276; rigidity and resiliency in, 277. *See also* Astral body; Bodies; Body

Free will: all-important concept of, 460; Alpha could never force your, 430; in the earth, 413

Freedom, and Saint Germain, *following* p. 484 (pp. 8–9 *in Sept. 12, 1992 letter*)

Freedom, Goddess of, *following* p. 484 (p. 13 *in Sept. 12, 1992 letter*)

FREEDOM 1992: has one goal, *following* p. 304 (p. 7 *in June 1, 1992 letter*); thoughtform for, 279. *See also* Conference(s)

Friday, first, 357

Friends, of God, 354, 355

Ganesha, 497

Garden of Eden, Maitreya's Mystery School known as the, 368

Gates, twelve, 257

Gathas, 460, 466; and Zarathustra, 454, 455, 456

Gautama Buddha: a co-relationship with, 267; crowned Lord of the World, 468; does a great deal of walking up and down the earth, 261; the first to respond to Sanat Kumara, 467; his etheric retreat called the Western Shamballa, *following* p. 304 (p. 2 *in June 1, 1992 letter*); at National Airport in Washington, D.C., 267; partook of rice milk before his meditation under the Bo tree, 271n.14; a strong heart-tie to, *following* p. 304 (p. 1 *in June 1, 1992 letter*); visualizing, 267. *See also* Buddha

Generations, true gap between, 508

Geology, Ascended Masters who are experts in, 397

Geothermal waters, in the earth, 429

God: be in awe of the indwelling Presence of, 508; can do anything, 297; contact with, 260, *following* p. 304 (p. 8 *in June 1, 1992 letter*); divine pity upon those who have no desire for, 442; doubt and denial of, 424; facilitator of your soul's union with, *following* p. 304 (p. 5 *in June 1, 1992 letter*); "God and my right," 265; God-identification, 424; as the great mother ship, 265; had you trusted in, 431; Inner, 356; inner walk with, 354; is in your temple, 508; is practical, 297; never leave off loving, 425; our Father-Mother, 298; the reality of you is, 267; sanctuary where you meet him daily, 443;

separation from, 359; things cannot get much worse without some reaction from, 416; in us, *following* p. 304 (p. 4 *in June 1, 1992 letter);* walk and talk with, 279; walks where you walk, 507; we will remake you in the image and likeness of, 388; within, *following* p. 304 (p. 1 *in June 1, 1992 letter); See also* Father; Godhood; Holy Spirit; I AM; I AM Presence; I AM THAT I AM; Mother(s), Divine; Son; Trinity

God consciousness, Lakshmi bestows, 498

Goddesses, four, 503. *See also* Deities

Godhead, four personalities of the, 359. *See also* God

Godhood, do not discount your, 389. *See also* God; I AM; I AM Presence; I AM THAT I AM

Gold rush, and human greed, 394

Golden age, of Aquarius, *following* p. 484 (p. 3 *in Sept. 12, 1992 letter). See also* Golden-age civilization

Golden-age civilization, on Atlantis, 367. *See also* Golden age

Golden fire, upon your crown chakras, 387. *See also* Second Ray; Yellow fire; Yellow flame

Good, and Evil in Zoroastrian theology, 459–60, 462, 463

Government: human, 373; those in the offices of, 379. *See also* House of Representatives

Grace, that you might ask of Mother Mary, 448

Grand Teton, connection of this place to the, 397

Grant, secured by Saint Germain, *following* p. 484 (pp. 4–5 *in Sept. 12, 1992 letter). See also* Dispensation

Great Central Sun: awakening of your experience in the, 380; replica of your Home in the, 421, 426; and the seraphim, 396; your birth in the, 429

Great Central Sun Magnet: the individual who is the focus of the, 389; replica of the, 380

Great Teams of Conquerors, 260

Great White Brotherhood, initiate of the, 287, 289

Greed, expiated, 394

Guatemala, earthquakes in, 394

Gun, is not a begging bowl, 258

Guru(s): descended from Sanat Kumara, 462; having the world as your, 431; the ideal, 494; mantle of, 277, 425; real worth of the, 256–57; your true, 261. *See also* Guru-chela relationship

Guru-chela relationship: with the Messenger, 432–33; shortening of the days for the elect in the, 257. *See also* Chela; Guru(s)

Hail Mary: mantra of the, 440; reestablishes Mother Mary's Electronic Presence over you, 449. *See also* Prayer(s); Rosaries; Rosary

Handwriting on the wall, 387

Handyman, adopting one quality of the, 253

Haoma ritual, in Zoroastrianism, 465

Happiness, greatest, 360

Harmony, God, and the 1964 Alaskan earthquake, 394

Harvest, hour of the, 371

Haurvatat, 459

Healers, seraphim are, 396, 474

Healing, 361. *See also* Resolution

Health: enjoyed by seraphim, 474;

regaining of your, 371
Health-care practitioners, 396
Heart(s): Beloved Omega on the secret chamber of the, 422–23; devotion to Mother Mary's, 444; Diamond Heart of El Morya, 363; Divine Presence in your, 422; expand your, 280; fat hardened in the, 276; how you expand the, 275–76; of an illumined soul, 428; of the Inner Retreat, *following* p. 304 (pp. 2, 3, 4 *in June 1, 1992 letter);* joy in your, 279; largess of, 445; lotus of the, 426–27; of the Messenger, 355; rituals of the, 423; a room that is a focus of the secret chamber of the, 476n.2; secret chamber of the, *following* p. 304 (p. 3 *in June 1, 1992 letter),* 468; ties to the secret chamber of Mother Mary's, 440; Twin, 441–42, 449n.3; Vishnu in the secret chamber of your, 508; visualizing the violet flame in and around the, 486; Zarathustra's retreat is a replica of the secret chamber of the, 472–73. *See also* Heart chakra; Immaculate Heart; Sacred Heart(s)
Heart chakra, 265; amethyst heart placed over, *following* p. 484 (p. 3 *in Sept. 12, 1992 letter);* expand the petals of the, 275; and the invocation of violet flame, 486; twelve-petaled, 468; your, *following* p. 304 (p. 3 *in June 1, 1992 letter); See also* Chakra(s); Heart(s)
Heat: for alchemy of the soul's transformation, 274; if it is too hot, 275; whereby you can be purged, 473
Helios, prophesied a great earthquake, 394. *See also* Helios and Vesta
Helios and Vesta, think of them each day as you greet the sun, 280. *See also* Helios
Hell: opening of the bowels of, 374; reserved for the devil and his angels, 298. *See also* Death and Hell
Hercules, freely asking his assistance, 449n.6. *See also* Elohim
Hermits, 256; and anchorites, 269
Herod, 370; and John the Baptist, 288, 291
Hindu Trinity, 399–400
Histories, unchronicled, 508. *See also* Past; Records; 35,000 years ago
Hokhmah, 353
Holy City, in the thoughtform for 1985, 266
Holy Spirit: anchoring more and more of the, 274; encouraged Christopher Columbus, *following* p. 484 (p. 7 *in Sept. 12, 1992 letter);* first stage of the receiving of the, 273; intensity of the, 277; may you be empowered by the, 260–61; peace with the, 359; a portion of the, 276; and Shiva, 399, 400; violation of the Light of the, 433; when you lose the, 279; in Zoroastrian theology, 458, 459, 460–61, 462, 463. *See also* God
Home: Gautama Buddha on, 256; in the Great Central Sun, 421, 426
Homing, Song of the, 265
Hope: and the anchor, 255–56, 266; Gautama Buddha on, 256–57, 258, 259; as the symbolic meaning of the anchor, 268–69
Horse, of King Vishtaspa, 456
House of Representatives, 440. *See also* Government

Human consciousness: is slow to adjust to abrupt changes, 362; if you do not want to be fooled by the, 278. *See also* Consciousness
Humanity, when you see the masses of, 259
Humility, 260
Hungry, balancing karma by feeding the, 258
Hutaosa, Queen, 456–58

I AM, within you is God, *following* p. 304 (p. 1 *in June 1, 1992 letter*). *See also* God; Godhood; I AM Presence; I AM THAT I AM
I AM Presence: and the Dharmakaya, 271n.3; keynote of, 265; knowledge of, *following* p. 484 (p. 2 *in Sept. 12, 1992 letter)*; leading authority in your life, 265; the prophet embodies the, 460; the rising action of the Omega flame and the descending Light of your, 430; the soul's union with the, 450–51n.11; star of your, 279; surrender all to your, 261; take the hand of your, 280. *See also* God; Godhood; I AM; I AM THAT I AM
I AM THAT I AM: cleavage between the soul and the, 357; Inner Buddha as the, 502; separation between the soul and the, 356. *See also* God; Godhood; I AM; I AM Presence
Idea, that the fallen ones have planted, 372
Identity, Divine, 249
Idolatry, El Morya on, 354
Idols, cast down your, 354
Ignorance: knot of, 505n.2; Shiva comes to save us from, 403
Illumination, 490; dispensation of, 378; Manjushri brings the gift of, 495; Sarasvati on, 501, 502–3, 503–4. *See also* Enlightenment; Understanding
Illusion, slayer of, 418
Immaculate Heart: all said at the recent conference encapsulated in Mother Mary's, 441; be representatives of Mother Mary's, 444; devotions to Mother Mary's, 446; novena to Mother Mary's, 440; veneration to the, 449n.3; your services to the, 358
Immortality: Lakshmi is associated with, 496; to put on, 276
Immovability, key to your increase of the Spirit of God, 280
Incarnation, Light for prolonged, 410. *See also* Life
India, all parties to the civilizations of, 365
Indra, represents the Self, 402, 497
Indulgence, a certain level of, 275
Infamy, has reached a high watermark, 416. *See also* Evil
Initiate: of the Great White Brotherhood, 287, 289; Zarathustra was an, 454–55. *See also* Chela
Initiation: compels you to break barriers, 277; karma allowed to descend in the form of, 278; key to the path of, 276; level of, 448; ship of, 271n.8; of Sonship and Christhood, 356. *See also* Test(s); Testing
Injustice: seeming, 278; sense of, 447
Inner Retreat: focuses at the, 426; Heart of, *following* p. 304 (pp. 2, 3, 4 *in June 1, 1992 letter)*; and the New Jerusalem in the thoughtform for 1985, 264–65; the "Place of Great Encounters," *following* p. 304 (pp. 2–3 *in June*

1, 1992 letter); Retreat of the Divine Mother over the, 265; your own, *following* p. 304 (p. 3 *in June 1, 1992 letter*)
Intensity, on the path, 277
Invocation, Messenger's, 281, 404–5, 469, 499
Iranian religion, traditional, 461
Isaiah, 285; prophesied the coming of John the Baptist, 286
Islam, and Zoroastrianism, 466

Jerome, and reincarnation, 292
Jesus: ascension of, 451n.11; devotion(s) to the Sacred Heart of, 441–42, 446; "did not many mighty works there for their unbelief," 424; the doctrine that he pays the whole price for our karma, 300; and the golden-age civilization of Atlantis, 357; his reign 35,000 years ago on Atlantis, 365; his request we take back the karma he has borne for us, 449n.6; his Sacred Heart in the thoughtform for 1985, 264–65, 266; his teaching on reincarnation, 285–99; "Jesus died for my sins," 300; make peace with, 359; in many incarnations, 366; people must choose Barabbas or, 358; perversion of the teachings of, 370; publishing abroad of the true teachings of, 374; rejection of the Son of God in the person of, 356–57; responded to Sanat Kumara, 467; Saint Joseph did not spare the rod with, 375; scenes in the New Testament where he protects his identity, 302–3n.9; services to the Sacred Heart of, 358; a strong heart-tie to, *following* p. 304 (p. 1 *in June 1,* *1992 letter*); those who say "We have no need of Jesus...," 356, 357; Universal Christ personified in, 356; veneration to the Sacred Heart of, 449n.3; was overshadowed, 371; will help you carry your karma, 301. *See also* Christ; Son of God
Joan of Arc, 448; prototypes of, 442
John the Baptist, 366; was Elijah come again, 285–99
Jophiel and Christine, you do not give them enough attention, 378. *See also* Archangels
Joseph, Saint, *following* p. 484 (pp. 1, 9 *in Sept. 12, 1992 letter*); did not spare the rod with Jesus, 375; mantle and Presence of, 371; Saint Germain as, 369
Journals, of the discovery of the Mind of God, 274
Journeys, at night, 509
Joy: and creation, *following* p. 304 (p. 6 *in June 1, 1992 letter*); in the Lord, *following* p. 304 (p. 7 *in June 1, 1992 letter*); of the Mystery School, 279; path of, *following* p. 304 (p. 6 *in June 1, 1992 letter*)
Judaism, and Zoroastrianism, 466
Judgment: betrayal of the LORD God's, 412; forces who perverted God's, *following* p. 484 (p. 13 *in Sept. 12, 1992 letter*); hour of the, 507; meted out through the Archangels, 354; that the fallen ones meted out, 368; upon those who know what they do, 413; turned to become the destroyer of souls, 357
Judgment call(s): for the binding of the dweller-on-the-threshold, 412; dictated by Jesus, 368
Justice: forces who perverted God's,

following p. 484 (p. 13 *in* Sept. 12, 1992 *letter*); scales of, 266
Justices, of the Supreme Court, 412–13
Justinius, Holy, 360

Kabbalah: birth of Evil in the, 463; perverted to imprison souls, 367–68
Kabir, words of, *following* p. 304 (p. 7 *in June 1, 1992 letter*)
Kailasa, Mount, *following* p. 304 (p. 2 *in June 1, 1992 letter*), 403
Kali, 503; Shiva's Shakti, 402–3
Karma(s): allowed to descend in the form of initiation, 278; and the ascension, 450–51n.11; balancing, 258, 446; balancing 51 percent of, 263; boulders and mountains of, 422; of caring for those in your care, 417; circle of your, 362; dark night of the soul of personal and planetary, 263; descent of, 285n; dispensation of bearing your own, 443; the doctrine that Jesus pays the whole price for our, 300; footprints of a past, 441; horrendous weight of untransmuted, 397; Jesus' request that we take back, 449n.6; Jesus will help you carry your, 301; law of, 458; mitigated and held back, 441; mitigation of world, 389; negative and positive, 410; opportunity for the balancing of, 487; remitted and retained, 260; responsibility for, 300; set forth in the Old and New Testament, 300; upon the Supreme Court justices for every child who is aborted, 413; that must be dealt with, 432; that you must balance, 432, 504; that you were shown, 430; and theologians, 299; those on Atlantis who balanced their karma and those who did not, 367; 25,800-year cycle of returning, 367n; when the Great Law decrees the balancing of, 487
Karmic cycles, on the Cosmic Clock, 496
Keeper of the Scrolls: angel(s) of the, 275, 430; chart of the, 360; explained, 477n.2
Keepers of the Flame: are fire-tenders, 468; know the heart of Saint Germain, *following* p. 484 (p. 8 *in Sept. 12, 1992 letter*); and smugness, 440–41
Keter, 353, 355, 358; you have called upon, 368
Keynote: Gautama Buddha's, 267; of each one's I AM Presence, 265
Khshathra Vairya, 459
King(s): and Lakshmi, 497; the office of, 497; representing the Christed one, 498
Knight, Holy Christ Self dressed as a, 442
Knowledge, 502; hunger for, 379; pass on true, 504; that your children and children's children do not have, 508
Krishna, Vishnu was incarnated as, 495–96
Kuan Yin, students who have answered the call of, 379
Kumaras, Seven Holy, 455
Kundalini yoga, 430
Kusti, in Zoroastrianism, 465
Kuthumi, and psychology, 359

Labors: from El Morya, 396; of the Elohim, 489
Laggards, who did begin as children

of the Light, 358
Lakshmi, 503; the Divine Mother in her manifestation as, 495–98; invoke, 509
Lamb, of God slain, 366
Lanello, closest to you, 433
Lanto, on the necessity of teaching children, *following* p. 304 (p. 3 *in June 2, 1992 letter*)
Lao Tzu, a strong heart-tie to, *following* p. 304 (p. 1 *in June 1, 1992 letter*)
Law: of feeding the beggars, 258; and Justice, 266; read to you each day, 410; Sarasvati articulates the wisdom of the, 493
Leaders, *following* p. 484 (p. 10 *in Sept. 12, 1992 letter*)
Leadership: positions of, 445; in this nation, 439
Leap, in consciousness, 362
Learning, Goddess of, 494
Lemuria, *following* p. 484 (p. 8 *in Sept. 12, 1992 letter*)
Letters, requesting a Guru-chela relationship, 432–33
Libra, sign of, 447
Lie, origin of the conflict between Truth and the, 460–62
Life, a review of this, 430. *See also* Incarnation; Lifetimes; Lives
Lifetimes, you have had thousands of, 278. *See also* Lives; Reincarnation
Light: of the Alpha and Omega flame in you merging, 430; borrowed, 358; companions of the Great Inner, *following* p. 304 (pp. 1–2, 4 *in June 1, 1992 letter*); concentration upon the Inner, 426–28; does purge, 273–74; how did you lose it, 367; Inner, *following* p. 304 (p. 3 *in June 1, 1992 letter*); if it is misqualified, 390; preparation to hold more, 377; when you increase in, 414. *See also* White light
Lightbearer(s): Alpha has called you to pray for the, 258; the star of the Body of, 279; who are searching and waiting for the Truth, 504; worked on by evil forces, 464
Listening ear, attuned to the Mind of God, 443
Lives: accountability for actions in all past, 300; you were shown the actions of past, 430. *See also* Lifetimes; Reincarnation
Lonely ones, children growing up as, 508
Longevity, your, 410
Lord of the World, office of, 468
Los Angeles, upheaval in, 374
Lotus: of the heart, 426–27; and Lakshmi, 496; Sarasvati sitting on a, 493, 494
Love: Beloved Omega on, 425; and discipline, 276; does come in 144,000 different flames, 280; flaming anchor of, 263–64; Light/Doctrine of Divine, *following* p. 304 (p. 4 *in June 1, 1992 letter*); that is a piercing fire, 279; universal, 467
Love Offering, Messenger's Blessing of the, 262
Lute, Sarasvati's, 494
Luxor, roll call at, 388

Magic carpet, of El Morya, 361
Maha Chohan, retreat of, 281
Mahadeva, 400
Maitreya: the anchor in his clipper ship, 264; clipper ship of, 271n.8; a little white bird in his heart chamber, 265; and Manjushri, 494–95; responded to Sanat

Kumara, 467; and the secret chamber of the heart, 476n.2

Maitreya's Mystery School: adversary who did betray you at, 368; those who advance in, 354; training of the Guru's of, 432; we have called you personally to, 273. *See also* Mystery School

Malachi, 285

Malkut, 355, 358

Maltese cross, Saint Germain's, 487

Man, hollowed-out, 472

Manchild, Divine, 444

Manjushri, Bodhisattva of Wisdom, 494–95

Manthran, 454

Mantra(s): fifth bija, 505n.2; and the flame, 486; handed down to us, 462; in Hinduism, 503; to the Mighty Threefold Flame of Life, 474; Sarasvati's, 495; that establish ties to Mother Mary's Heart, 440; will affect outer circumstances, 462. *See also* Call(s); Decree(s); Fiats

Map, of victory in every area of life, 391

Martha, 286

Mary, Mother: Catholic doctrine on the assumption of, 450n.10, 451n.11; a double portion of her Spirit, 445; has always cradled you, 446; on her tears, 450n.7; on the places of her appearances, 443; services to the Immaculate Heart of, 358; in this court, 440; veneration to the Immaculate Heart of, 449n.3; on why she weeps, 443

Mast, adopting one quality of the, 252

Masters, disciplining and love of the, 432. *See also* Ascended Master(s)

Mediator, Lakshmi as, 496

Medicine, violet flame as a, 488

Meditation, 388; upon the heart of an illumined soul, 428; on the lotus of the heart, 426–28

Melchizedek: priesthood of, 468; the requirement for studying under, 485; tithe to, 362

Memories, old, 273

Memory, and progress on the Path, 497

Mental belt, is highly polluted, 414. *See also* Mind(s)

Mercy, have, 260

Merlin,*following* p. 484 (p. 9 *in* Sept. 12, 1992 letter)

Messenger, 277; allow her to be who she is, 249; Beloved Omega on the, 425; and correction, 276; El Morya did pick her up as an orphan in the astral plane, 259; Guru-chela relationship with the, 432–33; heart of the, 355; a personal, 369; Saint Germain to send the,*following* p. 484 (p. 4 *in* Sept. 12, 1992 letter); and Sarasvati, 502; "two-way," 257; your access to the, 261; and your Holy Christ Self, 277; your personal, 278. *See also* Mother of the Flame; Prophet, Elizabeth Clare

Mexico, earthquake in, 394

Michael, Archangel, his Presence over you, 422. *See also* Archangels

Mind(s): disintegrating, 381; Evil, 460, 461, 463; good and evil, 467; the human, 276–77; mastery of your, 275; of the people, 378; as a steel trap, 443; that has gone out of the way, 276; the will to strengthen your, 278. *See also* Brain(s); Mental belt; Mind of God; Mindfulness; Subconscious

Mind of God, 380; glimpses of the,

274; listening ear attuned to the, 443; more of the penetration of the, 388

Mindfulness, and clear consciousness, 252. See also Mind(s)

Miracles: take place in the auras of the seraphim, 395; through the violet flame, 490; in your life, 268

Mission, begun long ago, *following* p. 484 (p. 12 *in Sept. 12, 1992 letter*)

Mohammed, a strong heart-tie to, *following* p. 304 (p. 1 *in June 1, 1992 letter*)

Moment, when all could be won or lost, 389. See also Time

Monasticism, 269

Money, hasty decisions to part with your, 464

Monotheist, Zarathustra as a, 455–56

Montessori Education Workshops, *following* p. 304 (pp. 1–3 *in June 2, 1992 letter*)

"Moonlight and Roses," the melody of, 267

Moses: on the Mount of Transfiguration, 294, 295, 296; a strong heart-tie to, *following* p. 304 (p. 1 *in June 1, 1992 letter);* was a practicing monotheist, 456

Moslems, and Zoroastrianism, 466

Mother(s), Divine, 509; in her manifestation as Lakshmi, 495–98; in her manifestation as Sarasvati, 493–95; is closest to her children, 507; karma of the misuse of the Light of the, 433; leading the armies of heaven, 448; to nurture you, 368; peace with the, 359; Sarasvati on the, 503; sorrow of the, 450n.7. See also God

Mother of the Flame, 423. See also Messenger; Prophet, Elizabeth Clare

Mount St. Helens, eruption of, 394

Mountain(s): that you climb, 448; Zarathustra's retreat deep within the, 473

Music, patroness of, 494

Mysteries, given by the inner voice, 270

Mystery School: joy of the, 279; why it is here, 274. See also Maitreya's Mystery School

Mystical paths, of the world's religions, *following* p. 304 (p. 5 *in June 1, 1992 letter,* 390, 504. See also Mysticism; Mystics

Mysticism: key to the path of, *following* p. 304 (p. 8 *in June 1, 1992 letter);* in Zoroastrianism, 466–67. See also Mystical paths; Mystics

Mystics: pursue the path of the, 390; spiritual life of the true, 398. See also Mystical paths; Mysticism

Nagasena: on the five qualities of the sea that must be adopted, 254–55; on the quality of the handyman that must be adopted, 253; on the quality of the mast that must be adopted, 252; on the three qualities of a ship that must be adopted, 250–51; on the three qualities of the navigator that must be adopted, 252–53; on the two qualities of the anchor that must be adopted, 251–52

Names, secrets for the unlocking of, 354

Nataraja, Shiva as, 403

Nation(s): political situation in this, 439; the reason for being of, 373; rosaries for the protection of this, 445. See also America

National Airport, Gautama Buddha at, 267

Navigator, three qualities of the, 252–53

New Jerusalem, and the Inner Retreat in the thoughtform for 1985, 264–65

New Testament: law of karma set forth in the, 300; teaching on reincarnation in the, 285–99. *See also* Scriptures

Newspapers, reflect that which is going on at inner levels, 509

Nicaragua, earthquakes in, 394

Nirmanakaya: defined, 271n.3; invoking Gautama Buddha's, 255

Nomads, predatory, 461

Nonbelief, 424

Nonresolution, 359

Novena(s): to the Immaculate Heart of Mary, 440; to the will of God and the Great Divine Director, 278. *See also* Prayer(s)

O Mighty Threefold Flame of Life, 478

Obedience, to the inner voice, 356

Octave, living in this, 422

Old Testament, law of karma set forth in, 300. *See also* Scriptures

Omega, the cord of life from the Heart of, 439

Omega flame, rising action of the, 430

Omri-Tas: his coming each month, 485–86; unprecedented dispensation of, 487; and the violet flame, 488

One hundred and forty-four thousand, volunteered to come with Sanat Kumara, 467

Opportunity, to turn the Dark Cycle around, *following* p. 484 (p. 2 *in Sept. 12, 1992 letter*)

Opposition, do not underestimate, 422

Oppressor, call for the binding of the, 423. *See also* Fallen ones; Tyrants

Order of Lord Zadkiel, 487

Organ(s): of the body, 380; strengthening of the, 431

Origen, 370

Origin, point of, 380

Orphan, see yourself as an, 259

Pacific Northwest, earthquake risk in the, 393

Pain: sensitivity to, 260; that far exceeds abortion, 416; to wean you from the pleasures of the world, 431

Parents: and Christed ones who have been lost, 370; patterns they have put upon you, 361; take over the functions of your, 362

Parvati, 503; Shiva's Shakti, 402, 403

Pashupati, 400

Past, karmic highways of a distant, 355. *See also* Histories; Records; 35,000 years ago

Pastoral communities, 461

Path: key to the, of initiation, 276; we could give you a much more intense, 277

Patience, everyone has established a certain level of, 275

Patriarchs, embody the Tree of Life, 353

Pattern, that is the key to creation, 255

Paul, his teaching on mutable and immutable bodies, 294–95

Peace, within your members, 359

Pearl of Wisdom, to give to individuals, 389

Pentecost, 260

People: evil, 464; put a patine of good over an evil core, 463

Persia: Archangels sent to the court in ancient, 457, 458; Zoroastrianism in, 465–66
Pharisees: and John the Baptist, 287; today's, 299–300
Philippines, earthquake in the, 392
Physicians, 396
Pilgrimages, sell song and rosary tapes in areas of, 444
Piscean age: Saint Germain on the, 366–67; those counseled and trained to play their role in the, 366. *See also* Pisces
Pisces: Saint Germain is not done with, *following* p. 484 (pp. 2, 4, 5 *in Sept. 12, 1992 letter);* Saint Germain's long ages of preparation for the age of, 365. *See also* Piscean age
Planet, belongs to you, 398. *See also* Earth
Pleasure, path of, *following* p. 304 (p. 6 *in June 1, 1992 letter)*
Political bodies, of the nations, 440. *See also* Government
Political situation, in this nation, 439
Politicians, *following* p. 484 (pp. 9, 10 *in Sept. 12, 1992 letter);* in government, 378–79
Poor: aid to the, 257; balancing karma by feeding the, 258
Pope Pius XII, defined the doctrine of the Assumption, 450n.10
Portia, and the forces who perverted God's justice and judgment, *following* p. 484 (p. 13 *in Sept. 12, 1992 letter)*
Pots, to fill with the violet flame, 488
Power: Lakshmi personifies royal, 496; multiplication of God's, 509; royal, 497; of Victory, 390; in your Mighty I AM Presence, 414
Pranayama, 388
Prayer(s): intercessory, 368n; mantras of perpetual, 440; the most sacred of Zoroastrian, 462; prayer vigil in this Community, 439; to start a spiral to turn the world around, 381; that you leave unspoken, 447. *See also* Hail Mary; Novena(s)
Pressure: greater and greater, 275; that we must apply, 274
Pride, spiritual, 357. *See also* Proud
Priest(s): decadence of some, 443; the office of, 497. *See also* Priest class; Priesthood
Priest class, who are not servants of the Light, 504. *See also* Priest(s); Priesthood
Priesthood, of Melchizedek, 485. *See also* Priest(s); Priest class
Principle(s): the four, 503; when there is a grasping of a cosmic, 274
Problems, God-resolution to the world's, 379
Process, of the purging, 273
Profession, what you have put into your, 370
Progress, and creation, *following* p. 304 (p. 6 *in June 1, 1992 letter)*
Prophecies: Ascended Master, 394; foreshadowing of, 442
Prophet(s): choose the hour when they reveal their mission, 289; embodies the I AM Presence, 460; embody the Tree of Life, 353; Zarathustra on the, 458; Zarathustra was a, 455
Prophet, Elizabeth Clare: on her career in the service of Saint Germain, *following* p. 484 (pp. 3–4 *in Sept. 12, 1992 letter);* her witness to Jesus' Heart within her heart, 426; on the mantle of her calling, *following* p. 304 (p. 5 *in June 1, 1992 letter);* and the office of the World Mother, 368n.

See also Messenger; Mother of the Flame
Proud, think they have come far enough on the path, 360. *See also* Pride
Psychology: books recommended whereby you might become masters of your own, 361; examine your, 396; old, outworn, rotten matrices of, 266; that must be dealt with, 432; we demand more than an understanding of, 361; where it stops, 359; your, 266, 445
Public good, serving the, 258
Public servants, 258
Pudding, Buddha's, 271n.14
Purging, the process of the, 273–74
Purity: lotus represents, 496; Sarasvati represents, 494

Qualities, anchor of Love to multiply God-qualities, 263–64. *See also* Virtue
Queen of Angels, may accord you a special grace or dispensation, 448

Ra, 497; explained, 500n.14
Rabbi, who tells his son to jump off the wall, 464
Radha, 496
Rai, 497; explained, 500n.14
Rain: of Alpha, 421; of Alpha and Omega, 410; for the clearing of ancient records, 377
Rainbow rays: for healing, 474; mantra to activate the, 474. *See also* Ray(s)
Rama, Vishnu was incarnated as, 495–96
Ray(s): and the flame, 472; that has descended and then sprung up as a flame, 486; the violet flame and the seven, 489–90. *See also* Rainbow rays; Second Ray; Yellow ray
Reasonings, 278
Rebuke, expecting the, 277
Records: must come to the surface and flow out, 273; rain for the clearing of ancient, 377. *See also* Histories; Past; 35,000 years ago
Regeneration, 410
Reincarnation: law of, 458; in the New Testament, 285–99; and theologians, 299; why God set up the system of, 297–98. *See also* Lifetimes; Lives
Reincarnation and Christianity, 292
Religion(s): mystical paths of the world's, *following* p. 304 (p. 5 *in June 1, 1992 letter),* 390, 504; oldest of the revealed, 453; traditional Iranian, 461; world's, *following* p. 304 (pp. 3, 4 *in June 1, 1992 letter). See also* Faiths; Islam; Theologians
Rescue mission, 381
Resolution: with the Father, 361; that you must come to, 359
Resurrection: bodily, 451n.11; at the end of time, 450n.10
Retreat(s): of the Maha Chohan, 281; Omri–Tas stops by at Zadkiel's, 486; violet flame garnered and preserved in the, 487; of Zarathustra, 472–73. *See also* Retreat of the Divine Mother; Royal Teton Retreat
Retreat of the Divine Mother: City Foursquare is the, 265; over the Royal Teton Ranch, 426, 509; over this place, 266; over this ranch, 281
Ribbons, golden, 391
Righteousness, in Zoroastrian theology, 462, 463, 467
Rigveda, 454

Ritual, and the violet flame, 486
River(s): the Sarasvati, 495; seven holy, 402
Roe v. Wade, Supreme Court agreed to uphold, 412
Role models, on the television, 508
Root race, seventh, 380, 446
Rope: and the anchor, 256; to tie you to Mother Mary's Heart, 440
Rosaries: *antahkarana* you build by the, 446; of the New Age, 443; perpetual, 439; for the protection of this nation, 445; pursue the, 448. *See also* Hail Mary; Rosary
Rosary: daily use of the, 446; the giving of the, 443; the long rosary and the Surrender Rosary, 448; when you regularly give the, 444. *See also* Hail Mary; Rosaries
Royal Teton Ranch: it is worth many lifetimes to stay near the, 411; Retreat of the Divine Mother over the, 426, 509; and the Western Shamballa, *following* p. 304 (p. 2 *in June 1, 1992 letter*)
Royal Teton Retreat: call to be taken to the, 373; gathering place of the, 418; you did go to the, 389
Rukmini, 496

Sacred fire: must be focused and employed by you, 378; not accessible when you are in a state of idolatry, 354. *See also* Fire
Sacred Heart(s): celebration of the five, 357; devotions to the, 446; of Jesus in the thoughtform for 1985, 264–65, 266; make it your goal to be that, 280; veneration to the, 449n.3; your services to the, 358
Sacred Ritual, for Transport and Holy Work, 411

Sadi, words of, *following* p. 304 (p. 7 *in June 1, 1992 letter*)
Saint(s): footprints of the, 373; in heaven, *following* p. 304 (pp. 4–5 *in June 1, 1992 letter*); how it must feel to be a great, 428
Saint Germain: chosen to father the Son of God in the Piscean age, 366; as Christopher Columbus, *following* p. 484 (pp. 5, 6, 10–11 *in Sept. 12, 1992 letter*); Electronic Presence of, *following* p. 484 (pp. 3, 4 *in Sept. 12, 1992 letter*); Elizabeth Clare Prophet on, *following* p. 484 (pp. 8–9, 12–13 *in Sept. 12, 1992 letter*); Elizabeth Clare Prophet on her career in the service of, *following* p. 484 (pp. 3–4 *in Sept. 12, 1992 letter*); and the eruption of Mount St. Helens, 394; his long ages of preparation for the age of Pisces, 365; on his many incarnations, 365; on his name, 369; his Presence over you, 371; principle of the mantra applied by, 503
Salamanders, fiery, 473. *See also* Elemental life
Sambhogakaya: defined, 271n.3; invoking Gautama Buddha's, 255
Samsara: defined, 271n.7; sea of, 257
Samuel, *following* p. 484 (p. 9 *in Sept. 12, 1992 letter*); Saint Germain's embodiment as, 365
San Francisco, earthquake in, 394
Sanat Kumara: Ahura Mazda is, 457, 458, 467; earthquakes following a dictation by, 394; Gurus descended from, 462; has saved you for this hour, 508; has sent El Morya to you personally, 360; his coming to earth, 472; his mission to Earth, 467–68; returned to Venus, 468; seed of, 353

Sanctissima, the answer to, 375
Sarah, 362, *following* p. 484 (p. 12 *in Sept. 12, 1992 letter*)
Sarasvati: the Divine Mother in her manifestation as, 493–95; is both Person and Principle, 503; mantle of the office of, 502; seed-syllable mantra of, 504
Saturday, first, 357
Saviouress, be, 508. *See also* Saviours
Saviours, becoming world, 449n.6. *See also* Saviouress
Scales: sign of the, 447; in the thoughtform for 1985, 264–65, 266
Science, and the sinking of Atlantis, 489
Scriptures: Christopher Columbus on, *following* p. 484 (p. 7 *in Sept. 12, 1992 letter);* in Sarasvati's hand, 493, 494. *See also* New Testament; Texts
Sea: being in a heavy storm at, 274; five qualities of the, 254–55; of violet flame, 487
Seat-of-the-soul chakra: soul seated in the, 422; spiral staircase from the, 423. *See also* Chakra(s)
Second Ray: legions of the, 389; for the quickening of the people, 381. *See also* Golden fire; Yellow fire; Yellow flame
Secret chamber: of the heart, *following* p. 304 (p. 3 *in June 1, 1992 letter),* 422–23, 468; of Mother Mary's Heart, 440; a retreat that is a replica of the, of the heart, 472–73; a room that is a focus of the, of the heart, 476n.2; Vishnu in the, of your heart, 508
Seed syllable(s): four, 503; Lakshmi's, 498; of Sarasvati, 495, 504
Seeds, planted within you, 261
Sefirot, 358, 414; Archangels embody the, 354; came forth on a descending scale, 366; contact with, 368; counterfeit set of the, 368; rise up the, 488; ten, 360
Self: dot of the original beginning of the not-self, 358; etheric and astral, 256; idolatry of the, 354; not-self, 268; sorrow of the deepest, 361; untransmuted forces of the not-self, 277; if you desire a new, 360
Self-knowledge, 502; and Aquarius, 374; fierceness of, 503
Self-mastery, Lord Shiva on, 415
Separation, from God, 359
Seraph, who attended your birth in the Great Central Sun, 429. *See also* Angel(s); Seraphim
Seraphim: best friends you ignore the most, 395; come with their rings upon rings of white fire, 379; cycling from the Great Central Sun, 474; Justinius on, 395–96; *sefirot* guarded and borne by, 360; who was with you in the hour of your birth in the Great Central Sun, 474. *See also* Angel(s); Seraph
Serapis, seraphim are of the order of, 395
Serpent, brazen, that the children of Israel looked upon, 266
Servant, is not greater than his lord, 258
Service, balancing karma by universal, 446
Shaivites, Western, 411
Shakespearean plays, *following* p. 484 (p. 8 *in Sept. 12, 1992 letter*)
Shakti, explained, 402
Shamballa: Sanat Kumara's retreat, 467; Western Shamballa, *following* p. 304 (p. 2 *in June 1, 1992 letter*), 373

Shambhu, 400
Shankara, 400
Sheet, that does traverse a cosmos, 381
Ship(s): and anchor, 265–66; anchor used by Maitreya in his clipper, 264; carry many anchors, 257; clipper, 266; of Maitreya, 271n.8; that is no longer on course, 276; three qualities of a, 250–51
Shiva, 399–404; attempted to move the Supreme Court justices on abortion, 413; be the negative polarity of, 409–10; the offer of his presence, 417; only make the call, "Shiva!" 415; places his image over the television, 417; on those whom he will work through, 415–16
Sinner(s): a poor, 259; souls who have become, 258
Sins, "Whosoever sins ye remit, they are remitted...," 260
Sirius, and Surya, 397
Sita, 496
Situation, that you may step out of, 432
666, the number, 397
Skinner, B. F., experiment of, 431
Slaughter, in Yugoslavia, 373–74
Slumber, some will awake as from a deep, 391
Snakeskin, opportunity for the shedding of the, 260
Society, that needs to serve, 258
Society's ladder, lowest rung of, 259
Solar-plexus chakra, and the violet flame, 488. *See also* Chakra(s)
Solitude. *See* Son(s) of the Solitude
Son: Inner, 356; making your peace with the, 361; violation of the Light of the, 433. *See also* Christ; Christ Self; God; Son of God
Son of God: bonding to the, 360; rejection of the, in the person of Jesus, 356–57; resolution with the, 359; Saint Germain chosen to father the, 366; those who deny the, 358. *See also* Christ; Christ Self; Jesus; Son
"Sonar" readings, of the astral sea, 257
Song(s): cassettes of, 443; of the Homing, 265; tapes to sell in areas of pilgrimages, 444
Son(s) of the Solitude, 287; explained, 302n.5
Sonship, initiation of, 356. *See also* Christhood; Son; Son of God
Soul: and the ascension, 450n.11; cleavage between the I AM THAT I AM and the, 357; death of the, 416; is most neglected, 433; journeys through many lifetimes, 297; may rise to the secret chamber of the heart, 422; separation between the I AM THAT I AM and the, 356
Soul journeys, at night, 509
Souls, "rub souls" with one another, 473
South America, Mother Mary speaks to those of, 446
Speech, right, 501. *See also* Word(s)
Spenta, in Zarathustra's theology, 458
Spenta Armaiti, 459
Spenta Mainyu, 458
Spiral, of the love of the Guru, 256
Spiral staircase, from the seat-of-the-soul chakra to the heart, 423
Spirit, key to your increase of the, 280
Spirits, "try the spirits," 463
Spiritual consciousness, center of, 426–27
Spiritual path, a worldwide awakening to the, 504
Spirituality, you are not satisfied with your present condition of, 417–18

Spiritualization, of consciousness, 274
Sri Lanka, retreat of the Maha Chohan at, 281
Star, that the Lightbearers will follow, 279
Stiff-necked generation, 355, 357
Stock market, sudden plummeting of the, 447
Stone, is not a begging bowl, 258
Storm, being at sea in a heavy, 274
Strength(s): know your, 431; regaining of your, 371
Students, in the retreats on the etheric octave, 487
Study Groups, twenty-four-hour marathon in your, 389
Stump, El Morya called the messenger to, *following* p. 484 (p. 4 *in Sept. 12, 1992 letter*)
Subconscious, substance in your, 469. *See also* Mind(s)
Subduction processes, 393
Substance: do not allow misqualified, to idle, 440; that has been in your subconscious and unconscious for aeons, 469; that the Holy Spirit does dislodge, 273. *See also* Energy
Sudra, in Zoroastrianism, 465
Suicide, spiritual, 298
Summer solstice, and your annual test, 278
Summit University: a period at, 371; students at, 379. *See also* Summit University students
Summit University students, Mother Mary speaks to, 442–43. *See also* Summit University
Sun, limitless light of the, 280
Sunbeams, of the Great Central Sun, 280
Supreme Court: agreed to uphold *Roe v. Wade*, 412–13; justices of the, 412–13

Surya, and Sirius, 397
Swan, of Sarasvati, 494
Sword: of discrimination, 276; of Manjushri, 495; to slay illusion, 418
Sympathies, human, 275

Tabor, God, and the 1964 Alaskan earthquake, 394
Talent, to pass to the next generation, 502
Tao, 497; explained, 500n.14
Tape recorders, to play the calls that you have given in the court, 279
Tapes, to give away and sell in areas of pilgrimages, 444. *See also* Cassettes
Tau, 497; explained, 500n.14
Teachers: false, 371; of righteousness, 260; wise, 277; your, 431
Teaching(s): are the foundation of Aquarius, *following* p. 484 (p. 2 *in Sept. 12, 1992 letter*); false, 371; of Jesus, 370, 374; pass it on to those who are interested, 504; preserving the, 445
Teaching Centers, twenty-four-hour marathon in your, 389
Tears, of Mother Mary, 450n.7
Television: and children, 417, 508; that which passes through the, 502
Tenderness, whereby you can hardly find a harsh feeling, 423
Terah, 354
Teresa of Avila, prayer of, 259
Test(s): passing your, 260; your annual, 278. *See also* Adversities; Initiation; Testing
Testing: of Christopher Columbus, *following* p. 484 (pp. 10–12 *in Sept. 12, 1992 letter*); these are hours of, 442. *See also* Adversities; Initiation; Test(s)

Texts, inspired by Gautama Buddha, 250
Theologians, and the doctrines of karma and reincarnation, 299
Thinking, old ways of, 273. *See also* Thought(s)
Third eye: origin of Shiva's, 403; raising the fire up to the point of the, 423; scorching power of Shiva's, 413; and that which passes through television sets, 502. *See also* Chakra(s); Third-eye chakra
Third-eye chakra, and the invocation of the violet flame, 486. *See also* Chakra(s); Third eye
35,000 years ago, when you walked away from the Son of God, 369
Thought(s): pure, 388; that are not your own, 372. *See also* Thinking
Thoughtform, for the year 1985, 264–65, 266
Thread of contact, that ties the soul to the Great White Brotherhood, 256
Threefold flame, 298; assisting you to balance the, 474; breathe upon the fire of the, 275; increase of light in your, 441; love in the secret place where it does burn, 423; mantra to the, 474; in the secret chamber of the heart, 468; some have snuffed out the, 260; sphere of the white fire that is the source of the, 503; that does burn in the heart of Alpha and Omega, 372; you have not yet mastered the, 473; in your heart, *following* p. 304 (p. 3 *in June 1, 1992 letter*). *See also* Divine spark
Throat chakra: guarding of the, 423; and the invocation of the violet flame, 486. *See also* Chakra(s)
Tiferet, 355, 358; bonding to, 360;

Saint Germain on the, 366
Time: buying, *following* p. 484 (p. 3 *in Sept. 12, 1992 letter*); moments in, 280. *See also* Moment
Timetable: in your chart, 360; of your life, 275
Tithe, of Abraham to Melchizedek, 362
Tolerance, everyone has established a certain level of, 275
Torch, is not being passed, 508
Toxic chemicals, 417
Transcendence, and Sarasvati, 494
Transfiguration: Elijah on the Mount of, 294–96; Moses on the Mount of, 294, 295, 296; our Lord's, 287–88, 289, 292, 295–96, 297
Translation: defined, 292n; of a soul to heaven, 292–93
Transmutation: intense and deep, 359; opportunity for, 487
Tree of Life: antithesis of the, 358; Christ midpoint on the, 366
Tribulations, of Christopher Columbus, *following* p. 484 (p. 12 *in Sept. 12, 1992 letter*). *See also* Adversities; Test(s); Testing
Trinity: Christian, 400; Hindu, 399–400
Trust: and friendship with God, 355; in God, 424; in other individuals, 431
Truth: fire was a symbol of, 465; origin of the conflict between the Lie and, 460–62; postponement of telling the, 289
Tube of light, to protect your momentum of the violet flame, 487
Twelve o'clock line, the Father on the, 503
25,800-year cycle, of returning karma, 367n
Twin flame(s): bird that sings the

love song of, 265; a seraphim who has an attachment to you and your, 474; your experiences in the Great Central Sun with your, 380
Two Witnesses, 443–44
Tyrants, many who are under, 259. See also Oppressor

Unconscious, substance in your, 469. See also Mind(s)
Understanding: and passing your tests, 260; psychology will take you to the place of, 359. See also Illumination
United States Naval Academy, an anchor at the, 263
Upanishad, *following* p. 304 (p. 6 *in June 1, 1992 letter*)

Vacation, at one of the places of Mother Mary's appearances, 443
Vedas, and Sarasvati, 495
Venus: devotees from, 472; Sanat Kumara returned to, 468
Vicarious atonement, doctrine of the, 300
Victory: in every area of life, 391; Mighty Victory on, 388; power of, 390; that which you can spiritually assimilate of, 391
Violet flame: calls to the, 412; candles of the, 490; coupled with the ruby fire and white light, 411; fifteen minutes a day, 301; garnering the, 487–88; has an aspect on each of the seven rays, 490; igniting a whole world with the, 488–89; knowledge of, *following* p. 484 (p. 2 *in Sept. 12, 1992 letter*); marathons will awaken and quicken some, 391; mastery of, 485; mystery of the, 488; preserved and garnered in the retreats of the Great White Brotherhood, 487; a reservoir of, 487; and the seven rays, 489–90; that earth can be given, 489; to transmute the burdens on elemental life, 394; on visualizing and using the, 486–87; what it can do, 489; will bring change about gently, 411
Virgo, sign of the Mother, 439–40
Virgo and Pelleur, delivered a warning of planetary upheaval, 394
Virtue, to be internalized, 255. See also Qualities
Vishnu, 399; invoke, 509; is the Christ Light, 498; and Lakshmi, 495–96; parallel to the principle of the Son, 495; in the person of your Holy Christ Self, 507; in the secret chamber of your heart, 508; Shakti of, 495
Vishtaspa, King, 456–58, 461
Visualization: much can be accomplished by, 259; of the violet flame, 486–87
Vohu Manah, 455, 459
Voice: inner, 270, 356; some have silenced the, of conscience, 260
Volcanic eruption(s), 393; in Alaska, 392; of Mount St. Helens, 394. See also Volcanic release
Volcanic release, in Alaska, 390. See also Volcanic eruption(s)

War: on this planet, 374; while you have a nation not besieged by, 442. See also Warfare
Warfare: against the evil ones, 457; global, 391. See also War
Waters: auspicious, 497–98; of everlasting Life, 429; the winning

of the, 402
Weaknesses, related to the weakest of your organs, 431
Wedding garment, that is the Deathless Solar Body, 450n.11
Wesak, the flame of, 261
Western Shamballa, 373; and Gautama Buddha, *following* p. 304 (p. 2 *in June 1, 1992 letter*)
Whips, for horses, 277
White, Sarasvati wears, 494
White fire: rings upon rings of, 379; those who will be a focus of, 411. *See also* White light
White light, and the transfiguration, 296. *See also* White fire
Will: test the, 278; that resides in the marrow of your bones, 256
Will of God: takes you across the karmic highways of a distant past, 355; will lead you to the very goal you desire, 360
Woe(s): fourth, 433, 489; three, 433
Woman, 369; clothed with the Sun, 444; protector of every, 369; violators of, 433
Wonderman, Saint Germain as, *following* p. 484 (p. 8 *in Sept. 12, 1992 letter*)
Word(s): Goddess of the, 493; many idle, 423. *See also* Speech
Work, of the ages, 264
World: another round in the, 369; how it will change, 373; it is possible to turn it around, 381; in transition, 381; as your guru, 431
World events, co-measurement of, 447
World Mother, office of, 368n
Wounds, your, 447
Wrath, let not the sun go down upon your, 411. *See also* Anger
Wretch, lying in the gutter, 259

Yellow fire: cloven tongues of, 382; imparting hope, 378; violet flame sprinkled with, 391. *See also* Golden fire; Second Ray; Yellow flame
Yellow flame, angels of the, 379. *See also* Golden fire; Second Ray; Yellow fire
Yellow ray, songs to the beings of the, 378. *See also* Golden fire; Second Ray; Yellow fire; Yellow flame
Yellowstone National Park, earthquakes in, 392
Yima, 461
Yoga, the key to bhakti, jnana, raja and karma yoga, 503
Yoga postures, 278
Yogi(s): Shiva as a, 401, 402; you are, 401–2. *See also* Yogin
Yogin: one quality of the handyman which must be adopted by, 253; qualities of a ship which a, must adopt, 250–51; qualities of the anchor which must be adopted by, 251–52; qualities of the navigator which must be adopted by the, 252–53; qualities of the sea which must be adopted by the, 254–55; quality of the mast which must be adopted by the, 252. *See also* Chela; Disciple
Yoke, of Jesus, 402
Youth: eternal, 410; regaining of your, 371
Yugoslavia: journeying to, 418; set your mark on, 509; slaughter in, 373–74; a spiritual work over, 389

Zadkiel, Archangel: Omri-Tas stops by at the retreat of, 486; Order of Lord Zadkiel, 487. *See also* Archangels

Zarathustra, 455; being in the presence of, 468; commanded angels to make war with hosts of Darkness, 271n.15; death of, 465; on his retreat, 472–73; his teaching, 458–63, 464–67; one with your Holy Christ Self, 475; a strong heart-tie to, *following* p. 304 (p. 1 *in June 1, 1992 letter);* and

Zoroastrianism, 453–58
Zohar, teachings of the, 368
Zoroaster, the Greek name for Zarathustra, 454. *See also* Zarathustra
Zoroastrianism: in Persia, 465–66; placed on the Eighth Ray chakra, 468; the teachings of, 458–63, 464–67; threefold ethic of, 465; and Zarathustra, 453–58

FOR MORE INFORMATION

We welcome you to learn more about the Teachings of the Ascended Masters. For a free catalog of books and tapes published by Summit University Press and for information about the weekly *Pearls of Wisdom,* the spiritual community at the Royal Teton Ranch, weekend seminars, quarterly conferences, annual ten-day summer retreats, Elizabeth Clare Prophet's cable TV shows, the Keepers of the Flame Fraternity, or the Ascended Masters' library and study center nearest you, write or call: Summit University Press, Dept. 470, Box 5000, Livingston, Montana 59047-5000 Telephone: (406) 222-8300.

Other Titles Published by Summit University Press

THE LOST YEARS OF JESUS
Documentary evidence of Jesus' 17-year journey to the East
By Elizabeth Clare Prophet

> *"Elizabeth Clare Prophet puts together the missing pieces in the life of the Master that have baffled biblical scholars for centuries."*
> —Jess Stearn, best-selling author of
> *Edgar Cayce—The Sleeping Prophet*

The Gospels record Jesus age 12 in the temple, then age 30 at the river Jordan. Where was he in the interim? Ancient Buddhist manuscripts say Jesus left Palestine and traveled to India, Nepal, Ladakh and Tibet. For the first time, Elizabeth Clare Prophet brings together the testimony of four eyewitnesses of these remarkable manuscripts plus three different translations of the texts. Illustrated with maps, drawings and 79 photos.

> Hardbound, 418 pp., color illustrations, #2080, $19.95
> Softbound, 418 pp., color illustrations, #1593, $14.95
> Pocketbook, 447 pp., black-and-white illustrations, #2156, $6.99

THE LOST TEACHINGS OF JESUS
By Mark L. Prophet and Elizabeth Clare Prophet

The Prophets prove that many of Jesus' original teachings are missing and that what was written down was tampered with by numerous editors or suppressed by "guardians of the faith." This landmark series reconstructs the lost teachings Jesus gave in public to the multitudes and in secret to his closest disciples—and answers questions that have puzzled readers of the Bible for centuries.

> Pocketbooks with black-and-white illustrations:
> Book 1: Missing Texts • Karma and Reincarnation. 384 pp., #2157, $5.99
> Book 2: Mysteries of the Higher Self. 352 pp., #2158, $5.99
> Book 3: Keys to Self-Transcendence. 352 pp., #2159, $5.99
> Book 4: Finding the God Within. 368 pp., #2160, $5.99

> Also published in a two-volume set with color illustrations:
> Vol. I 520 pp. Hardbound, #2075, $19.95 Softbound, #2040, $14.95
> Vol. II 650 pp. Hardbound, #2077, $21.95 Softbound, #2076, $16.95

PRAYER AND MEDITATION
By Jesus and Kuthumi

In this inspiring combination of Christian mysticism and Eastern meditation, Jesus Christ teaches the art of unceasing communion with God and the Tibetan mahatma Kuthumi teaches the way of higher meditation to open the heart to receive God's love, wisdom and strength. A practical guide for achieving spiritual renewal and overcoming adversity. 18 Chinese-style prints of world teachers.

> Softbound, 305 pp., #569, $10.95

Forbidden Mysteries of Enoch
Fallen Angels and the Origins of Evil
By Elizabeth Clare Prophet

Did fallen angels take on human form and teach man to build weapons of war? That is the thesis of the Book of Enoch—a story church fathers suppressed over a thousand years ago. It reveals that vengeful angels lusted after the "daughters of men," mated with them, and oppressed the people of earth. Mrs. Prophet examines the controversy surrounding the book and shows how it may be the missing link in our understanding of evil today. Includes the entire Book of Enoch, all the other Enoch texts, biblical parallels, and C. S. Lewis on bad angels. 32 illustrations by Gustave Doré.

Softbound, 495 pp., #1592, $14.95

Saint Germain On Alchemy
Formulas for Self-Transformation
Recorded by Mark L. Prophet and Elizabeth Clare Prophet

Alchemy is a powerful method of transformation. In this greatest of all self-help books, the Master Alchemist Saint Germain reveals techniques that can help you transform your life, your nation, your planet. He explains how you can harness energy to alter matter, create mental pictures to materialize objects, control your emotions, and get rid of anxiety. Contains a 117-page handbook of alchemical and spiritual terms plus sections on the mystical origins of the United States and Saint Germain as the Wonderman of Europe.

Pocketbook, 544 pp., #1835, $6.99

Dossier on the Ascension
The Story of the Soul's Acceleration into Higher Consciousness on the Path of Initiation
By Serapis Bey

The Ascended Master Serapis Bey shows that the soul's reunion with God through the ascension is the goal of life for all. He gives practical keys for spiritual growth that can help you earn your ascension and answers the ultimate questions about life after death. A profound look into the life of the soul, her purpose and destiny.

Softbound, 212 pp., #1038, $9.95

Available from Summit University Press, Dept. 470, Box 5000, Livingston, MT 59047-5000. Credit card orders call 800-245-5445 in the U.S.A. or 406-222-8300. Postage and handling charges: for orders up to $19.99 add $2.50; orders from $20 to $39.99 add $3.50; from $40 to $59.99 add $4.00; from $60 to $79.99 add $4.50; from $80 to $99.99 add $5.00 and for orders over $100 add 6% of the total. Prices and postage charges are subject to change.